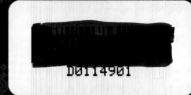

④

K
A
K
E
G
U
R
U
I

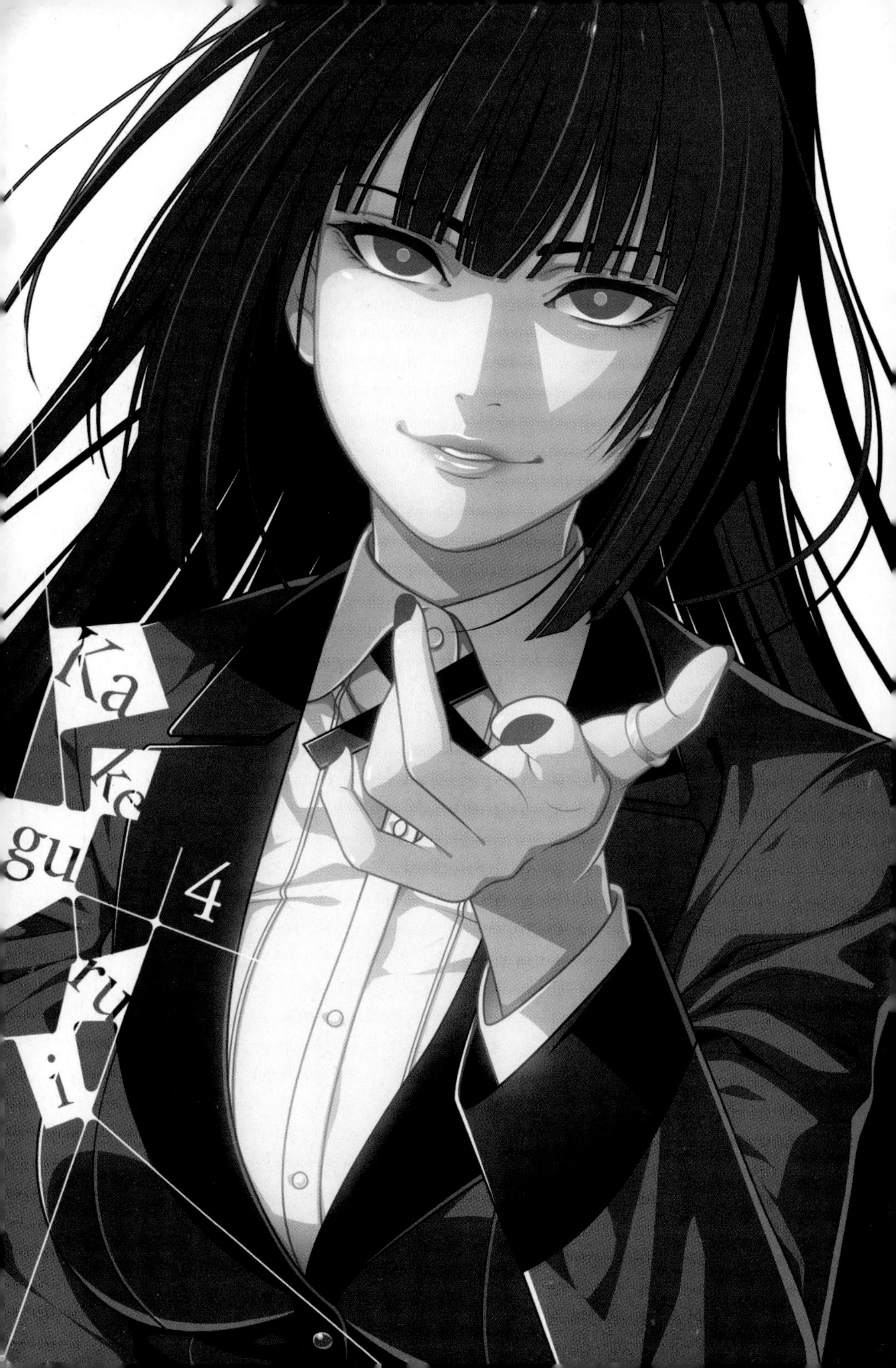
Kakegurui
4

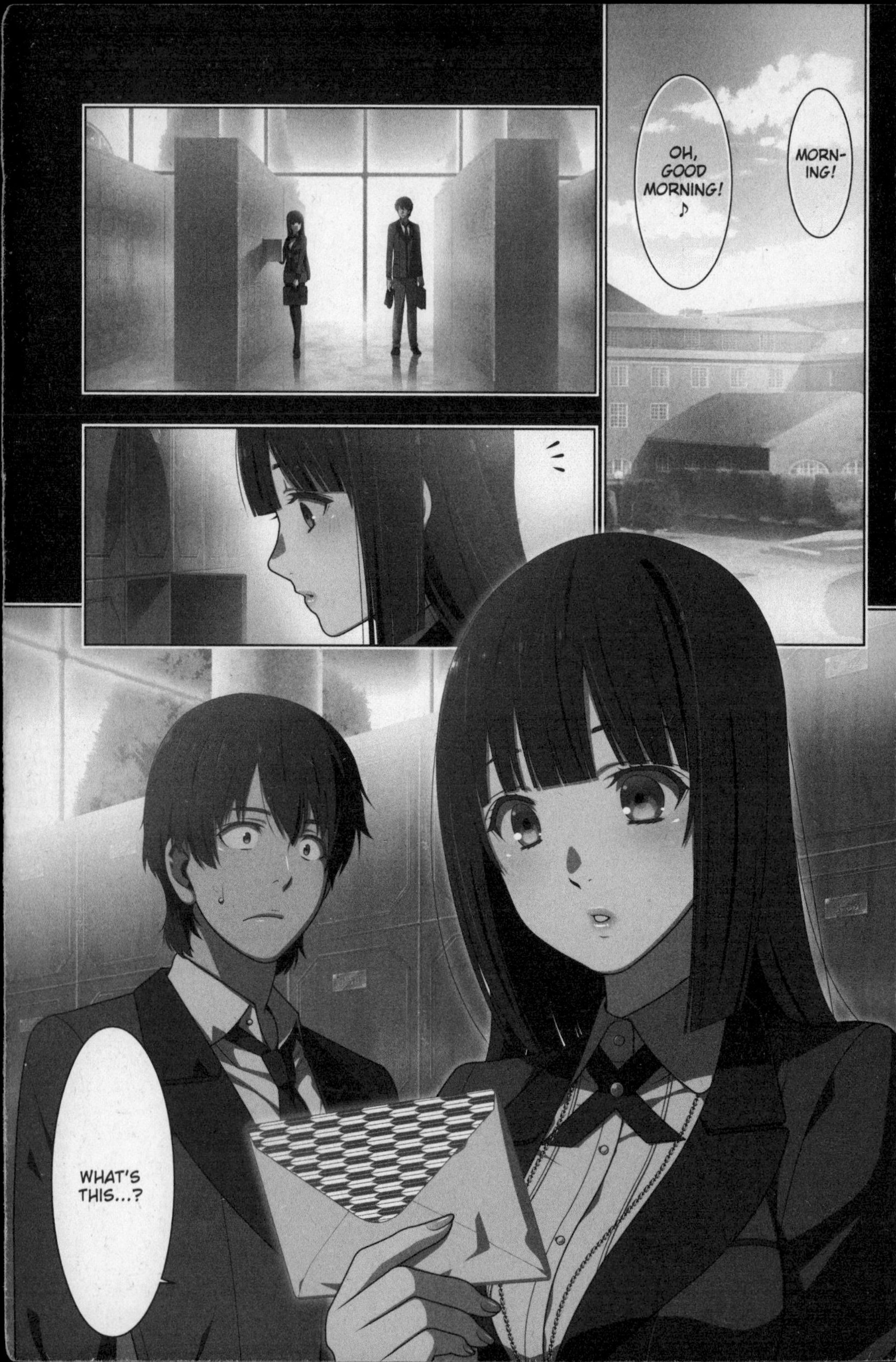
MORN-ING!
OH, GOOD MORNING! ♪
WHAT'S THIS...?

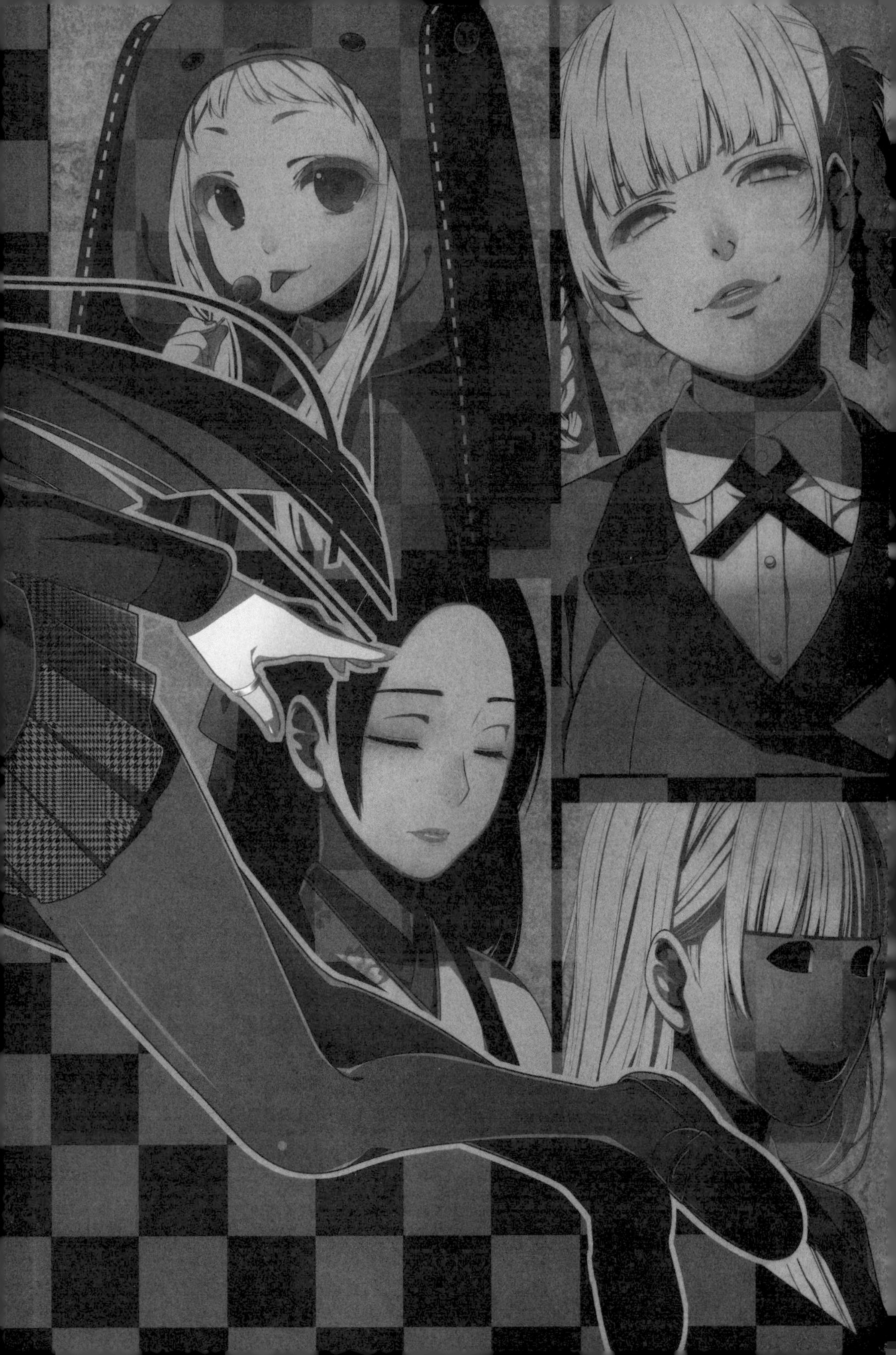

CHAPTER SEVENTEEN
THE LOVING GIRL

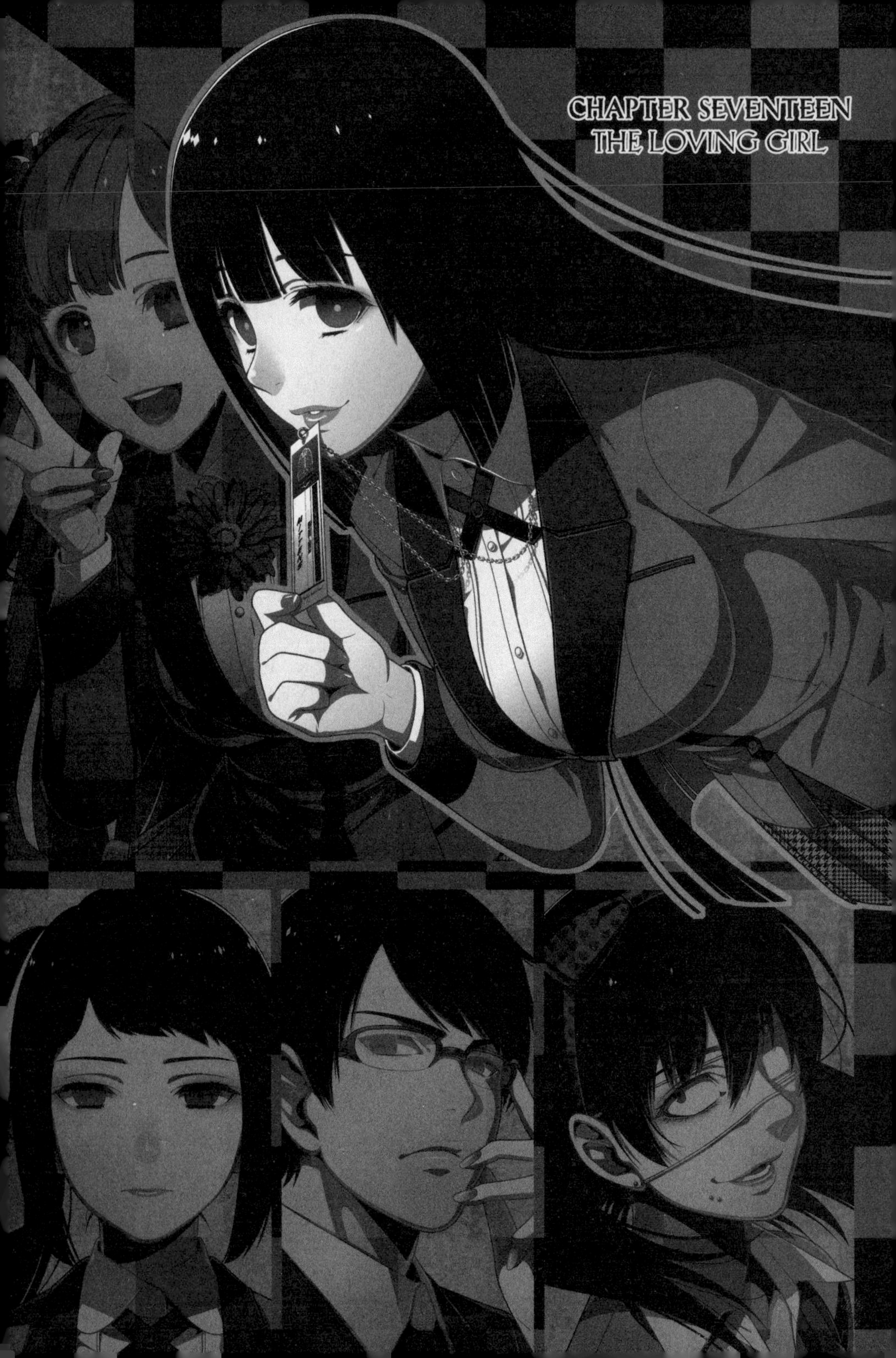

KAKEGURUI

— Compulsive Gambler —

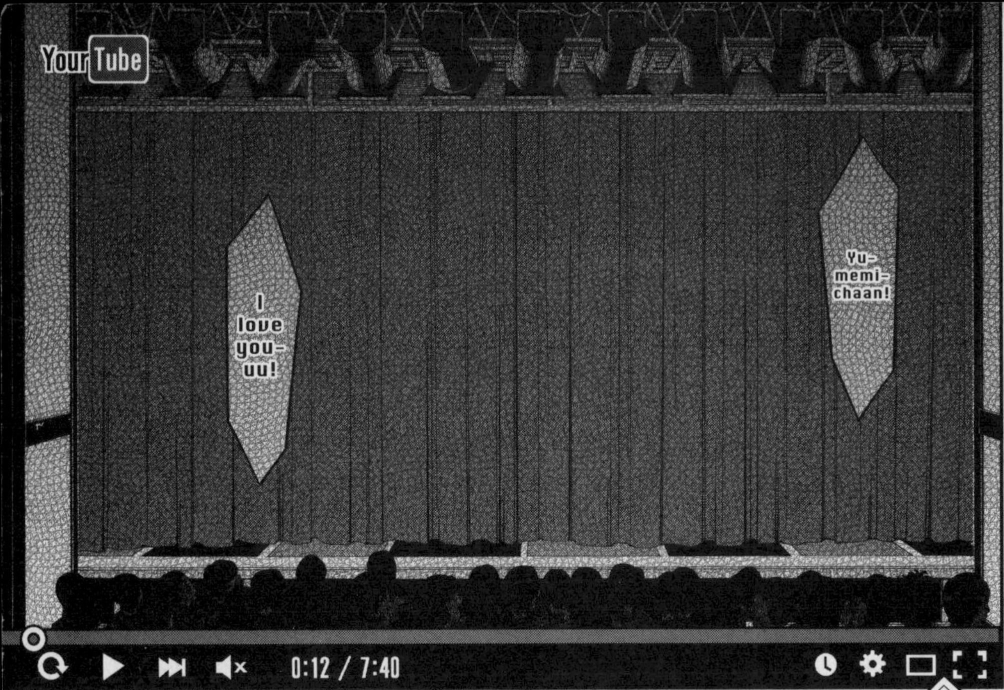
YourTube
Yu-memi-chaan!
I love you-uu!
0:12 / 7:40

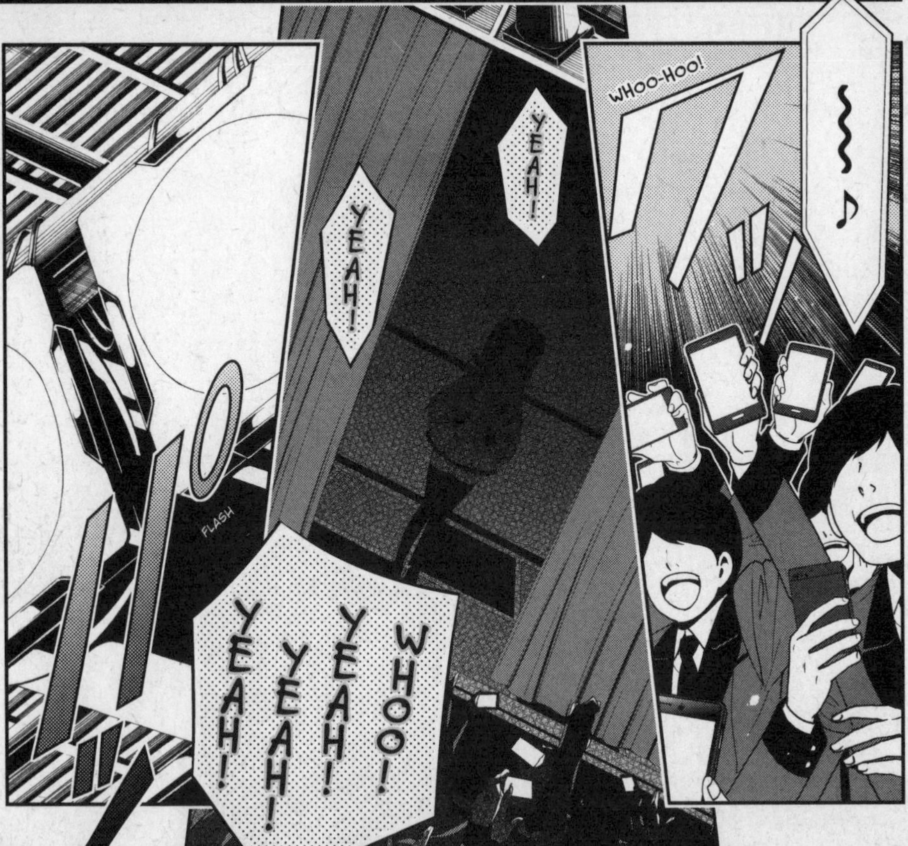

WHOO-HOO!
YEAH!
YEAH!
WHOOO! YEAH! YEAH! YEAH!
FLASH

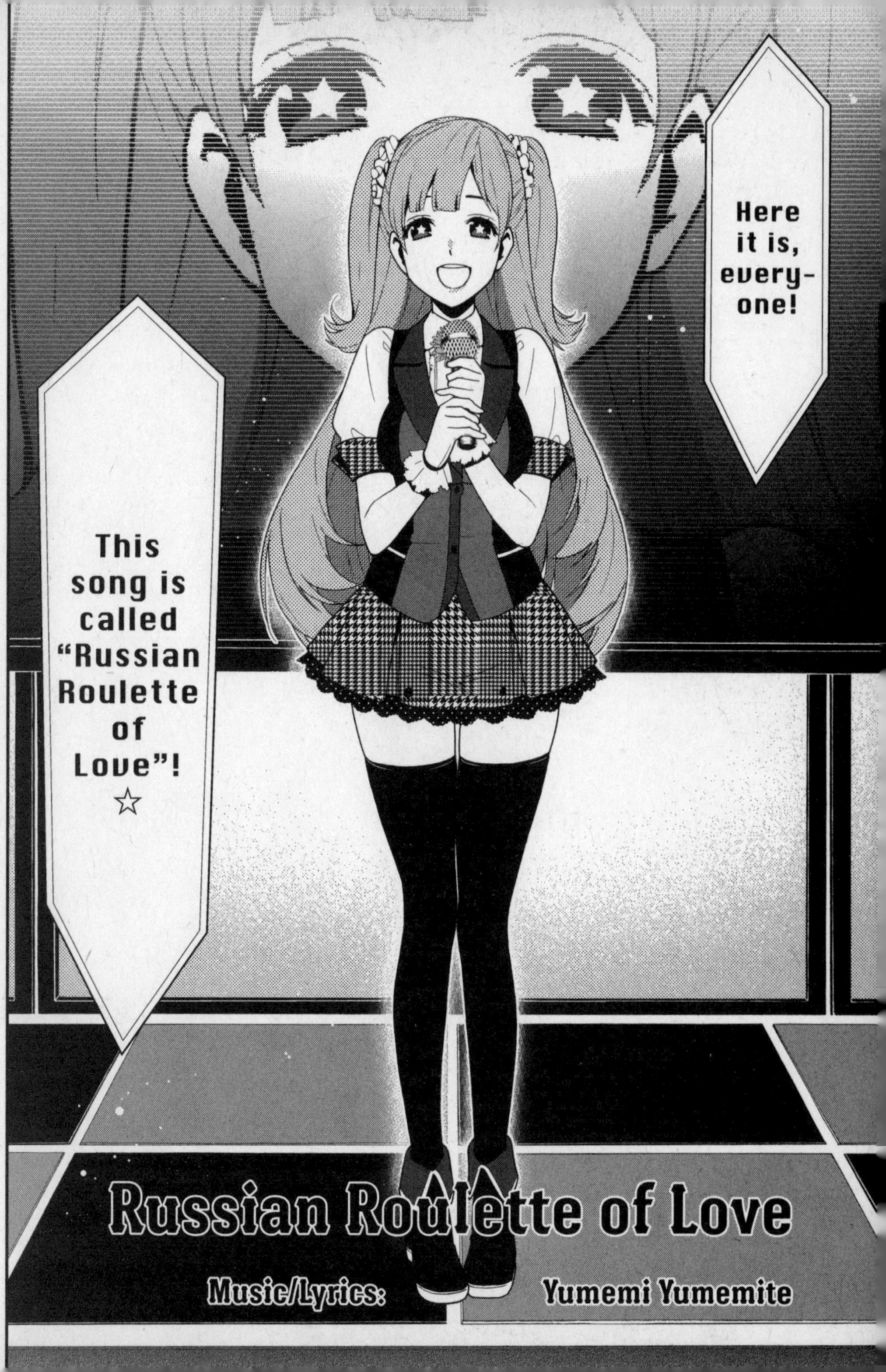
Here it is, everyone!
This song is called "Russian Roulette of Love"! ☆
Russian Roulette of Love
Music/Lyrics: Yumemi Yumemite

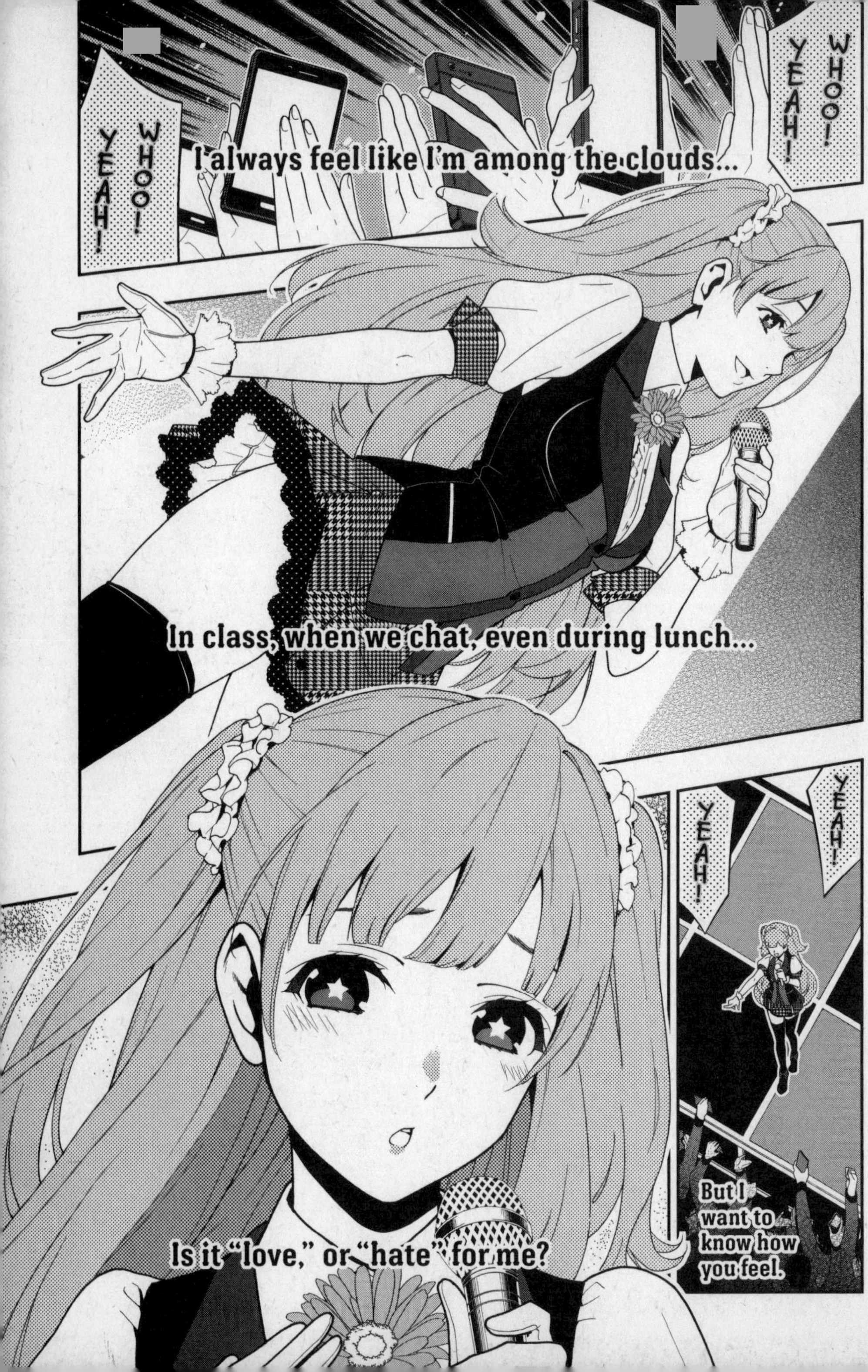
WHOO! YEAH!
I always feel like I'm among the clouds...
WHOO! YEAH!
In class, when we chat, even during lunch...
YEAH!
YEAH!
But I want to know how you feel.
Is it "love," or "hate" for me?

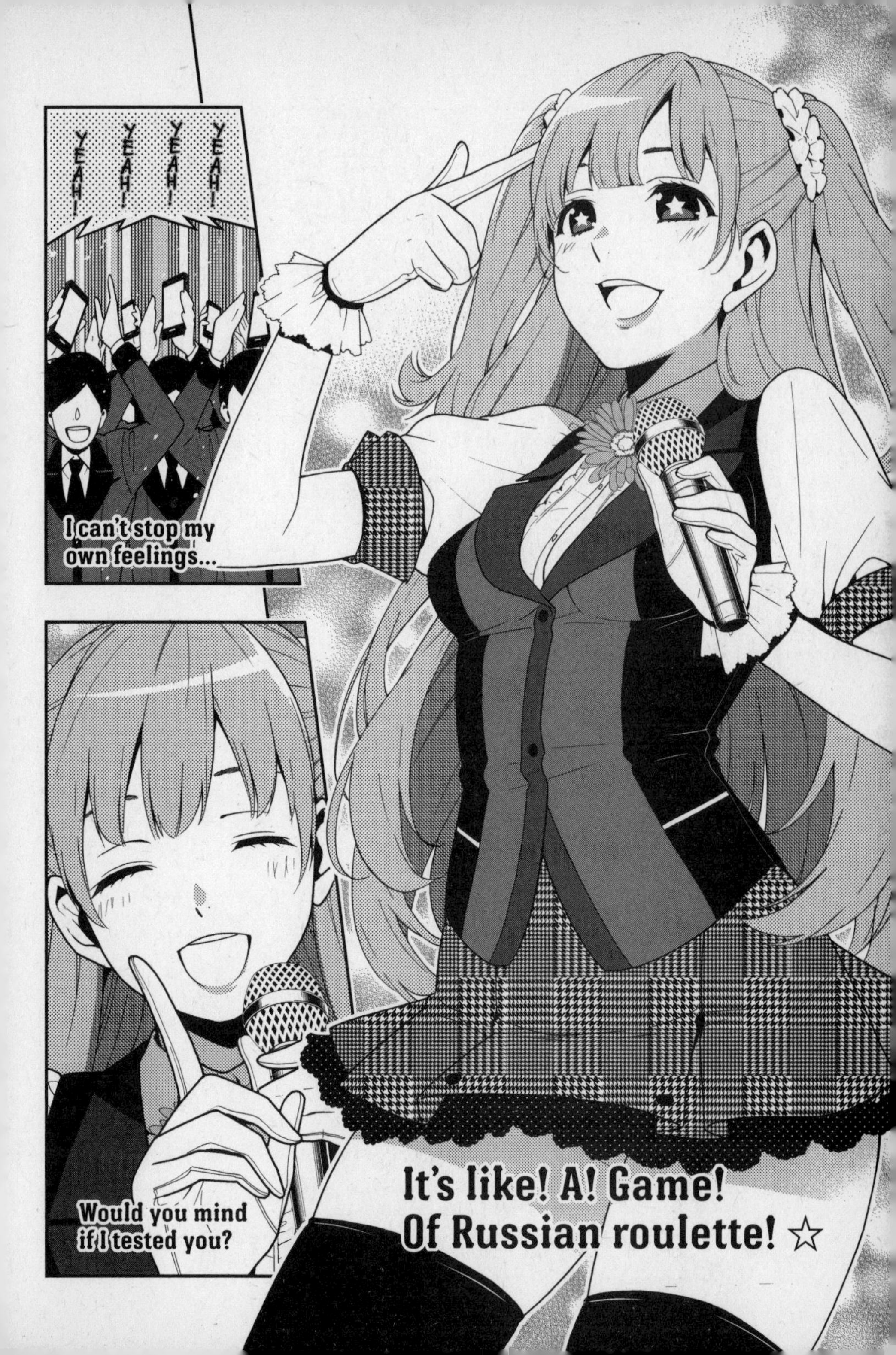
YEAH!
YEAH!
YEAH!
YEAH!
I can't stop my own feelings...
Would you mind if I tested you?
It's like! A! Game! Of Russian roulette! ☆

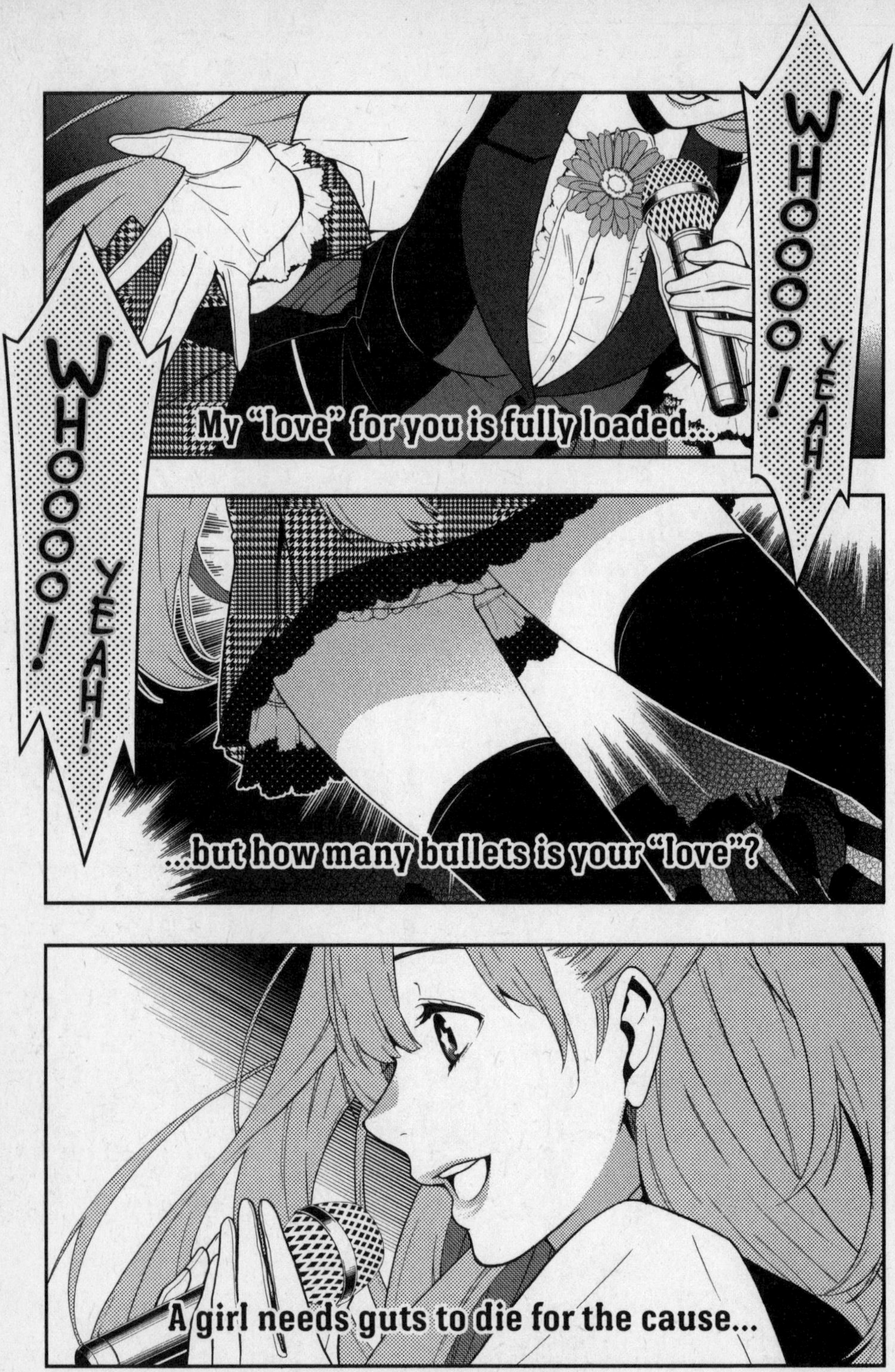
WHOOOOO! YEAH!
My "love" for you is fully loaded...
WHOOOOO! YEAH!
...but how many bullets is your "love"?
A girl needs guts to die for the cause...

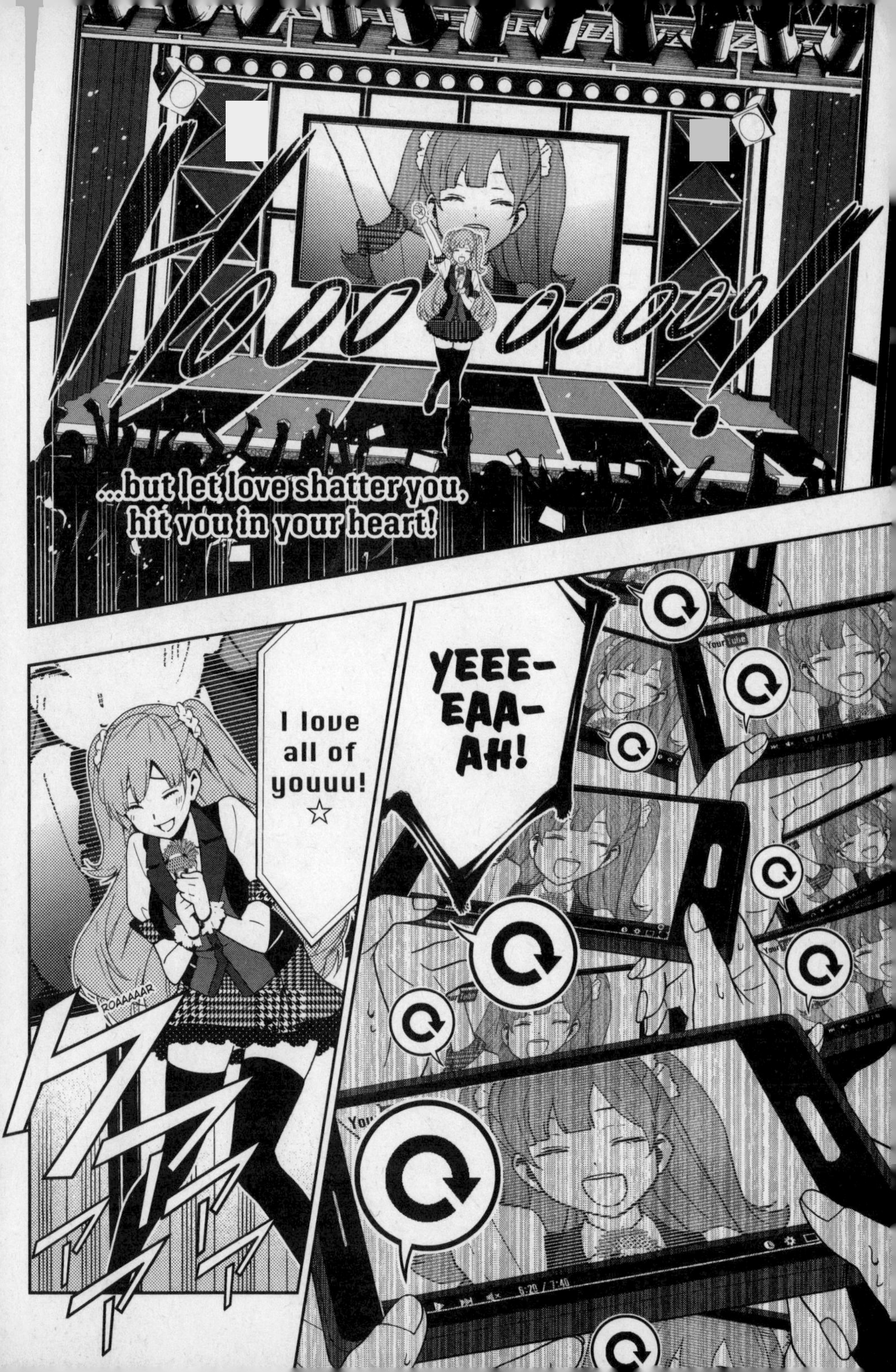
...but let love shatter you,
hit you in your heart!
YEEE-EAA-AH!
I love all of youuu! ☆
ROAAAAAR
6:20 / 7:40

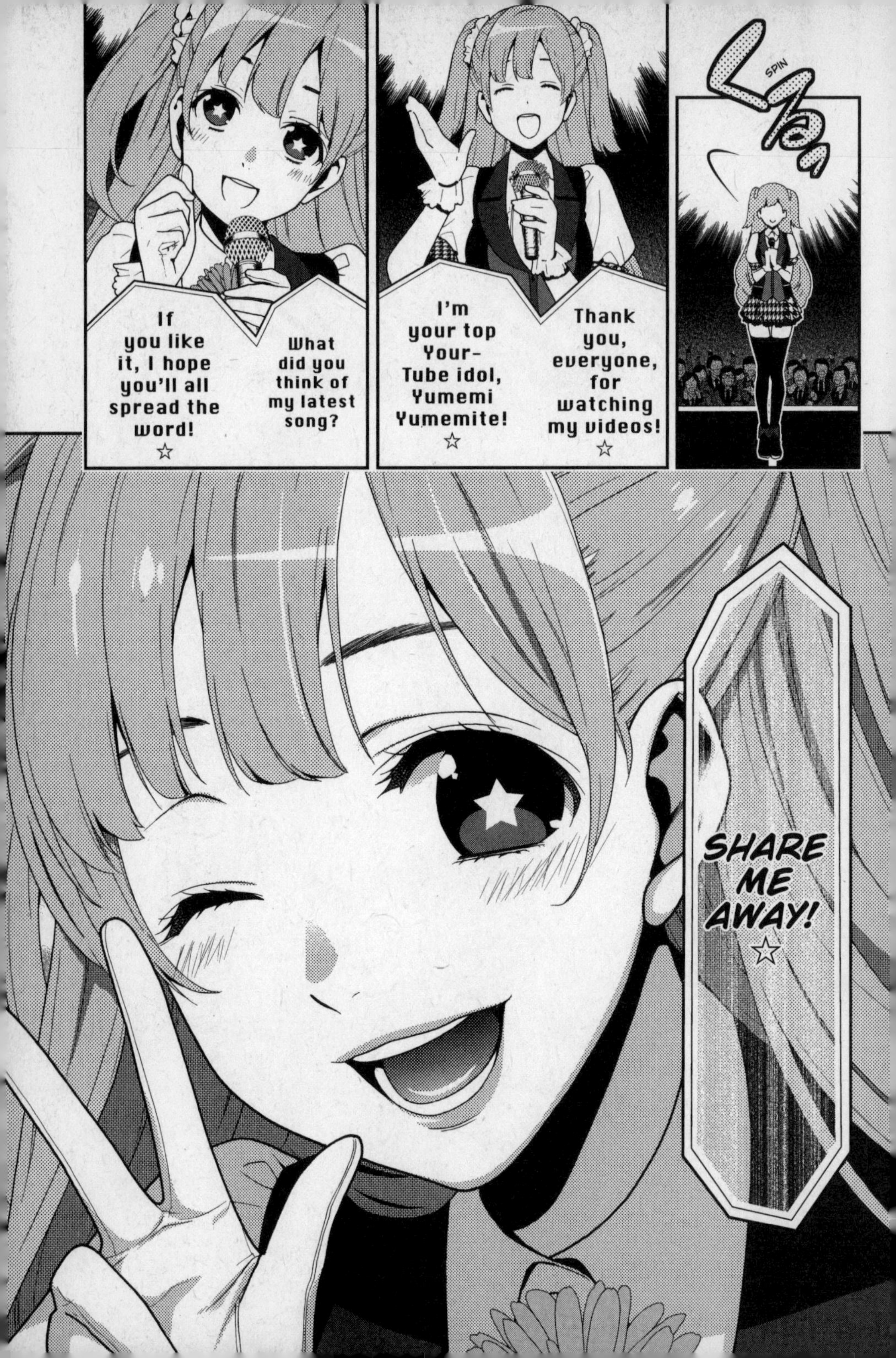
SPIN
Thank you, everyone, for watching my videos! ☆
I'm your top Your-Tube idol, Yumemi Yumemite! ☆
What did you think of my latest song?
If you like it, I hope you'll all spread the word! ☆
SHARE ME AWAY! ☆

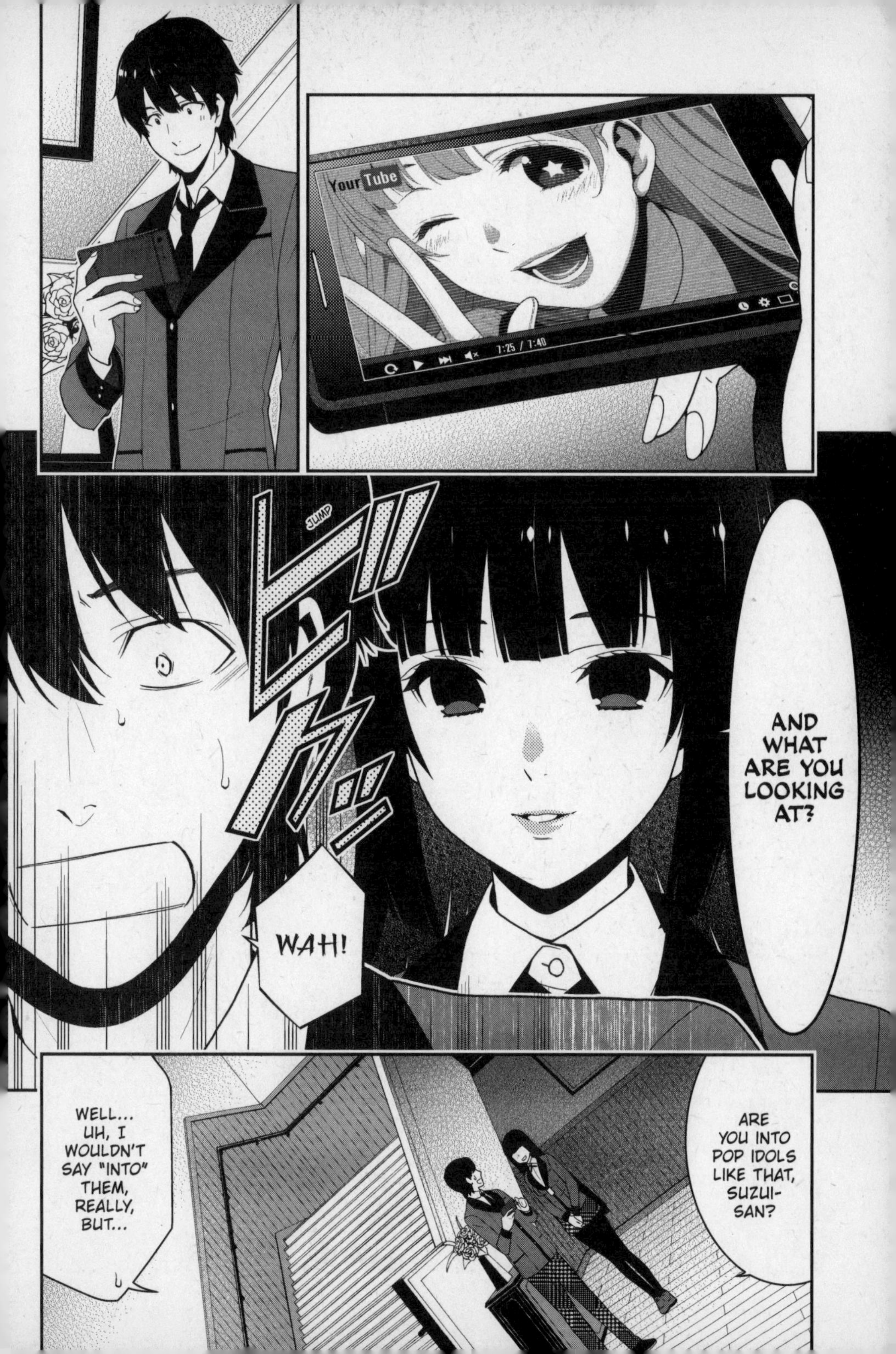
YourTube
7:25 / 7:40
AND WHAT ARE YOU LOOKING AT?
JUMP
WAH!
ARE YOU INTO POP IDOLS LIKE THAT, SUZUI-SAN?
WELL... UH, I WOULDN'T SAY "INTO" THEM, REALLY, BUT...

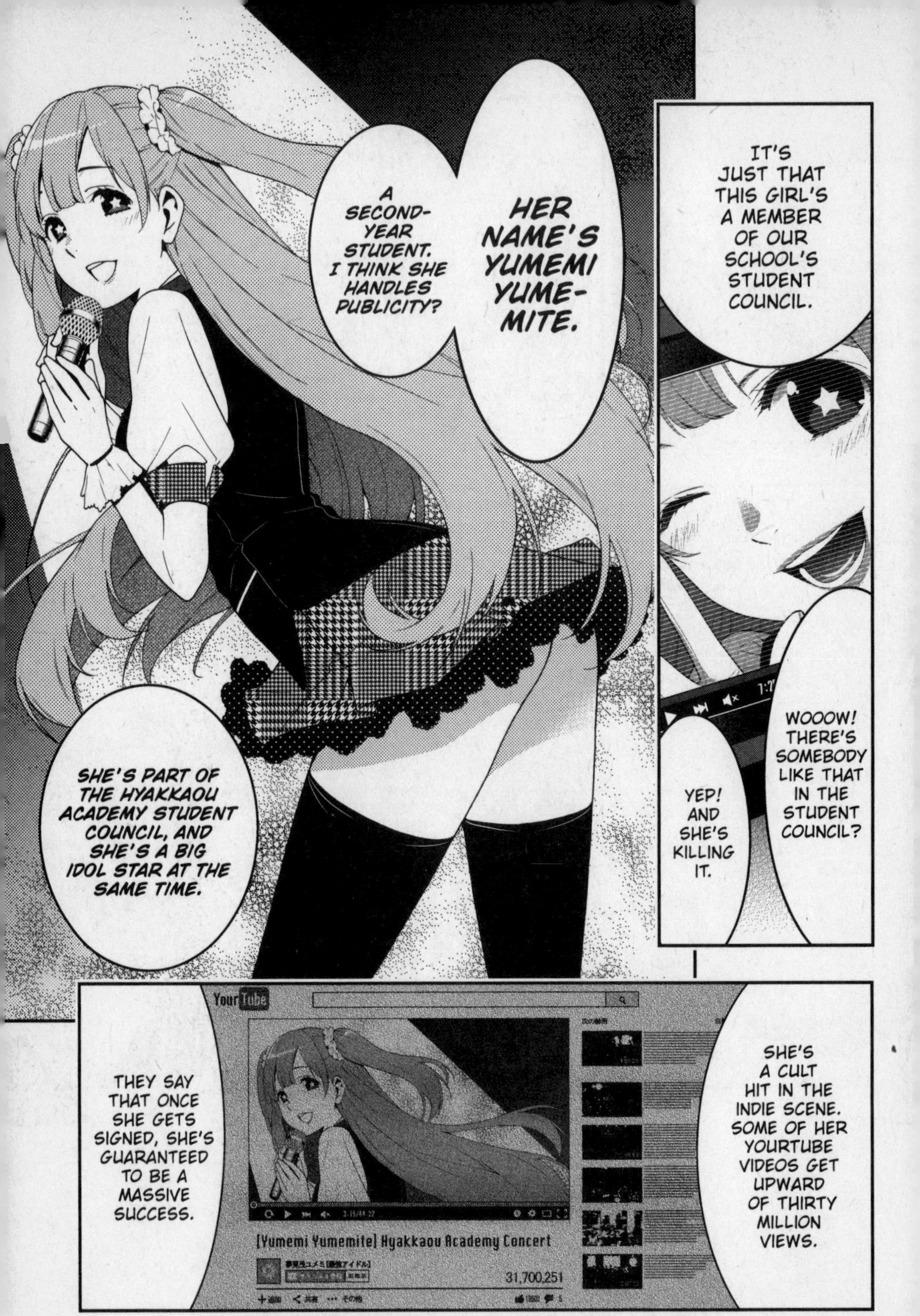
IT'S JUST THAT THIS GIRL'S A MEMBER OF OUR SCHOOL'S STUDENT COUNCIL.
WOOOW! THERE'S SOMEBODY LIKE THAT IN THE STUDENT COUNCIL?
YEP! AND SHE'S KILLING IT.
HER NAME'S YUMEMI YUMEMITE.
A SECOND-YEAR STUDENT. I THINK SHE HANDLES PUBLICITY?
SHE'S PART OF THE HYAKKAOU ACADEMY STUDENT COUNCIL, AND SHE'S A BIG IDOL STAR AT THE SAME TIME.
SHE'S A CULT HIT IN THE INDIE SCENE. SOME OF HER YOURTUBE VIDEOS GET UPWARD OF THIRTY MILLION VIEWS.
YourTube
[Yumemi Yumemite] Hyakkaou Academy Concert
31,700,251
THEY SAY THAT ONCE SHE GETS SIGNED, SHE'S GUARANTEED TO BE A MASSIVE SUCCESS.

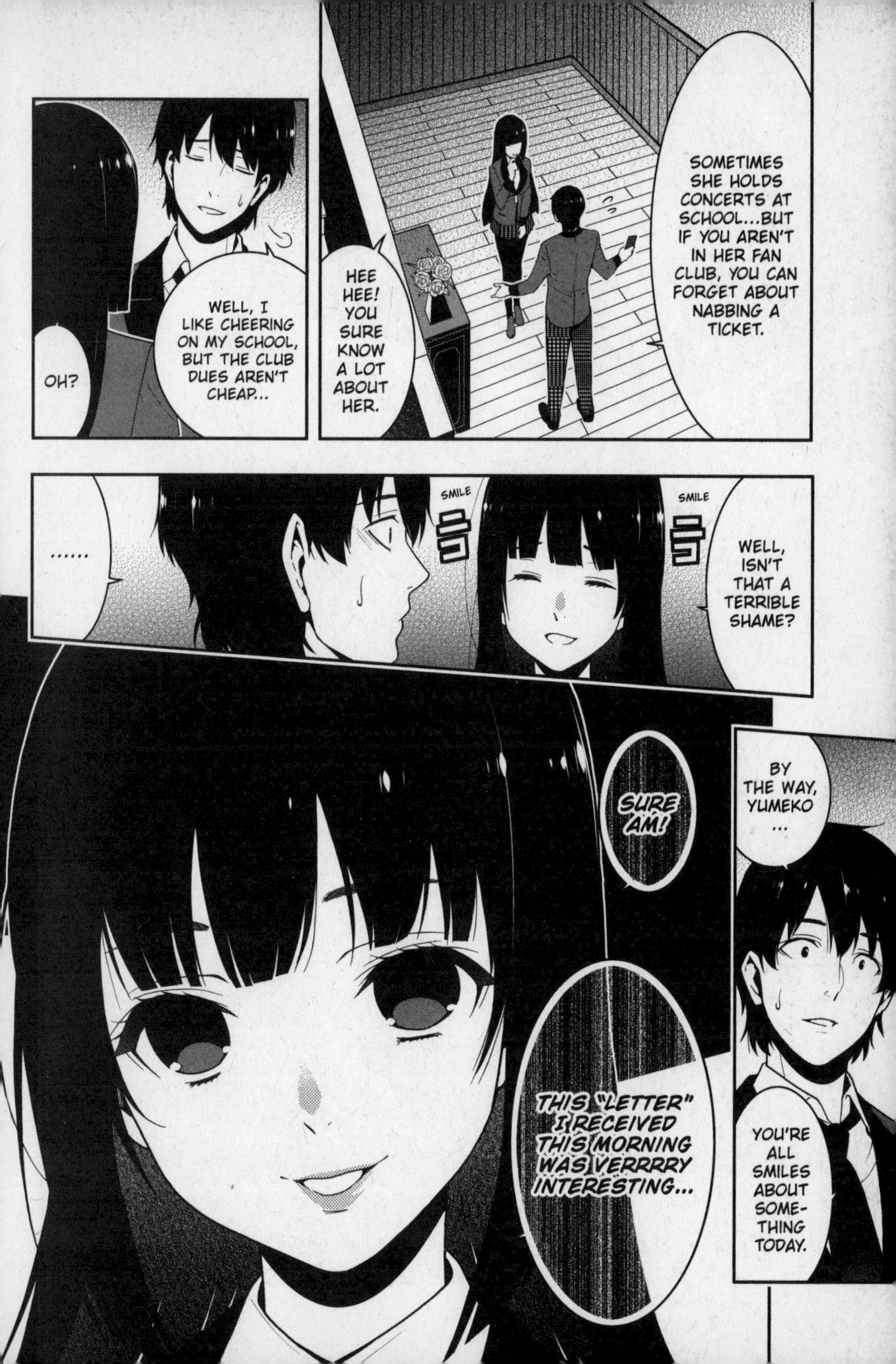
SOMETIMES SHE HOLDS CONCERTS AT SCHOOL...BUT IF YOU AREN'T IN HER FAN CLUB, YOU CAN FORGET ABOUT NABBING A TICKET.
HEE HEE! YOU SURE KNOW A LOT ABOUT HER.
WELL, I LIKE CHEERING ON MY SCHOOL, BUT THE CLUB DUES AREN'T CHEAP...
OH?
WELL, ISN'T THAT A TERRIBLE SHAME?
SMILE
SMILE
......
BY THE WAY, YUMEKO...
YOU'RE ALL SMILES ABOUT SOME-THING TODAY.
SURE AM!
THIS "LETTER" I RECEIVED THIS MORNING WAS VERRRRY INTERESTING...

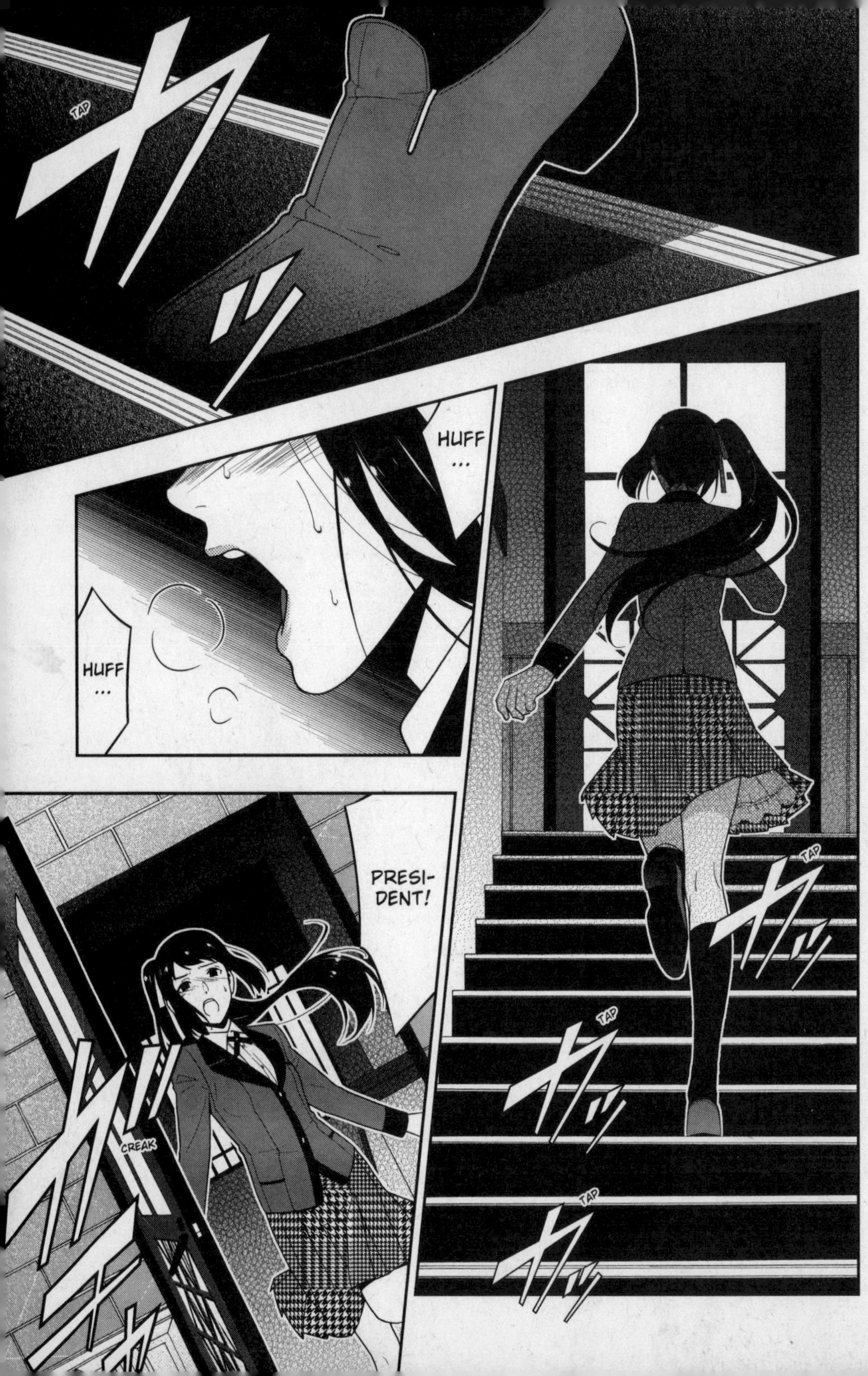
TAP
HUFF ...
TAP
TAP
TAP
HUFF ...
PRESI-DENT!
CREAK

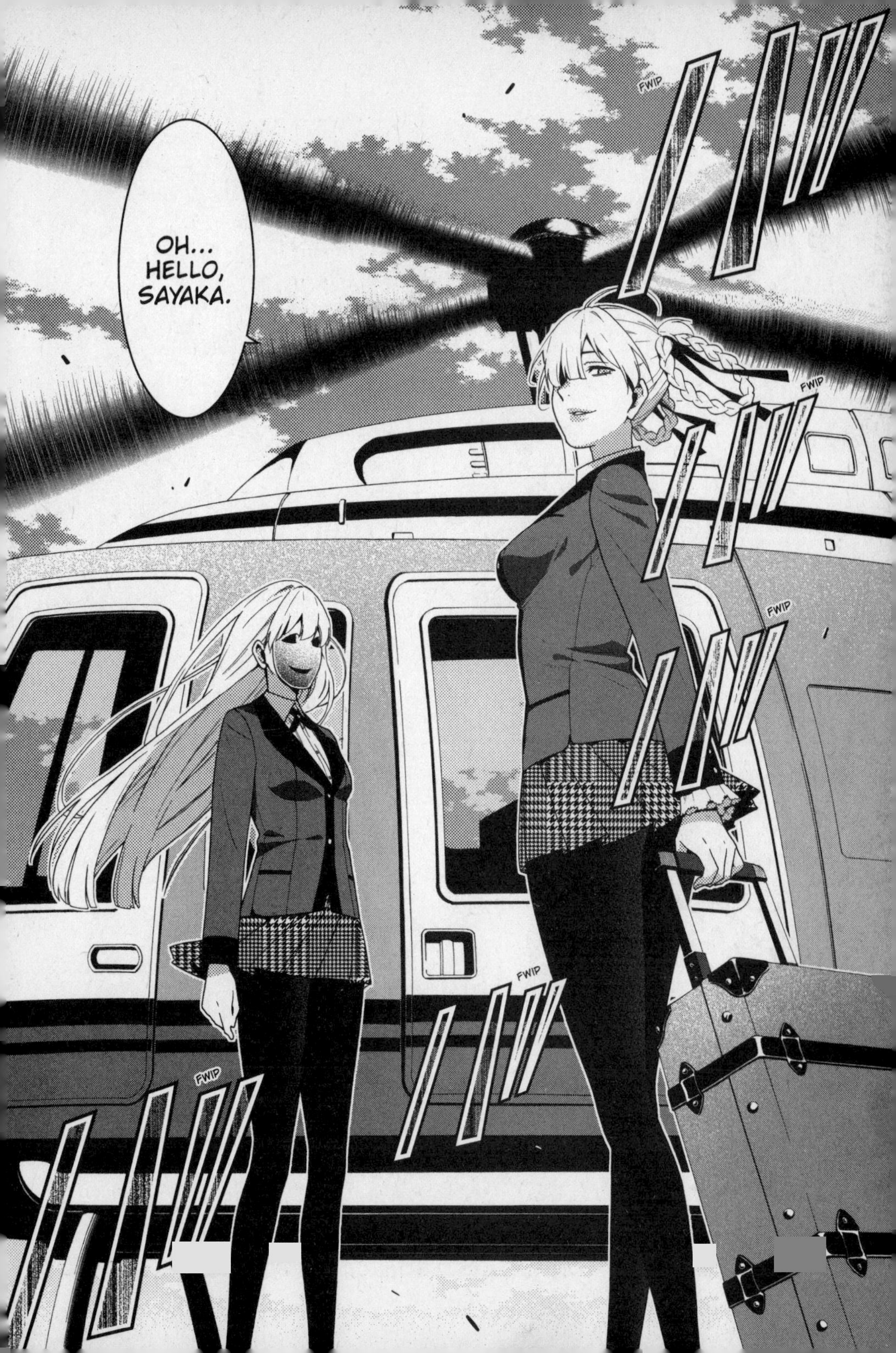
FWIP
FWIP
OH... HELLO, SAYAKA.
FWIP
FWIP
FWIP

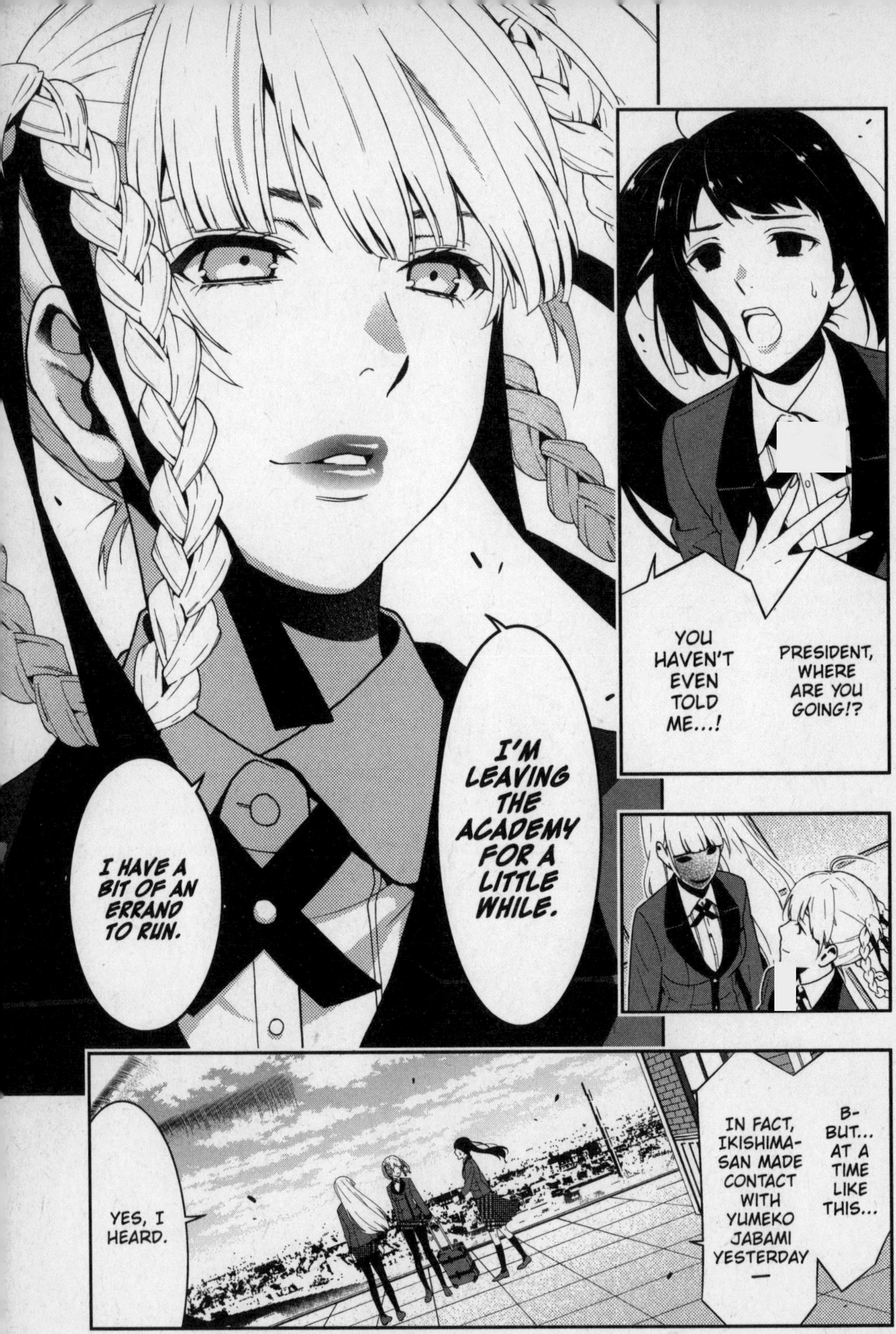
PRESIDENT, WHERE ARE YOU GOING!?
YOU HAVEN'T EVEN TOLD ME...!
I'M LEAVING THE ACADEMY FOR A LITTLE WHILE.
I HAVE A BIT OF AN ERRAND TO RUN.
B-BUT... AT A TIME LIKE THIS...
IN FACT, IKISHIMA-SAN MADE CONTACT WITH YUMEKO JABAMI YESTERDAY—
YES, I HEARD.

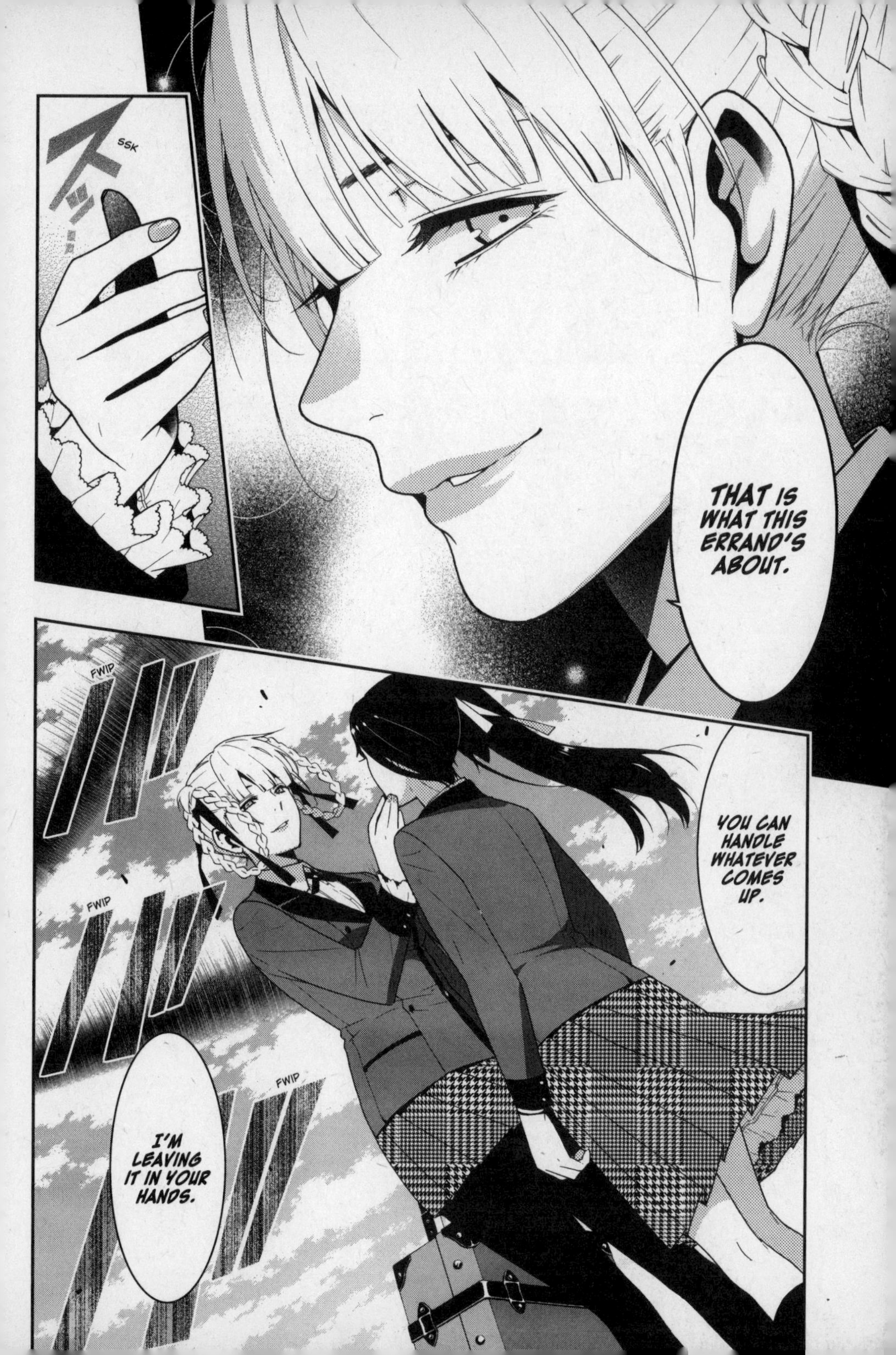
THAT IS WHAT THIS ERRAND'S ABOUT.
SSK
YOU CAN HANDLE WHATEVER COMES UP.
I'M LEAVING IT IN YOUR HANDS.
FWIP
FWIP
FWIP

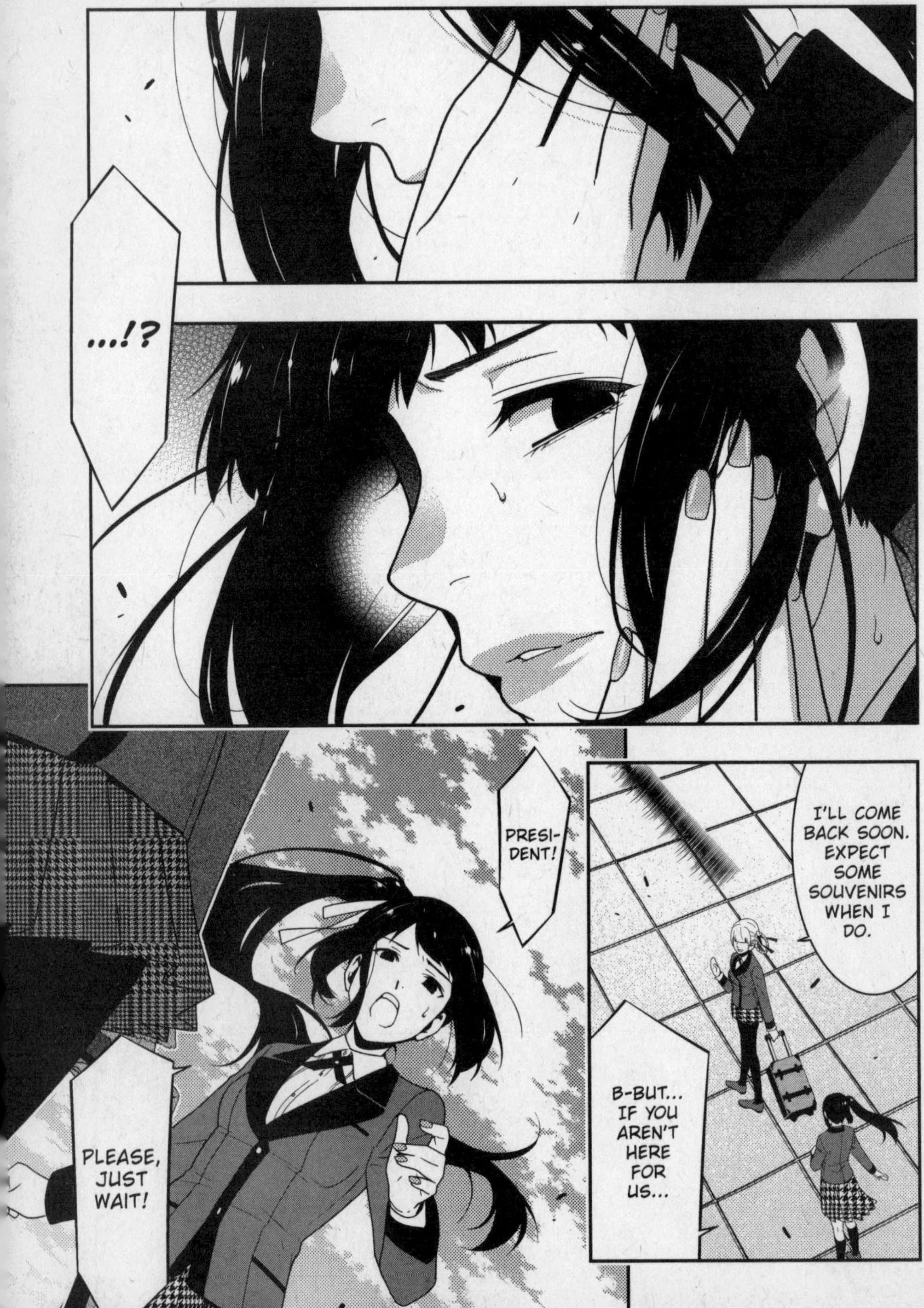
...!?
I'LL COME BACK SOON. EXPECT SOME SOUVENIRS WHEN I DO.
B-BUT... IF YOU AREN'T HERE FOR US...
PRESI-DENT!
PLEASE, JUST WAIT!

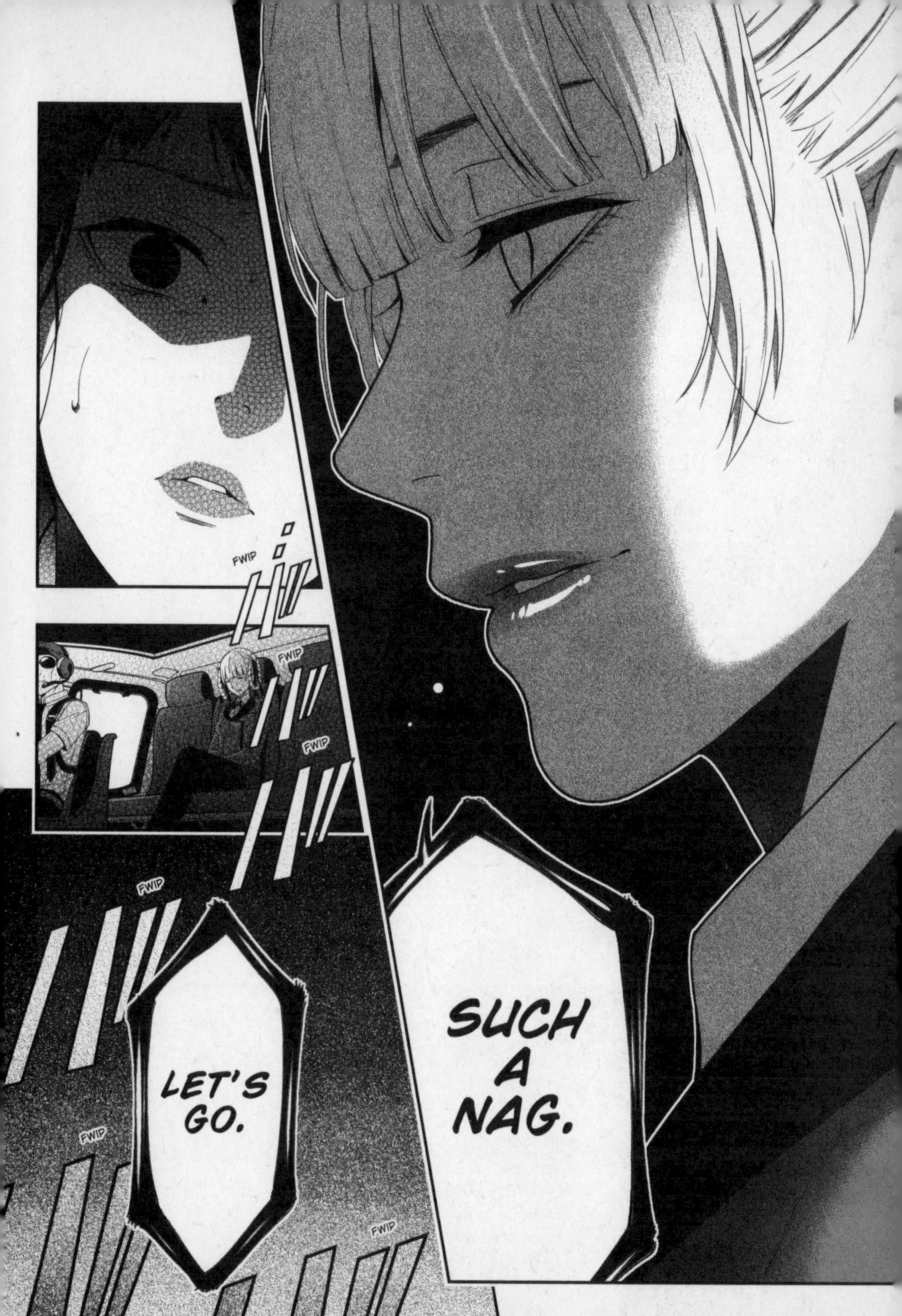
SUCH A NAG.
FWIP
FWIP
FWIP
FWIP
LET'S GO.
FWIP
FWIP

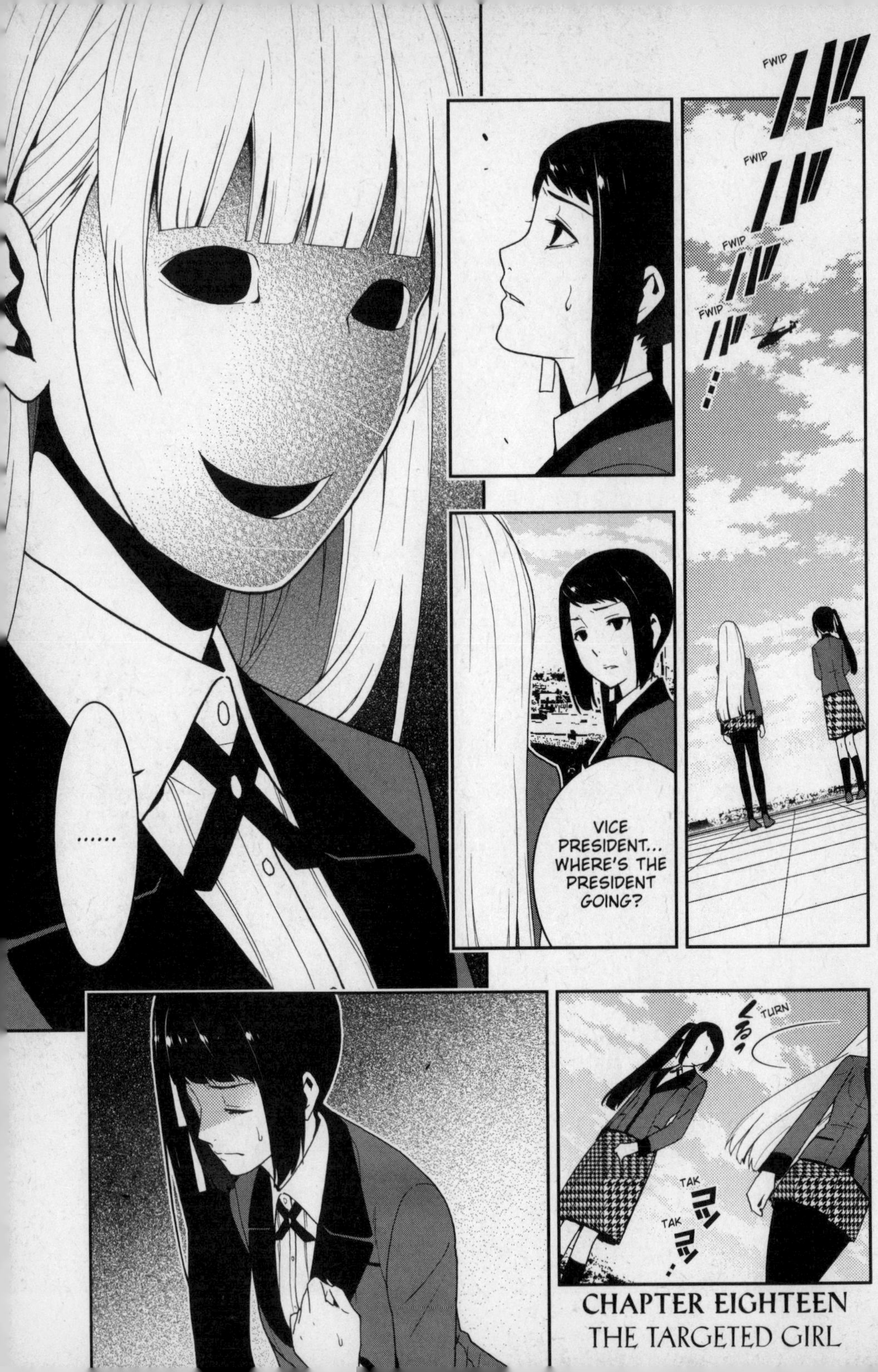
FWIP
FWIP
FWIP
FWIP
VICE PRESIDENT... WHERE'S THE PRESIDENT GOING?
......
TURN
TAK
TAK

CHAPTER EIGHTEEN
THE TARGETED GIRL

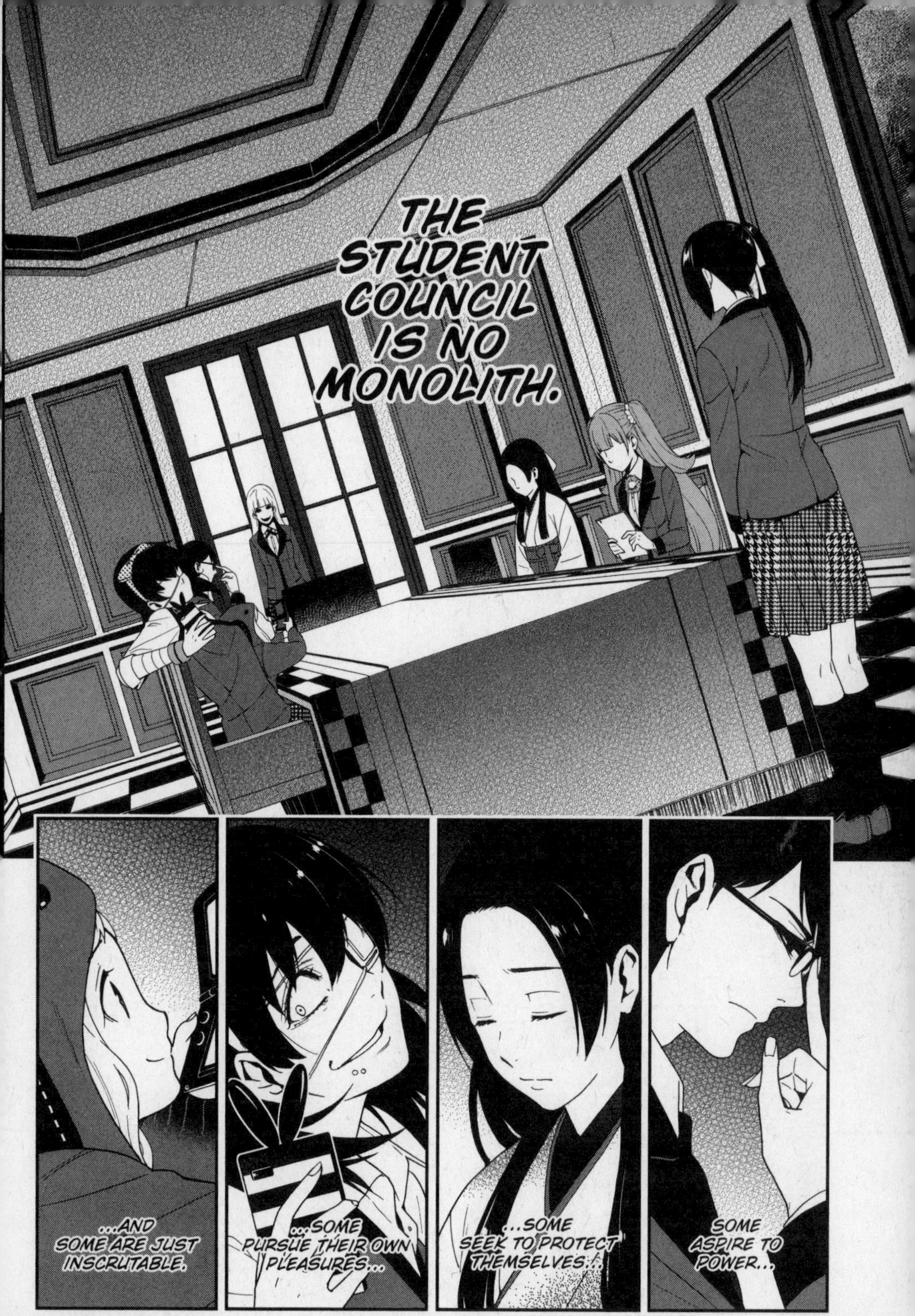
THE STUDENT COUNCIL IS NO MONOLITH.
SOME ASPIRE TO POWER...
...SOME SEEK TO PROTECT THEMSELVES...
...SOME PURSUE THEIR OWN PLEASURES...
...AND SOME ARE JUST INSCRUTABLE.

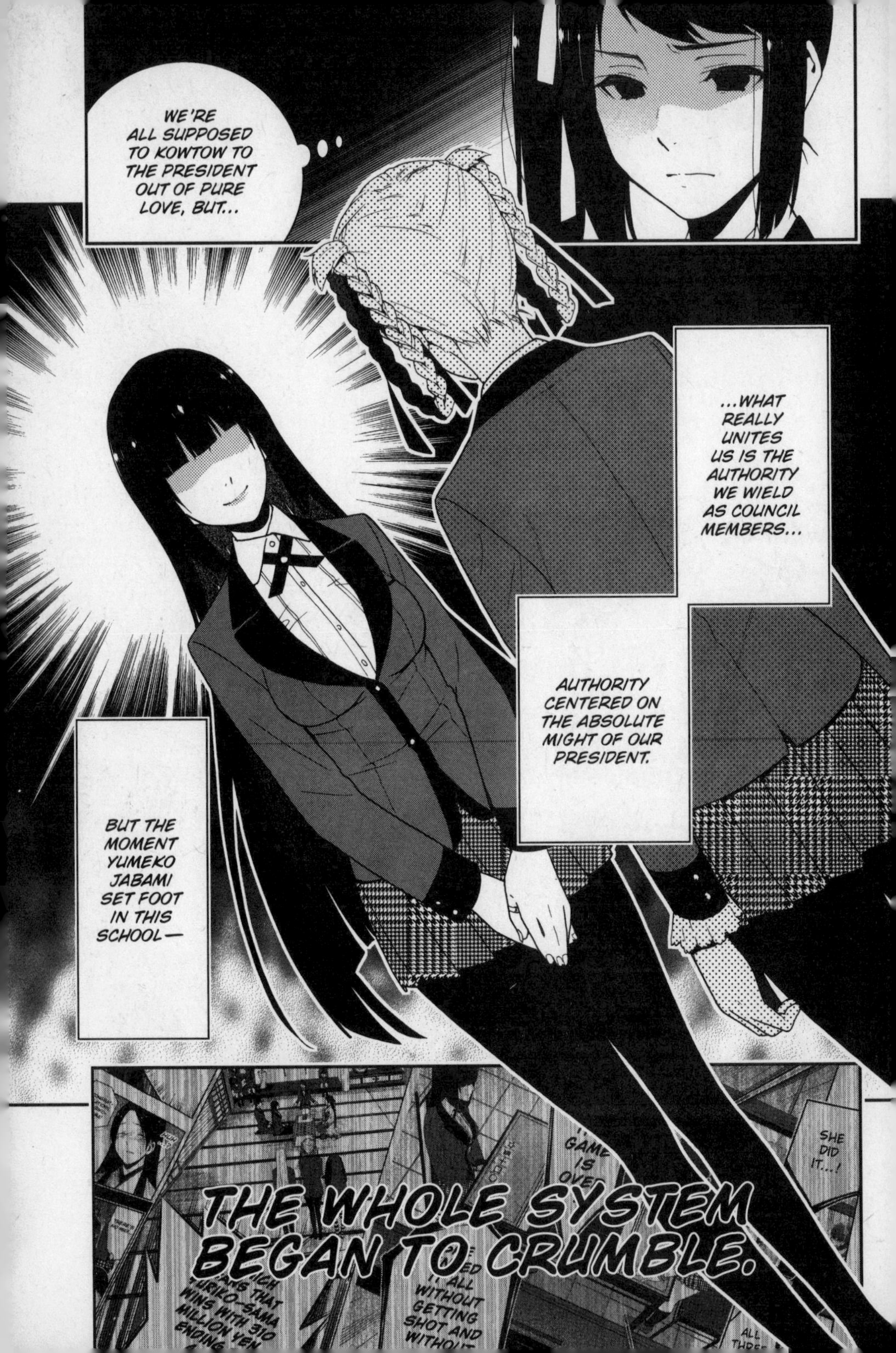
WE'RE ALL SUPPOSED TO KOWTOW TO THE PRESIDENT OUT OF PURE LOVE, BUT...
...WHAT REALLY UNITES US IS THE AUTHORITY WE WIELD AS COUNCIL MEMBERS...
AUTHORITY CENTERED ON THE ABSOLUTE MIGHT OF OUR PRESIDENT.
BUT THE MOMENT YUMEKO JABAMI SET FOOT IN THIS SCHOOL—
SHE DID IT...!
THE WHOLE SYSTEM BEGAN TO CRUMBLE.

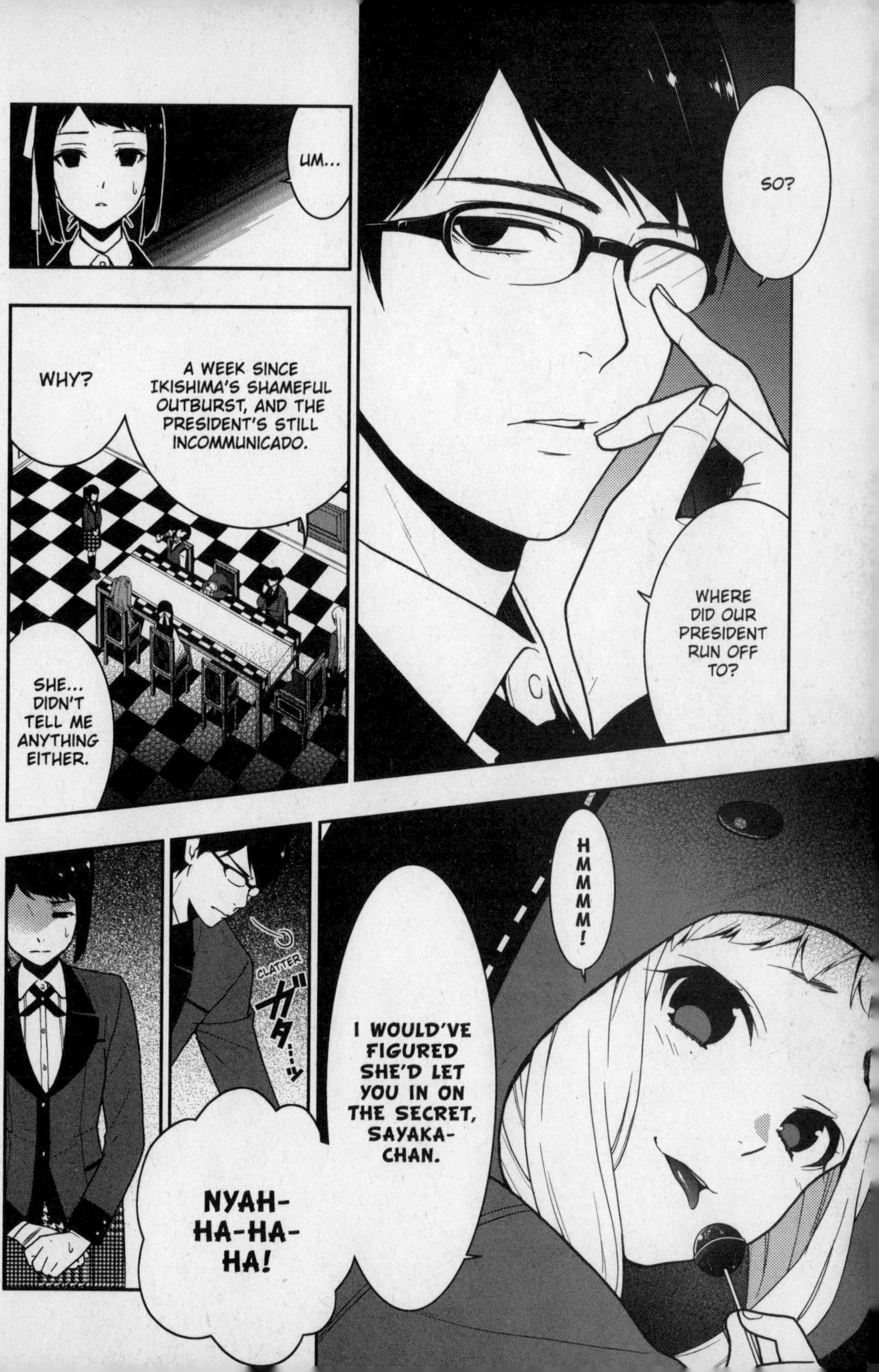
SO?
WHERE DID OUR PRESIDENT RUN OFF TO?
UM...
A WEEK SINCE IKISHIMA'S SHAMEFUL OUTBURST, AND THE PRESIDENT'S STILL INCOMMUNICADO.
WHY?
SHE... DIDN'T TELL ME ANYTHING EITHER.
HMMMM!
I WOULD'VE FIGURED SHE'D LET YOU IN ON THE SECRET, SAYAKA-CHAN.
NYAH-HA-HA-HA!
CLATTER
ガタ…ッ

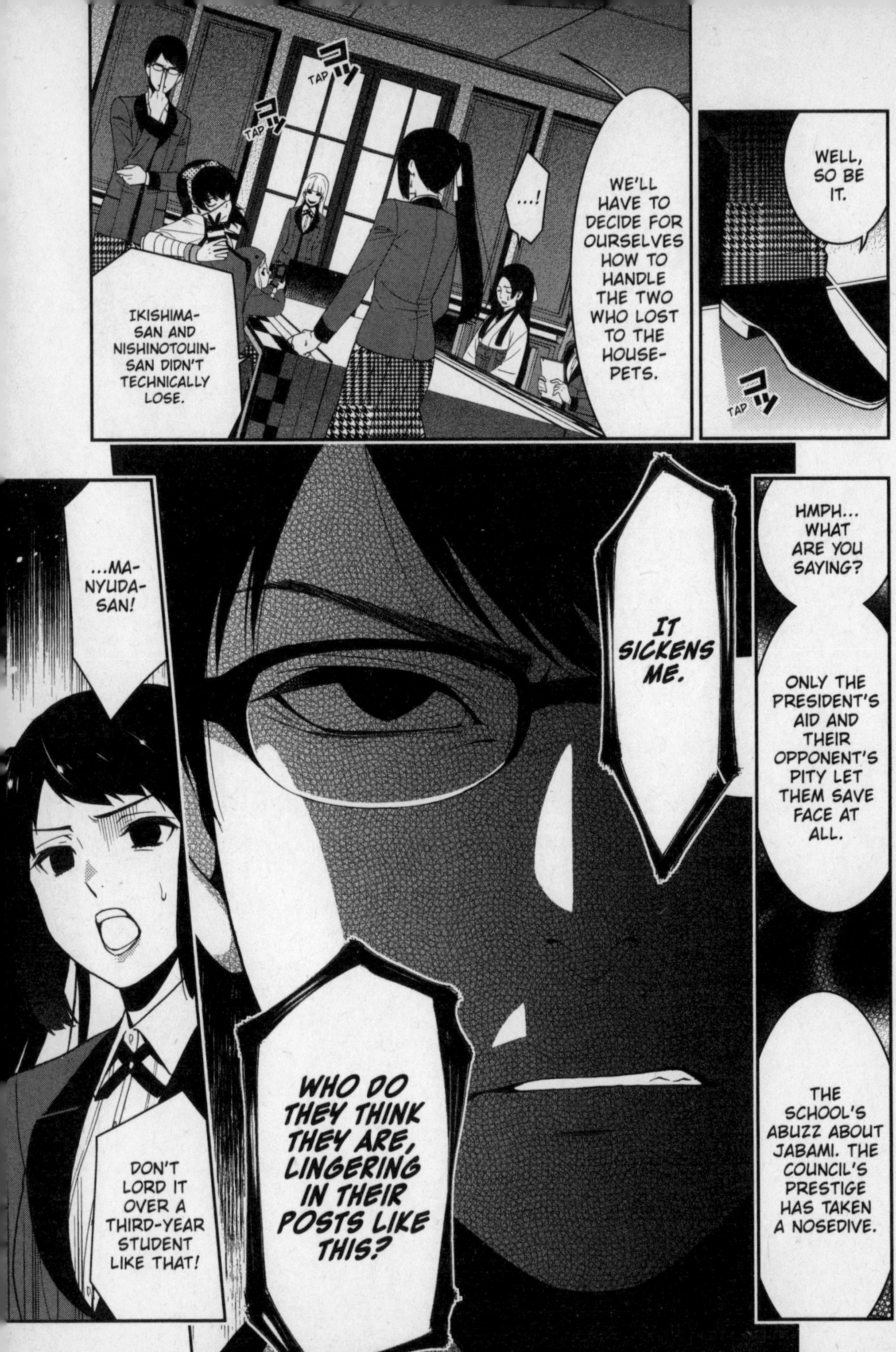
WELL, SO BE IT.
コツ TAP
WE'LL HAVE TO DECIDE FOR OURSELVES HOW TO HANDLE THE TWO WHO LOST TO THE HOUSE-PETS.
...!
コツ TAP
コツ TAP
IKISHIMA-SAN AND NISHINOTOUIN-SAN DIDN'T TECHNICALLY LOSE.
HMPH... WHAT ARE YOU SAYING?
ONLY THE PRESIDENT'S AID AND THEIR OPPONENT'S PITY LET THEM SAVE FACE AT ALL.
THE SCHOOL'S ABUZZ ABOUT JABAMI. THE COUNCIL'S PRESTIGE HAS TAKEN A NOSEDIVE.
IT SICKENS ME.
WHO DO THEY THINK THEY ARE, LINGERING IN THEIR POSTS LIKE THIS?
...MA-NYUDA-SAN!
DON'T LORD IT OVER A THIRD-YEAR STUDENT LIKE THAT!

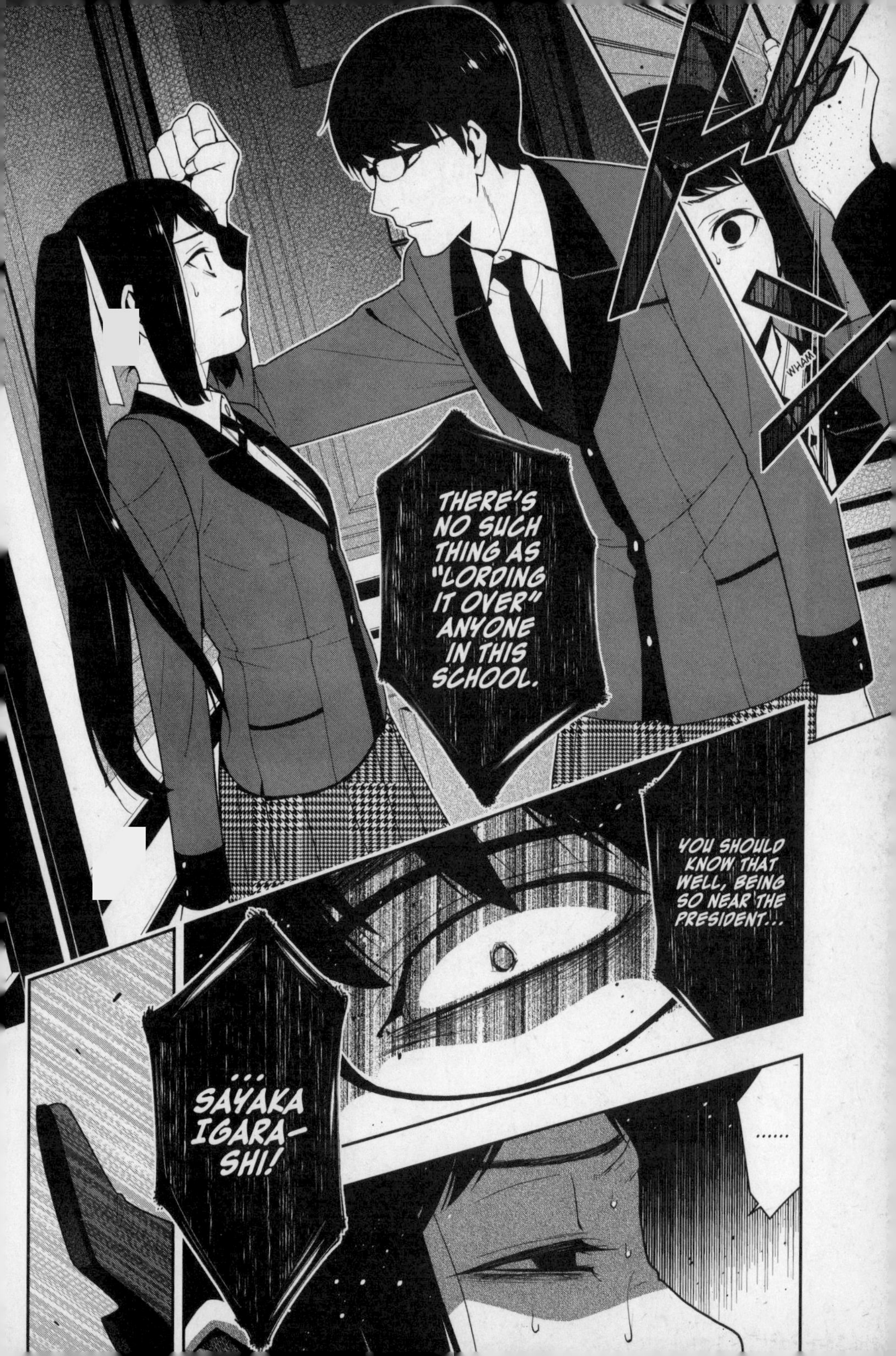
WHAM
THERE'S NO SUCH THING AS "LORDING IT OVER" ANYONE IN THIS SCHOOL.
YOU SHOULD KNOW THAT WELL, BEING SO NEAR THE PRESIDENT...
......
... SAYAKA IGARASHI!

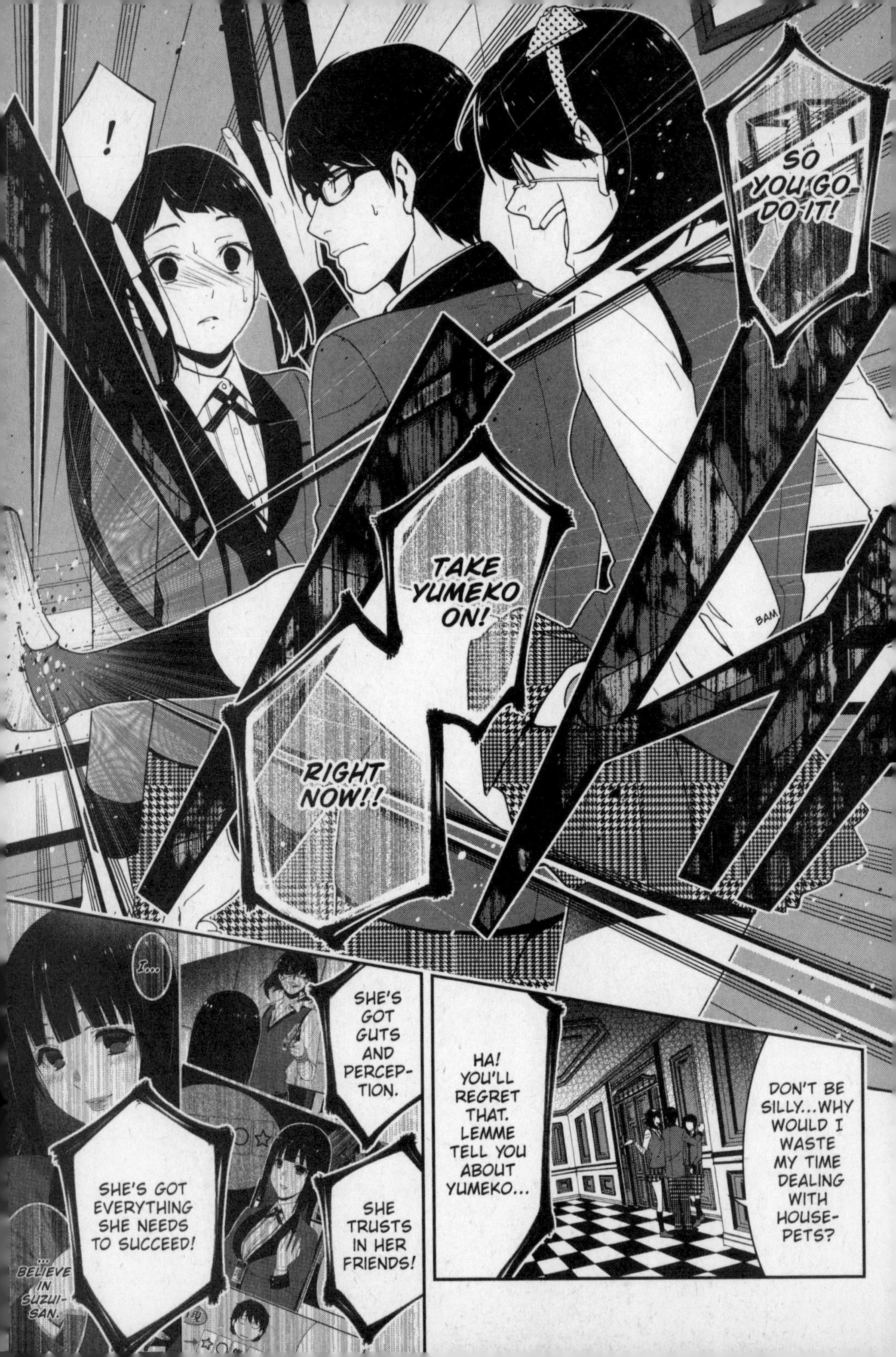
SO YOU GO DO IT!
!
TAKE YUMEKO ON!
BAM
RIGHT NOW!!
DON'T BE SILLY...WHY WOULD I WASTE MY TIME DEALING WITH HOUSE-PETS?
HA! YOU'LL REGRET THAT. LEMME TELL YOU ABOUT YUMEKO...
SHE'S GOT GUTS AND PERCEP-TION.
I...
SHE TRUSTS IN HER FRIENDS!
SHE'S GOT EVERYTHING SHE NEEDS TO SUCCEED!
...BELIEVE IN SUZUI-SAN.

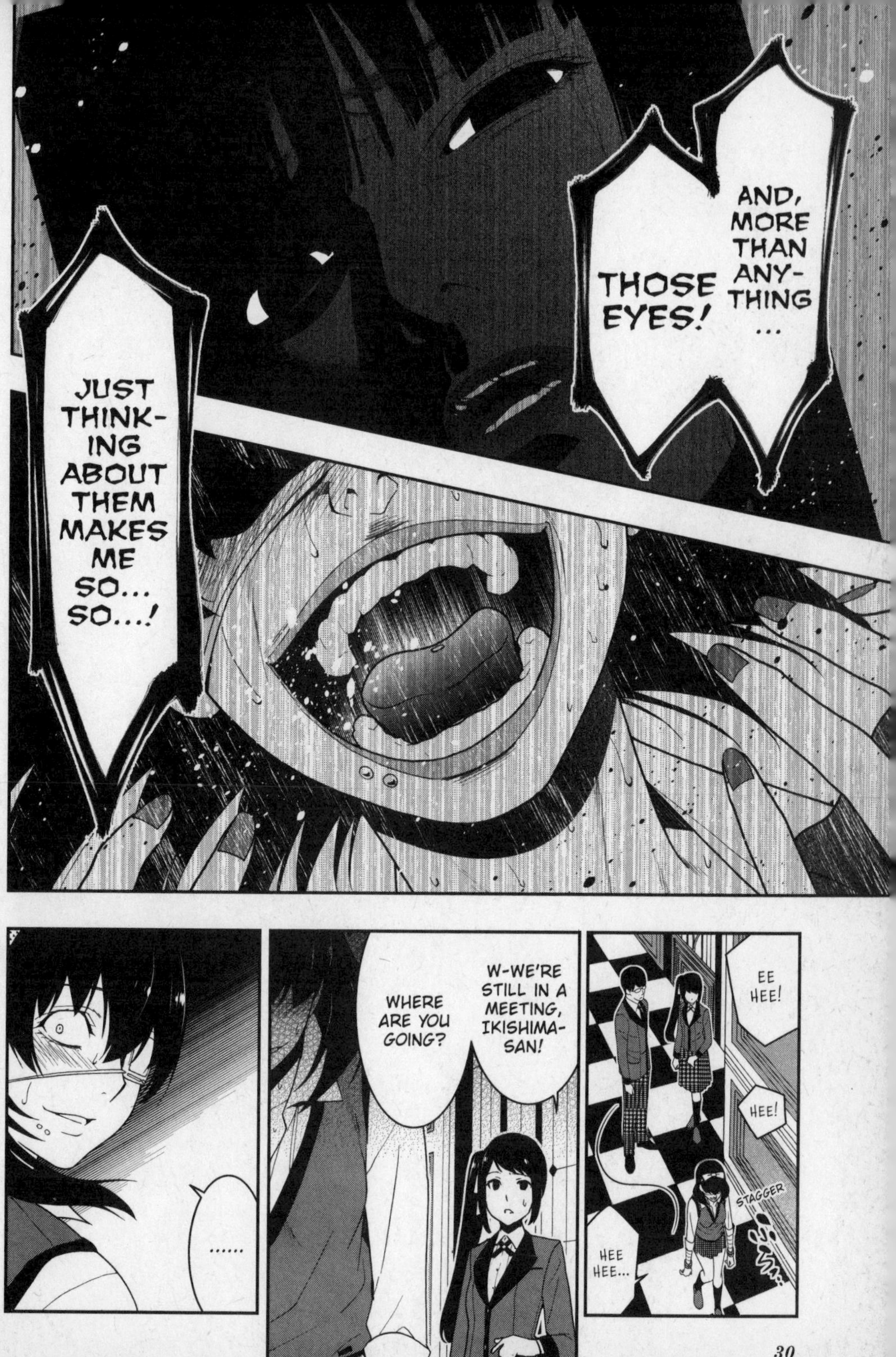
AND, MORE THAN ANYTHING... THOSE EYES!
JUST THINKING ABOUT THEM MAKES ME SO... SO...!
EE HEE!
HEE!
STAGGER
HEE HEE...
W-WE'RE STILL IN A MEETING, IKISHIMA-SAN!
WHERE ARE YOU GOING?
......

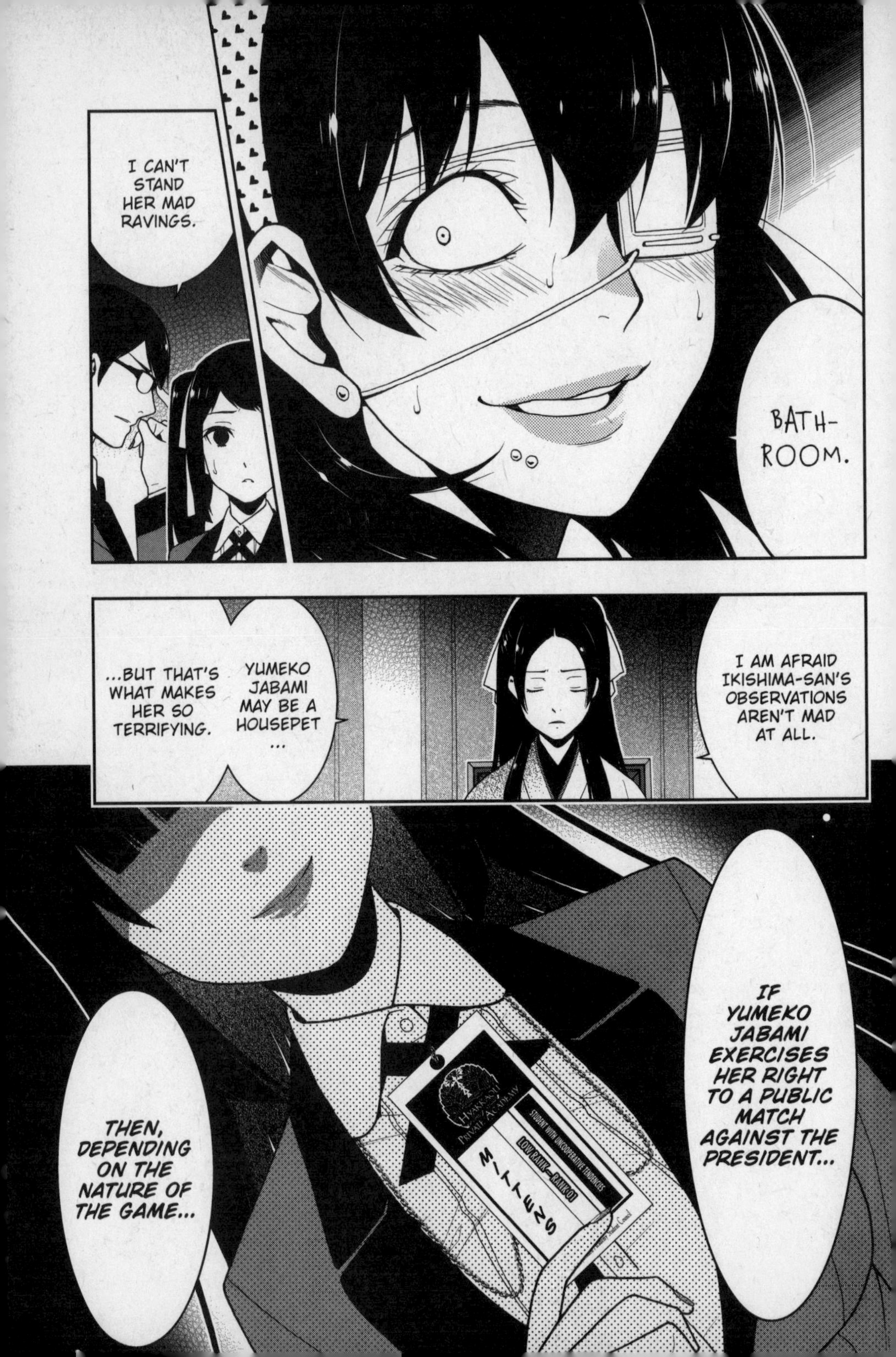
BATH-ROOM.
I CAN'T STAND HER MAD RAVINGS.
I AM AFRAID IKISHIMA-SAN'S OBSERVATIONS AREN'T MAD AT ALL.
YUMEKO JABAMI MAY BE A HOUSEPET ...
...BUT THAT'S WHAT MAKES HER SO TERRIFYING.
IF YUMEKO JABAMI EXERCISES HER RIGHT TO A PUBLIC MATCH AGAINST THE PRESIDENT...
THEN, DEPENDING ON THE NATURE OF THE GAME...

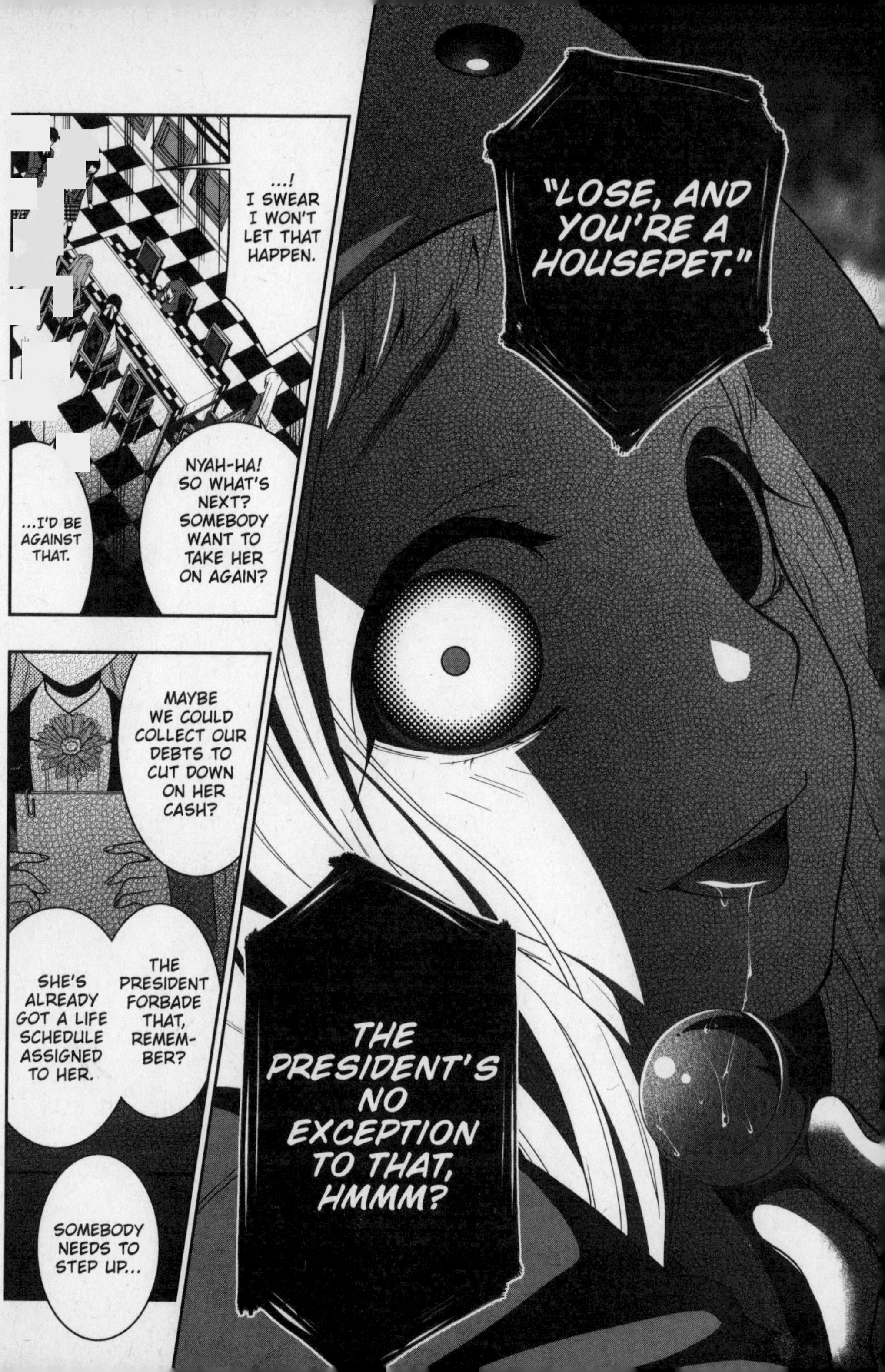
"LOSE, AND YOU'RE A HOUSEPET."
THE PRESIDENT'S NO EXCEPTION TO THAT, HMMM?
...! I SWEAR I WON'T LET THAT HAPPEN.
NYAH-HA! SO WHAT'S NEXT? SOMEBODY WANT TO TAKE HER ON AGAIN?
...I'D BE AGAINST THAT.
MAYBE WE COULD COLLECT OUR DEBTS TO CUT DOWN ON HER CASH?
THE PRESIDENT FORBADE THAT, REMEMBER?
SHE'S ALREADY GOT A LIFE SCHEDULE ASSIGNED TO HER.
SOMEBODY NEEDS TO STEP UP...

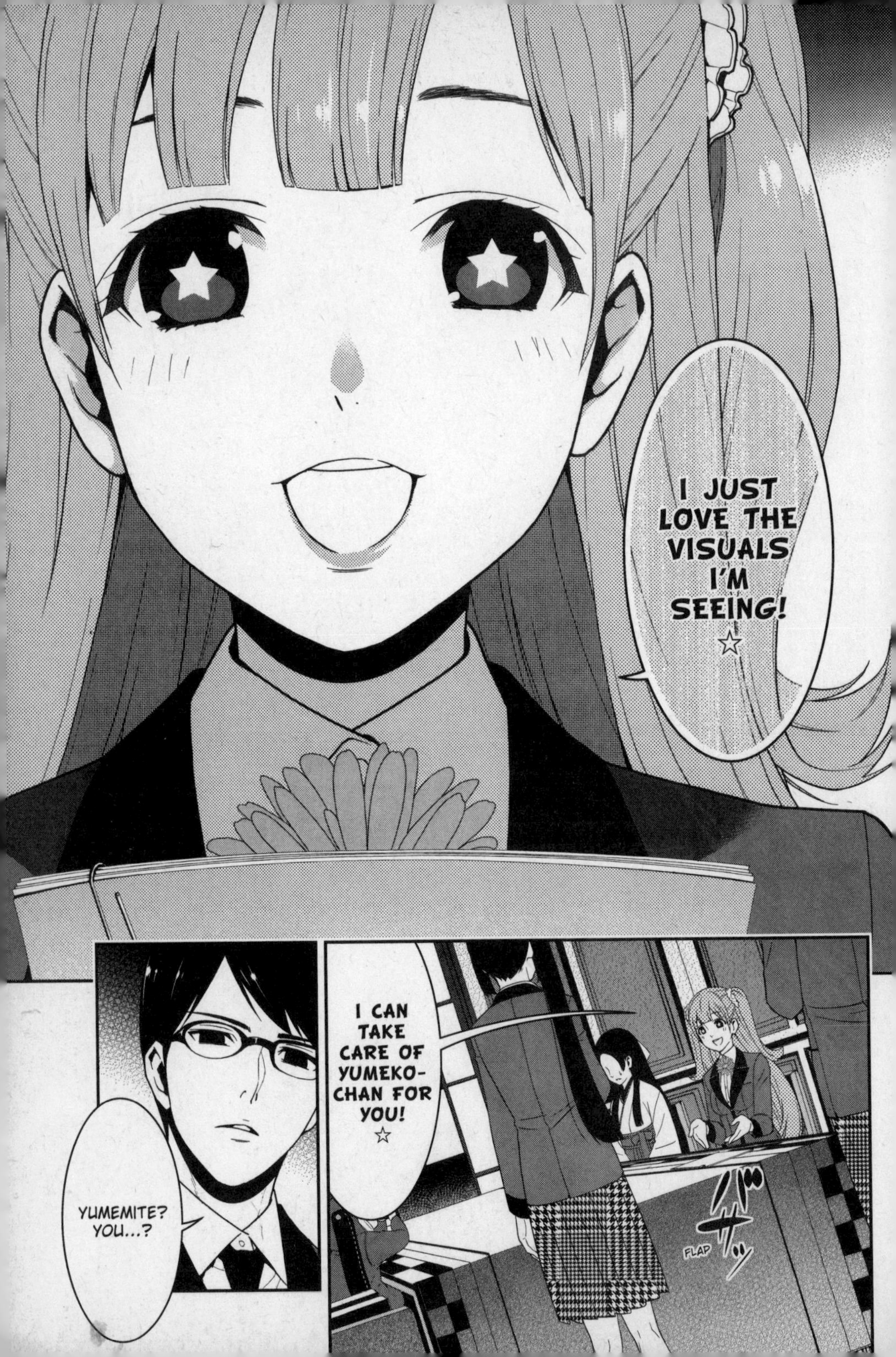
I JUST LOVE THE VISUALS I'M SEEING! ☆
I CAN TAKE CARE OF YUMEKO-CHAN FOR YOU! ☆
FLAP
YUMEMITE? YOU...?

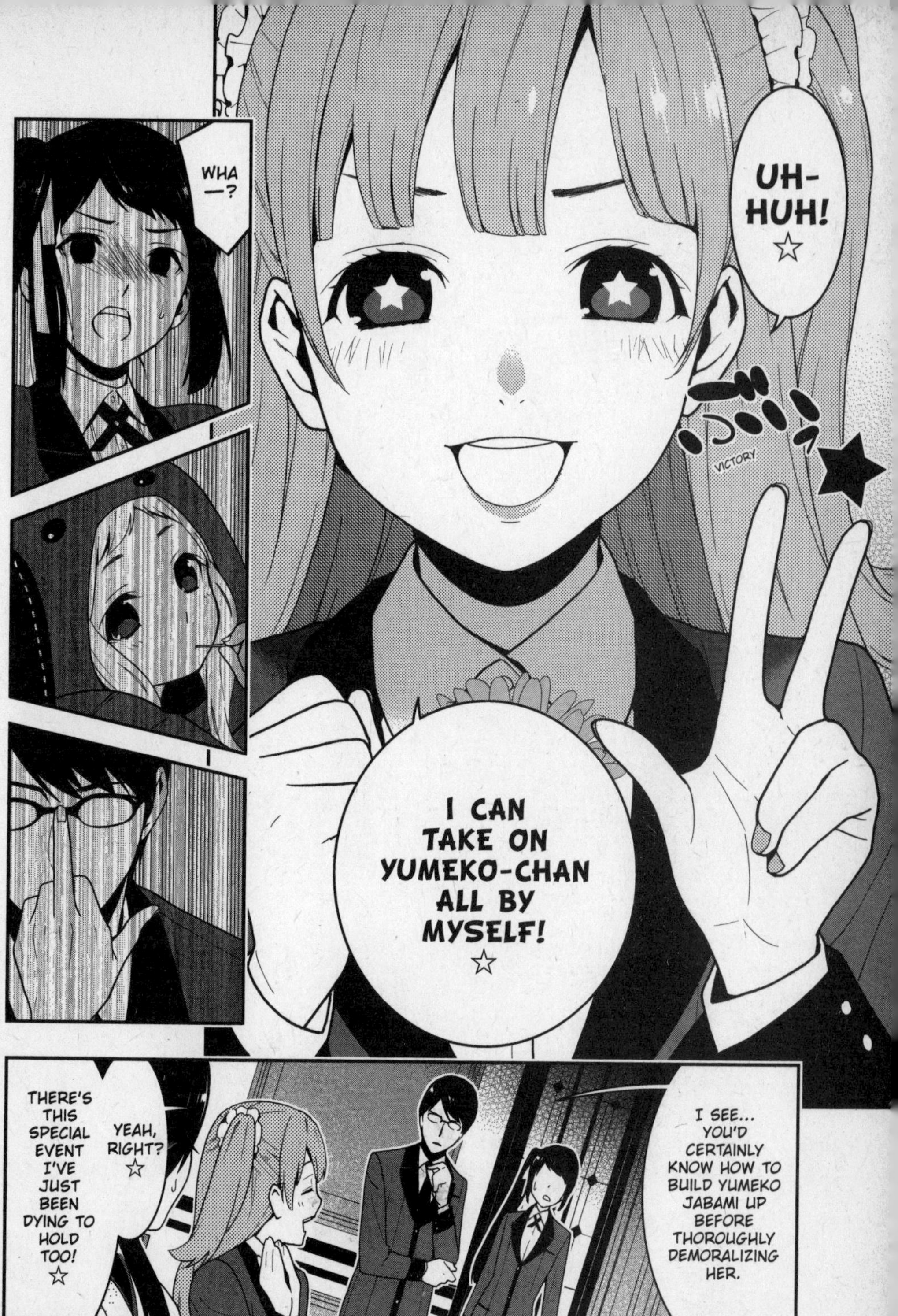
UH-HUH! ☆
VICTORY
I CAN TAKE ON YUMEKO-CHAN ALL BY MYSELF! ☆
WHA—?
I SEE... YOU'D CERTAINLY KNOW HOW TO BUILD YUMEKO JABAMI UP BEFORE THOROUGHLY DEMORALIZING HER.
YEAH, RIGHT? ☆
THERE'S THIS SPECIAL EVENT I'VE JUST BEEN DYING TO HOLD TOO! ☆

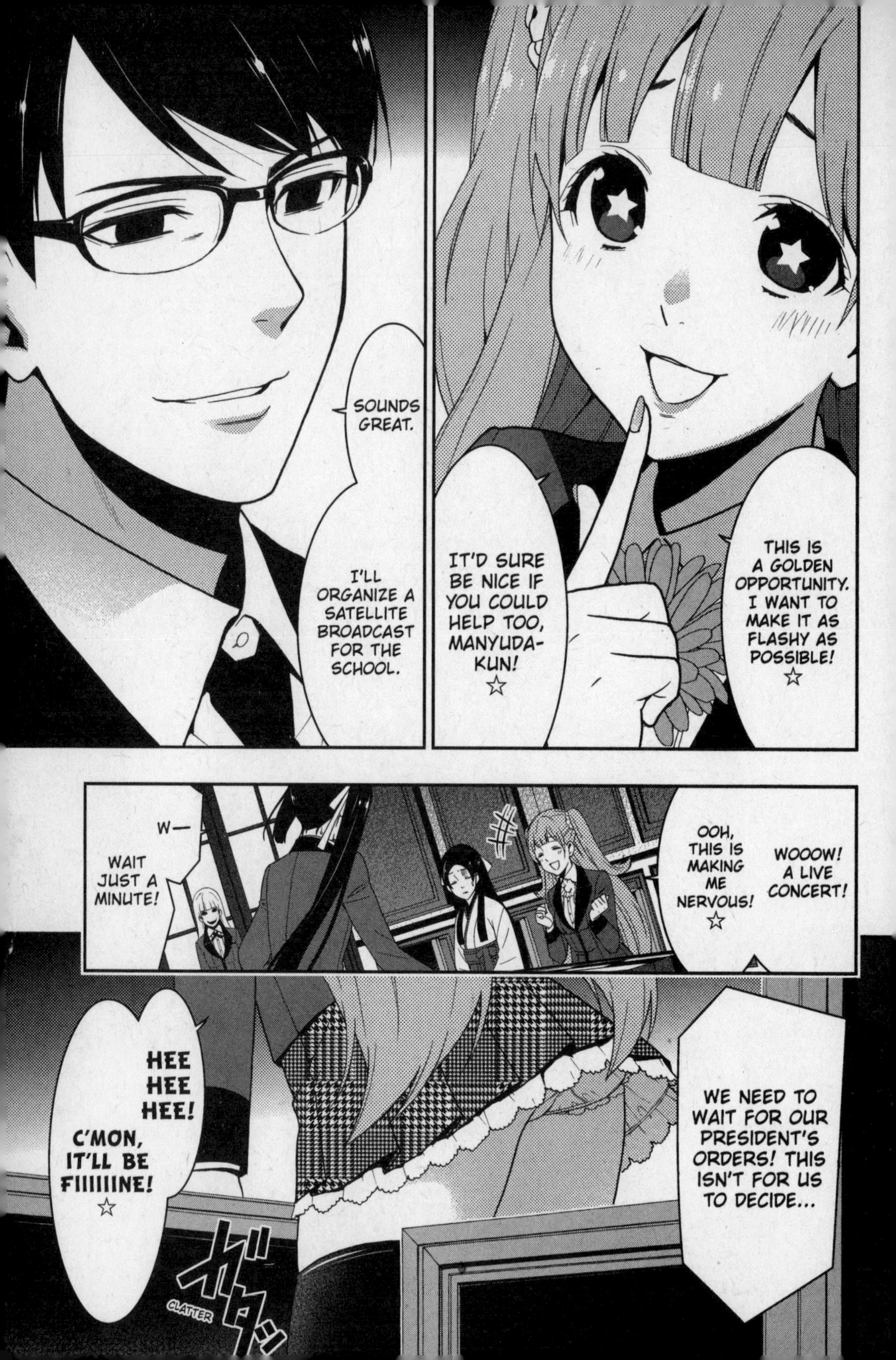
THIS IS A GOLDEN OPPORTUNITY. I WANT TO MAKE IT AS FLASHY AS POSSIBLE! ☆
IT'D SURE BE NICE IF YOU COULD HELP TOO, MANYUDA-KUN! ☆
SOUNDS GREAT.
I'LL ORGANIZE A SATELLITE BROADCAST FOR THE SCHOOL.
WOOOW! A LIVE CONCERT!
OOH, THIS IS MAKING ME NERVOUS! ☆
W—
WAIT JUST A MINUTE!
WE NEED TO WAIT FOR OUR PRESIDENT'S ORDERS! THIS ISN'T FOR US TO DECIDE...
HEE HEE HEE! C'MON, IT'LL BE FIIIIIINE! ☆
CLATTER

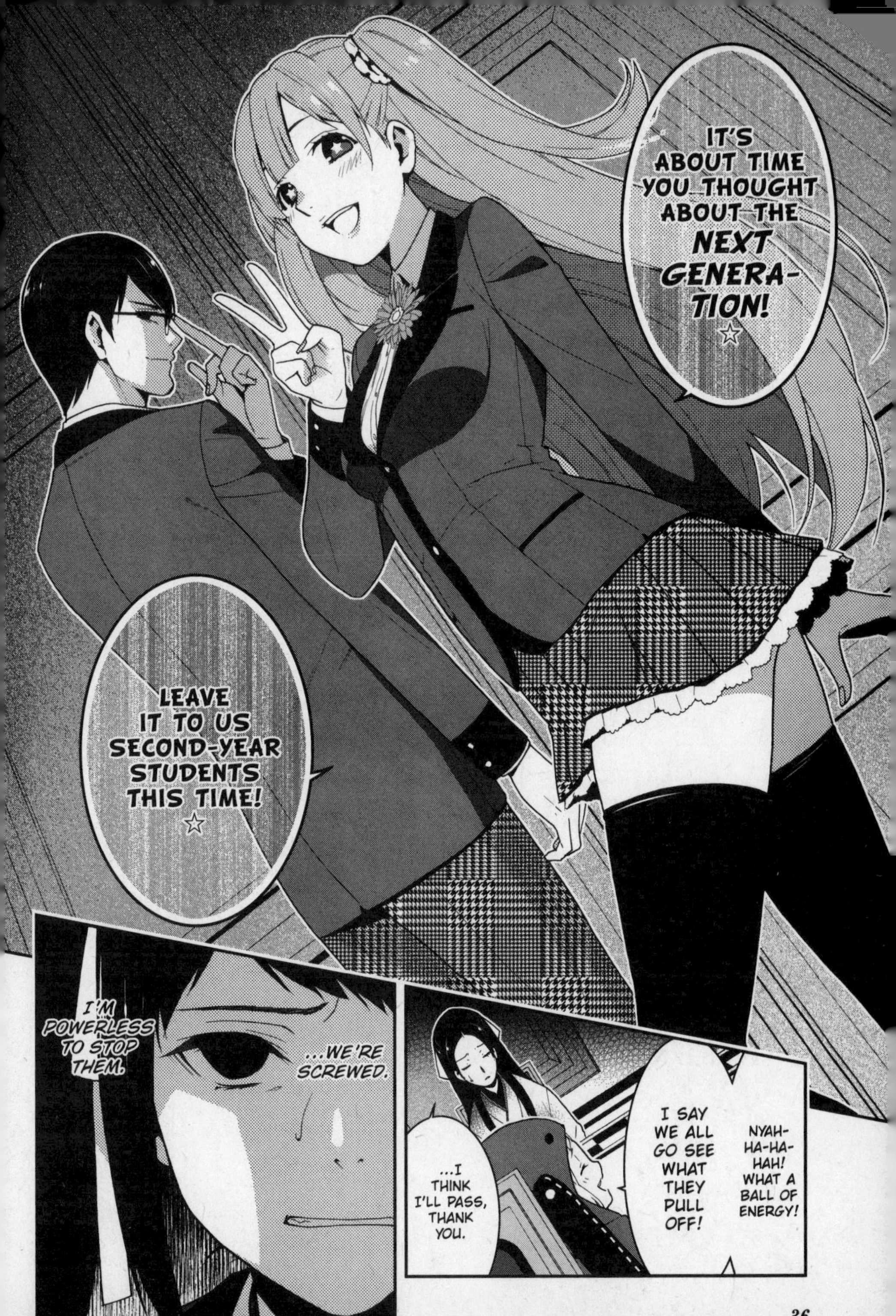
IT'S ABOUT TIME YOU THOUGHT ABOUT THE NEXT GENERATION! ☆
LEAVE IT TO US SECOND-YEAR STUDENTS THIS TIME! ☆
NYAH-HA-HAH! WHAT A BALL OF ENERGY!
I SAY WE ALL GO SEE WHAT THEY PULL OFF!
...I THINK I'LL PASS, THANK YOU.
...WE'RE SCREWED.
I'M POWERLESS TO STOP THEM.

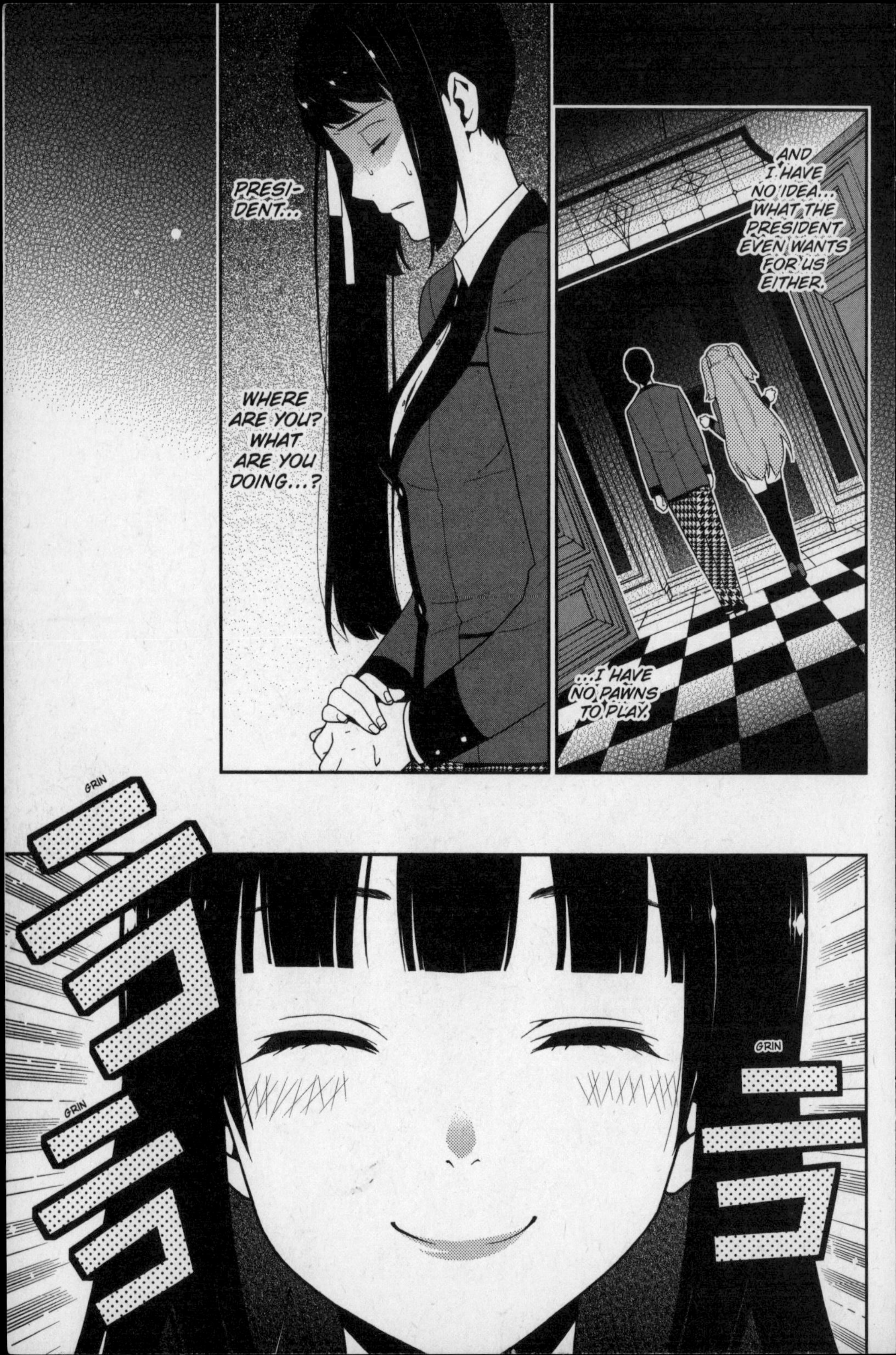

AND I HAVE NO IDEA... WHAT THE PRESIDENT EVEN WANTS FOR US EITHER.
...I HAVE NO PAWNS TO PLAY.
PRESI-DENT...
WHERE ARE YOU? WHAT ARE YOU DOING...?
GRIN
GRIN
GRIN

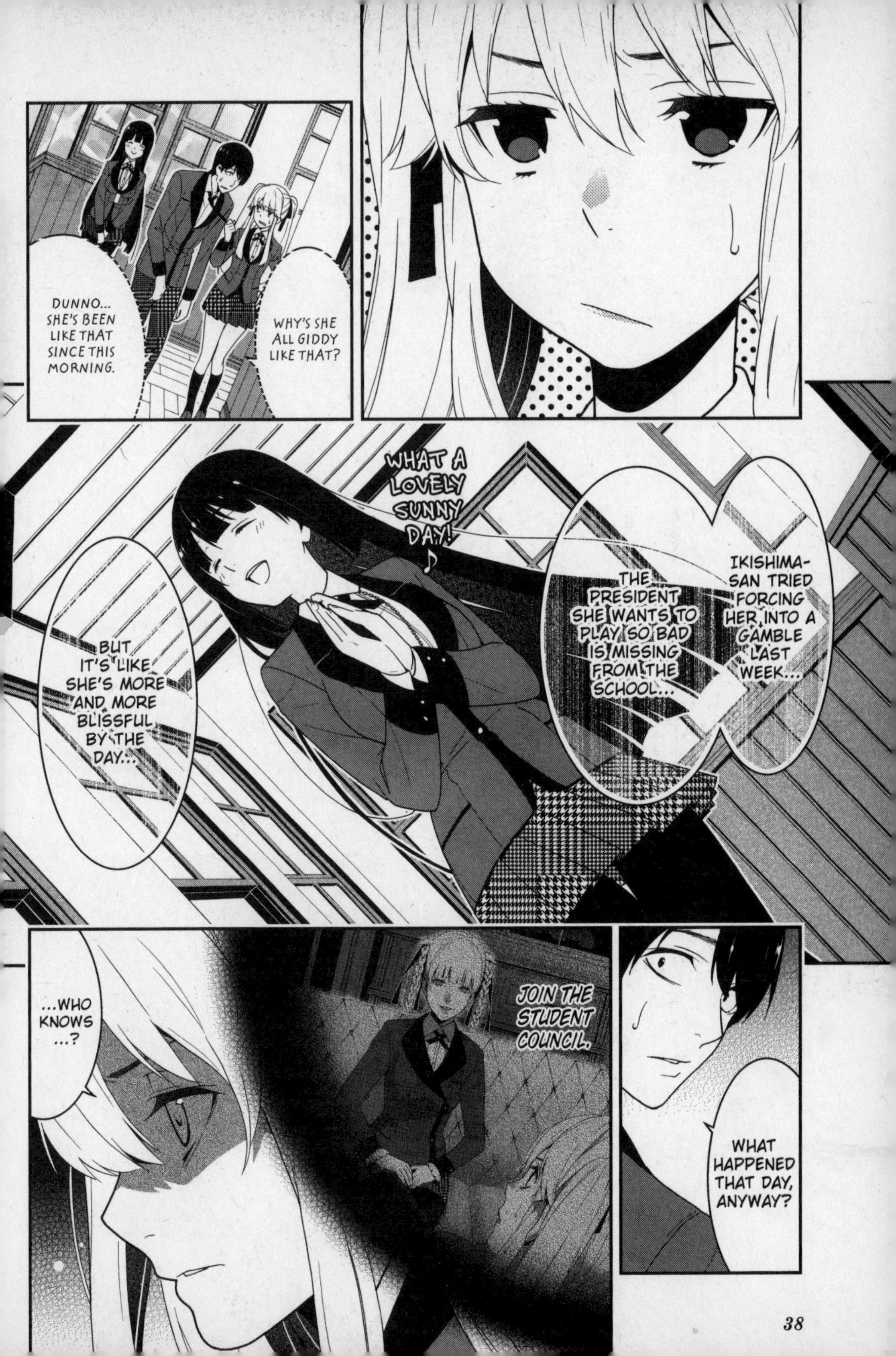
WHY'S SHE ALL GIDDY LIKE THAT?
DUNNO... SHE'S BEEN LIKE THAT SINCE THIS MORNING.
IKISHIMA-SAN TRIED FORCING HER INTO A GAMBLE LAST WEEK...
THE PRESIDENT SHE WANTS TO PLAY SO BAD IS MISSING FROM THE SCHOOL...
WHAT A LOVELY SUNNY DAY! ♪
BUT IT'S LIKE SHE'S MORE AND MORE BLISSFUL BY THE DAY...
WHAT HAPPENED THAT DAY, ANYWAY?
JOIN THE STUDENT COUNCIL.
...WHO KNOWS ...?

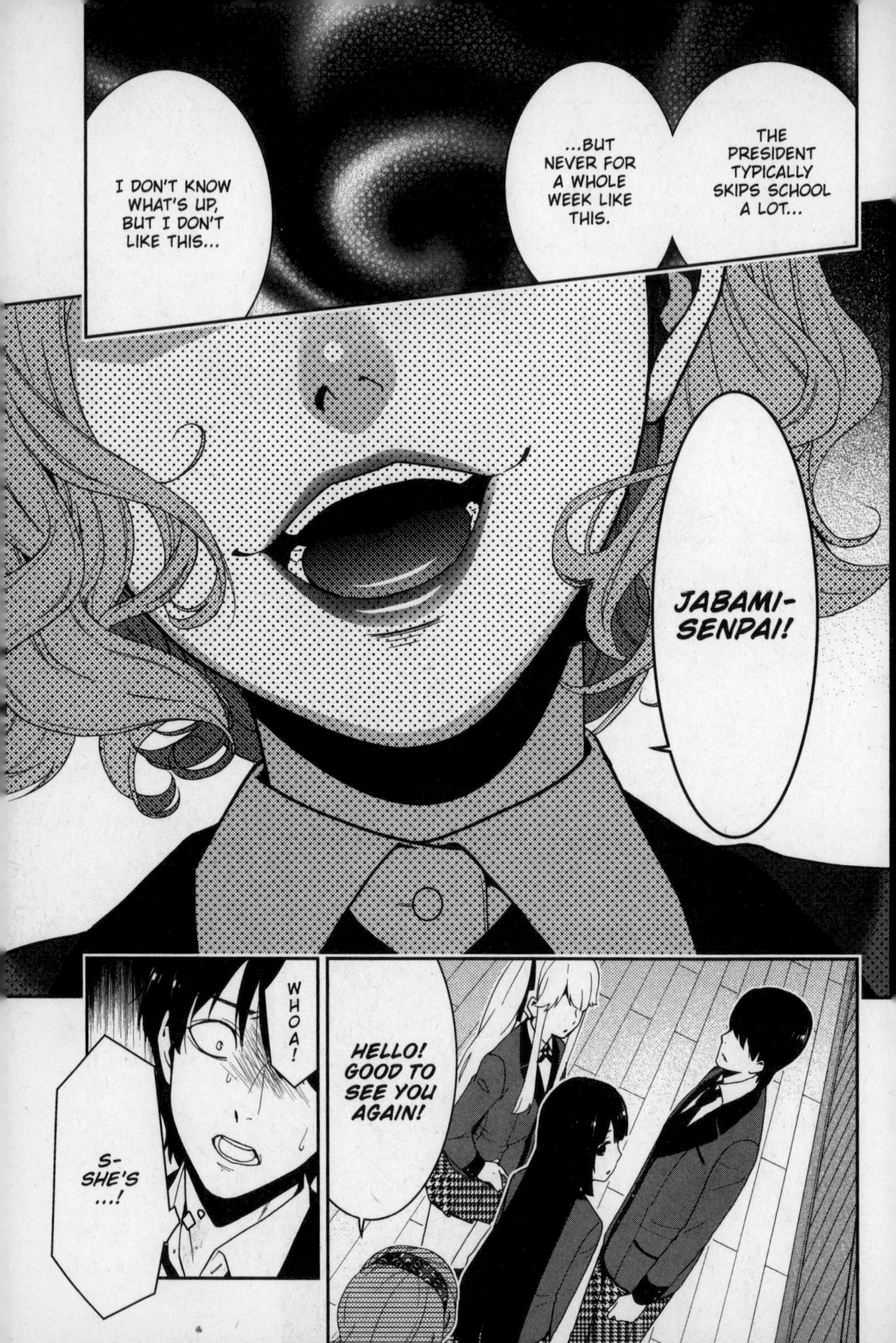
THE PRESIDENT TYPICALLY SKIPS SCHOOL A LOT...
...BUT NEVER FOR A WHOLE WEEK LIKE THIS.
I DON'T KNOW WHAT'S UP, BUT I DON'T LIKE THIS...
JABAMI-SENPAI!
HELLO! GOOD TO SEE YOU AGAIN!
WHOA!
S-SHE'S ...!

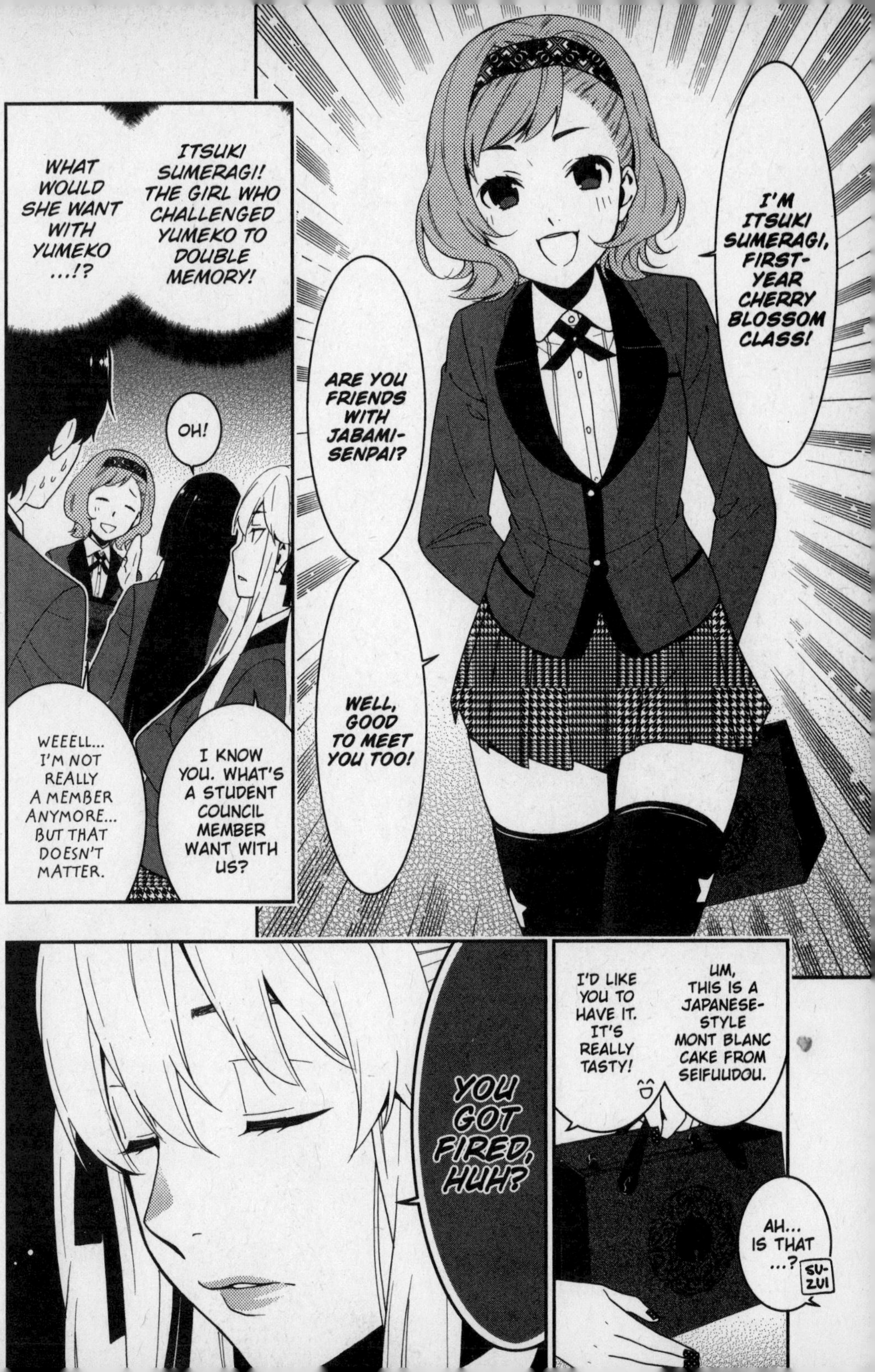
I'M ITSUKI SUMERAGI, FIRST-YEAR CHERRY BLOSSOM CLASS!
ARE YOU FRIENDS WITH JABAMI-SENPAI?
WELL, GOOD TO MEET YOU TOO!
ITSUKI SUMERAGI! THE GIRL WHO CHALLENGED YUMEKO TO DOUBLE MEMORY!
WHAT WOULD SHE WANT WITH YUMEKO ...!?
OH!
I KNOW YOU. WHAT'S A STUDENT COUNCIL MEMBER WANT WITH US?
WEEELL... I'M NOT REALLY A MEMBER ANYMORE... BUT THAT DOESN'T MATTER.
UM, THIS IS A JAPANESE-STYLE MONT BLANC CAKE FROM SEIFUUDOU.
I'D LIKE YOU TO HAVE IT. IT'S REALLY TASTY!
AH... IS THAT ...?
SU-ZUI
YOU GOT FIRED, HUH?

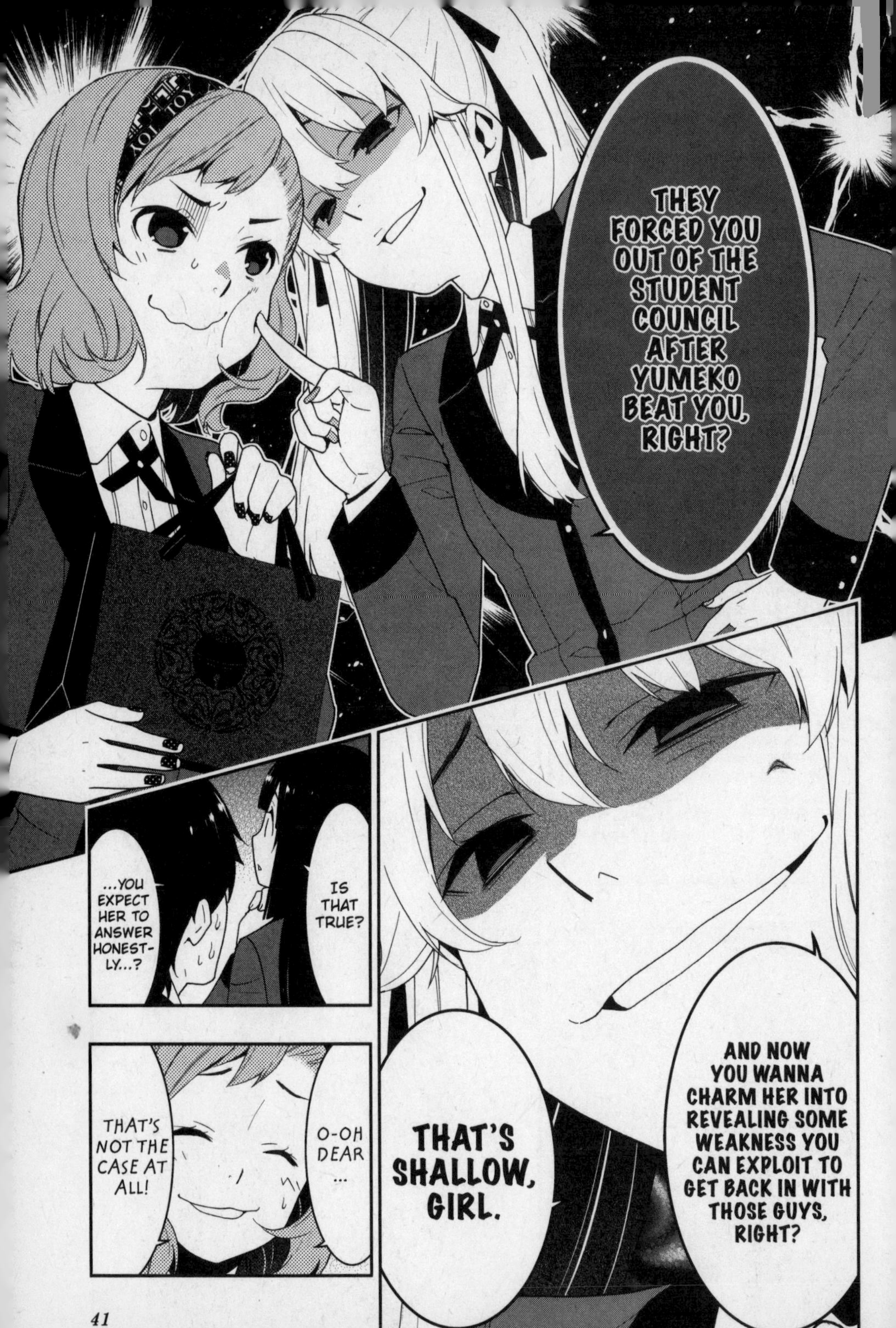
THEY FORCED YOU OUT OF THE STUDENT COUNCIL AFTER YUMEKO BEAT YOU, RIGHT?
AND NOW YOU WANNA CHARM HER INTO REVEALING SOME WEAKNESS YOU CAN EXPLOIT TO GET BACK IN WITH THOSE GUYS, RIGHT?
THAT'S SHALLOW, GIRL.
IS THAT TRUE?
...YOU EXPECT HER TO ANSWER HONESTLY...?
O-OH DEAR...
THAT'S NOT THE CASE AT ALL!

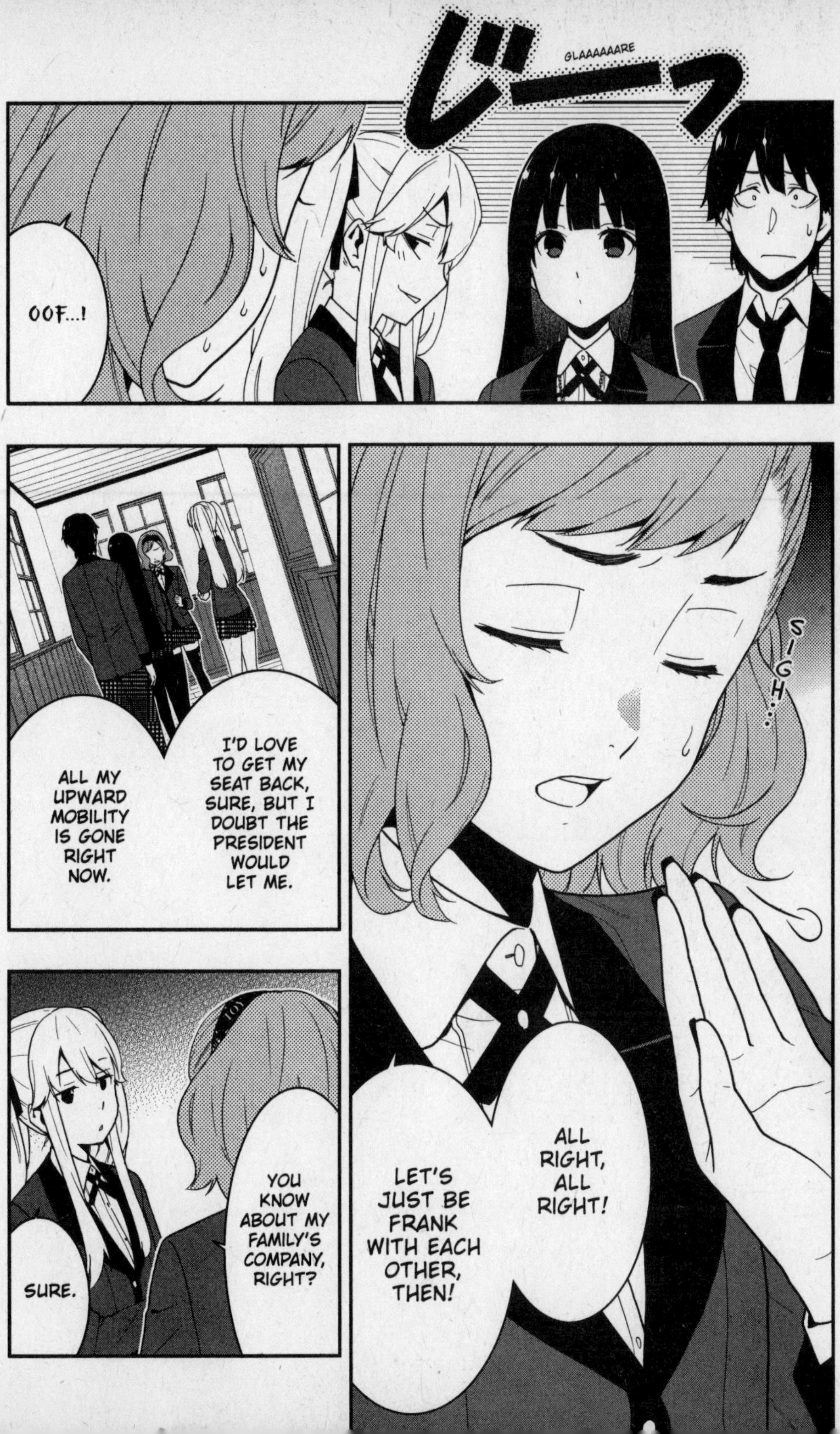
GLAAAAAARE
OOF...!
SIGH...
ALL RIGHT, ALL RIGHT!
LET'S JUST BE FRANK WITH EACH OTHER, THEN!
I'D LOVE TO GET MY SEAT BACK, SURE, BUT I DOUBT THE PRESIDENT WOULD LET ME.
ALL MY UPWARD MOBILITY IS GONE RIGHT NOW.
YOU KNOW ABOUT MY FAMILY'S COMPANY, RIGHT?
SURE.

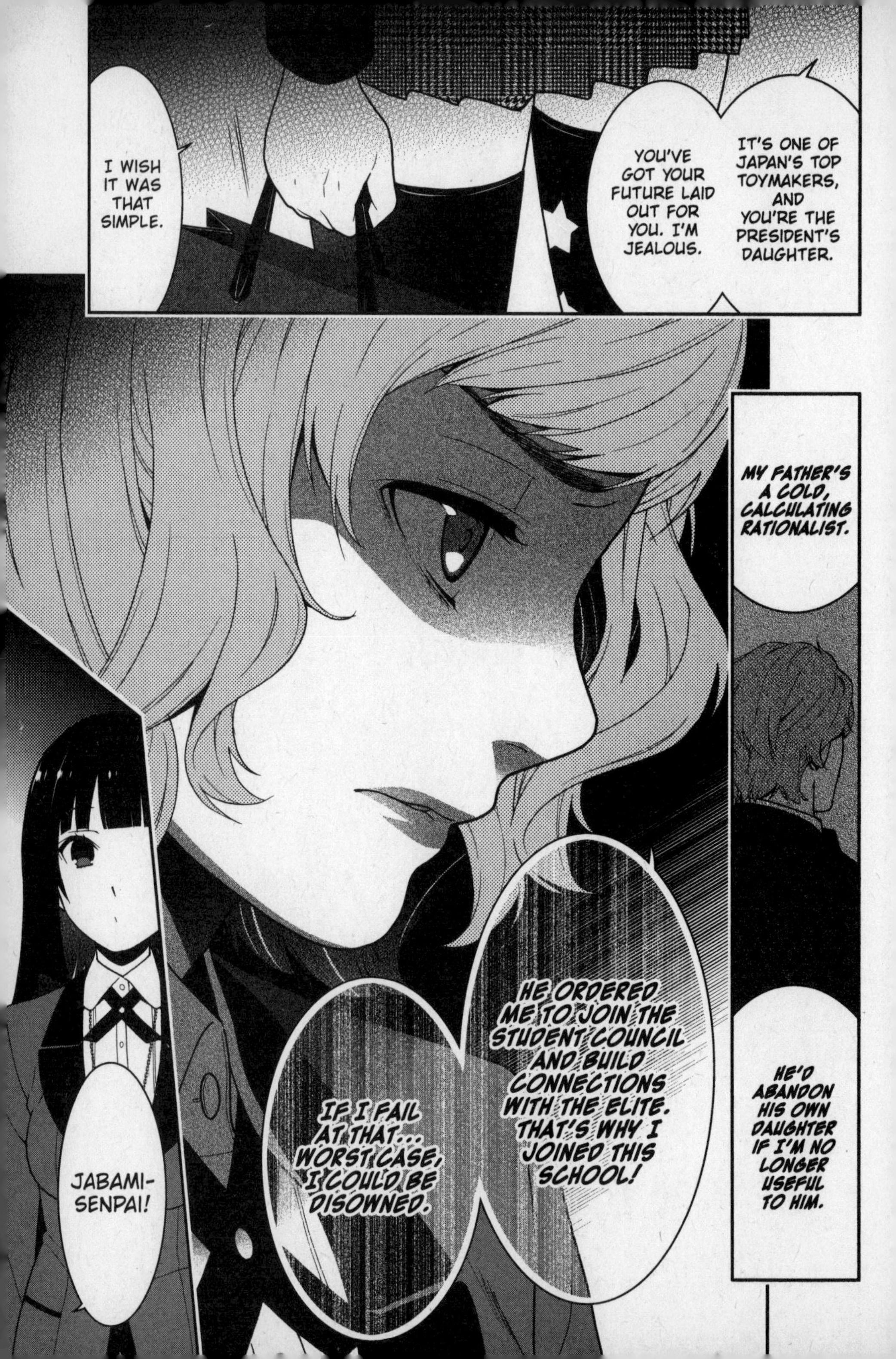
IT'S ONE OF JAPAN'S TOP TOYMAKERS, AND YOU'RE THE PRESIDENT'S DAUGHTER.
YOU'VE GOT YOUR FUTURE LAID OUT FOR YOU. I'M JEALOUS.
I WISH IT WAS THAT SIMPLE.
MY FATHER'S A COLD, CALCULATING RATIONALIST.
HE'D ABANDON HIS OWN DAUGHTER IF I'M NO LONGER USEFUL TO HIM.
HE ORDERED ME TO JOIN THE STUDENT COUNCIL AND BUILD CONNECTIONS WITH THE ELITE. THAT'S WHY I JOINED THIS SCHOOL!
IF I FAIL AT THAT... WORST CASE, I COULD BE DISOWNED.
JABAMI-SENPAI!

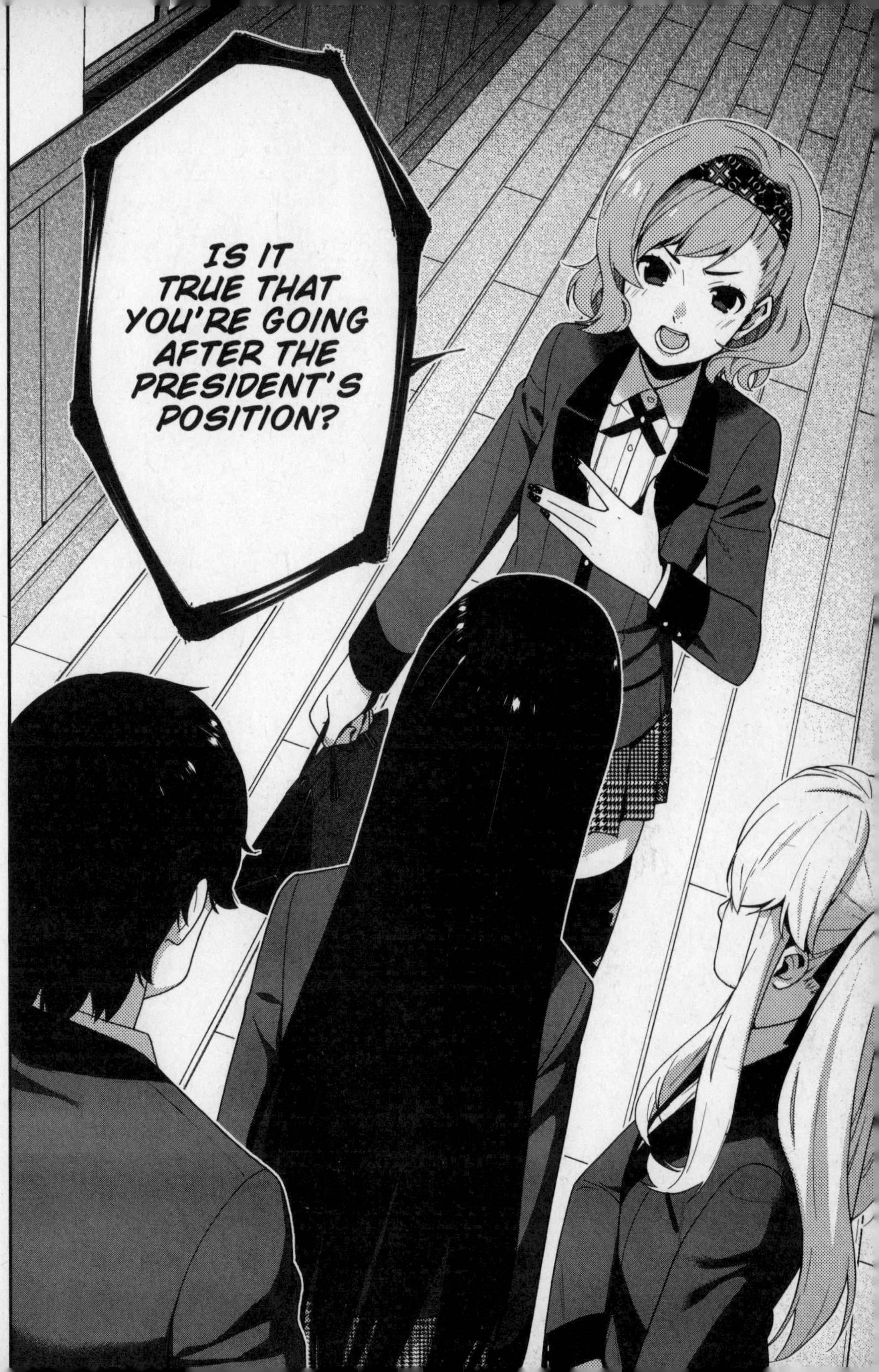
IS IT TRUE THAT YOU'RE GOING AFTER THE PRESIDENT'S POSITION?

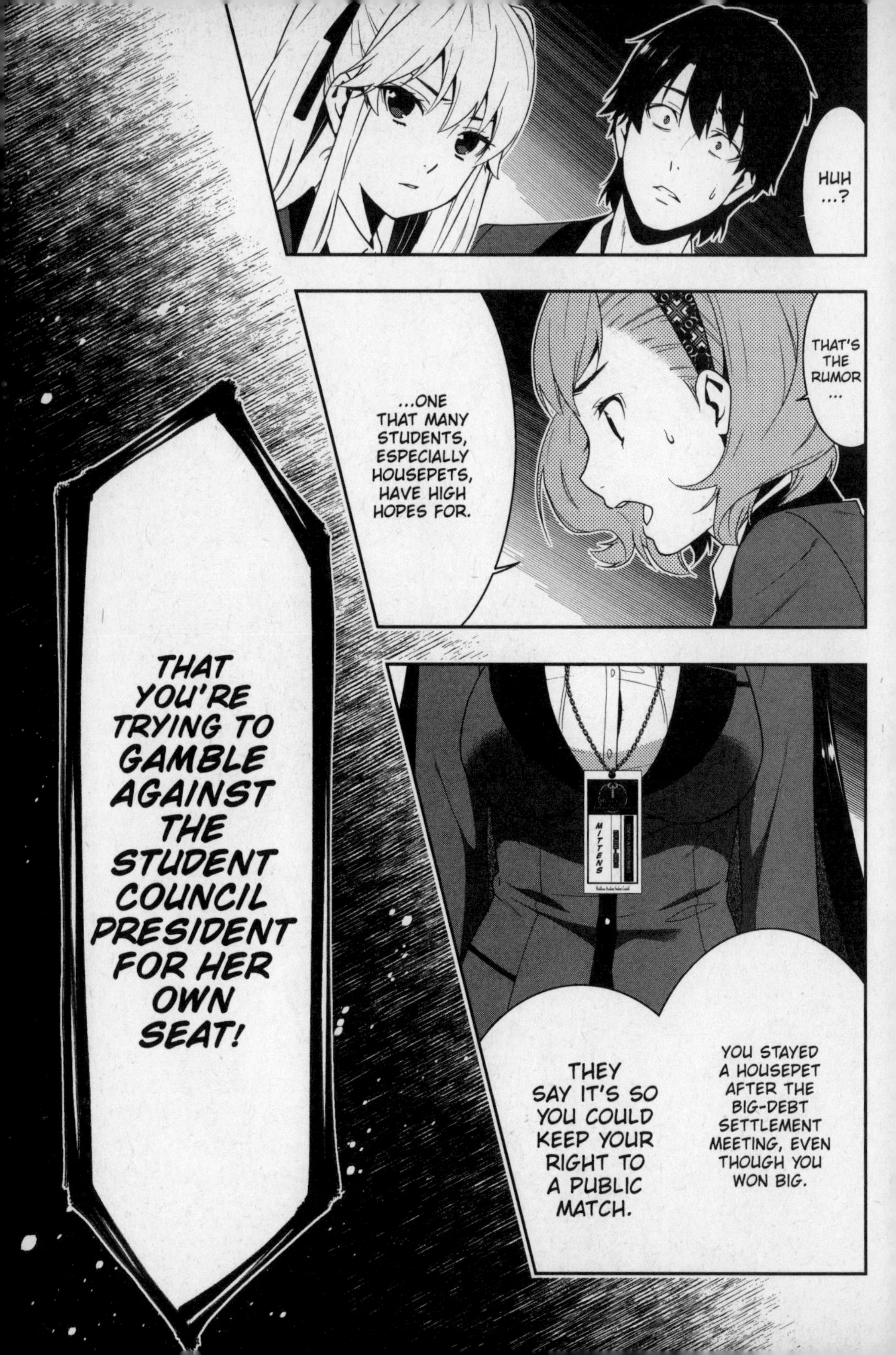
HUH ...?
THAT'S THE RUMOR ...
...ONE THAT MANY STUDENTS, ESPECIALLY HOUSEPETS, HAVE HIGH HOPES FOR.
MITTENS
YOU STAYED A HOUSEPET AFTER THE BIG-DEBT SETTLEMENT MEETING, EVEN THOUGH YOU WON BIG.
THEY SAY IT'S SO YOU COULD KEEP YOUR RIGHT TO A PUBLIC MATCH.
THAT YOU'RE TRYING TO GAMBLE AGAINST THE STUDENT COUNCIL PRESIDENT FOR HER OWN SEAT!

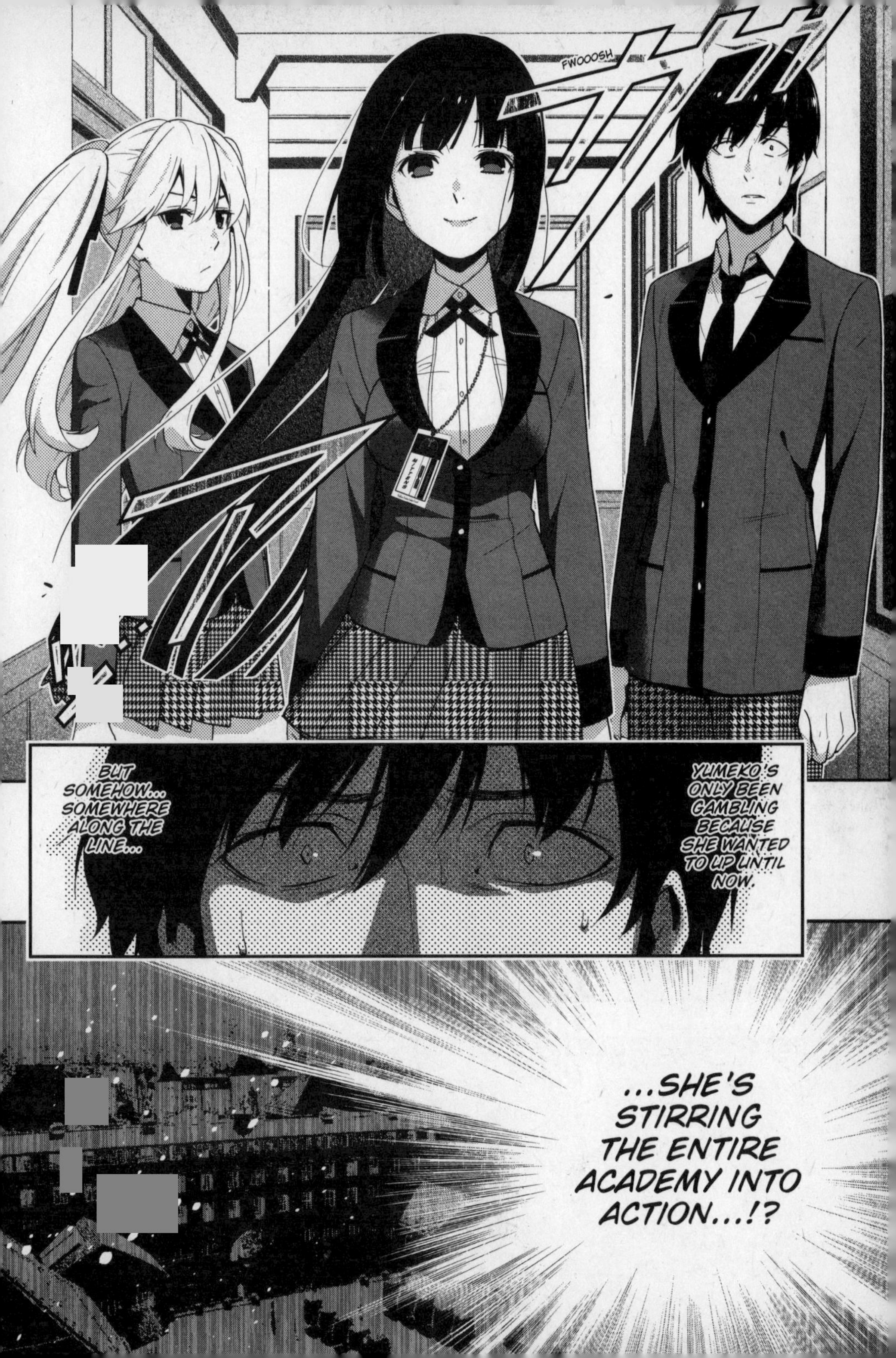
FWOOOSH
YUMEKO'S ONLY BEEN GAMBLING BECAUSE SHE WANTED TO UP UNTIL NOW.
BUT SOMEHOW... SOMEWHERE ALONG THE LINE...
...SHE'S STIRRING THE ENTIRE ACADEMY INTO ACTION...!?

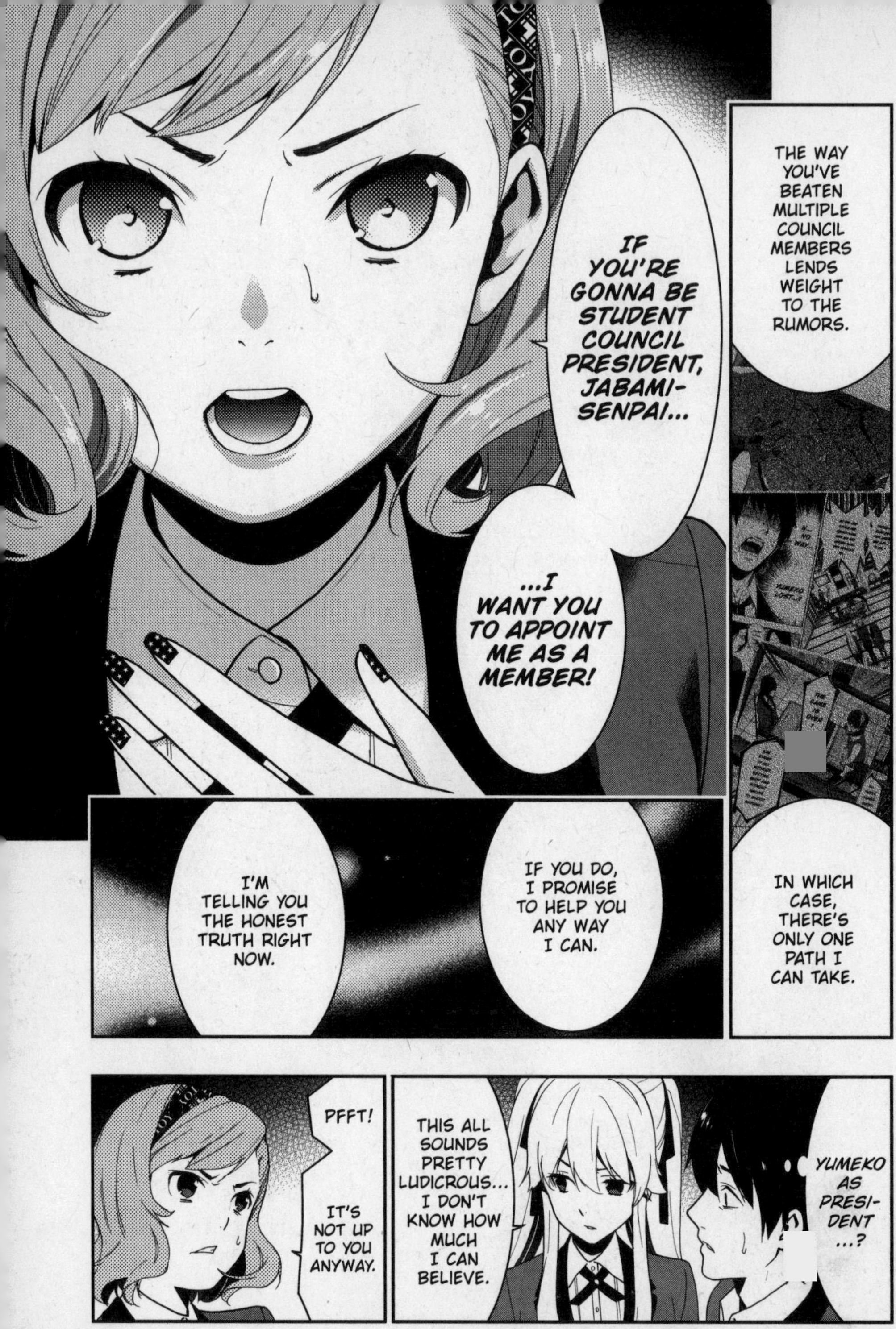
THE WAY YOU'VE BEATEN MULTIPLE COUNCIL MEMBERS LENDS WEIGHT TO THE RUMORS.
IN WHICH CASE, THERE'S ONLY ONE PATH I CAN TAKE.
IF YOU'RE GONNA BE STUDENT COUNCIL PRESIDENT, JABAMI-SENPAI...
...I WANT YOU TO APPOINT ME AS A MEMBER!
IF YOU DO, I PROMISE TO HELP YOU ANY WAY I CAN.
I'M TELLING YOU THE HONEST TRUTH RIGHT NOW.
YUMEKO AS PRESI-DENT ...?
THIS ALL SOUNDS PRETTY LUDICROUS... I DON'T KNOW HOW MUCH I CAN BELIEVE.
PFFT!
IT'S NOT UP TO YOU ANYWAY.

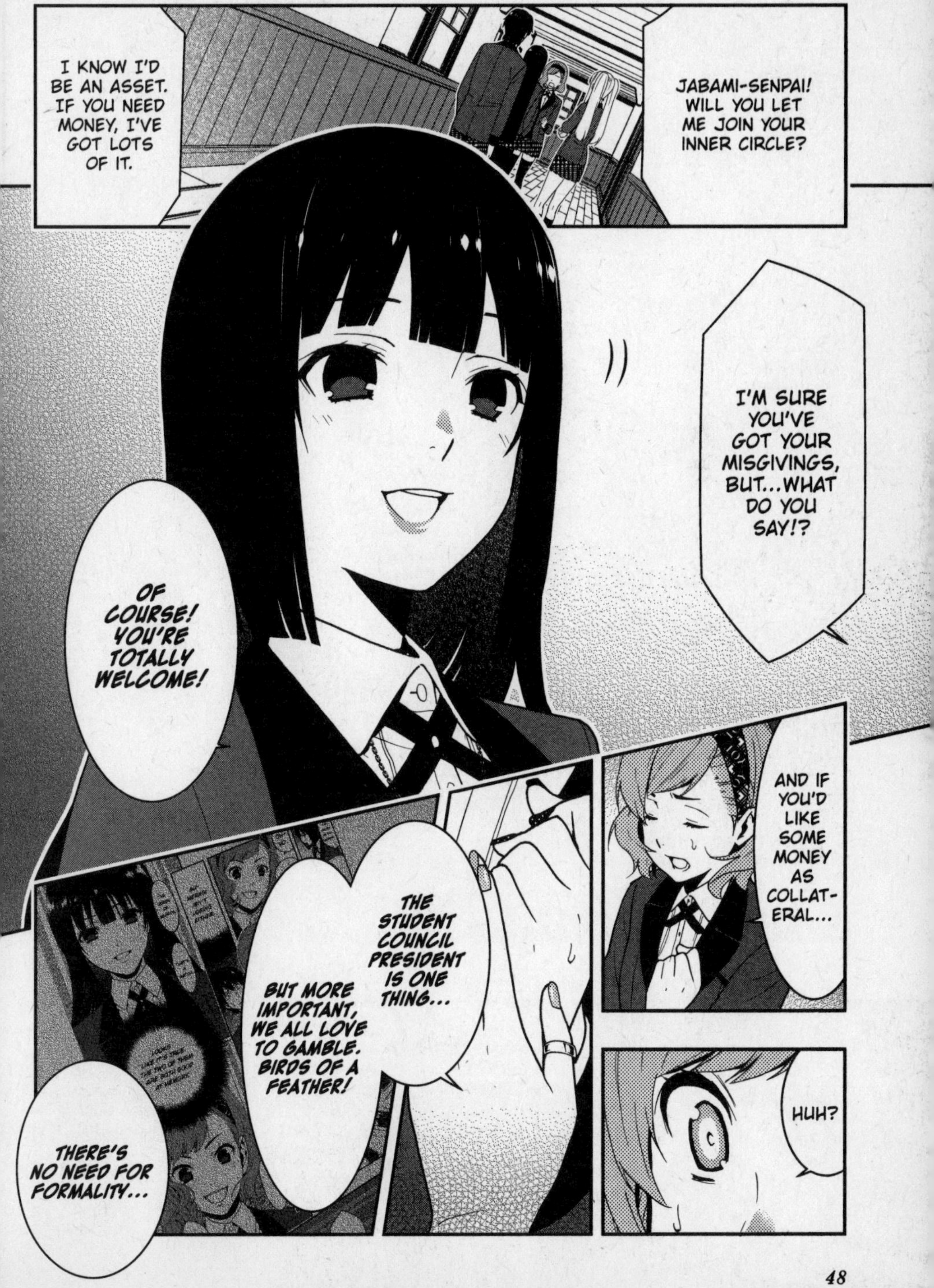
JABAMI-SENPAI! WILL YOU LET ME JOIN YOUR INNER CIRCLE?
I KNOW I'D BE AN ASSET. IF YOU NEED MONEY, I'VE GOT LOTS OF IT.
I'M SURE YOU'VE GOT YOUR MISGIVINGS, BUT...WHAT DO YOU SAY!?
OF COURSE! YOU'RE TOTALLY WELCOME!
AND IF YOU'D LIKE SOME MONEY AS COLLAT-ERAL...
HUH?
THE STUDENT COUNCIL PRESIDENT IS ONE THING...
BUT MORE IMPORTANT, WE ALL LOVE TO GAMBLE. BIRDS OF A FEATHER!
THERE'S NO NEED FOR FORMALITY...

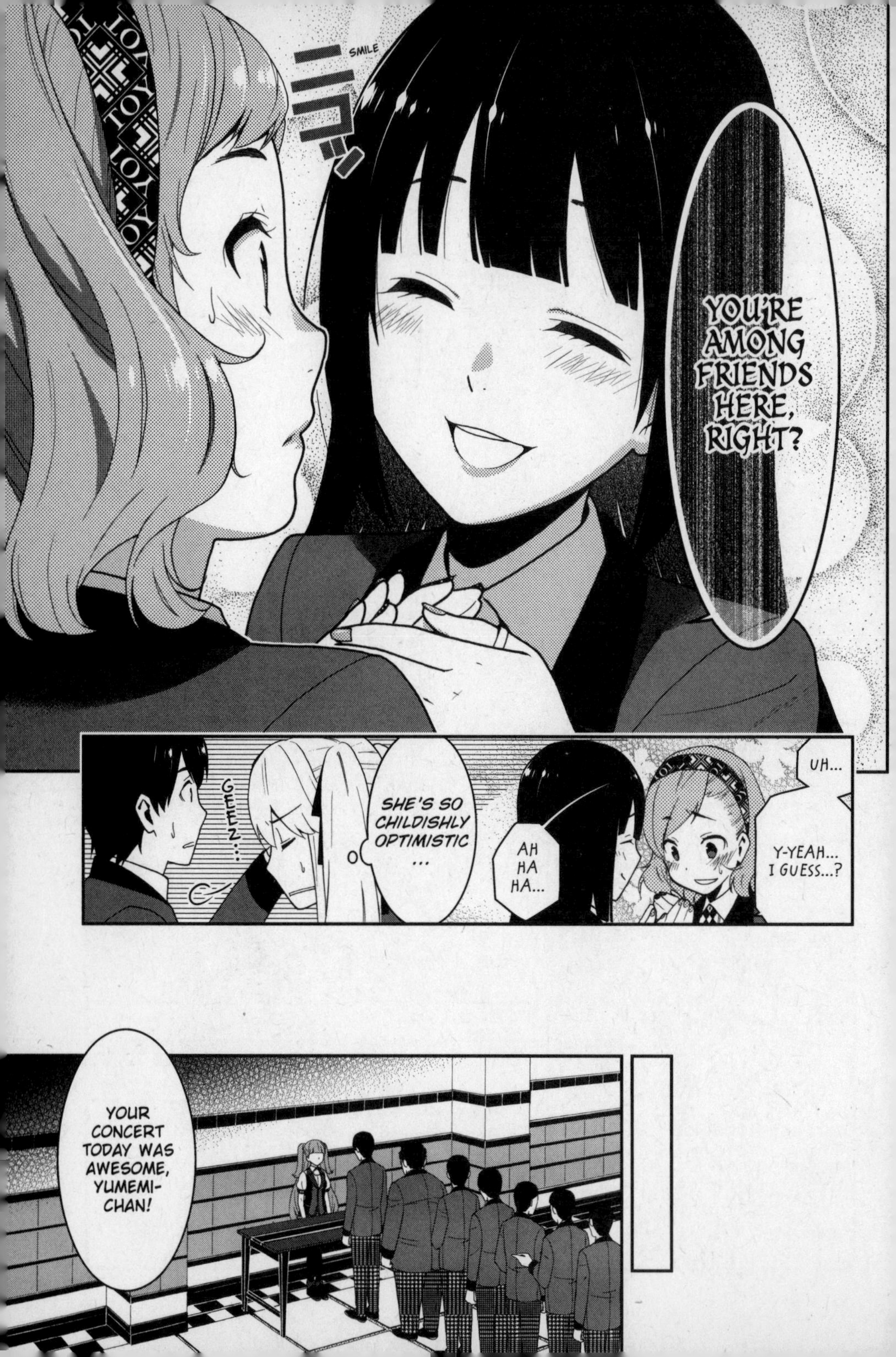
SMILE
YOU'RE AMONG FRIENDS HERE, RIGHT?
UH...
Y-YEAH... I GUESS...?
AH HA HA...
SHE'S SO CHILDISHLY OPTIMISTIC ...
GEEZ...
YOUR CONCERT TODAY WAS AWESOME, YUMEMI-CHAN!

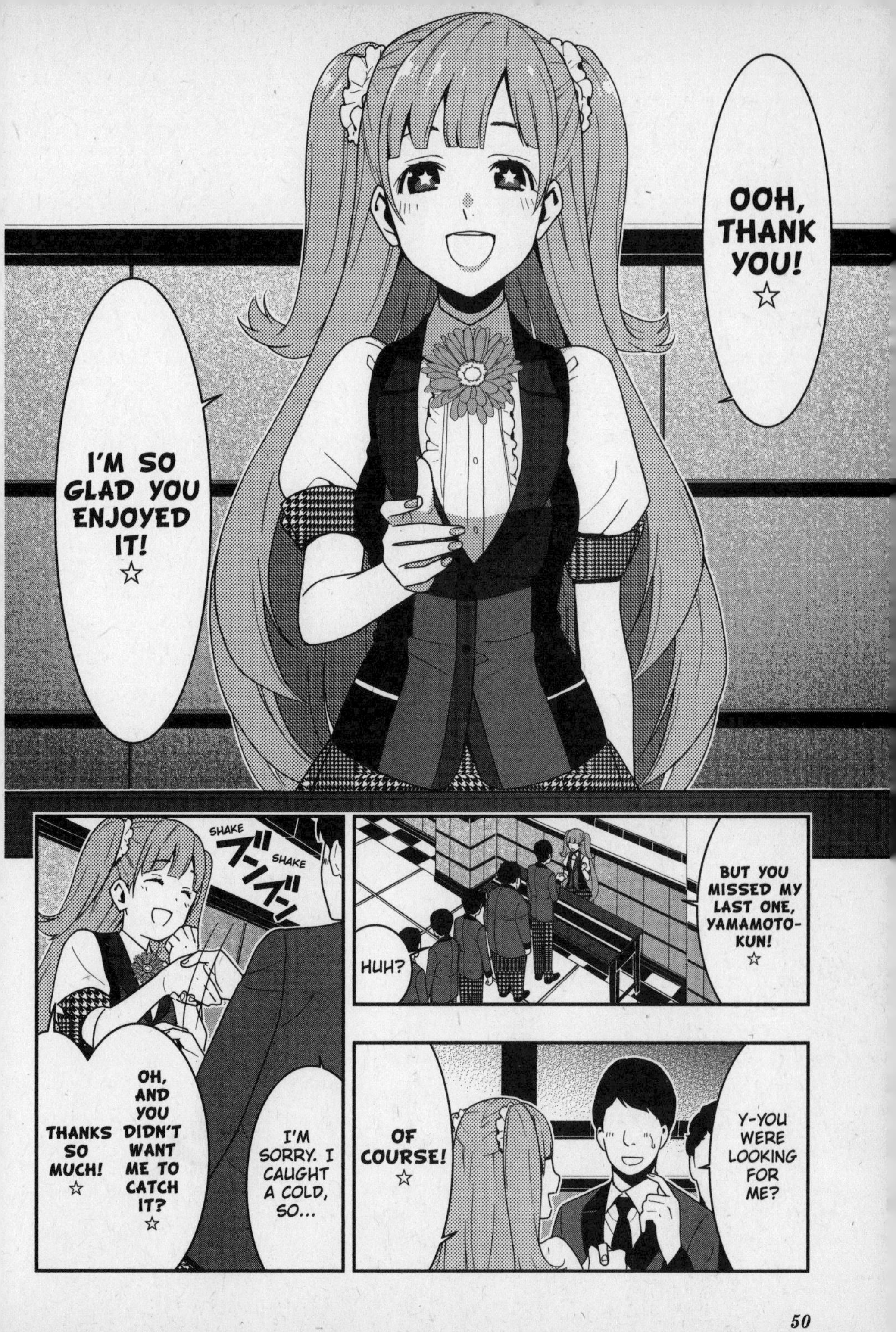
OOH, THANK YOU! ☆
I'M SO GLAD YOU ENJOYED IT! ☆
BUT YOU MISSED MY LAST ONE, YAMAMOTO-KUN! ☆
HUH?
Y-YOU WERE LOOKING FOR ME?
OF COURSE! ☆
SHAKE
SHAKE
I'M SORRY. I CAUGHT A COLD, SO...
OH, AND YOU DIDN'T WANT ME TO CATCH IT? ☆
THANKS SO MUCH! ☆

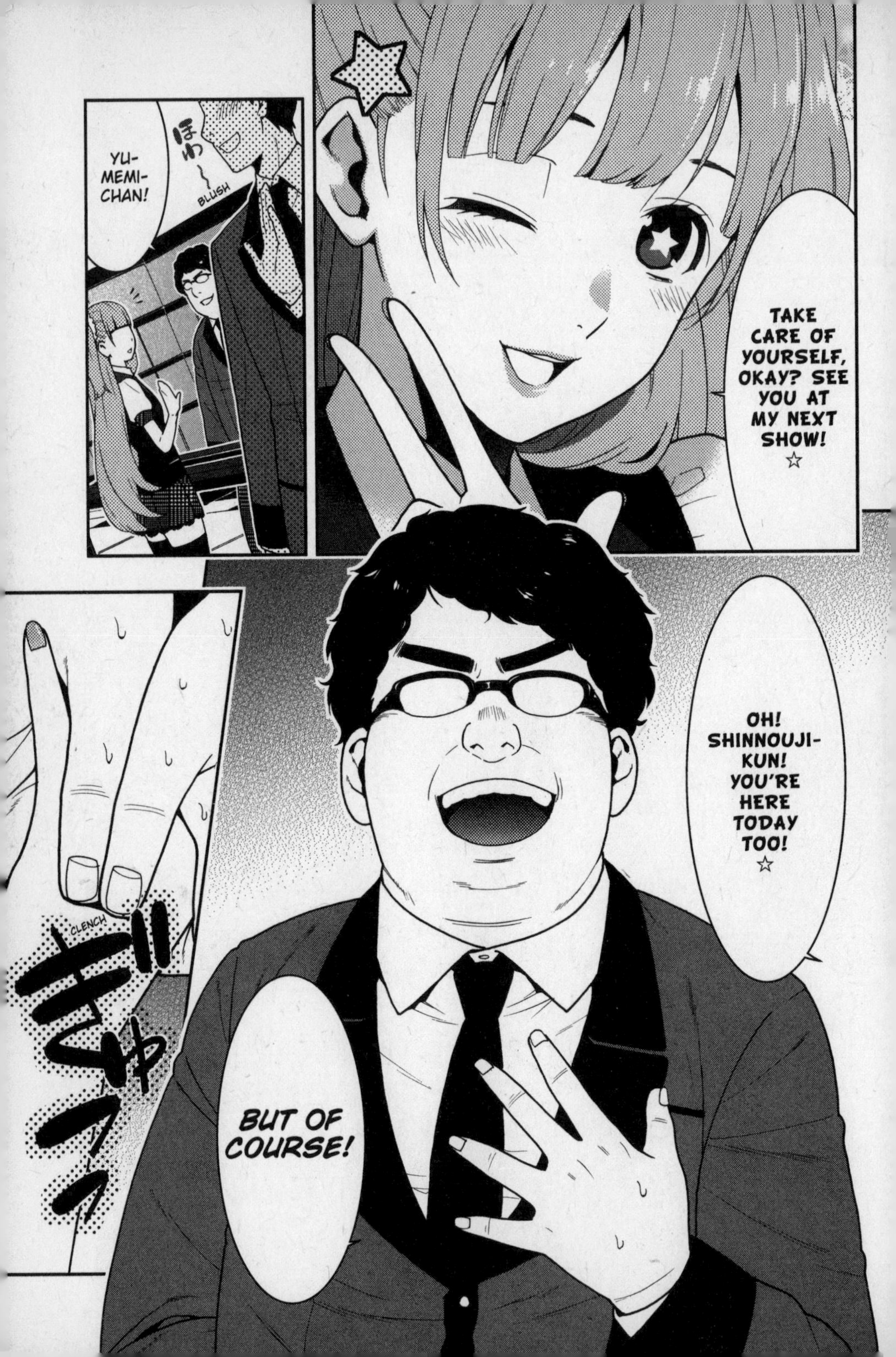
TAKE CARE OF YOURSELF, OKAY? SEE YOU AT MY NEXT SHOW! ☆
ほわ～
BLUSH
YU-MEMI-CHAN!
OH! SHINNOUJI-KUN! YOU'RE HERE TODAY TOO! ☆
BUT OF COURSE!
ぎゅっ
CLENCH

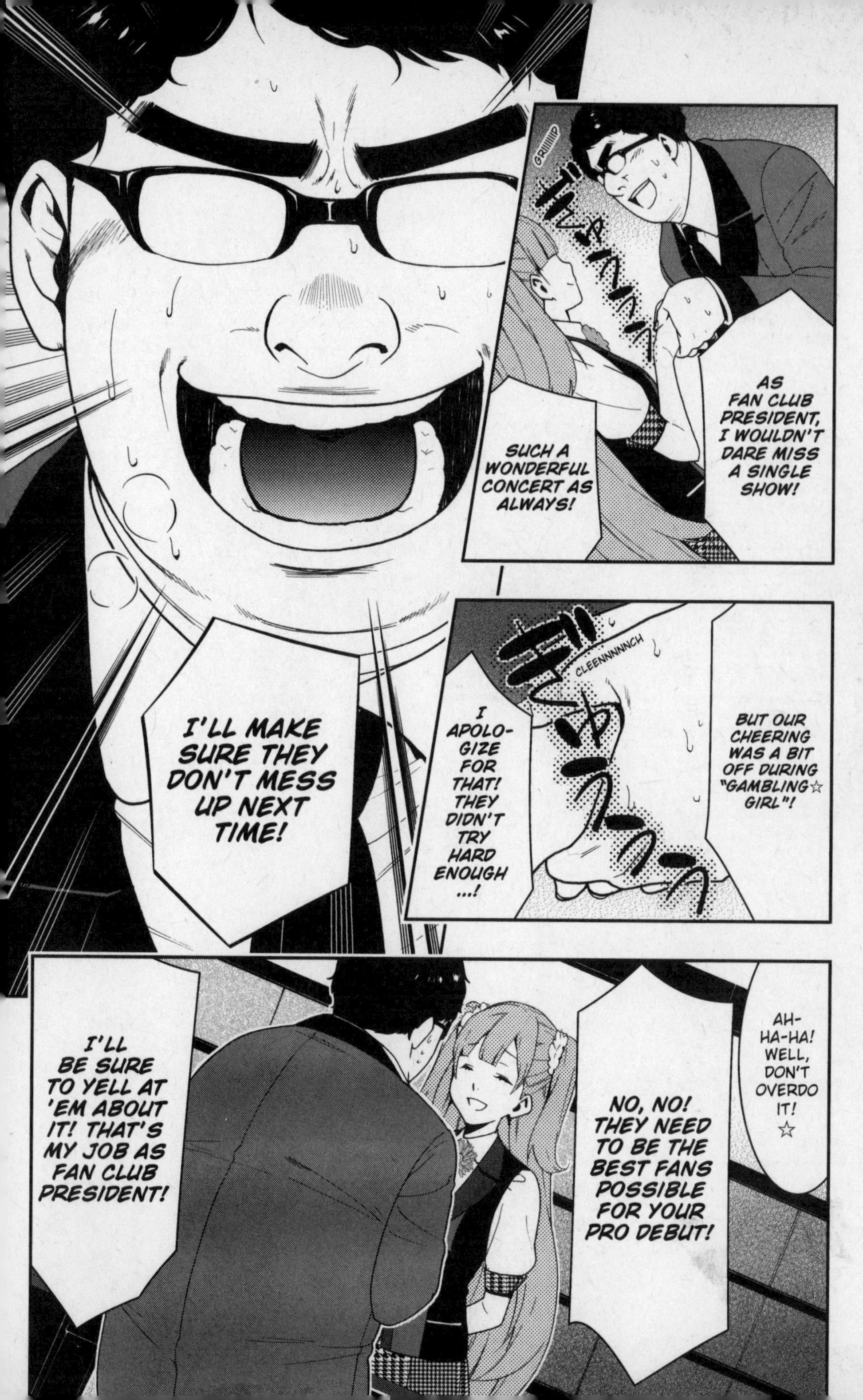
GRIIIIP
AS FAN CLUB PRESIDENT, I WOULDN'T DARE MISS A SINGLE SHOW!
SUCH A WONDERFUL CONCERT AS ALWAYS!
CLEENNNNNCH
BUT OUR CHEERING WAS A BIT OFF DURING "GAMBLING☆GIRL"!
I APOLO-GIZE FOR THAT! THEY DIDN'T TRY HARD ENOUGH ...!
I'LL MAKE SURE THEY DON'T MESS UP NEXT TIME!
AH-HA-HA! WELL, DON'T OVERDO IT! ☆
NO, NO! THEY NEED TO BE THE BEST FANS POSSIBLE FOR YOUR PRO DEBUT!
I'LL BE SURE TO YELL AT 'EM ABOUT IT! THAT'S MY JOB AS FAN CLUB PRESIDENT!

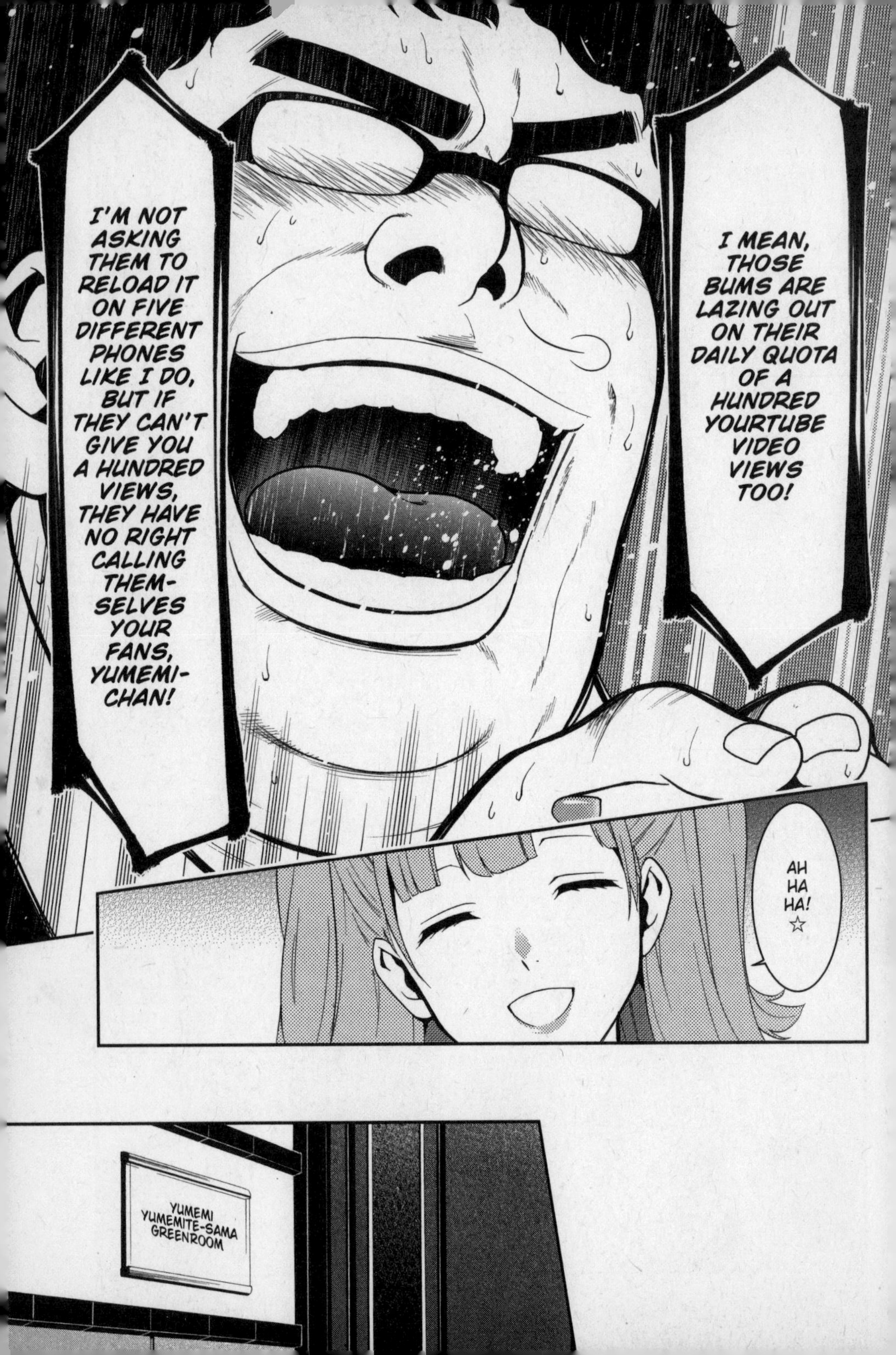
I MEAN, THOSE BUMS ARE LAZING OUT ON THEIR DAILY QUOTA OF A HUNDRED YOURTUBE VIDEO VIEWS TOO!
I'M NOT ASKING THEM TO RELOAD IT ON FIVE DIFFERENT PHONES LIKE I DO, BUT IF THEY CAN'T GIVE YOU A HUNDRED VIEWS, THEY HAVE NO RIGHT CALLING THEM-SELVES YOUR FANS, YUMEMI-CHAN!
AH HA HA! ☆
YUMEMI YUMEMITE-SAMA GREENROOM

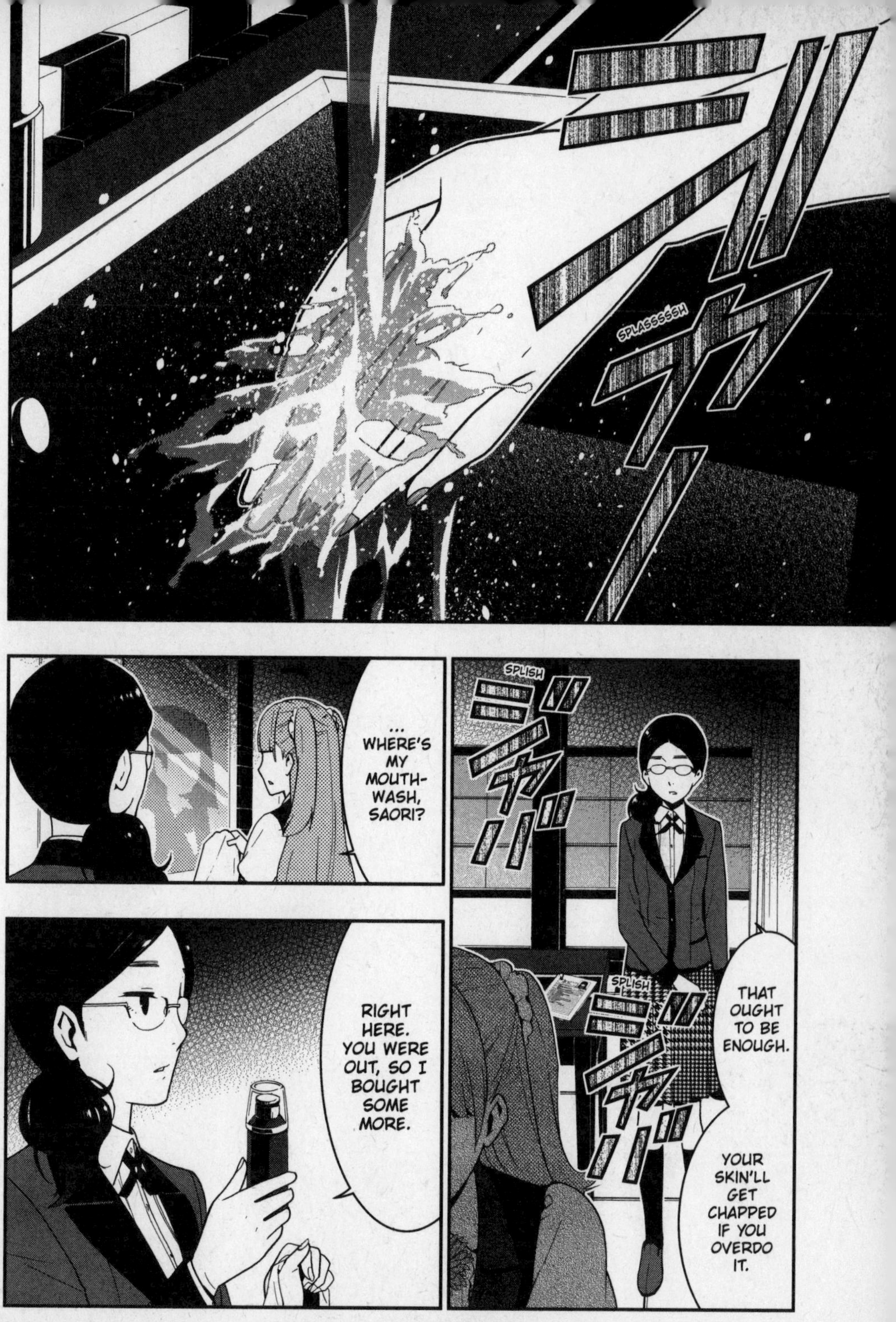
SPLASSSSSH
SPLISH
SPLISH
THAT OUGHT TO BE ENOUGH.
YOUR SKIN'LL GET CHAPPED IF YOU OVERDO IT.
... WHERE'S MY MOUTH-WASH, SAORI?
RIGHT HERE. YOU WERE OUT, SO I BOUGHT SOME MORE.

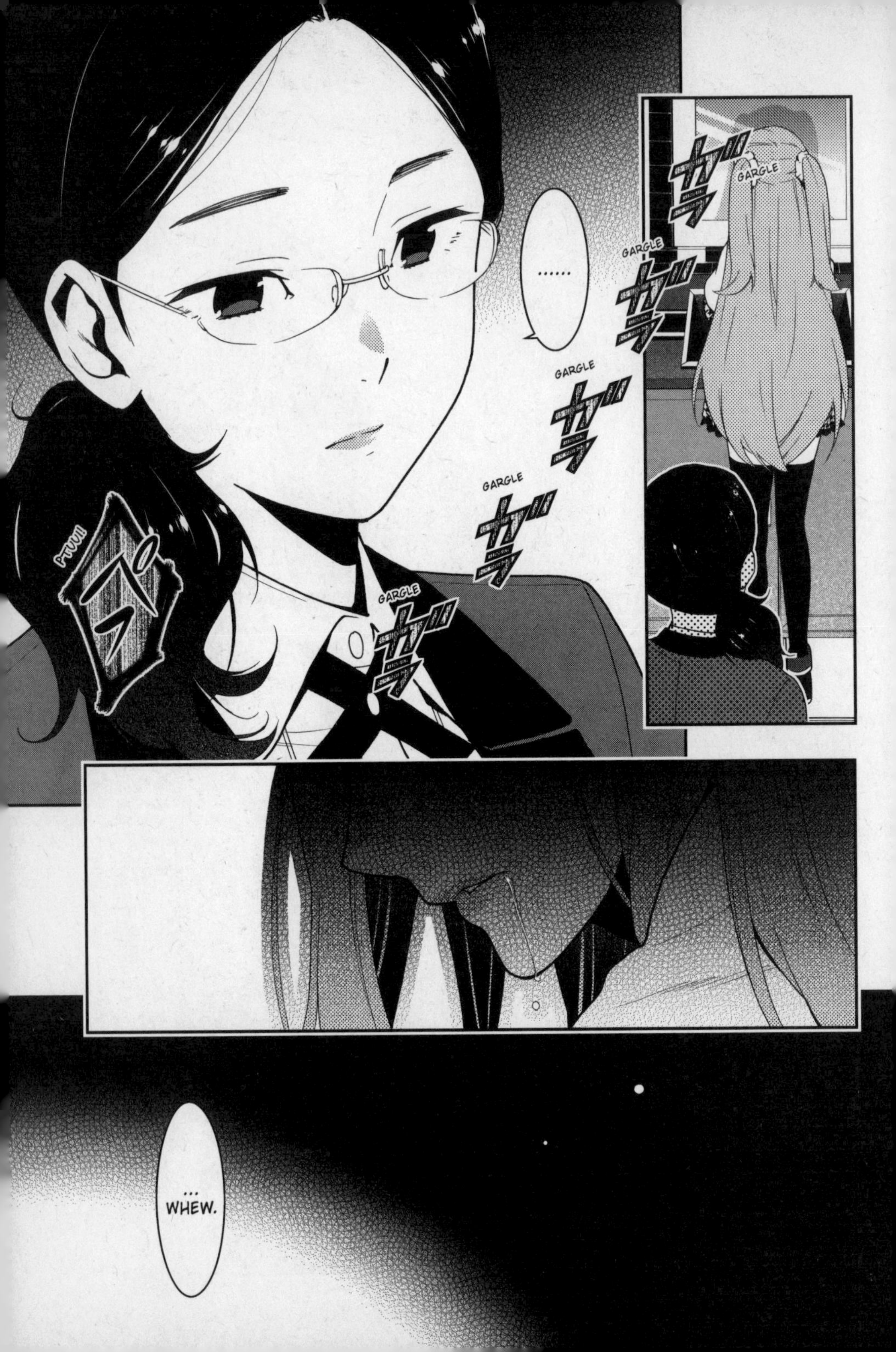
GARGLE
GARGLE
GARGLE
GARGLE
GARGLE
......
PTUU!!
... WHEW.

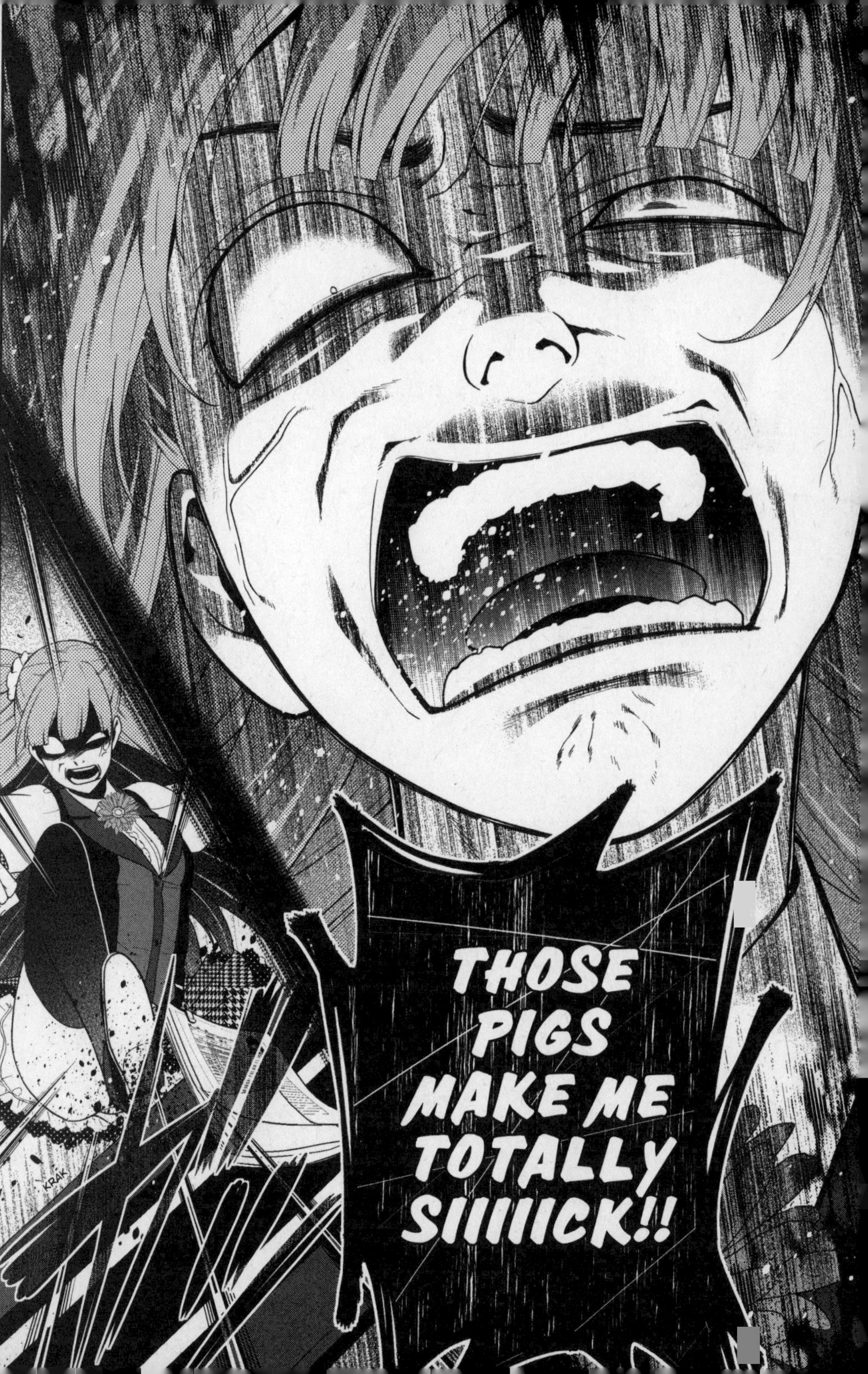
THOSE PIGS MAKE ME TOTALLY SIIIIICK!!
KRAK

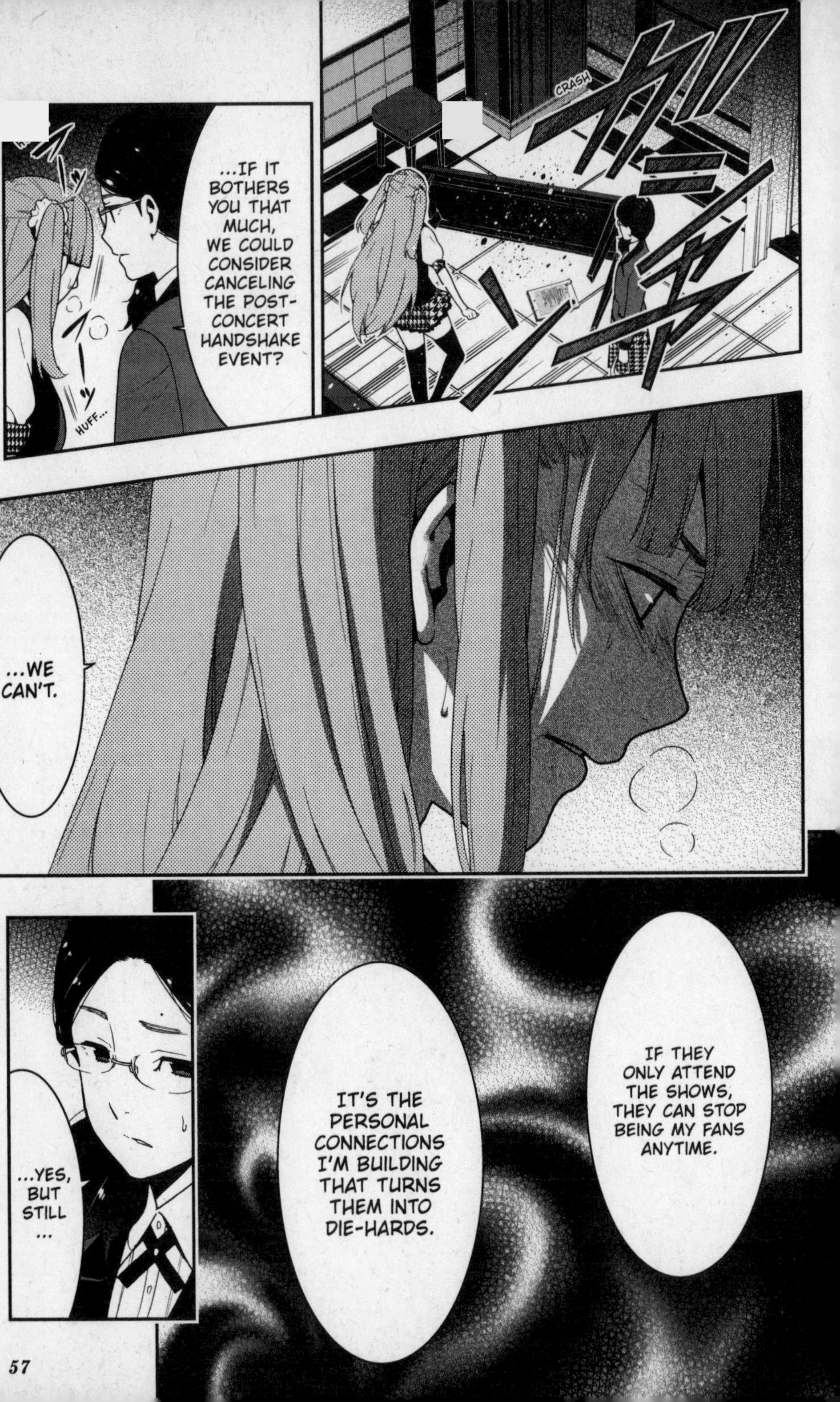
CRASH
...IF IT BOTHERS YOU THAT MUCH, WE COULD CONSIDER CANCELING THE POST-CONCERT HANDSHAKE EVENT?
HUFF...
...WE CAN'T.
IF THEY ONLY ATTEND THE SHOWS, THEY CAN STOP BEING MY FANS ANYTIME.
IT'S THE PERSONAL CONNECTIONS I'M BUILDING THAT TURNS THEM INTO DIE-HARDS.
...YES, BUT STILL ...

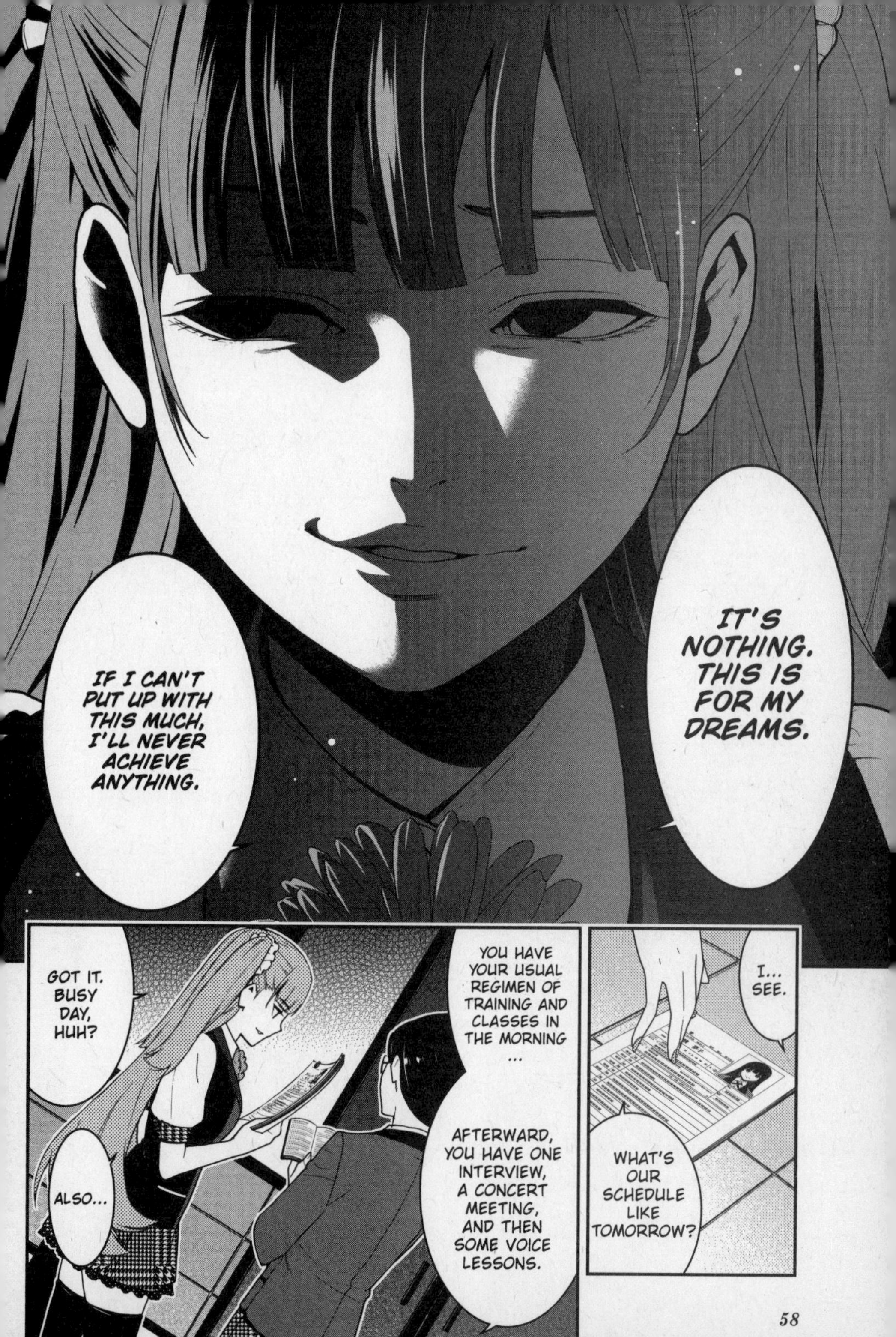
IT'S NOTHING. THIS IS FOR MY DREAMS.
IF I CAN'T PUT UP WITH THIS MUCH, I'LL NEVER ACHIEVE ANYTHING.
I... SEE.
WHAT'S OUR SCHEDULE LIKE TOMORROW?
YOU HAVE YOUR USUAL REGIMEN OF TRAINING AND CLASSES IN THE MORNING...
AFTERWARD, YOU HAVE ONE INTERVIEW, A CONCERT MEETING, AND THEN SOME VOICE LESSONS.
GOT IT. BUSY DAY, HUH?
ALSO...

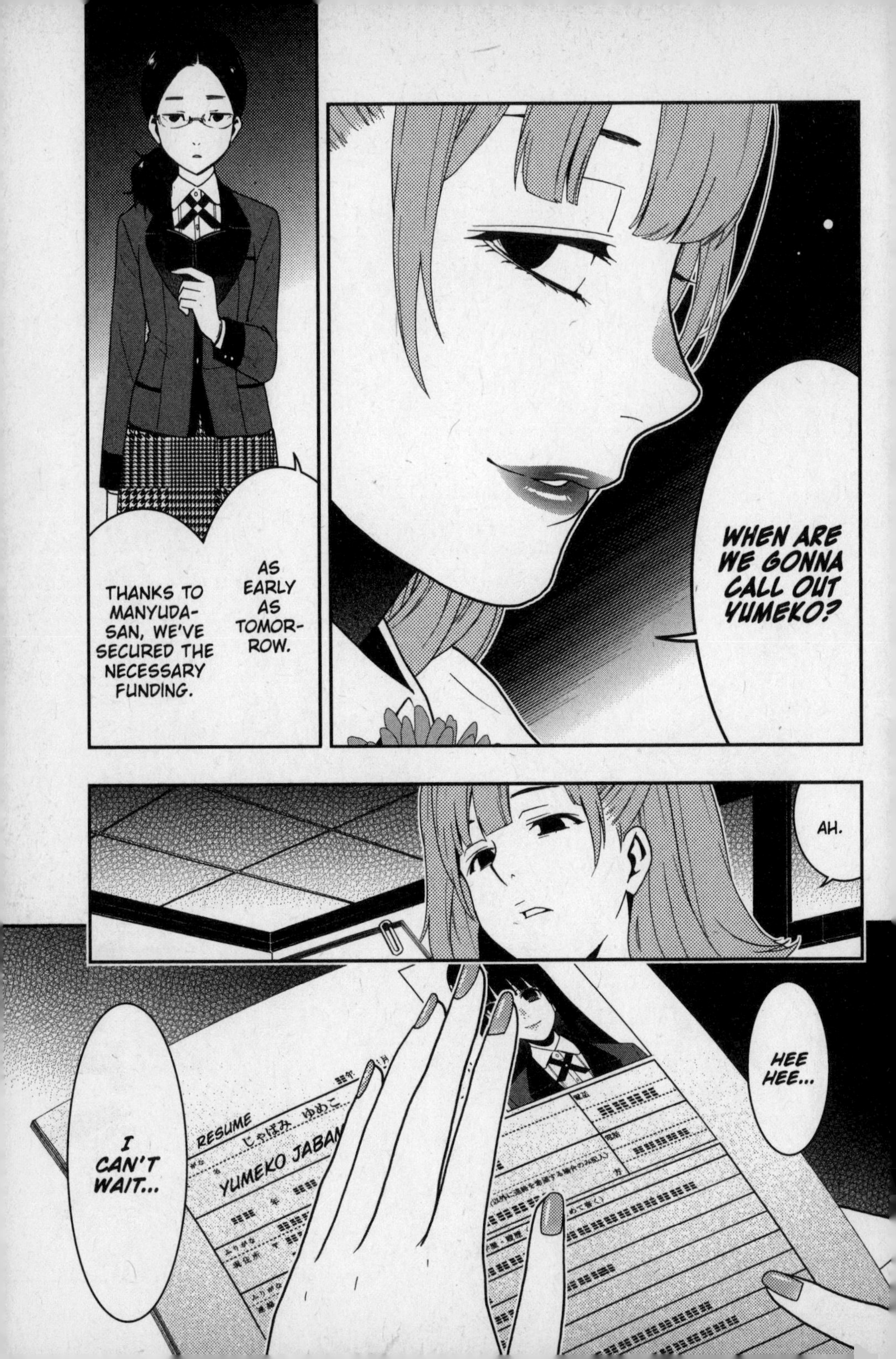
WHEN ARE WE GONNA CALL OUT YUMEKO?
AS EARLY AS TOMORROW.
THANKS TO MANYUDA-SAN, WE'VE SECURED THE NECESSARY FUNDING.
AH.
HEE HEE...
I CAN'T WAIT...
RESUME
じゃばみ ゆめこ

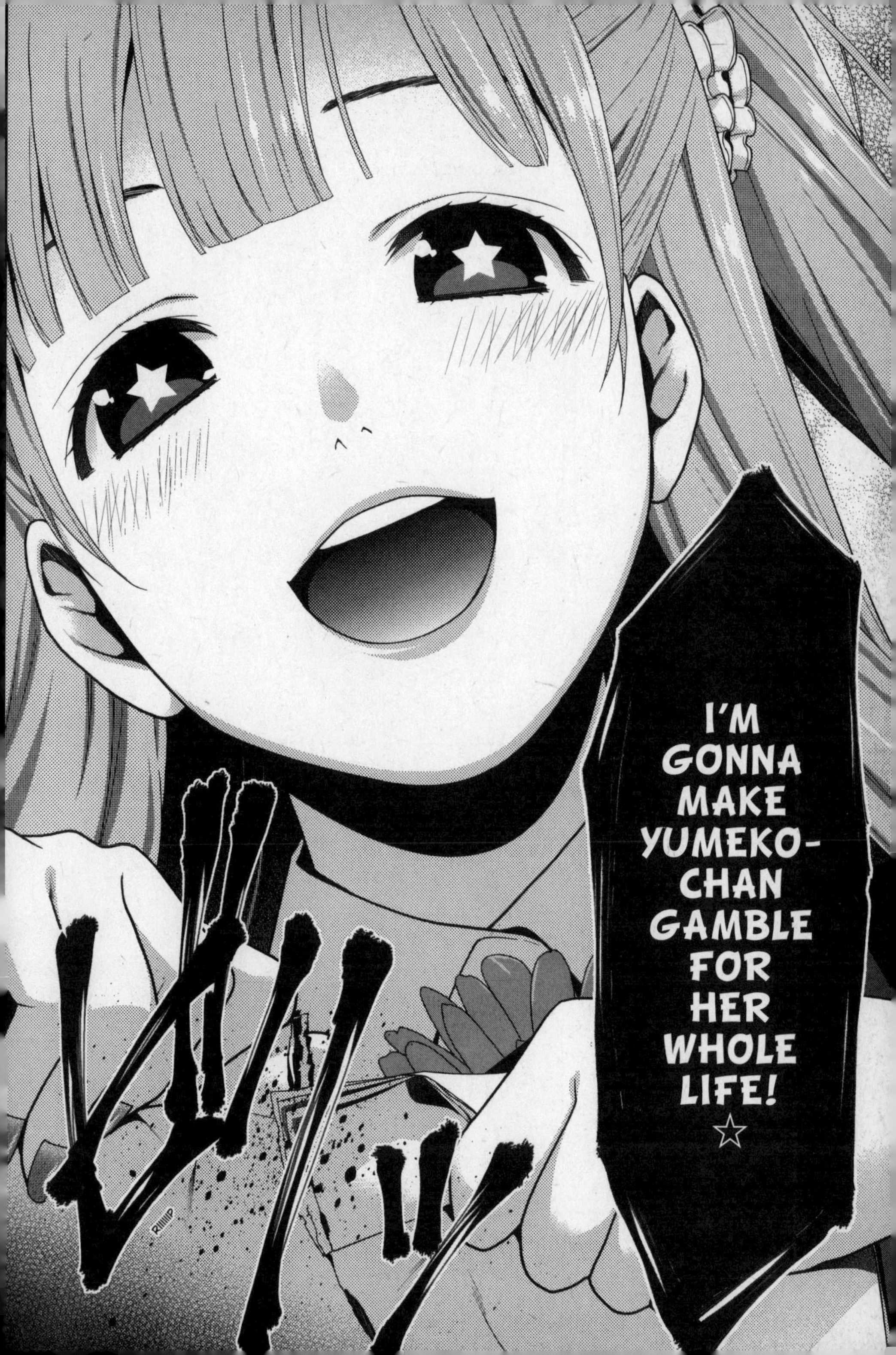
I'M GONNA MAKE YUMEKO-CHAN GAMBLE FOR HER WHOLE LIFE! ☆
RIIIIIP

KAKEGURUI

— Compulsive Gambler —

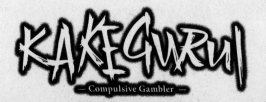

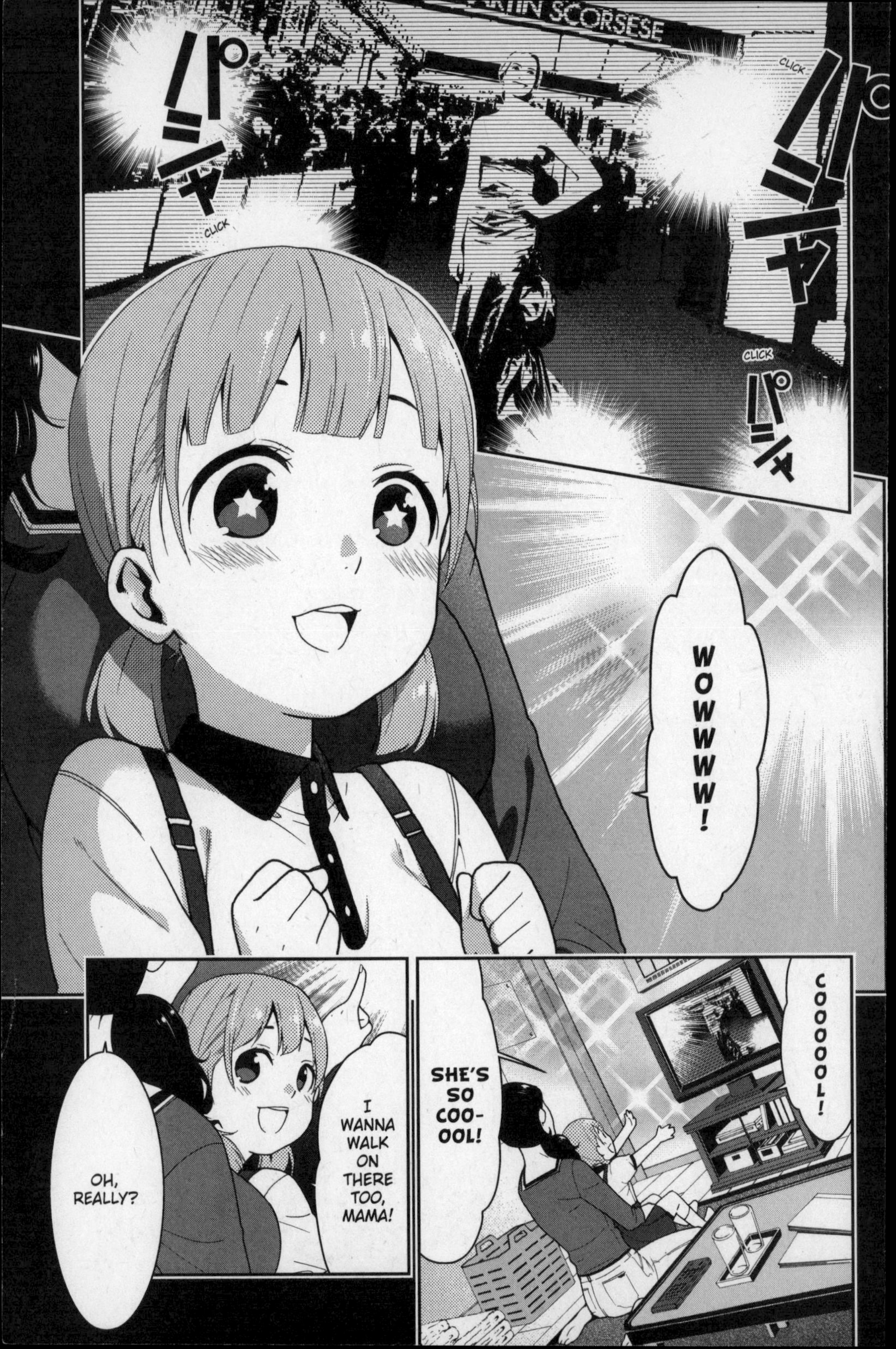
CLICK
パシャ
CLICK
パシャ
パシャ
CLICK
WOWWWWW!
COOOOOOL!
SHE'S SO COO-OOL!
I WANNA WALK ON THERE TOO, MAMA!
OH, REALLY?

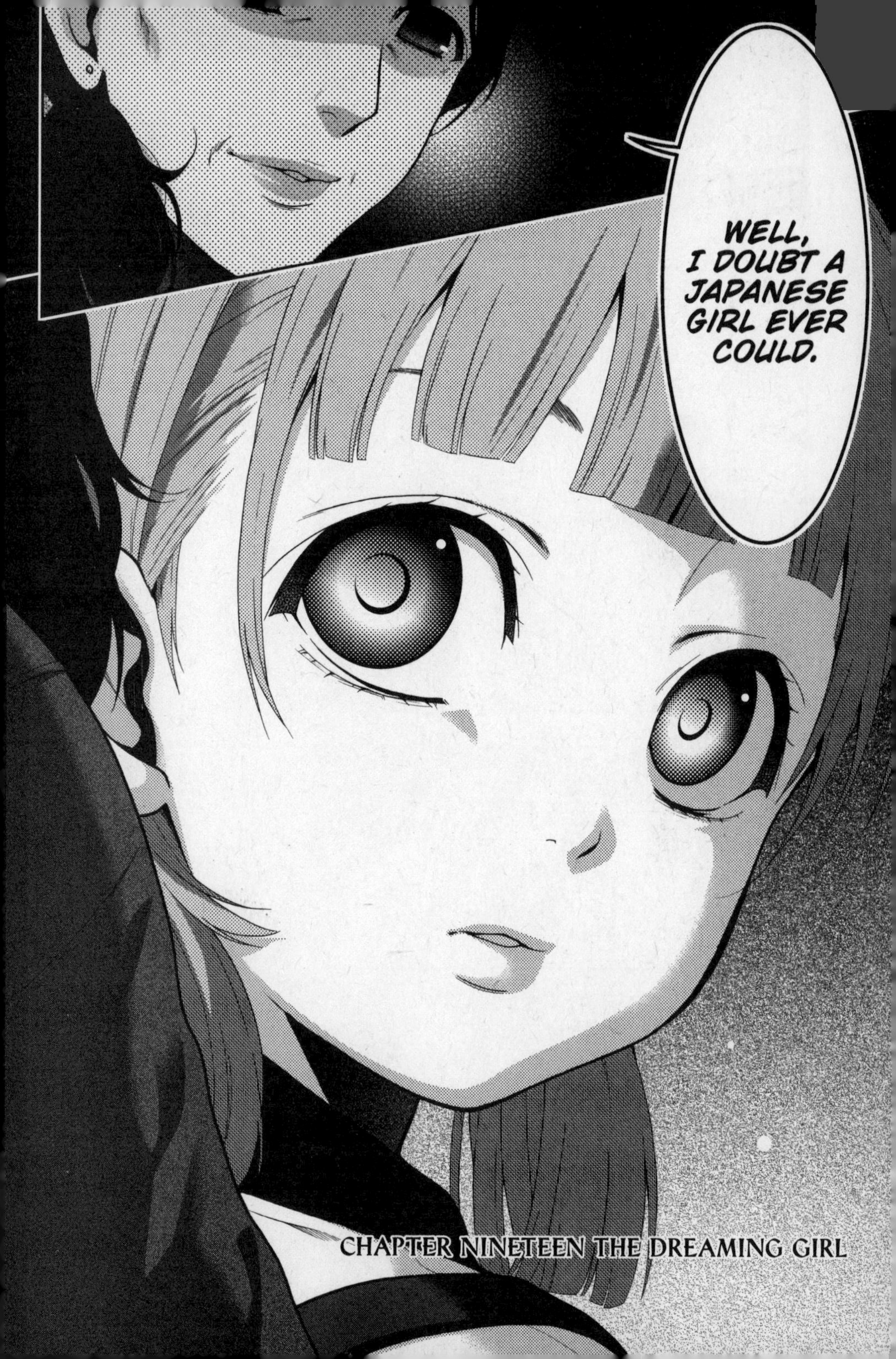
WELL, I DOUBT A JAPANESE GIRL EVER COULD.
CHAPTER NINETEEN THE DREAMING GIRL

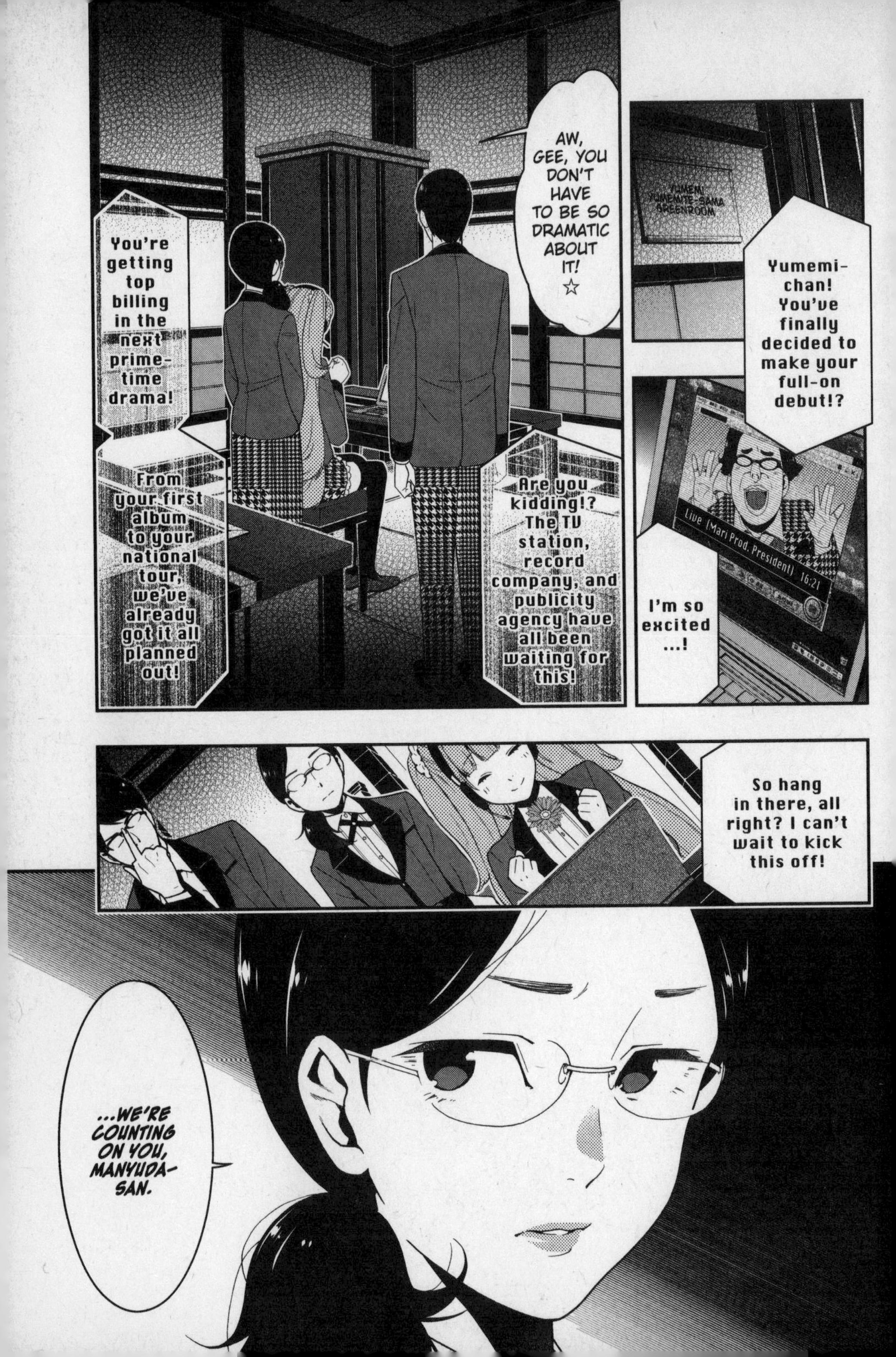

YUMEMI YUMEMITE-SAMA GREENROOM
Yumemi-chan! You've finally decided to make your full-on debut!?
Live (Mari Prod. President) 16:21
I'm so excited ...!
You're getting top billing in the next prime-time drama!
From your first album to your national tour, we've already got it all planned out!
AW, GEE, YOU DON'T HAVE TO BE SO DRAMATIC ABOUT IT! ☆
Are you kidding!? The TV station, record company, and publicity agency have all been waiting for this!
So hang in there, all right? I can't wait to kick this off!
...WE'RE COUNTING ON YOU, MANYUDA-SAN.

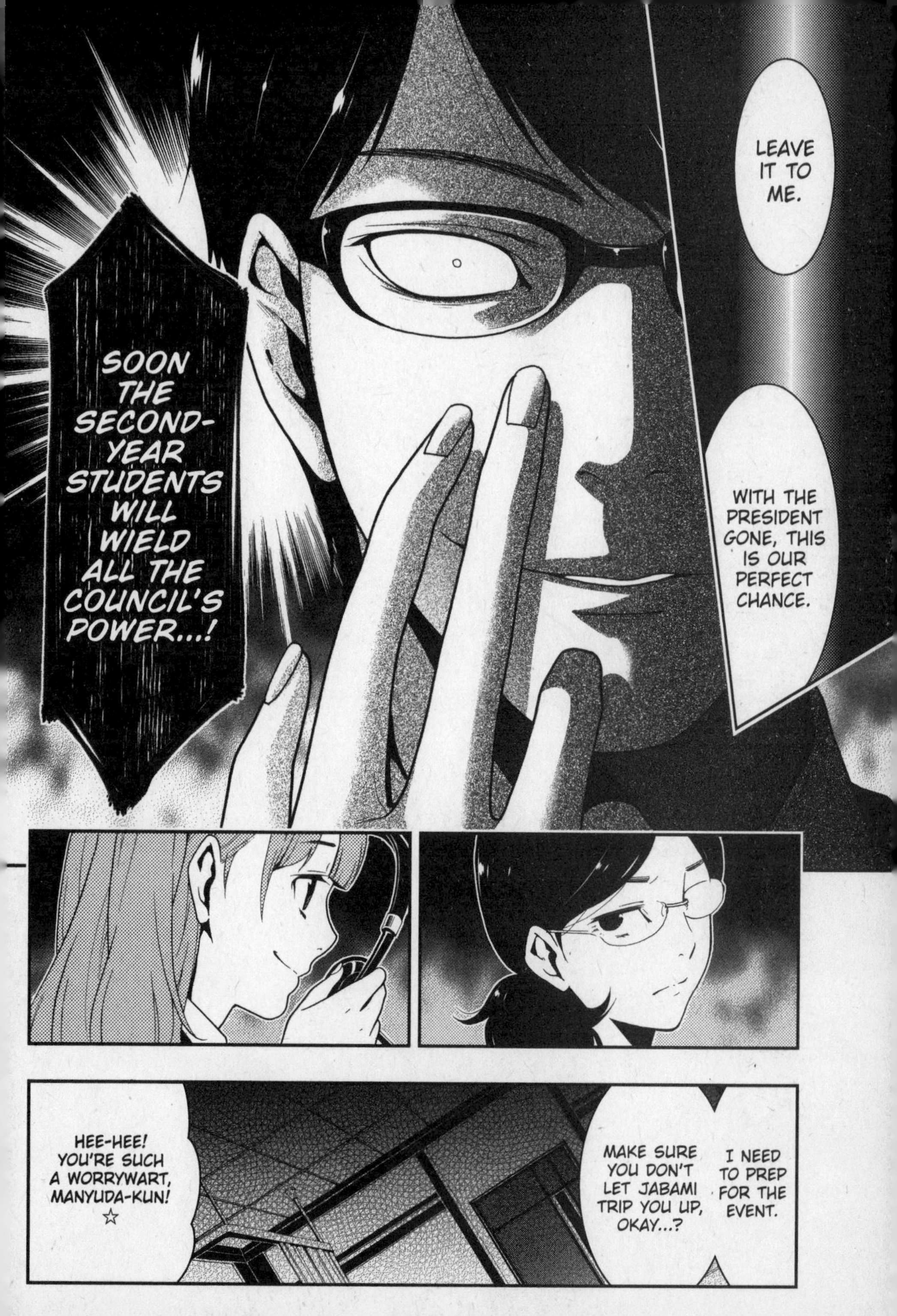
LEAVE IT TO ME.
WITH THE PRESIDENT GONE, THIS IS OUR PERFECT CHANCE.
SOON THE SECOND-YEAR STUDENTS WILL WIELD ALL THE COUNCIL'S POWER...!
I NEED TO PREP FOR THE EVENT.
MAKE SURE YOU DON'T LET JABAMI TRIP YOU UP, OKAY...?
HEE-HEE! YOU'RE SUCH A WORRYWART, MANYUDA-KUN! ☆

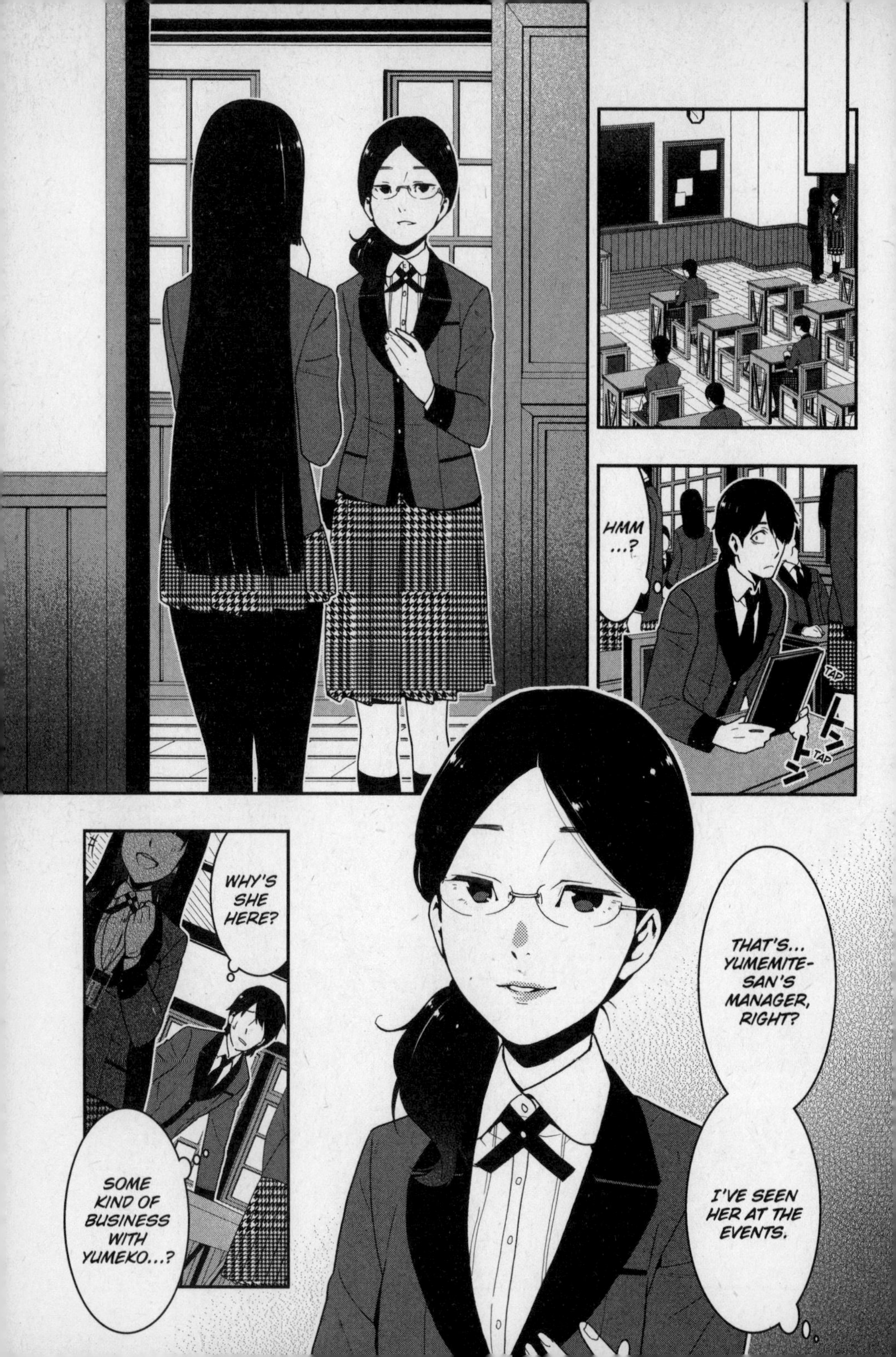
HMM ...?
TAP
TAP
THAT'S... YUMEMITE-SAN'S MANAGER, RIGHT?
I'VE SEEN HER AT THE EVENTS.
WHY'S SHE HERE?
SOME KIND OF BUSINESS WITH YUMEKO...?

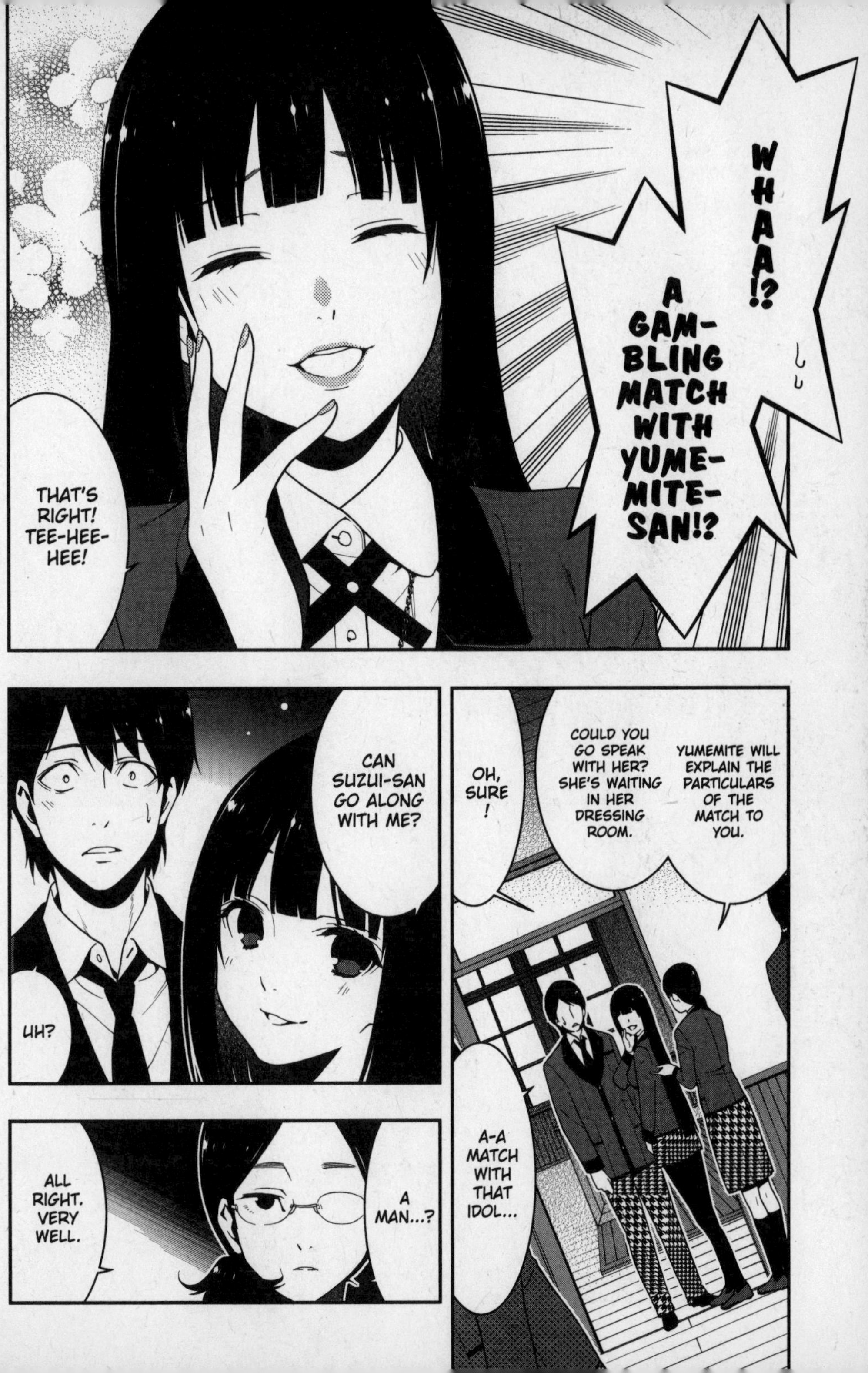
WHAA!?
A GAM-BLING MATCH WITH YUME-MITE-SAN!?
THAT'S RIGHT! TEE-HEE-HEE!
YUMEMITE WILL EXPLAIN THE PARTICULARS OF THE MATCH TO YOU.
COULD YOU GO SPEAK WITH HER? SHE'S WAITING IN HER DRESSING ROOM.
OH, SURE!
A-A MATCH WITH THAT IDOL...
CAN SUZUI-SAN GO ALONG WITH ME?
UH?
A MAN...?
ALL RIGHT. VERY WELL.

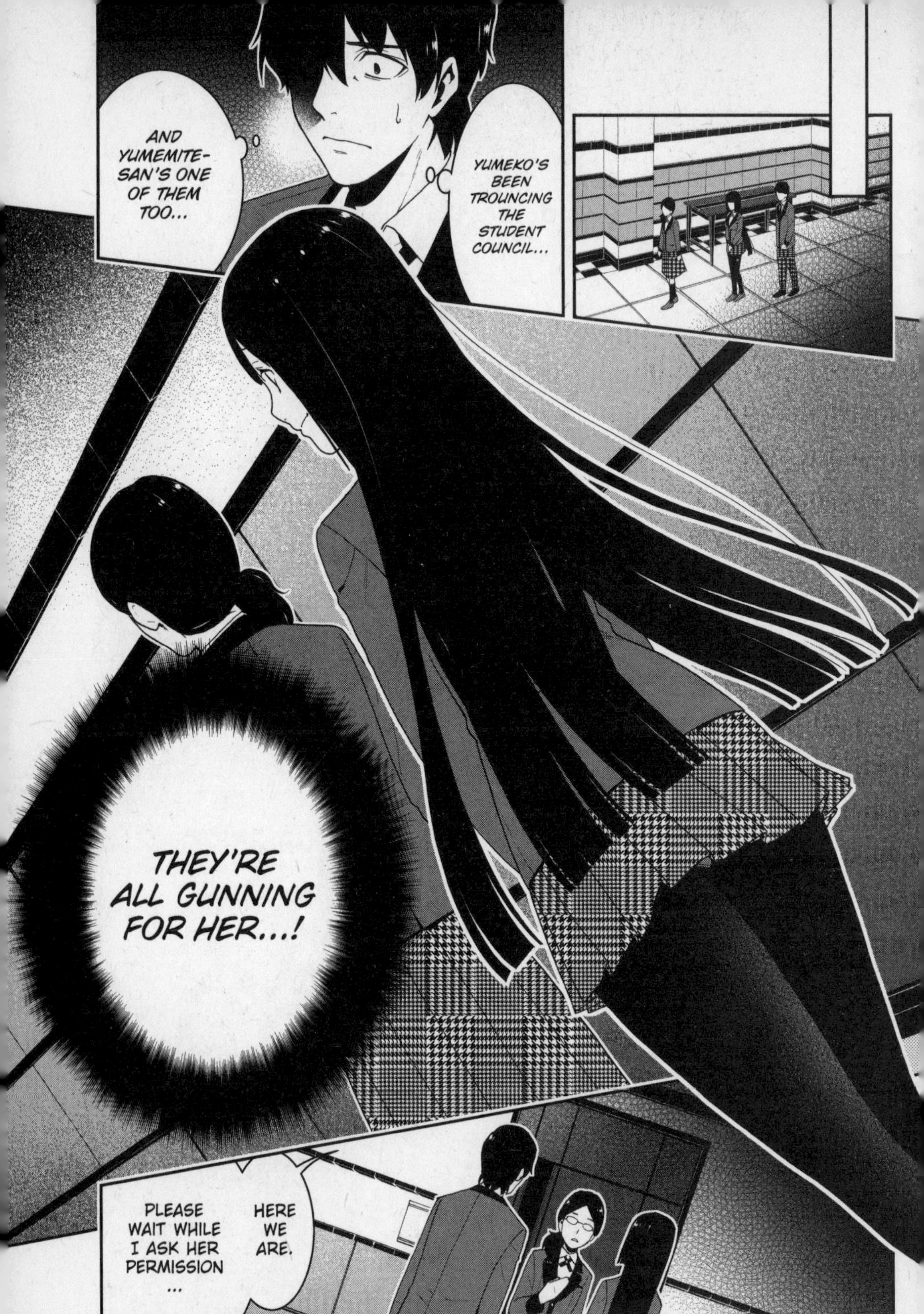
YUMEKO'S BEEN TROUNCING THE STUDENT COUNCIL...
AND YUMEMITE-SAN'S ONE OF THEM TOO...
THEY'RE ALL GUNNING FOR HER...!
HERE WE ARE.
PLEASE WAIT WHILE I ASK HER PERMISSION ...

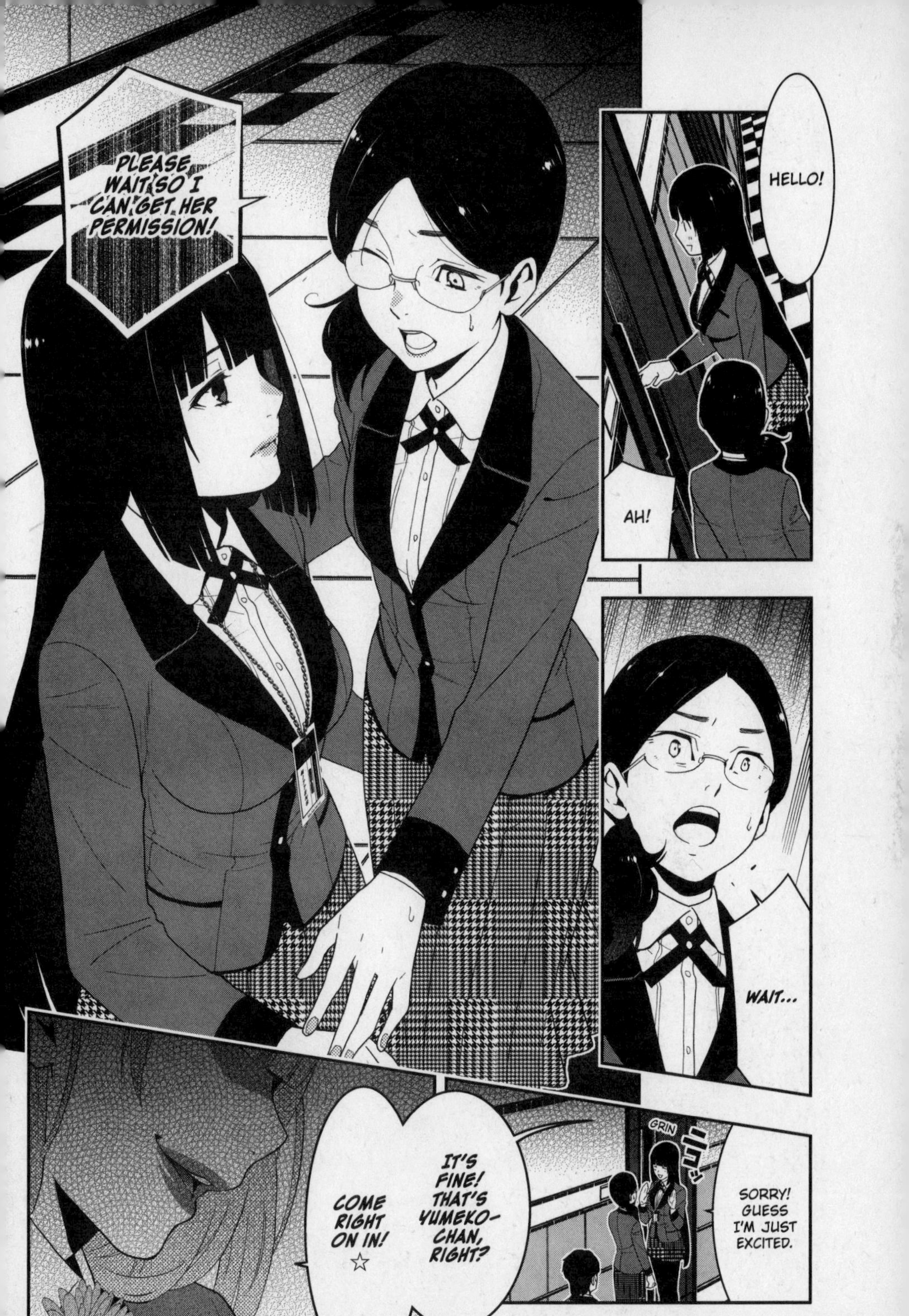
HELLO!
AH!
WAIT...
PLEASE WAIT SO I CAN GET HER PERMISSION!
GRIN
SORRY! GUESS I'M JUST EXCITED.
IT'S FINE! THAT'S YUMEKO-CHAN, RIGHT?
COME RIGHT ON IN! ☆

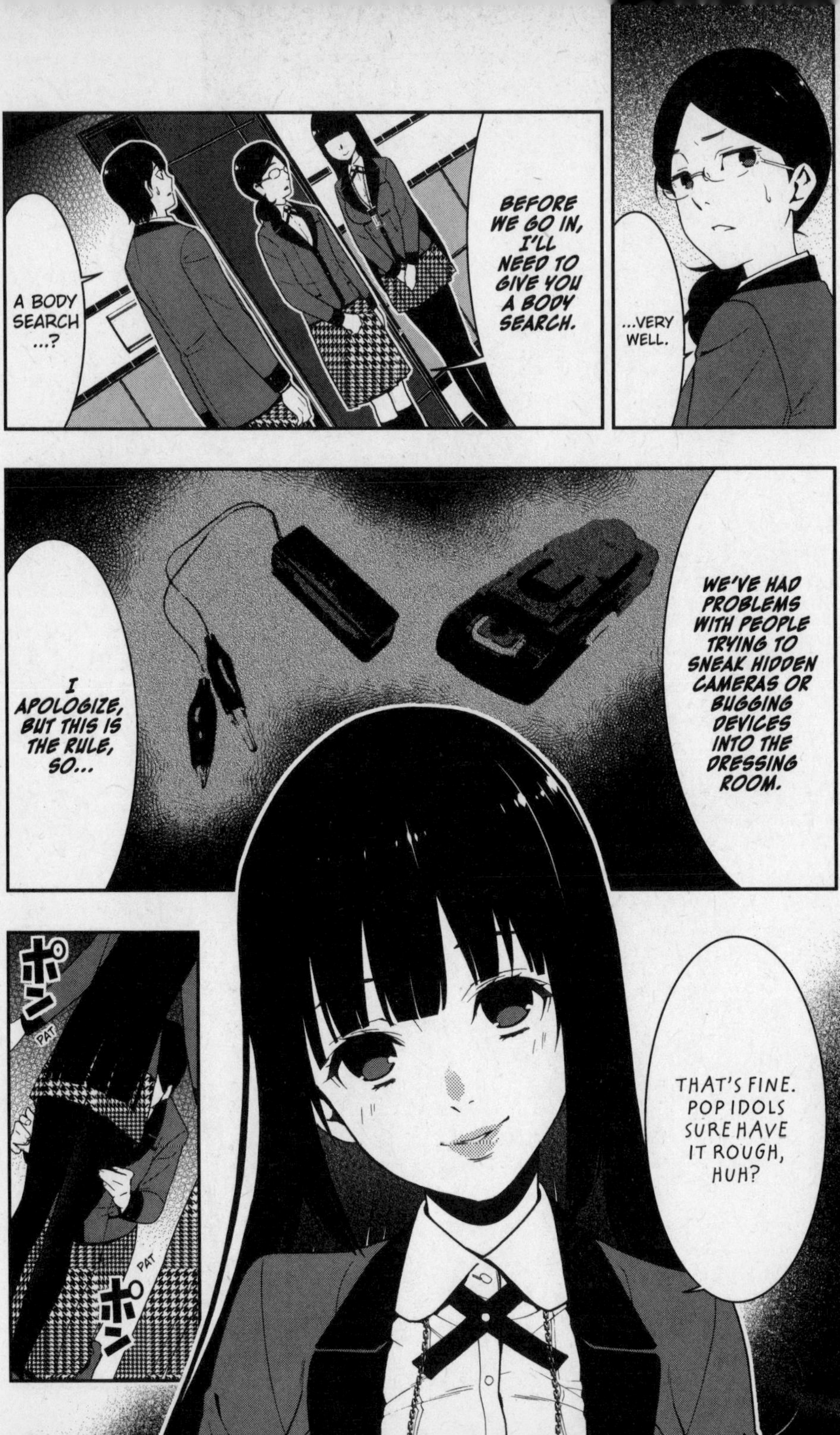
...VERY WELL.
BEFORE WE GO IN, I'LL NEED TO GIVE YOU A BODY SEARCH.
A BODY SEARCH ...?
WE'VE HAD PROBLEMS WITH PEOPLE TRYING TO SNEAK HIDDEN CAMERAS OR BUGGING DEVICES INTO THE DRESSING ROOM.
I APOLOGIZE, BUT THIS IS THE RULE, SO...
THAT'S FINE. POP IDOLS SURE HAVE IT ROUGH, HUH?
ポン
PAT
ポン
PAT

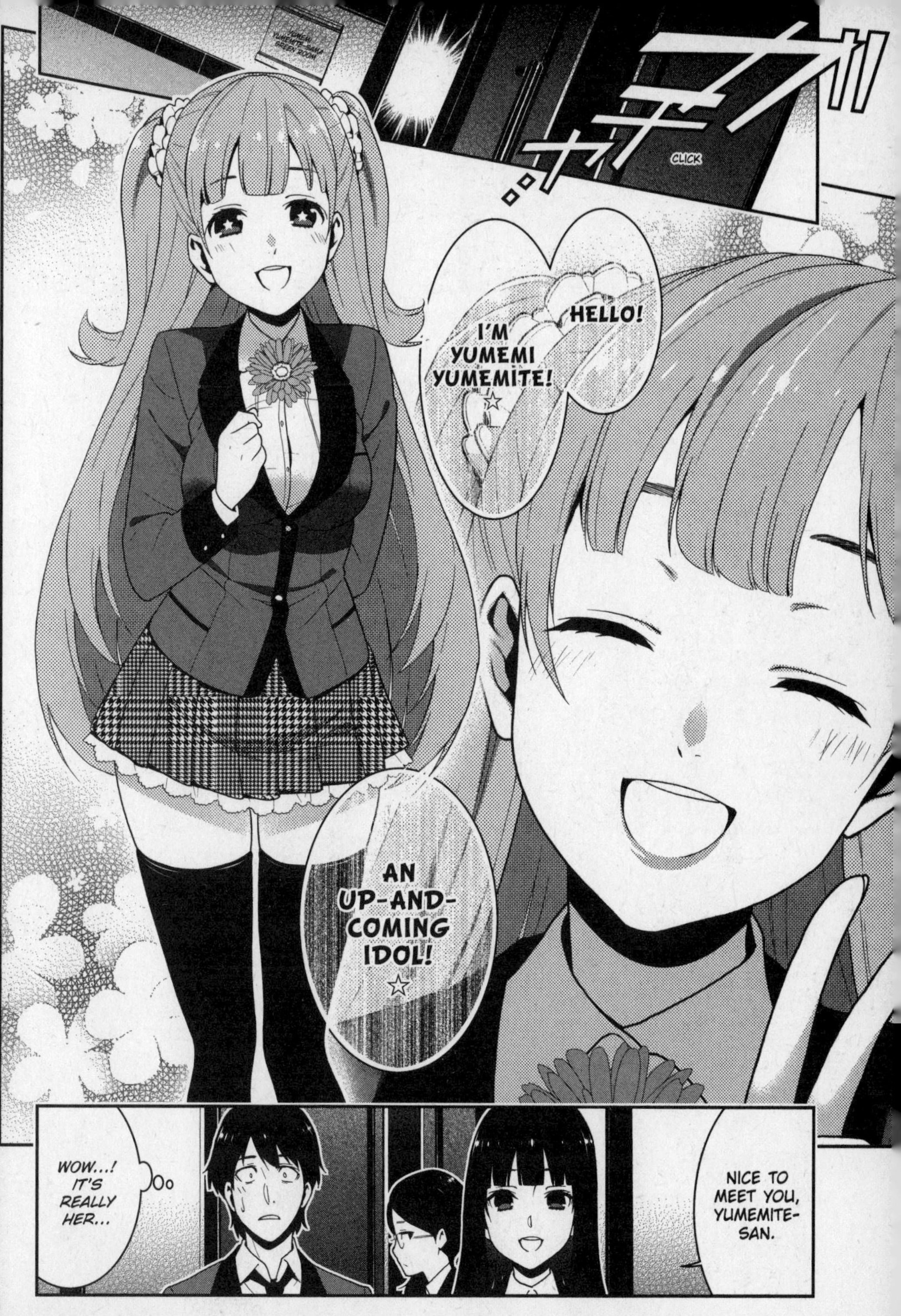
YUMEMI YUMEMITE-SAMA GREEN ROOM
ガチャ
CLICK
HELLO!
I'M YUMEMI YUMEMITE! ☆
AN UP-AND-COMING IDOL! ☆
NICE TO MEET YOU, YUMEMITE-SAN.
WOW...! IT'S REALLY HER...

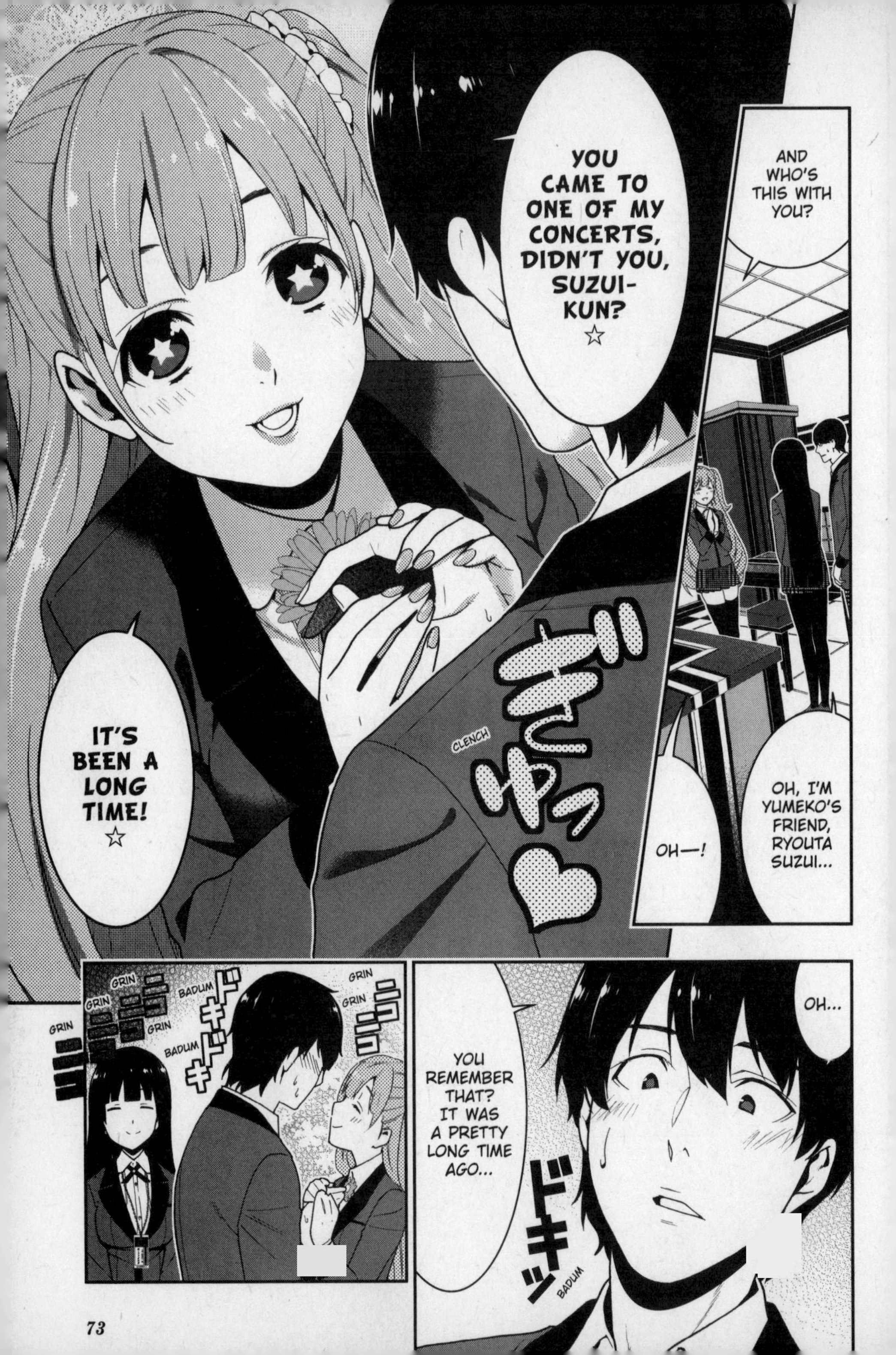
AND WHO'S THIS WITH YOU?
OH, I'M YUMEKO'S FRIEND, RYOUTA SUZUI...
OH—!
YOU CAME TO ONE OF MY CONCERTS, DIDN'T YOU, SUZUI-KUN? ☆
IT'S BEEN A LONG TIME! ☆
CLENCH
OH...
YOU REMEMBER THAT? IT WAS A PRETTY LONG TIME AGO...
BADUM
GRIN
GRIN
BADUM
GRIN
GRIN
GRIN
BADUM
GRIN

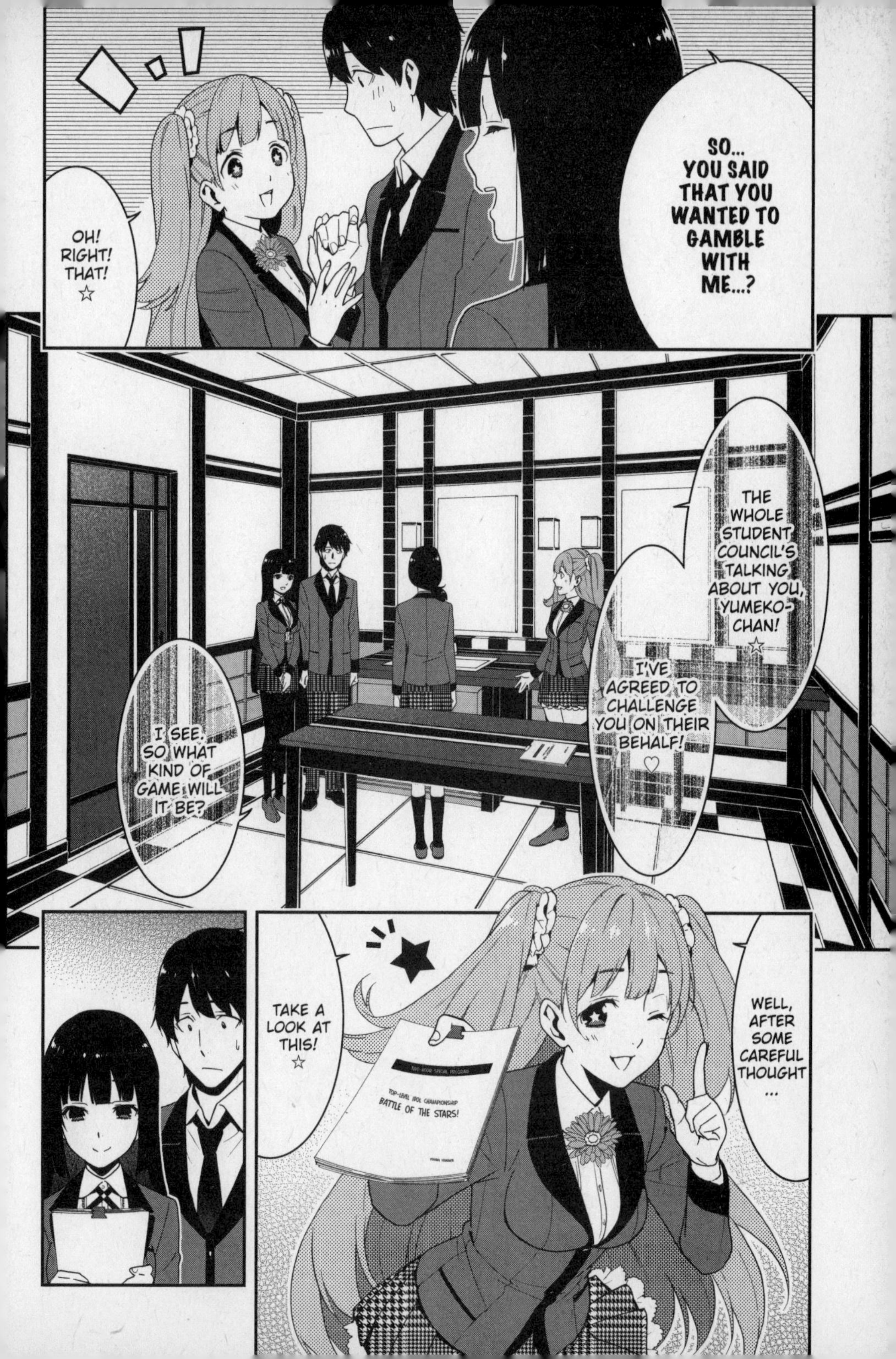
SO... YOU SAID THAT YOU WANTED TO GAMBLE WITH ME...?
OH! RIGHT! THAT! ☆
THE WHOLE STUDENT COUNCIL'S TALKING ABOUT YOU, YUMEKO-CHAN! ☆
I'VE AGREED TO CHALLENGE YOU ON THEIR BEHALF! ♡
I SEE. SO WHAT KIND OF GAME WILL IT BE?
WELL, AFTER SOME CAREFUL THOUGHT...
TAKE A LOOK AT THIS! ☆
TOP-LEVEL IDOL CHAMPIONSHIP
BATTLE OF THE STARS!

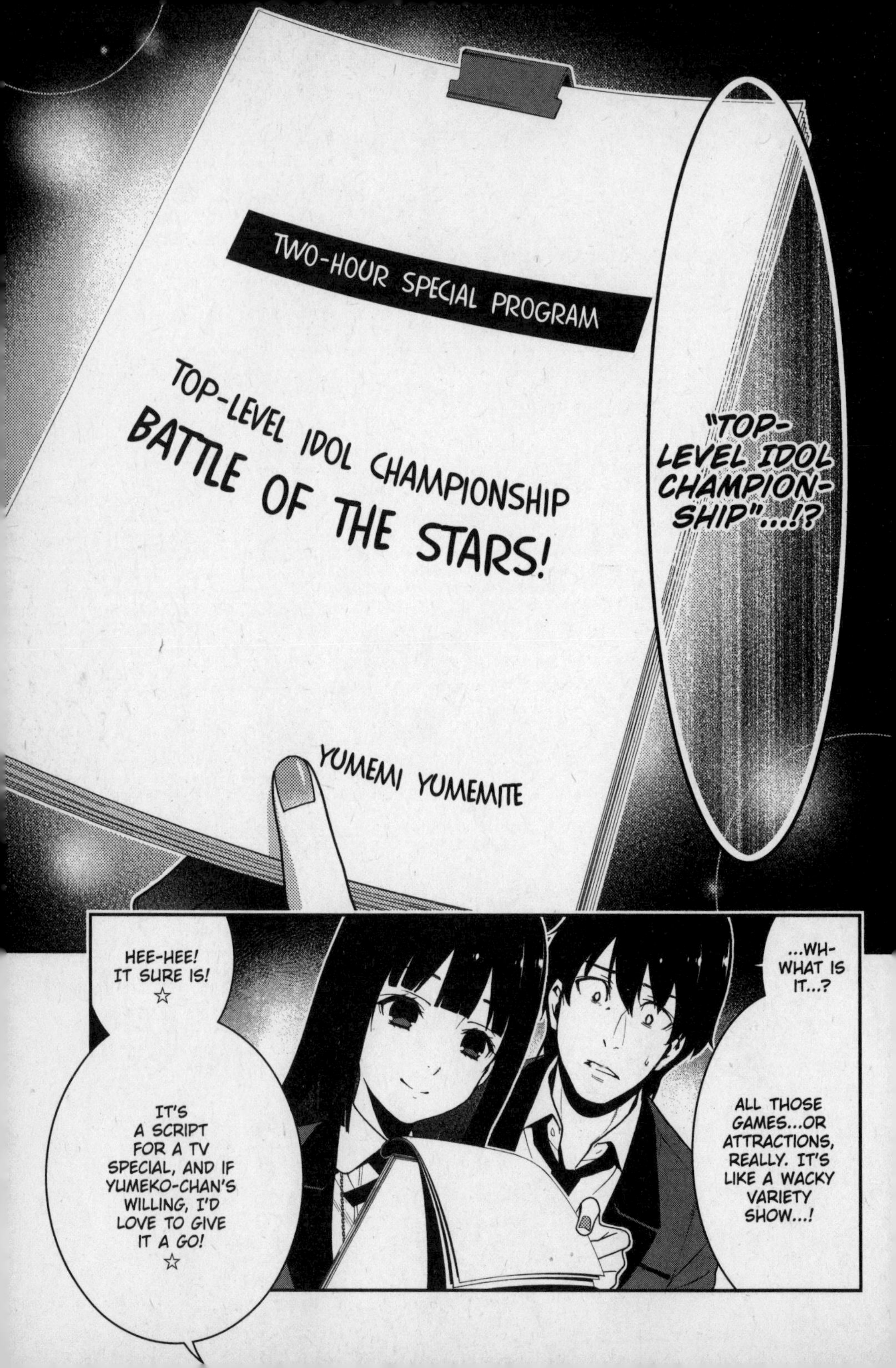

TWO-HOUR SPECIAL PROGRAM
TOP-LEVEL IDOL CHAMPIONSHIP BATTLE OF THE STARS!
YUMEMI YUMEMITE
"TOP-LEVEL IDOL CHAMPION-SHIP"...!?
...WH-WHAT IS IT...?
ALL THOSE GAMES...OR ATTRACTIONS, REALLY. IT'S LIKE A WACKY VARIETY SHOW...!
HEE-HEE! IT SURE IS! ☆
IT'S A SCRIPT FOR A TV SPECIAL, AND IF YUMEKO-CHAN'S WILLING, I'D LOVE TO GIVE IT A GO! ☆

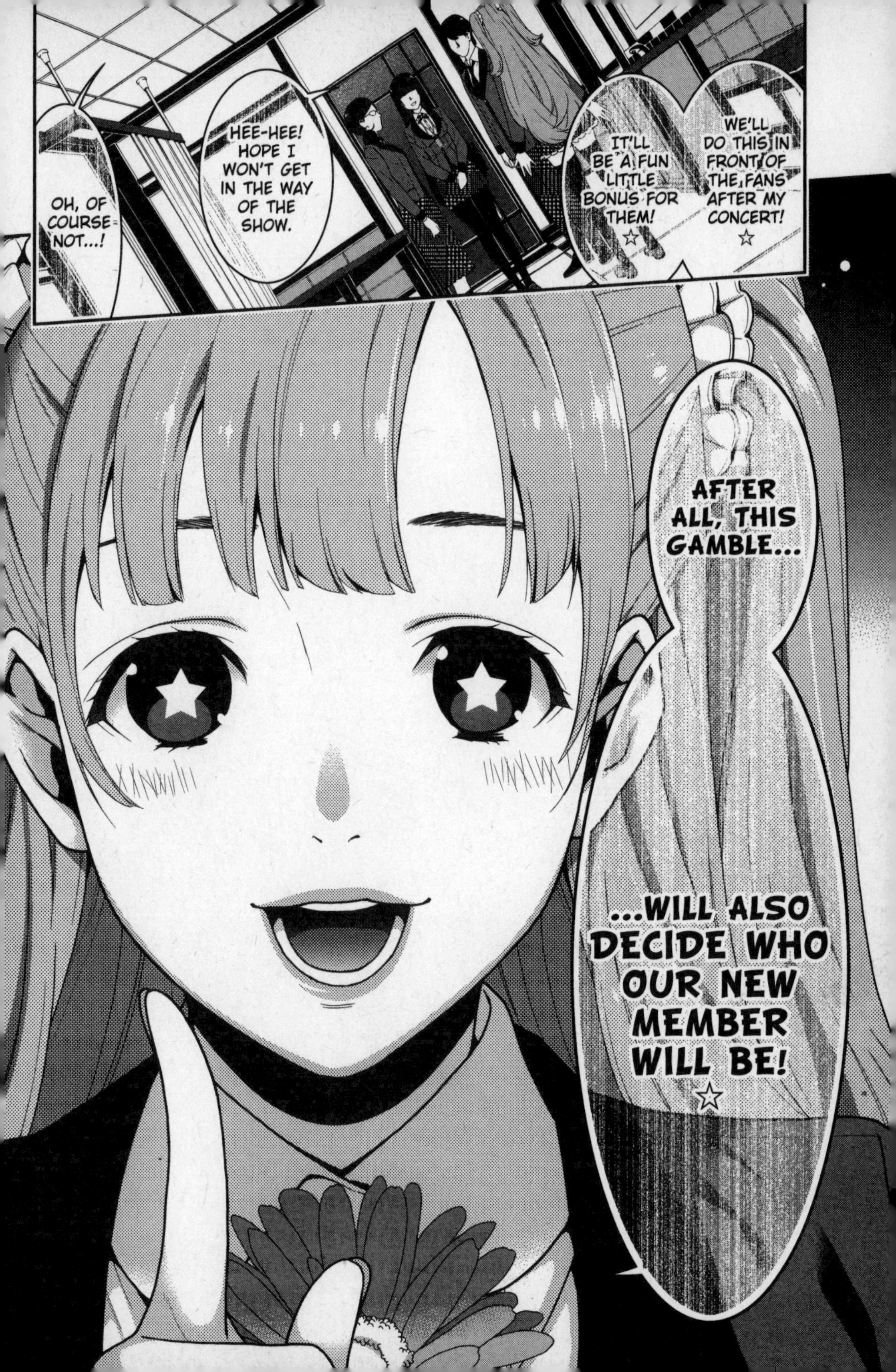
WE'LL DO THIS IN FRONT OF THE FANS AFTER MY CONCERT! ☆
IT'LL BE A FUN LITTLE BONUS FOR THEM! ☆
HEE-HEE! HOPE I WON'T GET IN THE WAY OF THE SHOW.
OH, OF COURSE NOT...!
AFTER ALL, THIS GAMBLE...
...WILL ALSO DECIDE WHO OUR NEW MEMBER WILL BE! ☆

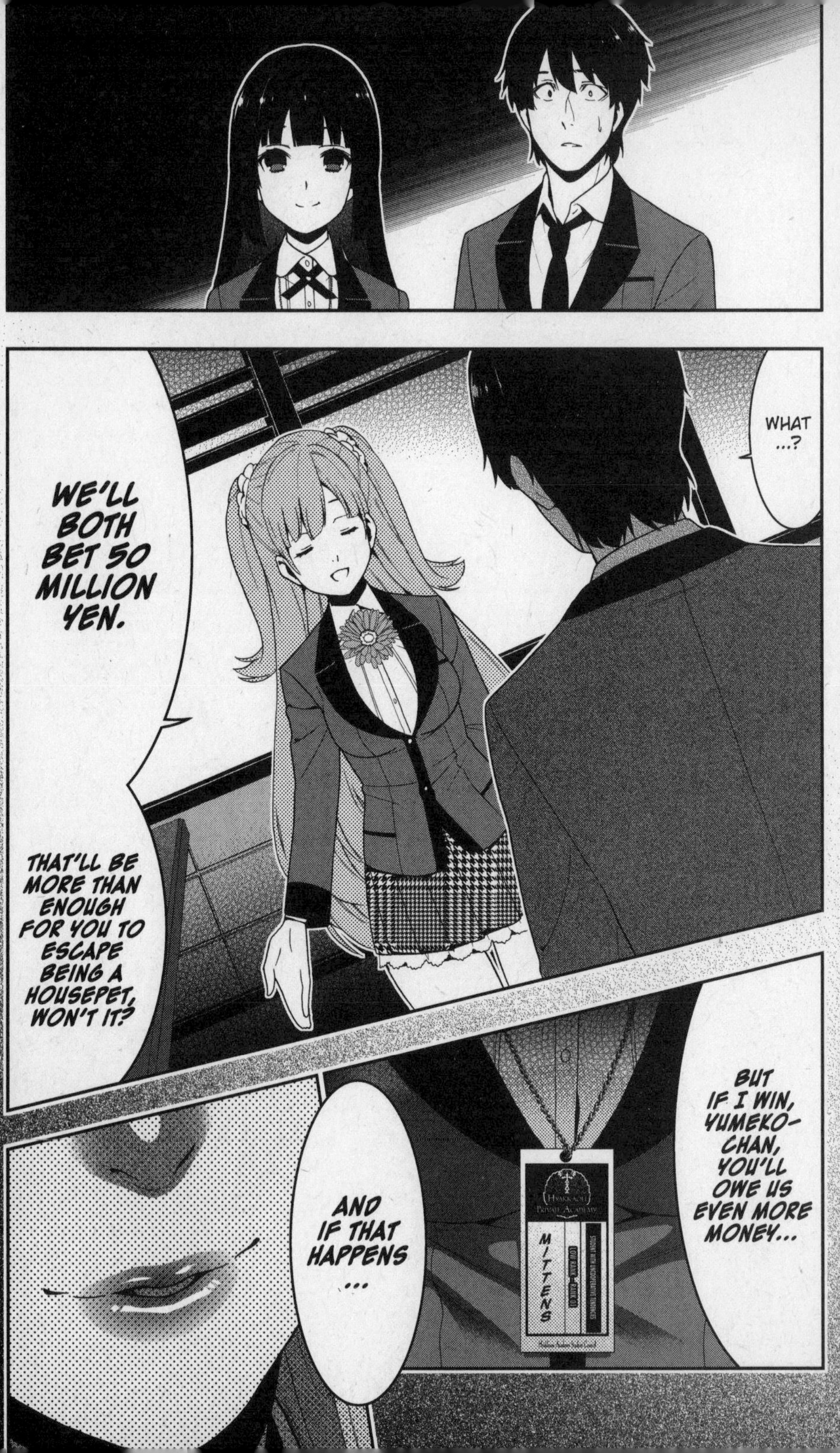
WHAT ...?
WE'LL BOTH BET 50 MILLION YEN.
THAT'LL BE MORE THAN ENOUGH FOR YOU TO ESCAPE BEING A HOUSEPET, WON'T IT?
BUT IF I WIN, YUMEKO-CHAN, YOU'LL OWE US EVEN MORE MONEY...
HYAKKAOU PRIVATE ACADEMY
MITTENS
AND IF THAT HAPPENS ...

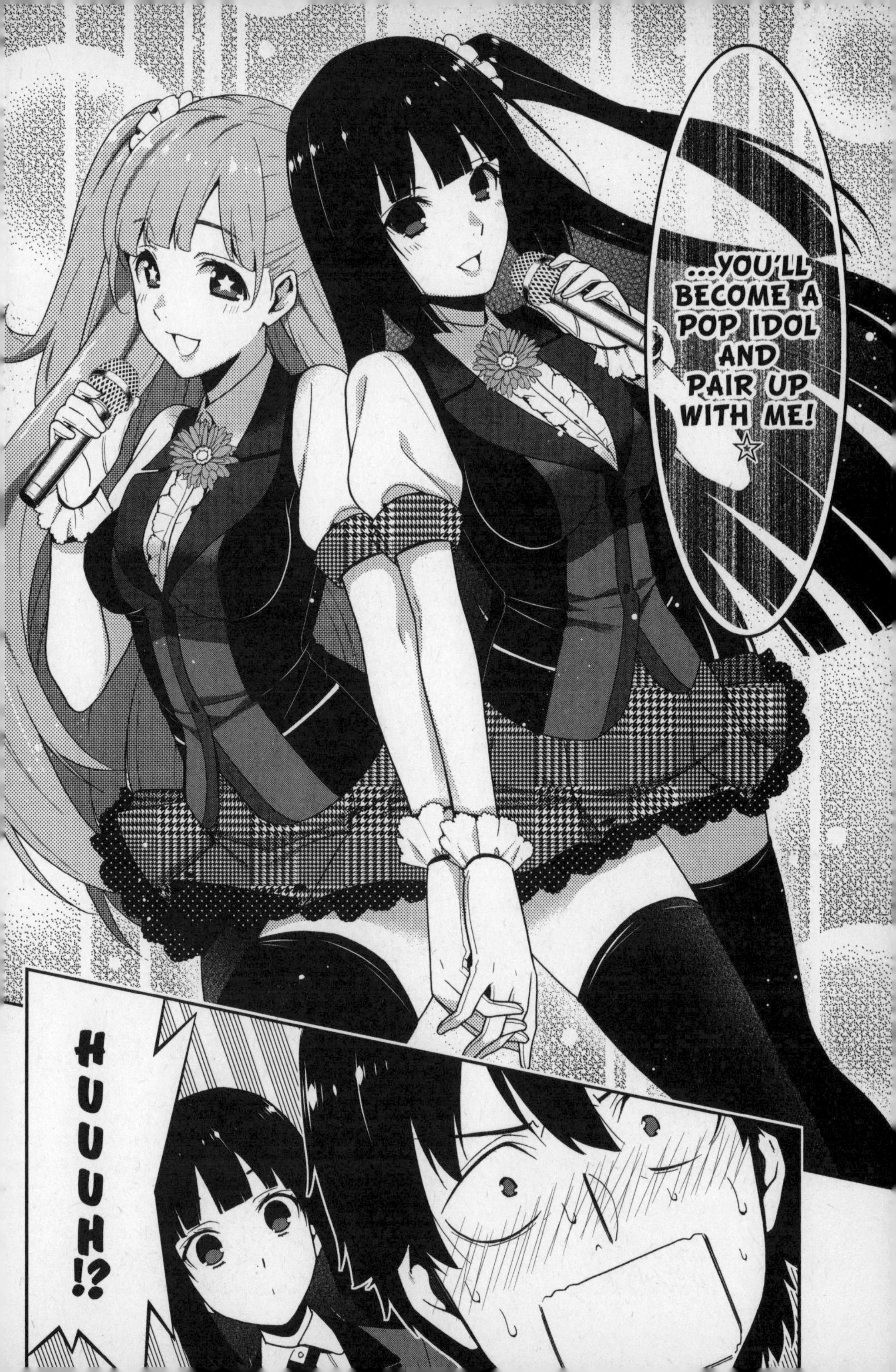
...YOU'LL BECOME A POP IDOL AND PAIR UP WITH ME! ☆
HUUUUH!?

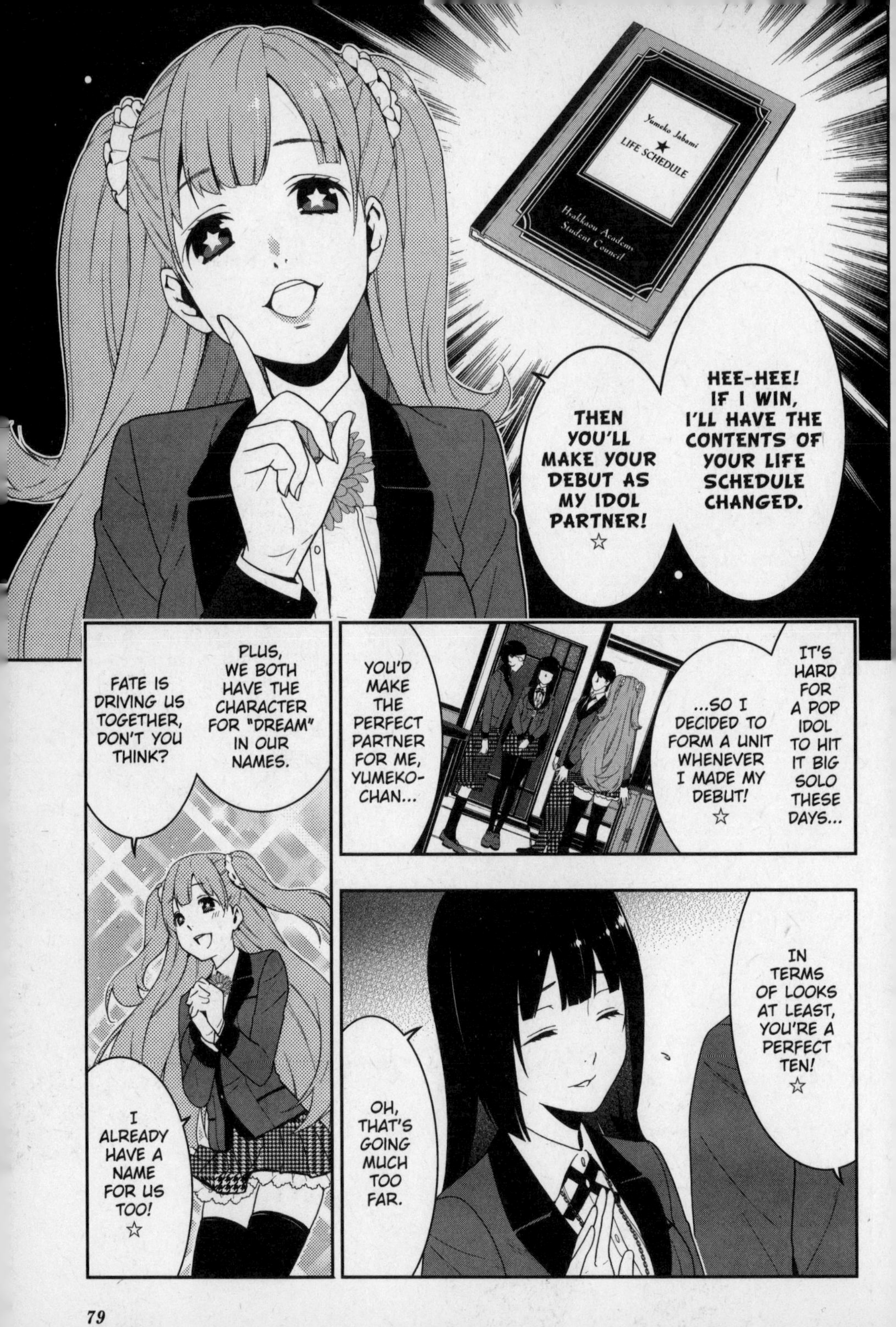
Yumeko Jabami
★
LIFE SCHEDULE
Hyakkaou Academy
Student Council
HEE-HEE! IF I WIN, I'LL HAVE THE CONTENTS OF YOUR LIFE SCHEDULE CHANGED.
THEN YOU'LL MAKE YOUR DEBUT AS MY IDOL PARTNER! ☆
IT'S HARD FOR A POP IDOL TO HIT IT BIG SOLO THESE DAYS...
...SO I DECIDED TO FORM A UNIT WHENEVER I MADE MY DEBUT! ☆
YOU'D MAKE THE PERFECT PARTNER FOR ME, YUMEKO-CHAN...
IN TERMS OF LOOKS AT LEAST, YOU'RE A PERFECT TEN! ☆
OH, THAT'S GOING MUCH TOO FAR.
PLUS, WE BOTH HAVE THE CHARACTER FOR "DREAM" IN OUR NAMES.
FATE IS DRIVING US TOGETHER, DON'T YOU THINK?
I ALREADY HAVE A NAME FOR US TOO! ☆

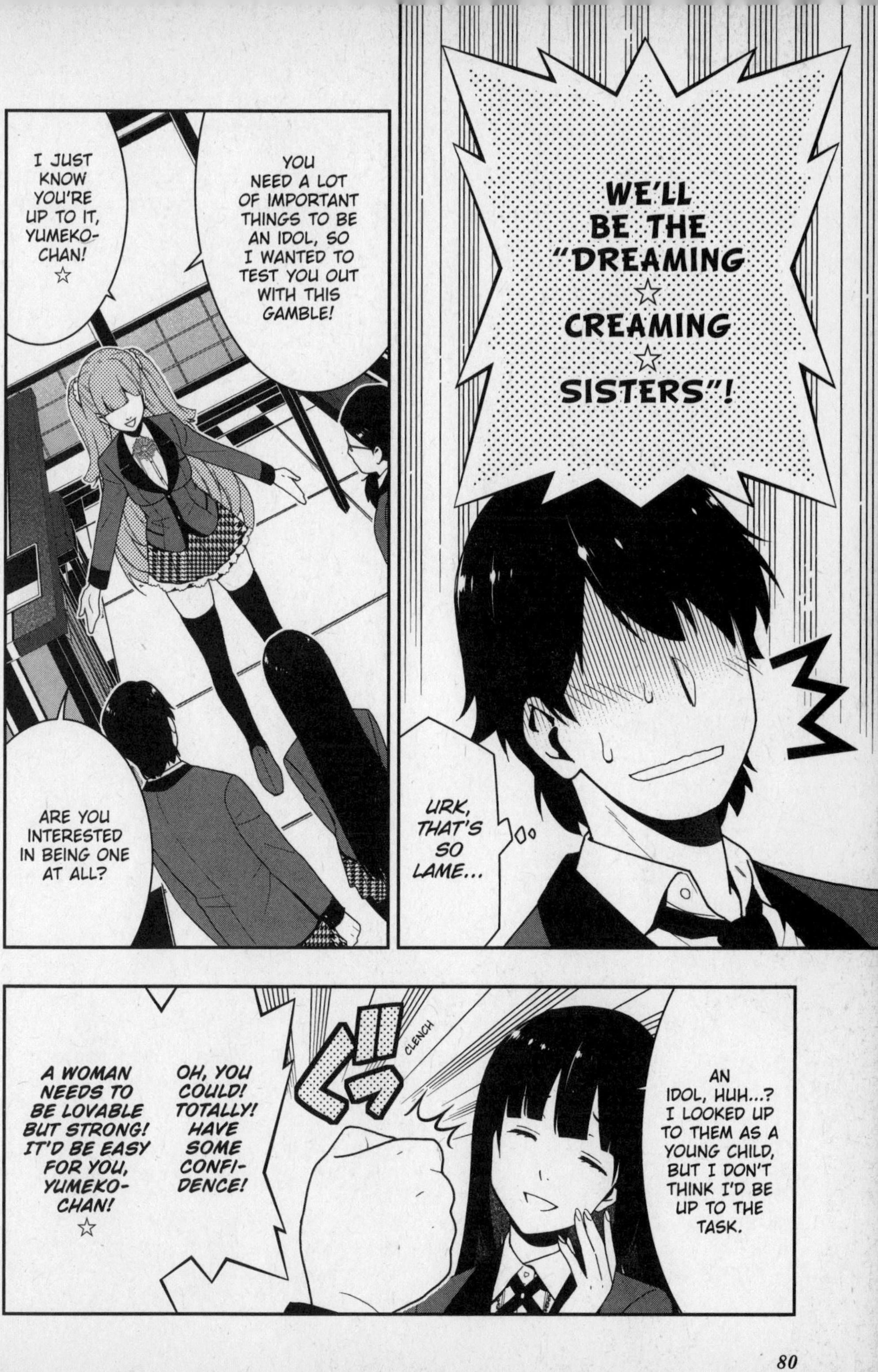
WE'LL BE THE "DREAMING ☆ CREAMING ☆ SISTERS"!
URK, THAT'S SO LAME...
YOU NEED A LOT OF IMPORTANT THINGS TO BE AN IDOL, SO I WANTED TO TEST YOU OUT WITH THIS GAMBLE!
I JUST KNOW YOU'RE UP TO IT, YUMEKO-CHAN! ☆
ARE YOU INTERESTED IN BEING ONE AT ALL?
AN IDOL, HUH...? I LOOKED UP TO THEM AS A YOUNG CHILD, BUT I DON'T THINK I'D BE UP TO THE TASK.
CLENCH
OH, YOU COULD! TOTALLY! HAVE SOME CONFI-DENCE!
A WOMAN NEEDS TO BE LOVABLE BUT STRONG! IT'D BE EASY FOR YOU, YUMEKO-CHAN! ☆

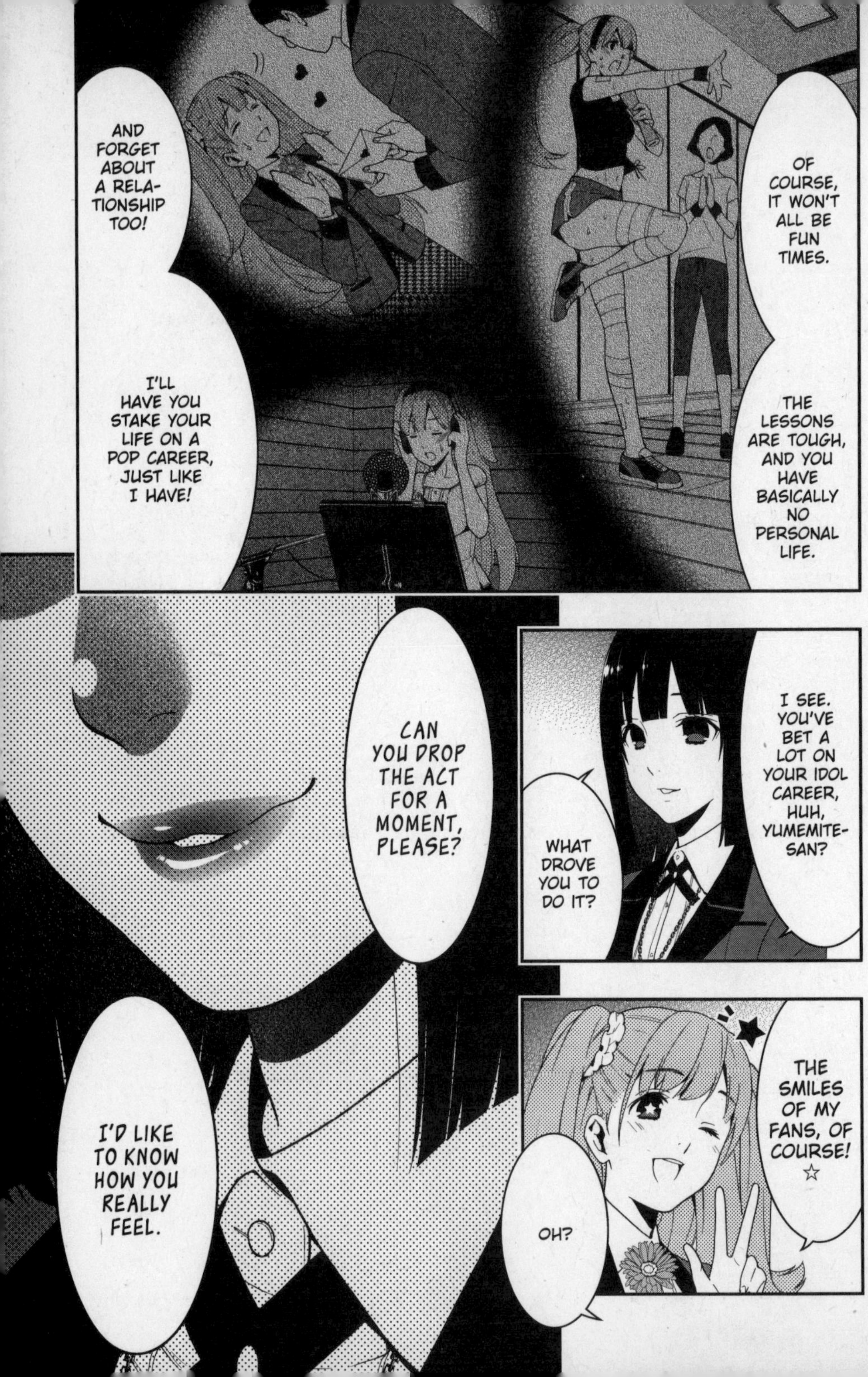
OF COURSE, IT WON'T ALL BE FUN TIMES.
THE LESSONS ARE TOUGH, AND YOU HAVE BASICALLY NO PERSONAL LIFE.
AND FORGET ABOUT A RELATIONSHIP TOO!
I'LL HAVE YOU STAKE YOUR LIFE ON A POP CAREER, JUST LIKE I HAVE!
I SEE. YOU'VE BET A LOT ON YOUR IDOL CAREER, HUH, YUMEMITE-SAN?
WHAT DROVE YOU TO DO IT?
THE SMILES OF MY FANS, OF COURSE! ☆
OH?
CAN YOU DROP THE ACT FOR A MOMENT, PLEASE?
I'D LIKE TO KNOW HOW YOU REALLY FEEL.

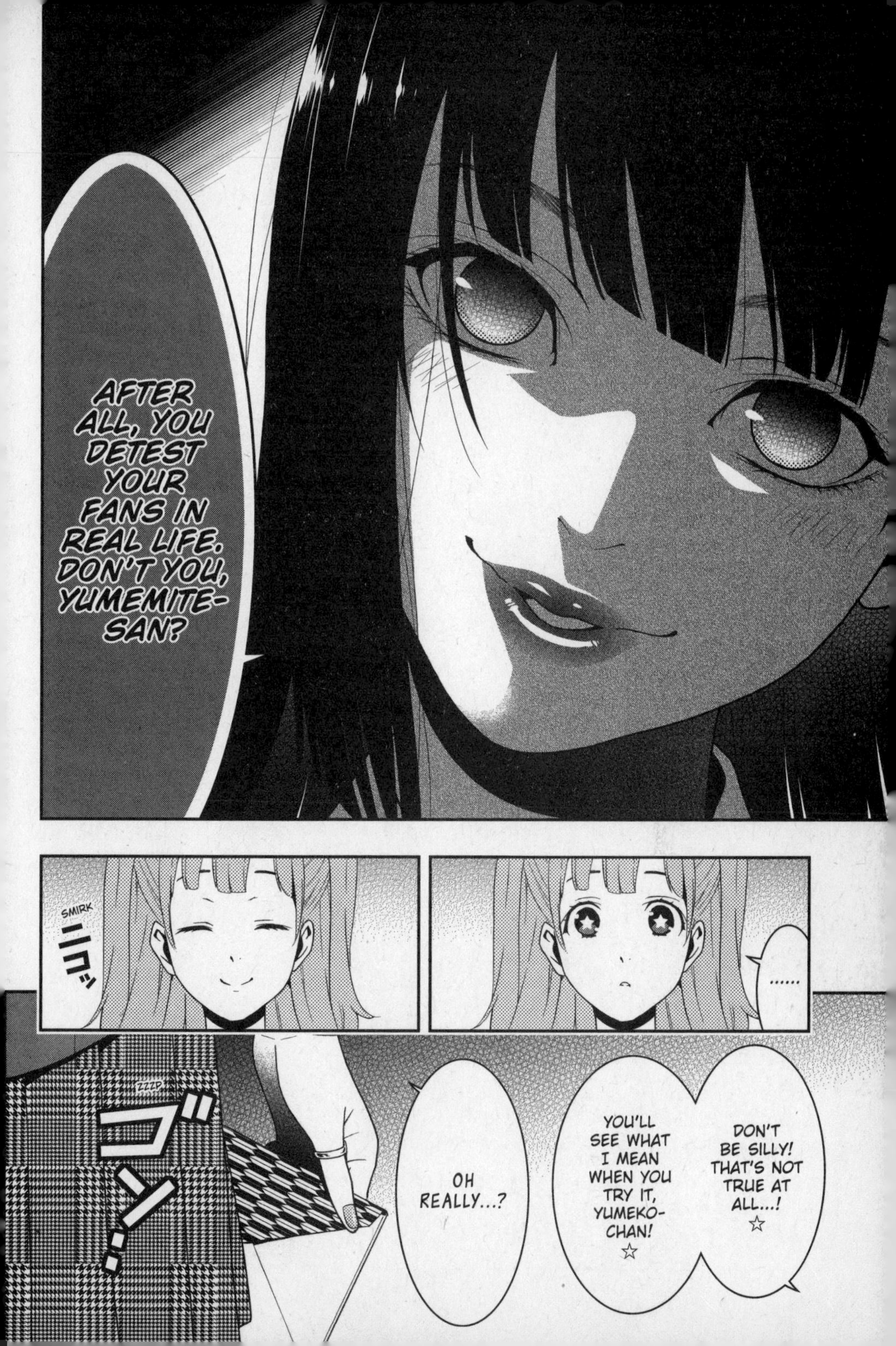
AFTER ALL, YOU DETEST YOUR FANS IN REAL LIFE. DON'T YOU, YUMEMITE-SAN?
......
SMIRK
ニコッ
DON'T BE SILLY! THAT'S NOT TRUE AT ALL...! ☆
YOU'LL SEE WHAT I MEAN WHEN YOU TRY IT, YUMEKO-CHAN! ☆
OH REALLY...?
ZZZP
ゴソッ...

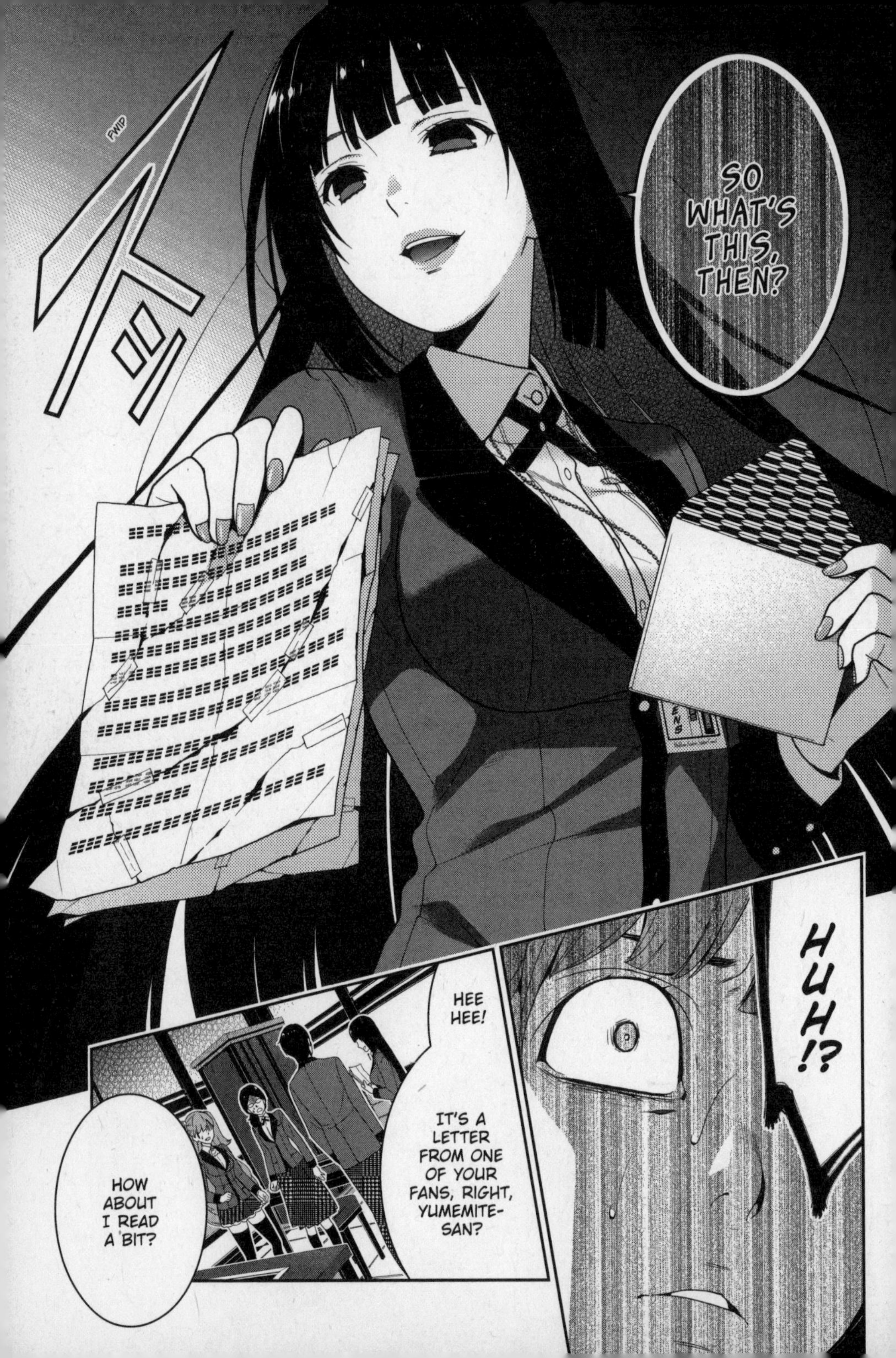
PWIP
SO WHAT'S THIS, THEN?
HUH!?
HEE HEE!
IT'S A LETTER FROM ONE OF YOUR FANS, RIGHT, YUMEMITE-SAN?
HOW ABOUT I READ A BIT?

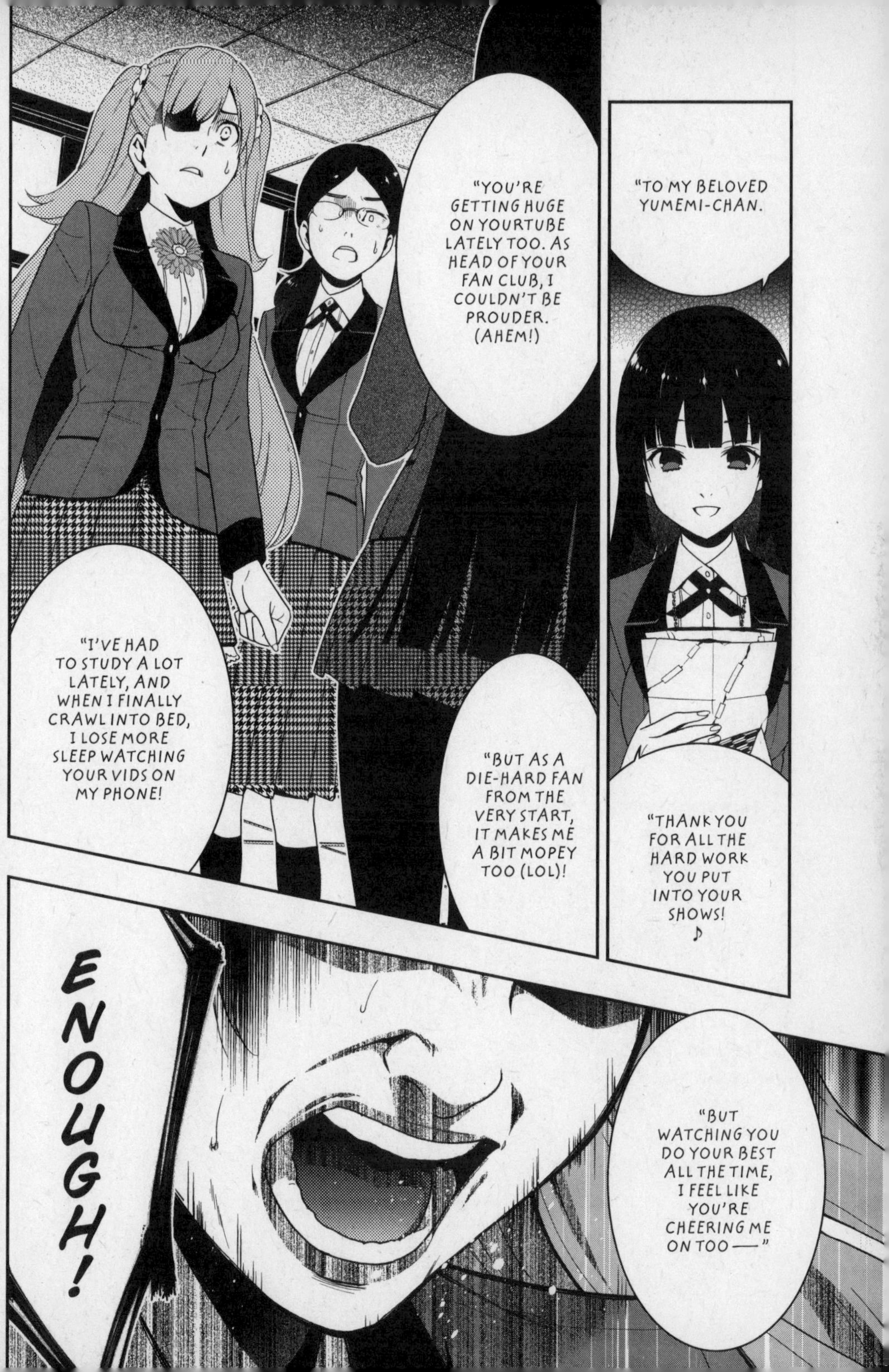
"TO MY BELOVED YUMEMI-CHAN.
"THANK YOU FOR ALL THE HARD WORK YOU PUT INTO YOUR SHOWS! ♪
"YOU'RE GETTING HUGE ON YOURTUBE LATELY TOO. AS HEAD OF YOUR FAN CLUB, I COULDN'T BE PROUDER. (AHEM!)
"BUT AS A DIE-HARD FAN FROM THE VERY START, IT MAKES ME A BIT MOPEY TOO (LOL)!
"I'VE HAD TO STUDY A LOT LATELY, AND WHEN I FINALLY CRAWL INTO BED, I LOSE MORE SLEEP WATCHING YOUR VIDS ON MY PHONE!
"BUT WATCHING YOU DO YOUR BEST ALL THE TIME, I FEEL LIKE YOU'RE CHEERING ME ON TOO—"
ENOUGH!

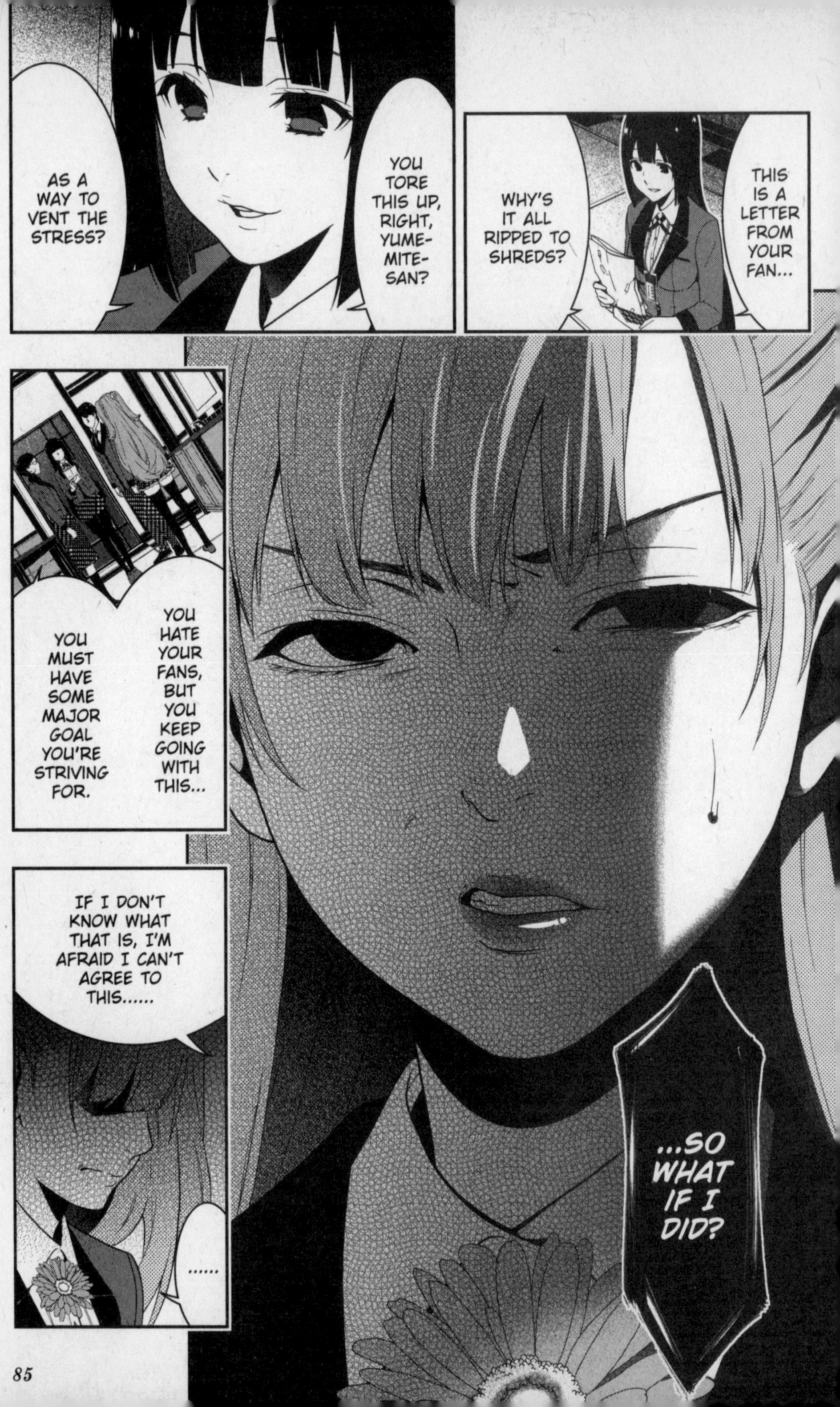
THIS IS A LETTER FROM YOUR FAN...
WHY'S IT ALL RIPPED TO SHREDS?
YOU TORE THIS UP, RIGHT, YUME-MITE-SAN?
AS A WAY TO VENT THE STRESS?
...SO WHAT IF I DID?
YOU HATE YOUR FANS, BUT YOU KEEP GOING WITH THIS...
YOU MUST HAVE SOME MAJOR GOAL YOU'RE STRIVING FOR.
IF I DON'T KNOW WHAT THAT IS, I'M AFRAID I CAN'T AGREE TO THIS......
......

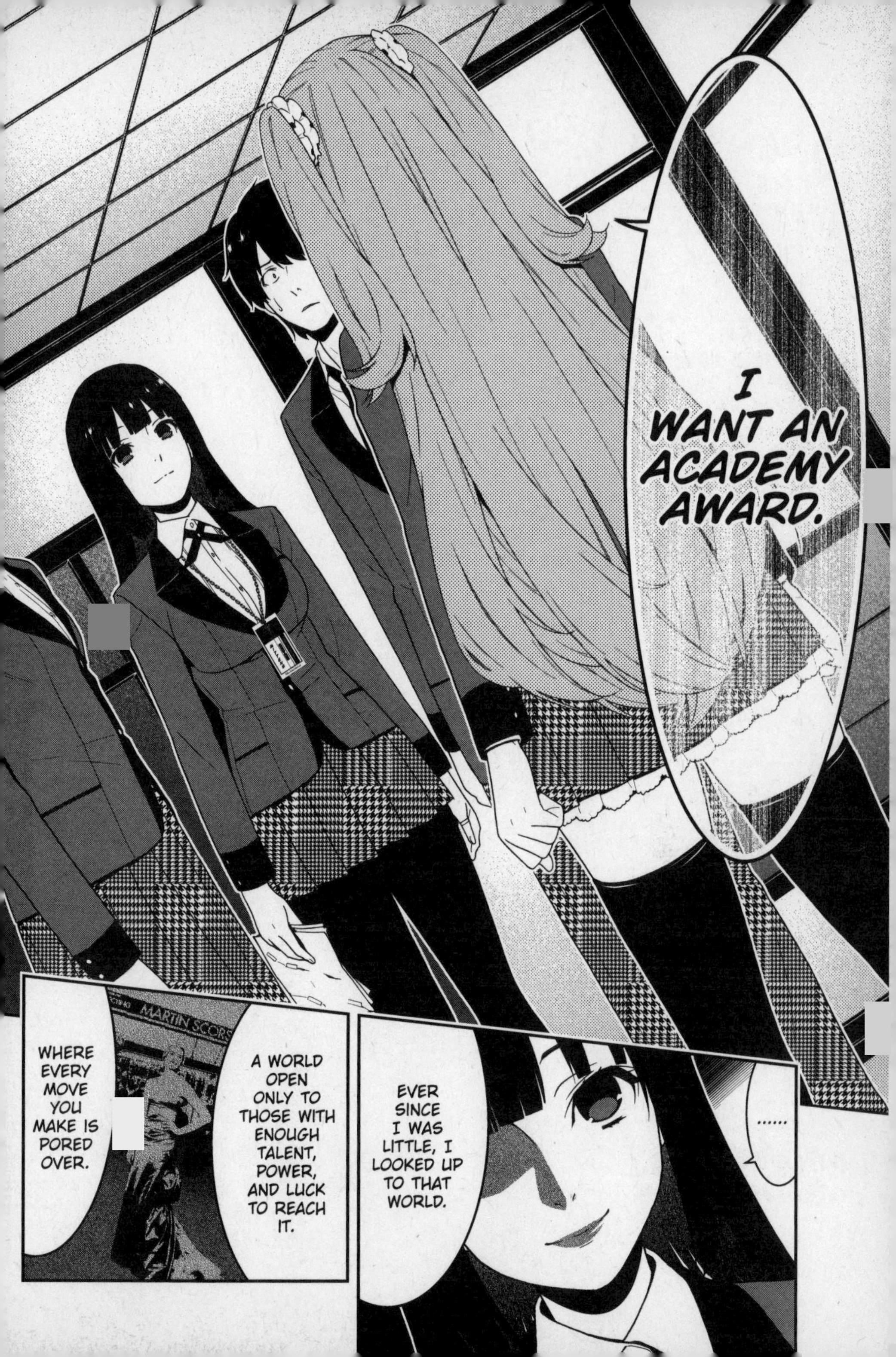
I WANT AN ACADEMY AWARD.
......
EVER SINCE I WAS LITTLE, I LOOKED UP TO THAT WORLD.
A WORLD OPEN ONLY TO THOSE WITH ENOUGH TALENT, POWER, AND LUCK TO REACH IT.
WHERE EVERY MOVE YOU MAKE IS PORED OVER.

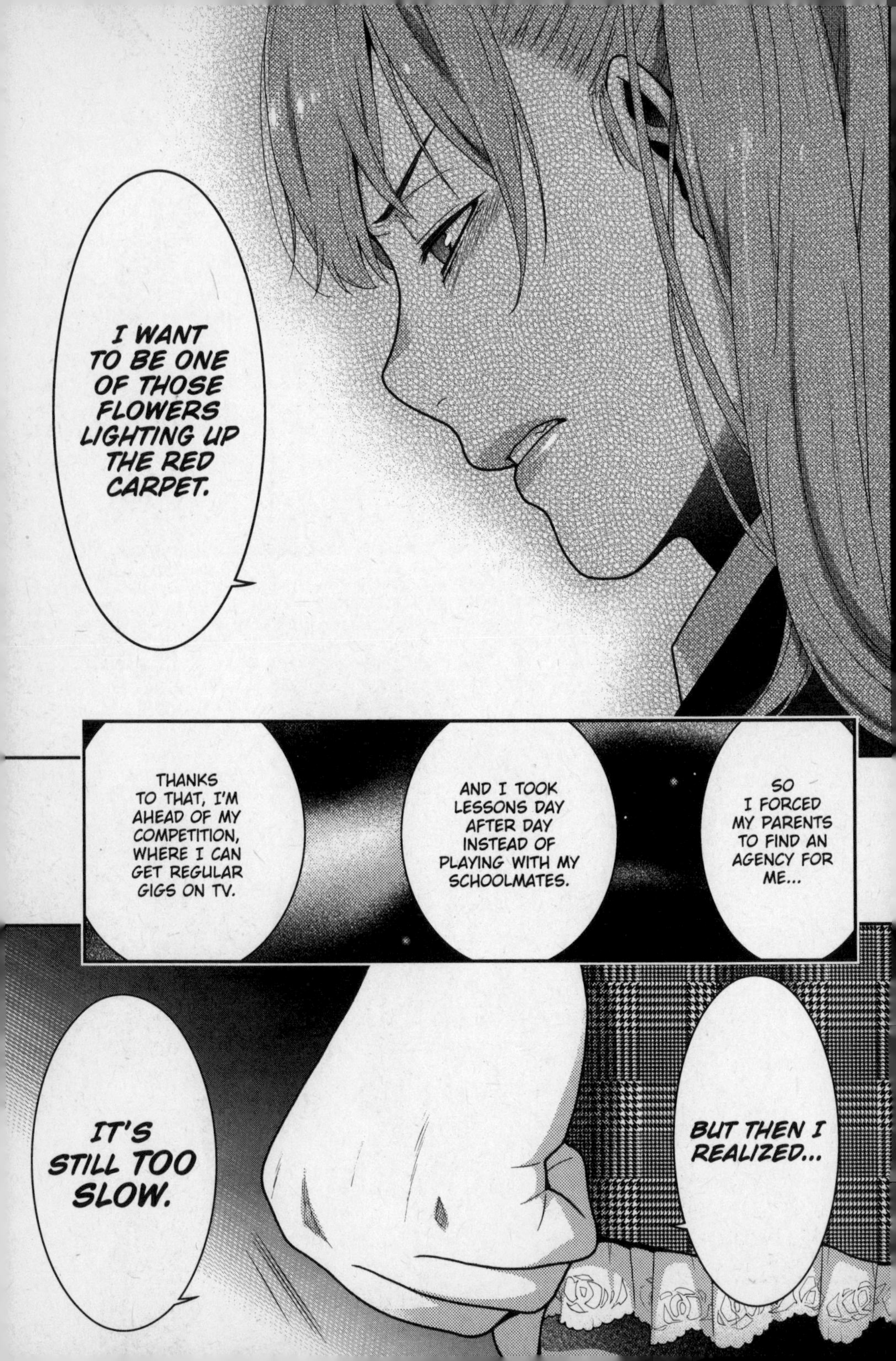
I WANT TO BE ONE OF THOSE FLOWERS LIGHTING UP THE RED CARPET.
SO I FORCED MY PARENTS TO FIND AN AGENCY FOR ME...
AND I TOOK LESSONS DAY AFTER DAY INSTEAD OF PLAYING WITH MY SCHOOLMATES.
THANKS TO THAT, I'M AHEAD OF MY COMPETITION, WHERE I CAN GET REGULAR GIGS ON TV.
BUT THEN I REALIZED...
IT'S STILL TOO SLOW.

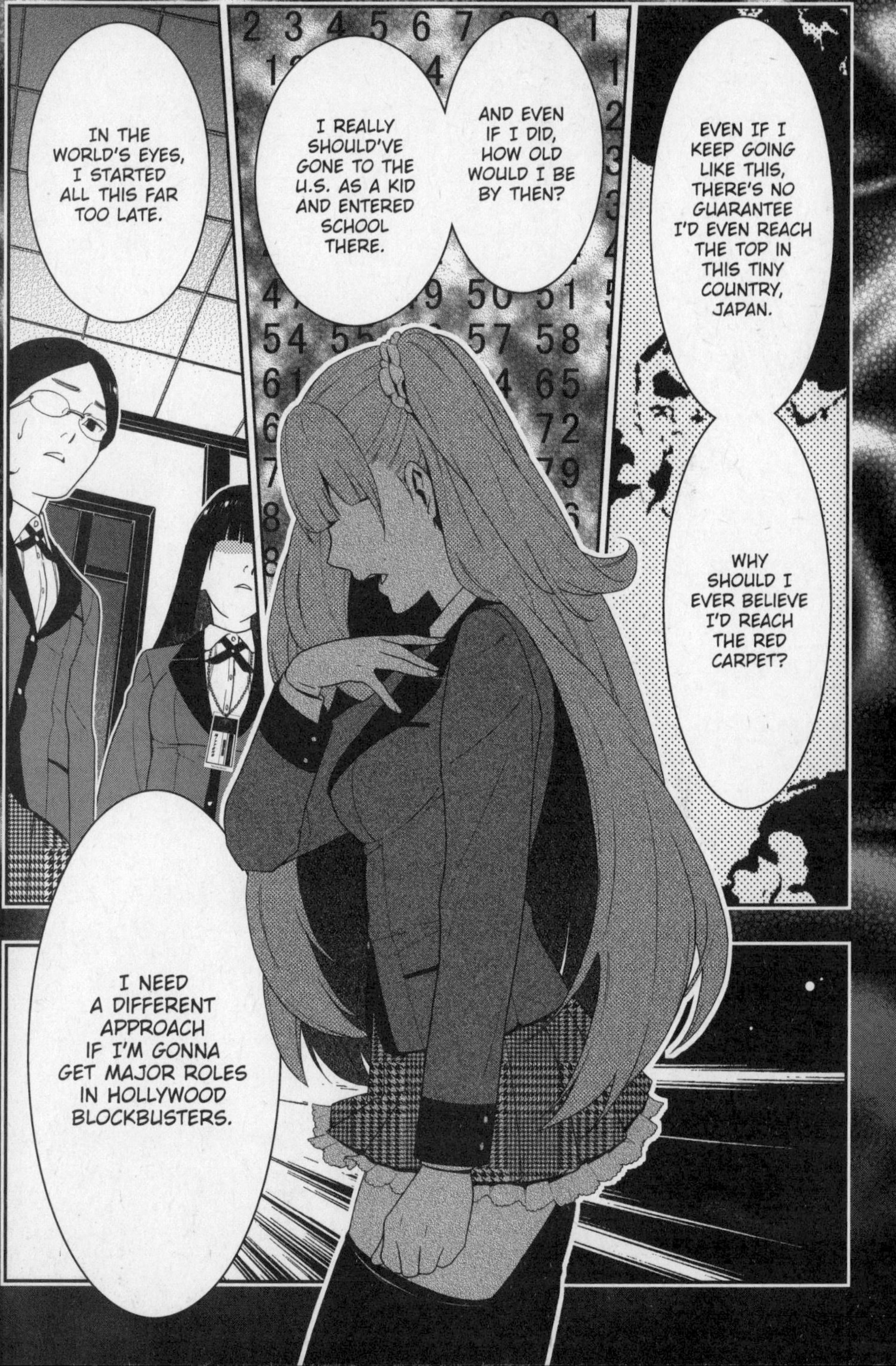
EVEN IF I KEEP GOING LIKE THIS, THERE'S NO GUARANTEE I'D EVEN REACH THE TOP IN THIS TINY COUNTRY, JAPAN.
WHY SHOULD I EVER BELIEVE I'D REACH THE RED CARPET?
I REALLY SHOULD'VE GONE TO THE U.S. AS A KID AND ENTERED SCHOOL THERE.
AND EVEN IF I DID, HOW OLD WOULD I BE BY THEN?
IN THE WORLD'S EYES, I STARTED ALL THIS FAR TOO LATE.
I NEED A DIFFERENT APPROACH IF I'M GONNA GET MAJOR ROLES IN HOLLYWOOD BLOCKBUSTERS.

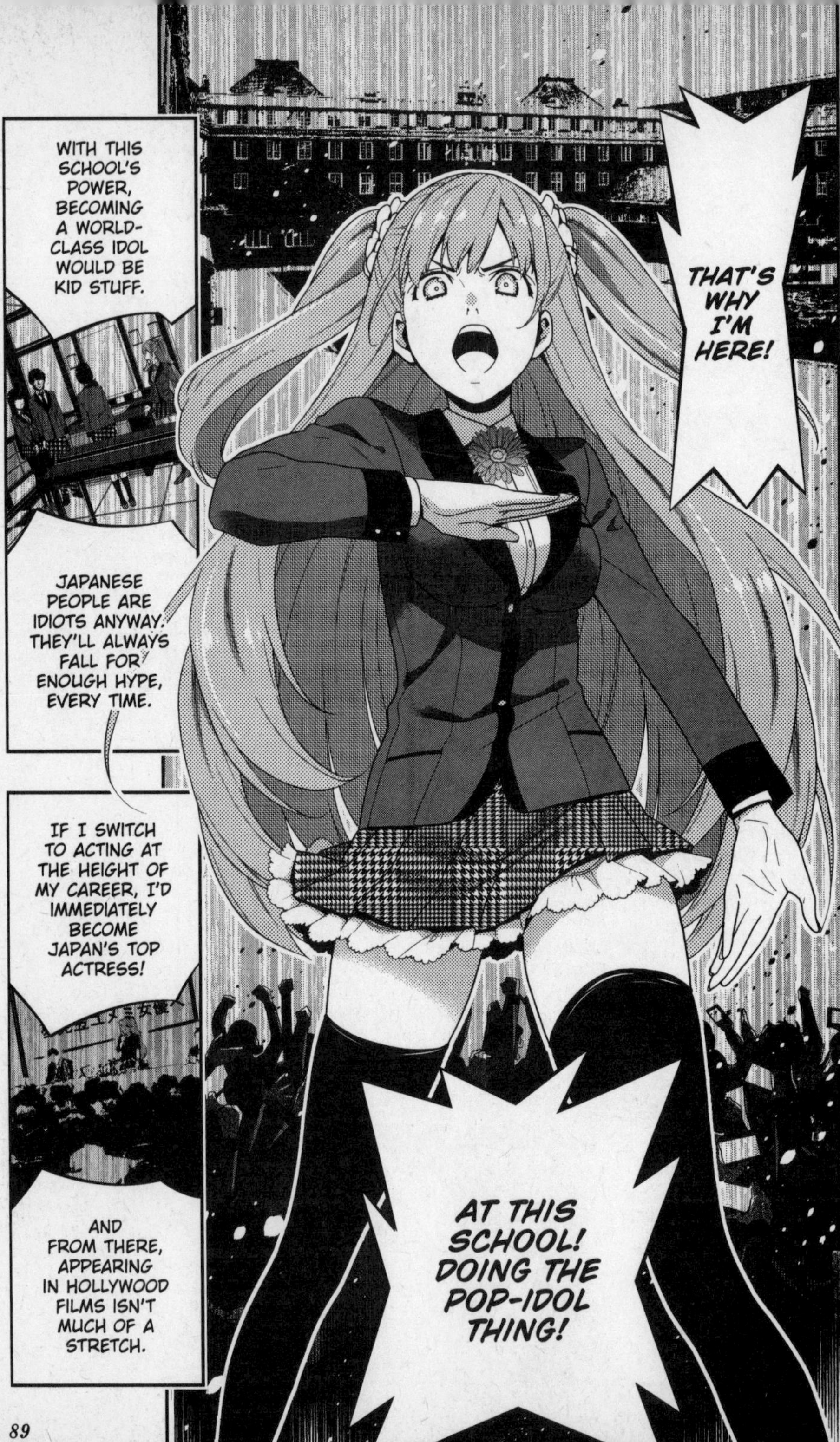
THAT'S WHY I'M HERE!
AT THIS SCHOOL! DOING THE POP-IDOL THING!
WITH THIS SCHOOL'S POWER, BECOMING A WORLD-CLASS IDOL WOULD BE KID STUFF.
JAPANESE PEOPLE ARE IDIOTS ANYWAY. THEY'LL ALWAYS FALL FOR ENOUGH HYPE, EVERY TIME.
IF I SWITCH TO ACTING AT THE HEIGHT OF MY CAREER, I'D IMMEDIATELY BECOME JAPAN'S TOP ACTRESS!
AND FROM THERE, APPEARING IN HOLLYWOOD FILMS ISN'T MUCH OF A STRETCH.

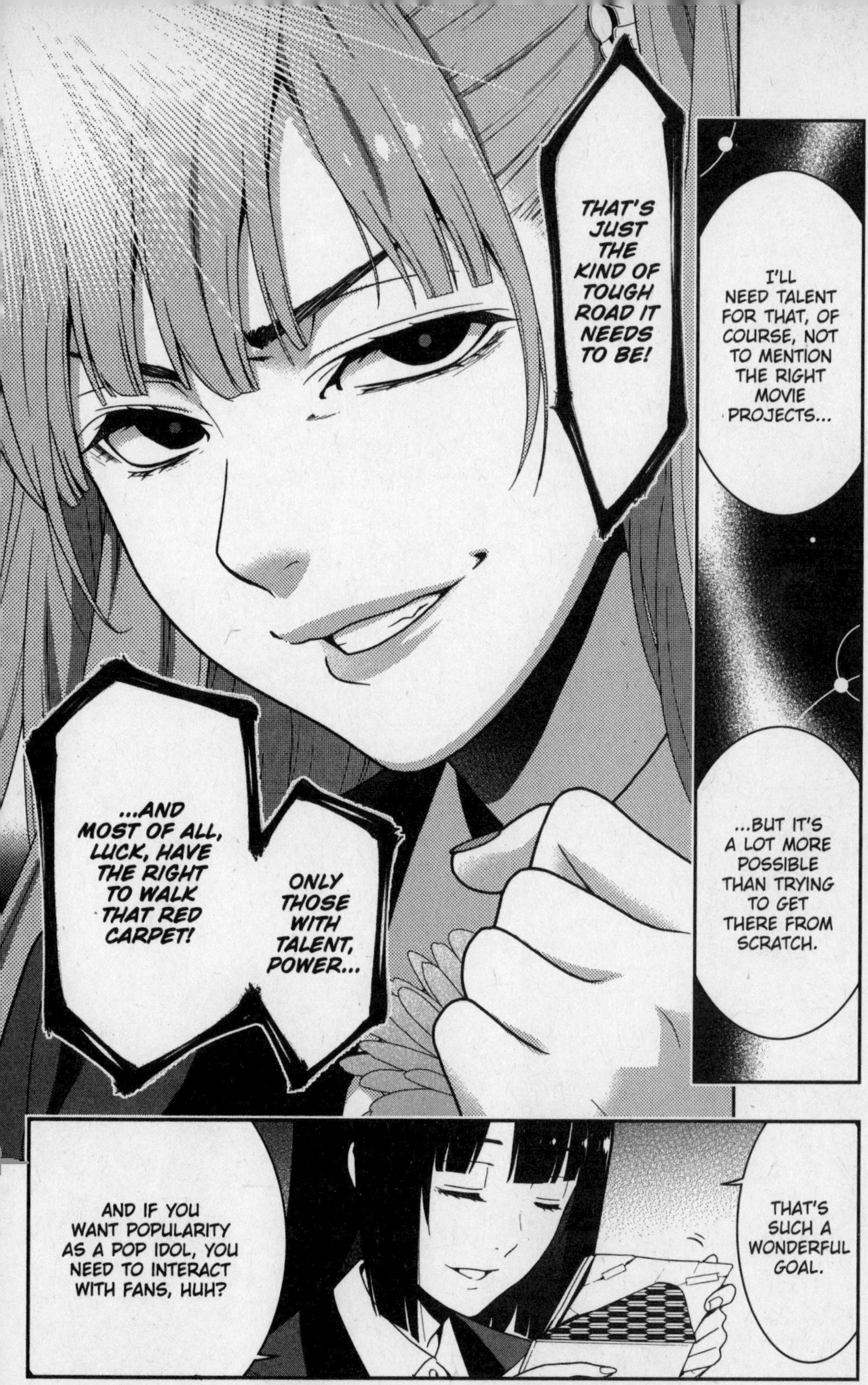
I'LL NEED TALENT FOR THAT, OF COURSE, NOT TO MENTION THE RIGHT MOVIE PROJECTS...
...BUT IT'S A LOT MORE POSSIBLE THAN TRYING TO GET THERE FROM SCRATCH.
THAT'S JUST THE KIND OF TOUGH ROAD IT NEEDS TO BE!
ONLY THOSE WITH TALENT, POWER...
...AND MOST OF ALL, LUCK, HAVE THE RIGHT TO WALK THAT RED CARPET!
THAT'S SUCH A WONDERFUL GOAL.
AND IF YOU WANT POPULARITY AS A POP IDOL, YOU NEED TO INTERACT WITH FANS, HUH?

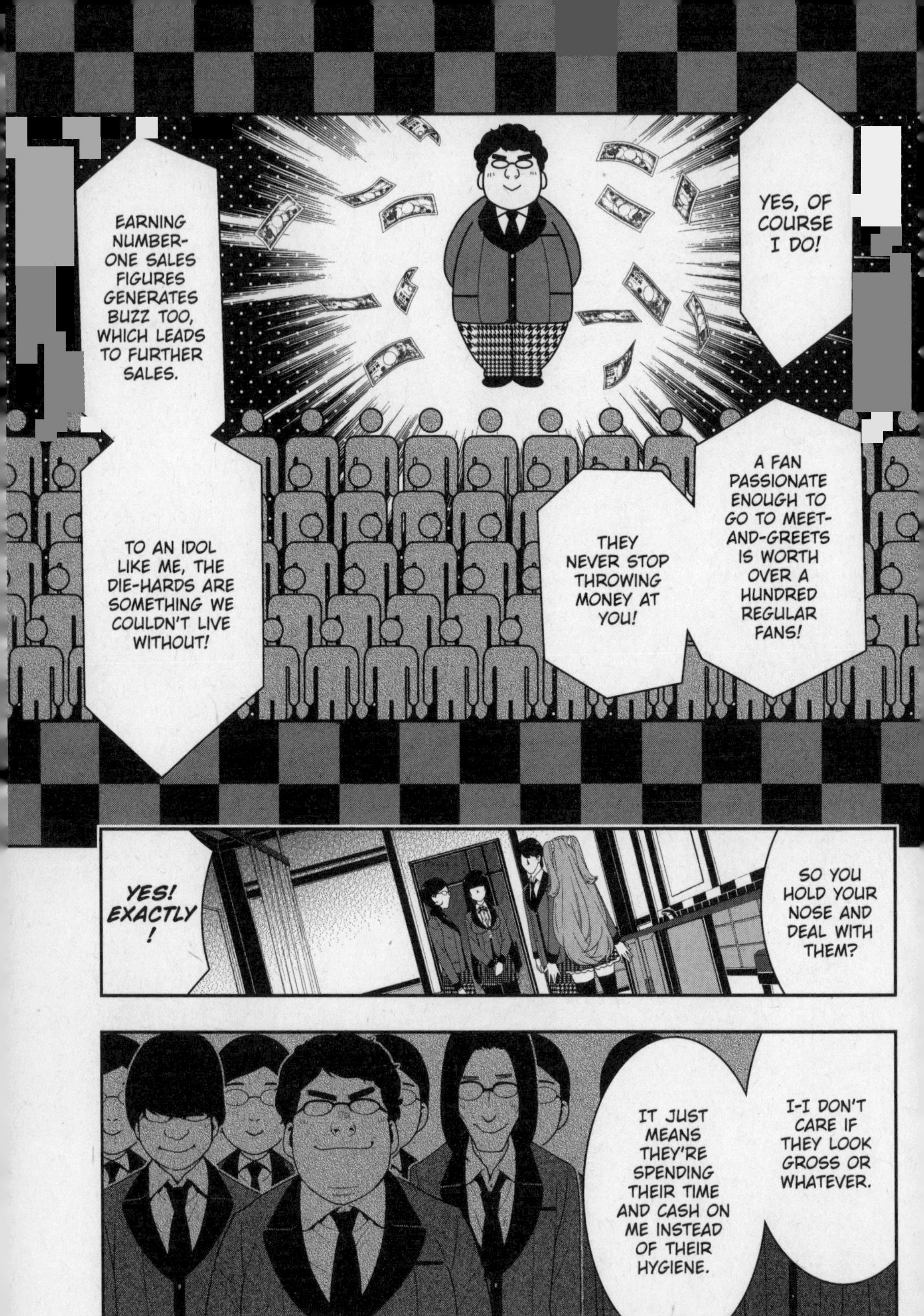

YES, OF COURSE I DO!
EARNING NUMBER-ONE SALES FIGURES GENERATES BUZZ TOO, WHICH LEADS TO FURTHER SALES.
TO AN IDOL LIKE ME, THE DIE-HARDS ARE SOMETHING WE COULDN'T LIVE WITHOUT!
A FAN PASSIONATE ENOUGH TO GO TO MEET-AND-GREETS IS WORTH OVER A HUNDRED REGULAR FANS!
THEY NEVER STOP THROWING MONEY AT YOU!
SO YOU HOLD YOUR NOSE AND DEAL WITH THEM?
YES! EXACTLY!
I-I DON'T CARE IF THEY LOOK GROSS OR WHATEVER.
IT JUST MEANS THEY'RE SPENDING THEIR TIME AND CASH ON ME INSTEAD OF THEIR HYGIENE.

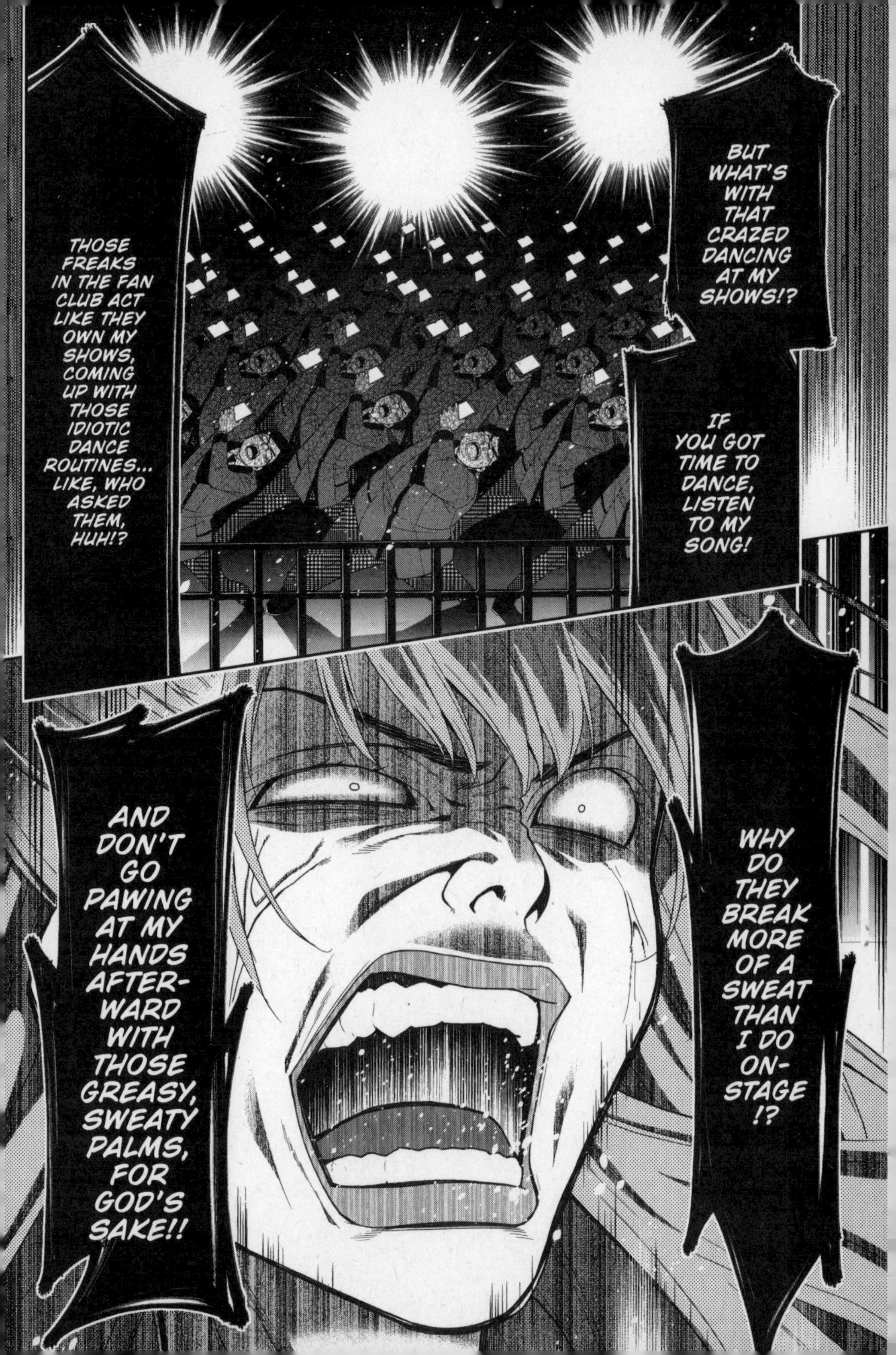
BUT WHAT'S WITH THAT CRAZED DANCING AT MY SHOWS!?
IF YOU GOT TIME TO DANCE, LISTEN TO MY SONG!
THOSE FREAKS IN THE FAN CLUB ACT LIKE THEY OWN MY SHOWS, COMING UP WITH THOSE IDIOTIC DANCE ROUTINES... LIKE, WHO ASKED THEM, HUH!?
WHY DO THEY BREAK MORE OF A SWEAT THAN I DO ON-STAGE!?
AND DON'T GO PAWING AT MY HANDS AFTER-WARD WITH THOSE GREASY, SWEATY PALMS, FOR GOD'S SAKE!!

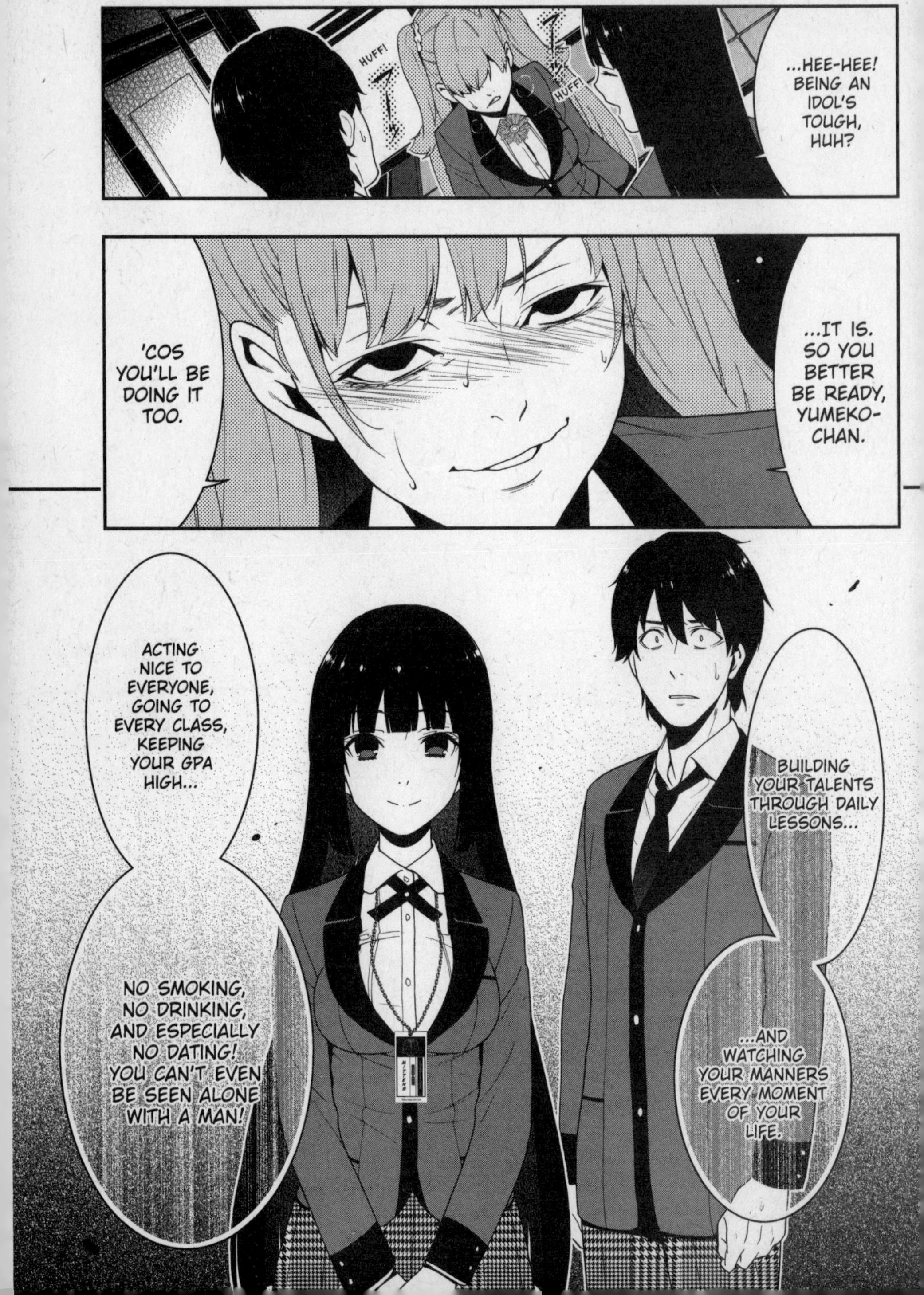
...HEE-HEE! BEING AN IDOL'S TOUGH, HUH?
HUFF!
HUFF!
...IT IS. SO YOU BETTER BE READY, YUMEKO-CHAN.
'COS YOU'LL BE DOING IT TOO.
ACTING NICE TO EVERYONE, GOING TO EVERY CLASS, KEEPING YOUR GPA HIGH...
BUILDING YOUR TALENTS THROUGH DAILY LESSONS...
NO SMOKING, NO DRINKING, AND ESPECIALLY NO DATING! YOU CAN'T EVEN BE SEEN ALONE WITH A MAN!
...AND WATCHING YOUR MANNERS EVERY MOMENT OF YOUR LIFE.

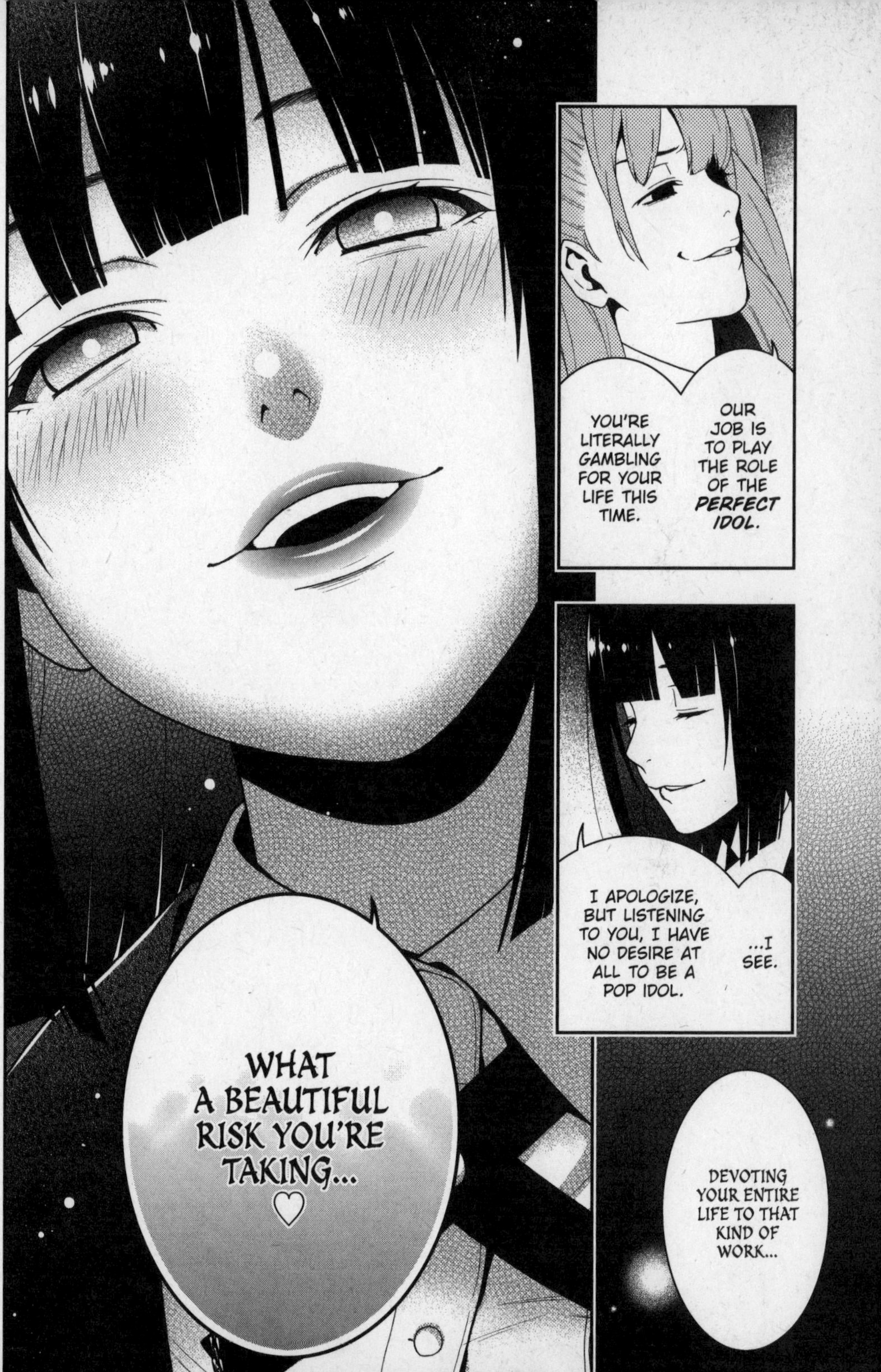
OUR JOB IS TO PLAY THE ROLE OF THE *PERFECT IDOL*.
YOU'RE LITERALLY GAMBLING FOR YOUR LIFE THIS TIME.
...I SEE.
I APOLOGIZE, BUT LISTENING TO YOU, I HAVE NO DESIRE AT ALL TO BE A POP IDOL.
DEVOTING YOUR ENTIRE LIFE TO THAT KIND OF WORK...
WHAT A BEAUTIFUL RISK YOU'RE TAKING... ♡

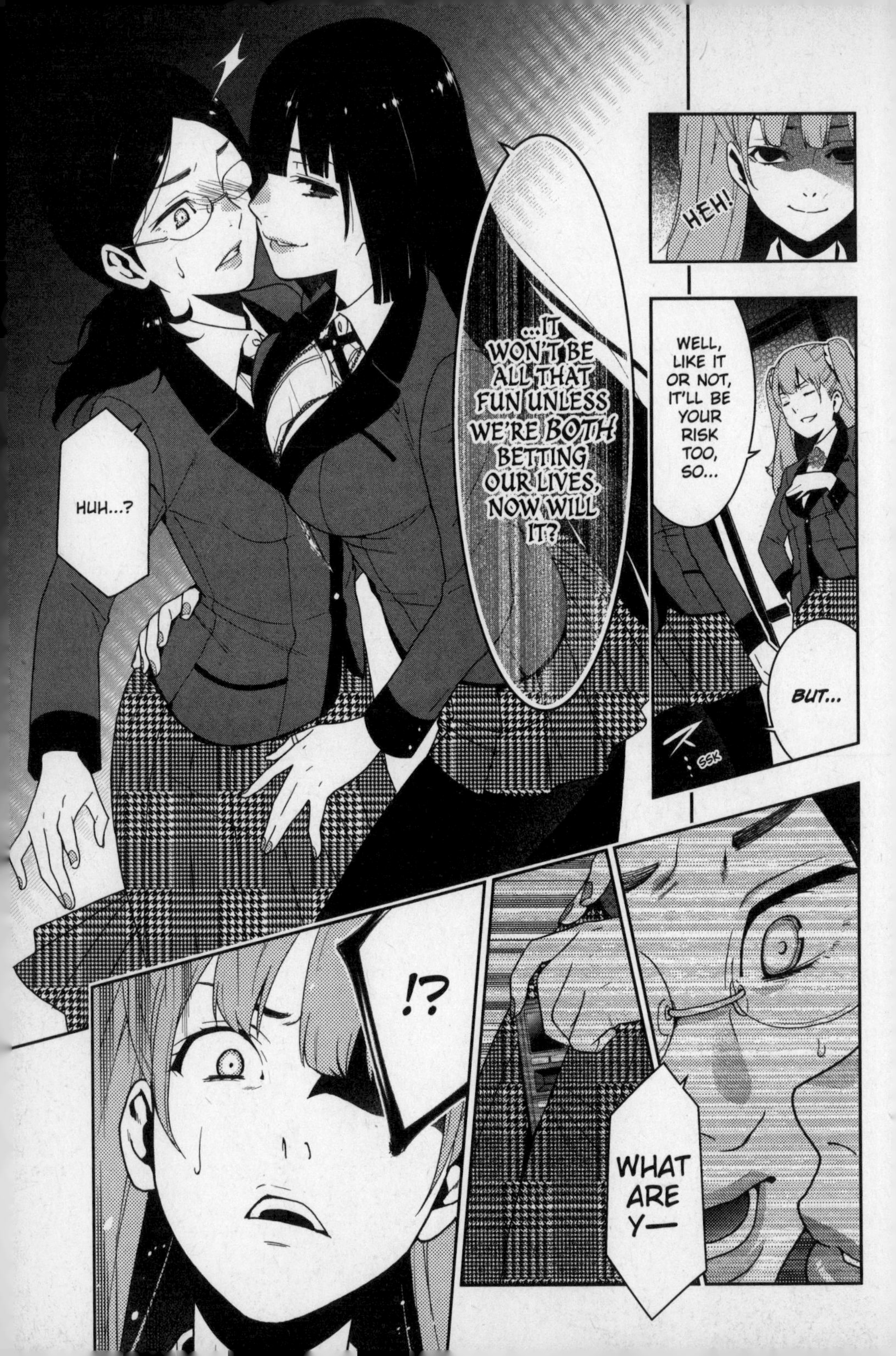
HEH!
WELL, LIKE IT OR NOT, IT'LL BE YOUR RISK TOO, SO...
BUT...
SSK
...IT WON'T BE ALL THAT FUN UNLESS WE'RE BOTH BETTING OUR LIVES, NOW WILL IT?
HUH...?
WHAT ARE Y—
!?

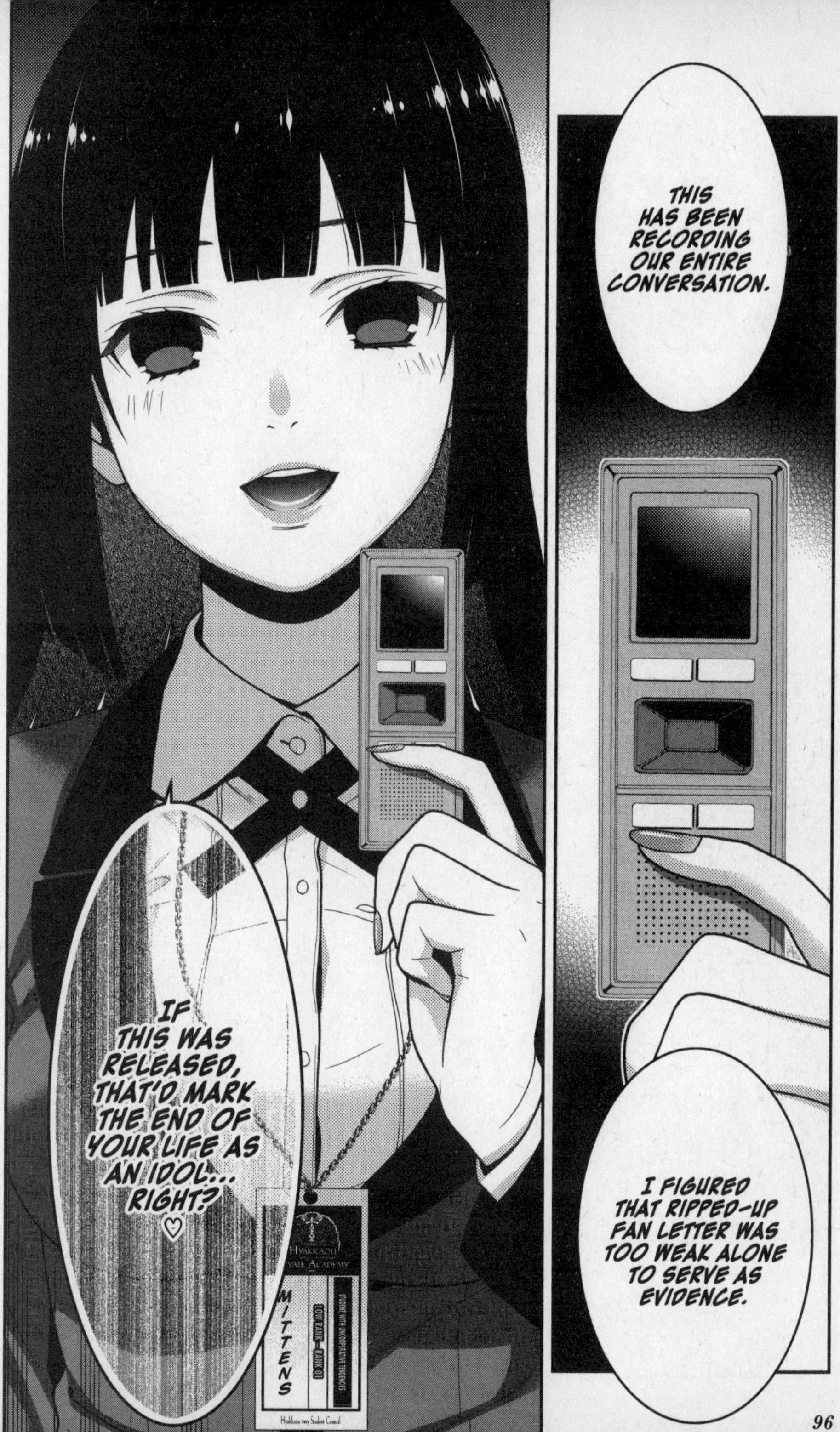
THIS HAS BEEN RECORDING OUR ENTIRE CONVERSATION.
I FIGURED THAT RIPPED-UP FAN LETTER WAS TOO WEAK ALONE TO SERVE AS EVIDENCE.
IF THIS WAS RELEASED, THAT'D MARK THE END OF YOUR LIFE AS AN IDOL... RIGHT? ♡
MITTENS

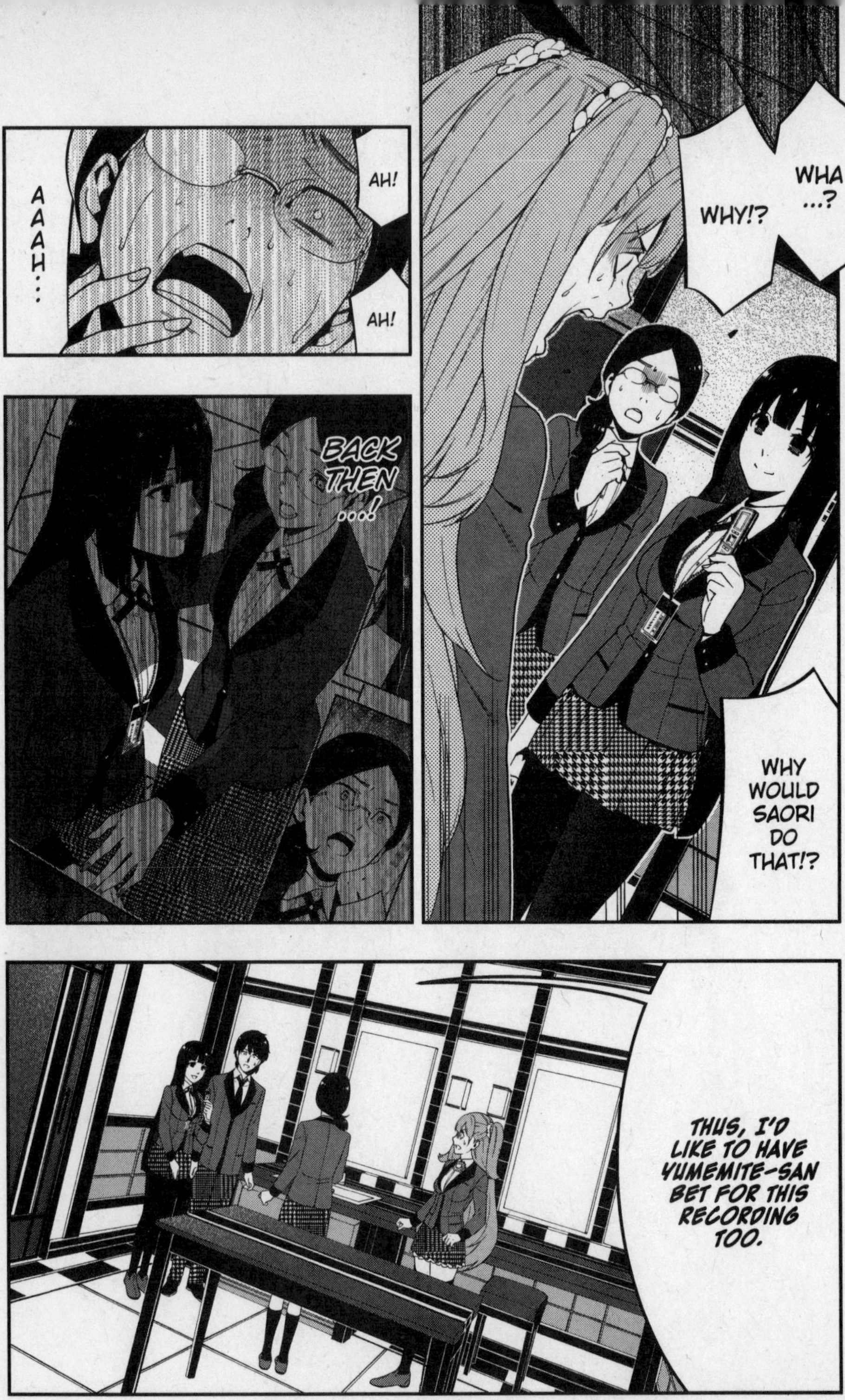
WHA ...?
WHY!?
WHY WOULD SAORI DO THAT!?
AH!
AAAAH...
AH!
BACK THEN ....!
THUS, I'D LIKE TO HAVE YUMEMITE-SAN BET FOR THIS RECORDING TOO.

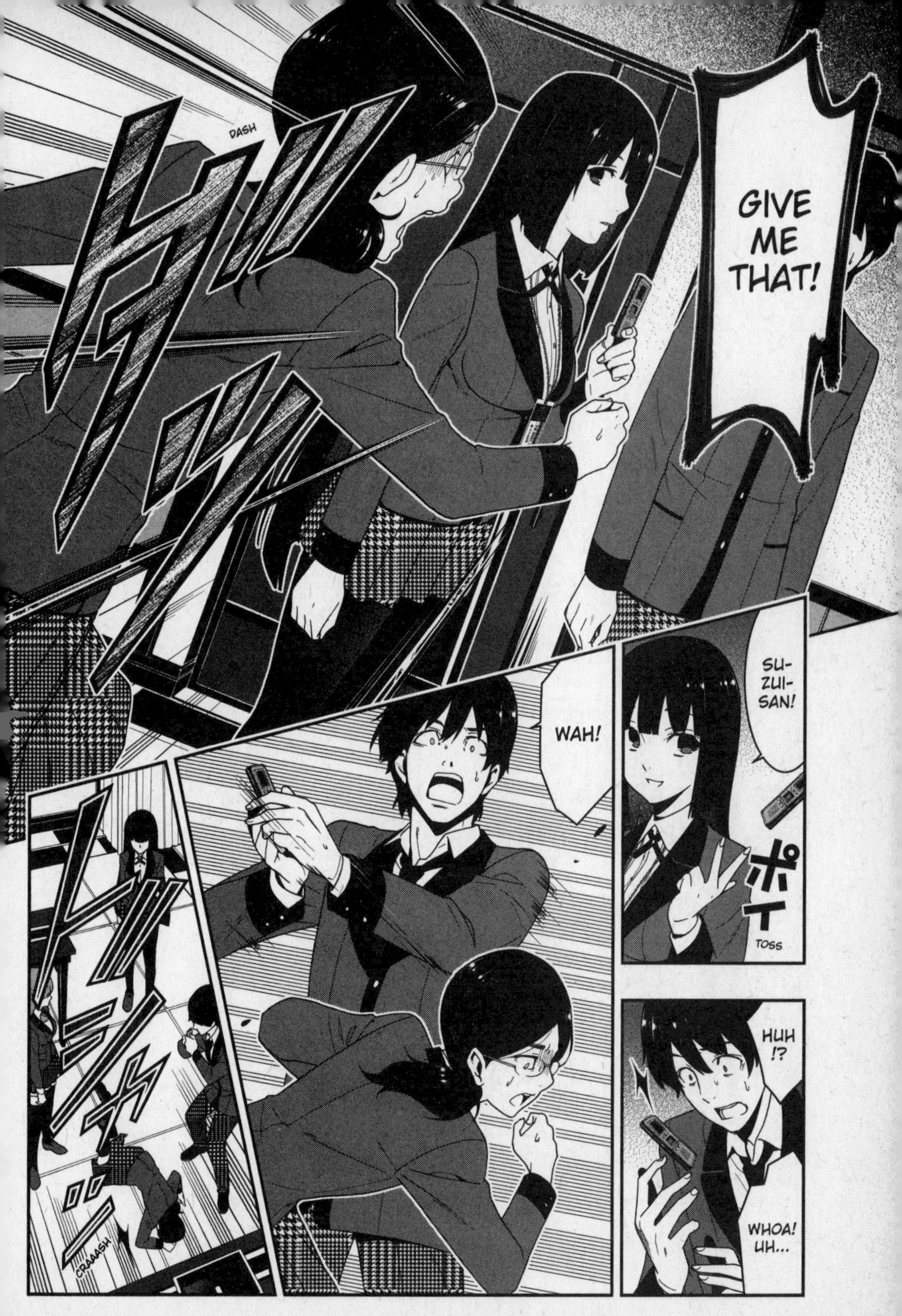
GIVE ME THAT!
DASH
SU-ZUI-SAN!
TOSS
HUH!?
WHOA! UH...
WAH!
CRAAASH

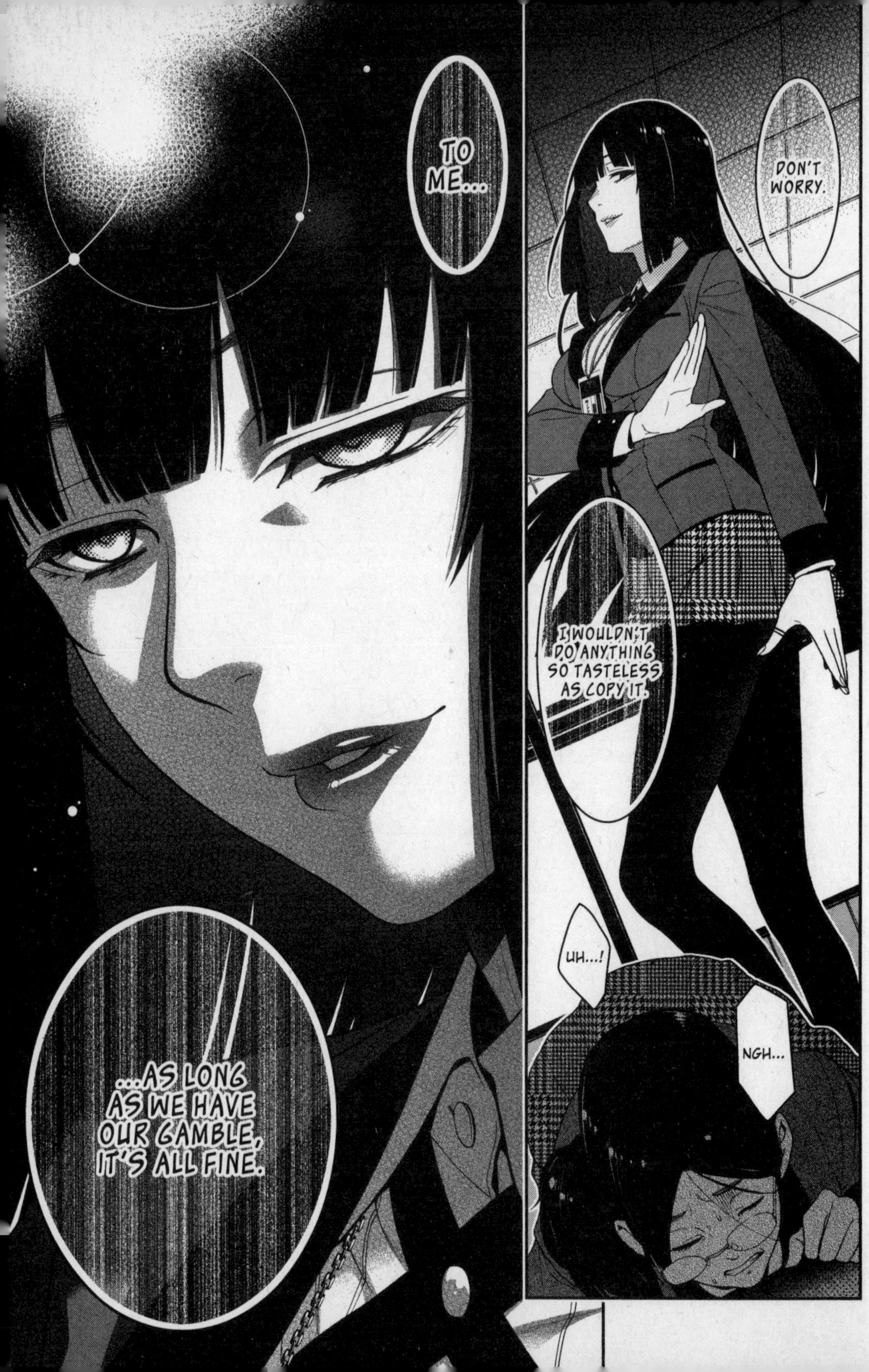
DON'T WORRY.
I WOULDN'T DO ANYTHING SO TASTELESS AS COPY IT.
UH...!
NGH...
TO ME...
...AS LONG AS WE HAVE OUR GAMBLE, IT'S ALL FINE.

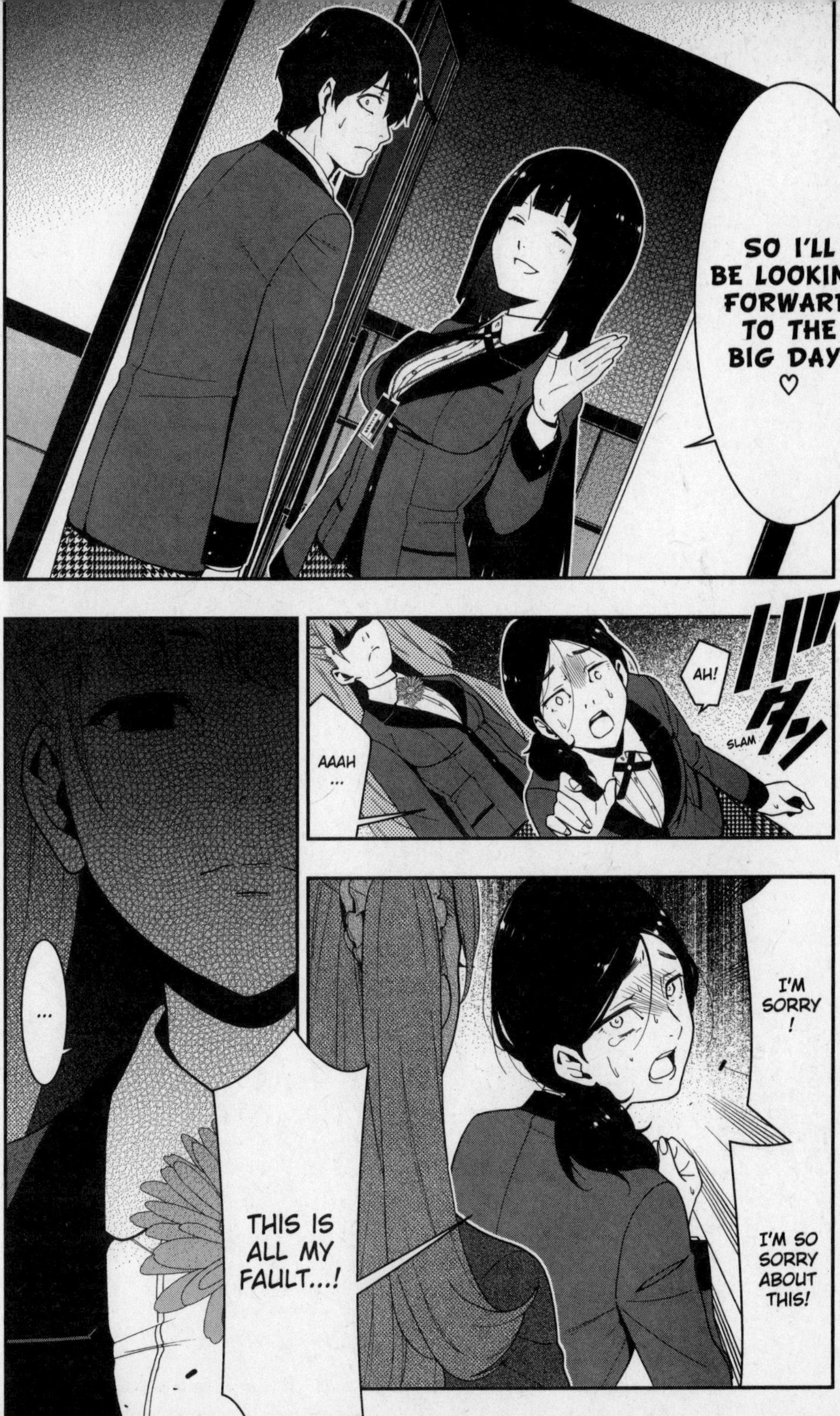
SO I'LL BE LOOKING FORWARD TO THE BIG DAY! ♡
バタン
SLAM
AH!
AAAH ...
I'M SORRY!
I'M SO SORRY ABOUT THIS!
THIS IS ALL MY FAULT...!
...

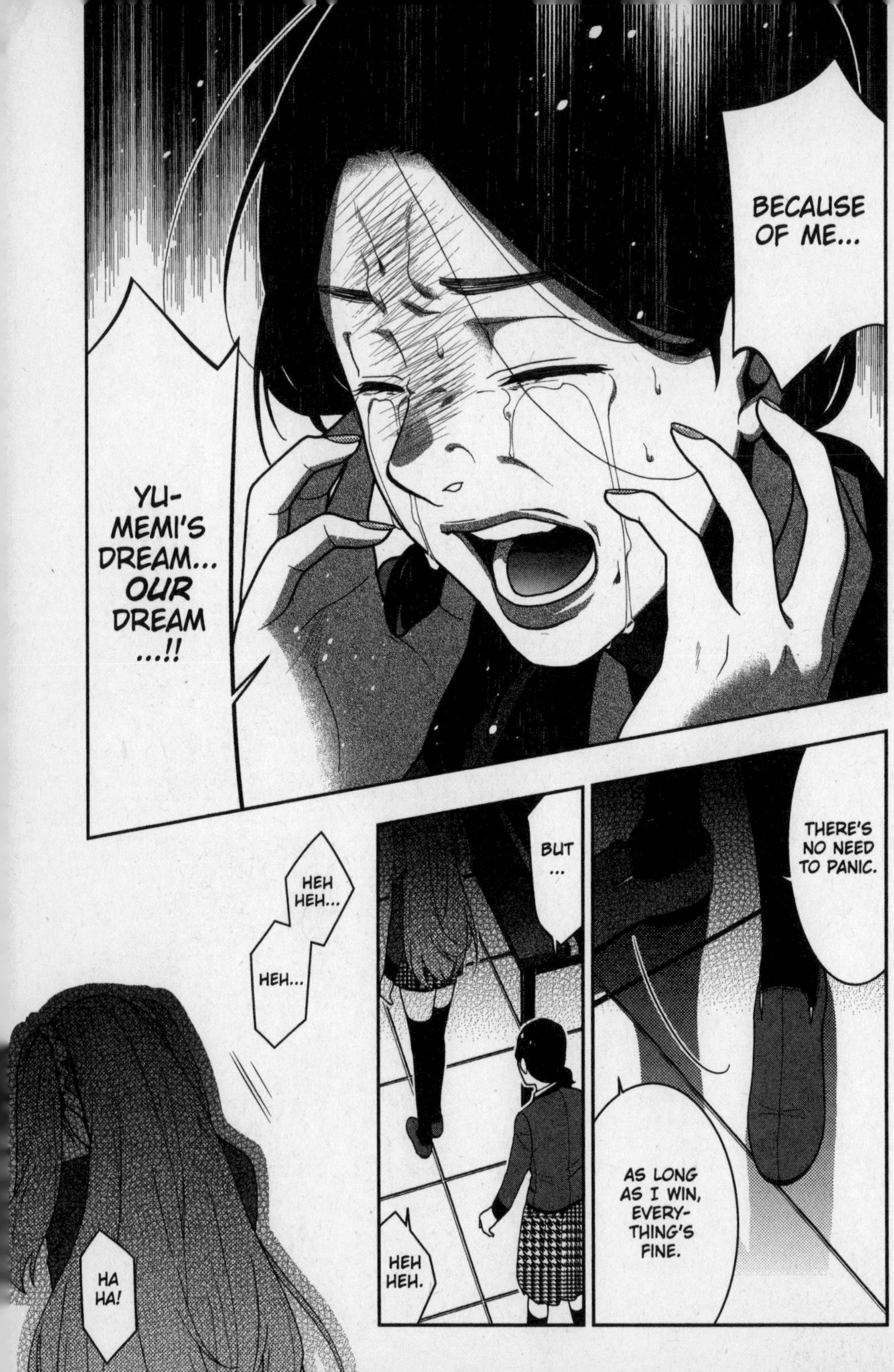

BECAUSE OF ME...
YU-MEMI'S DREAM... OUR DREAM ...!!
THERE'S NO NEED TO PANIC.
AS LONG AS I WIN, EVERY-THING'S FINE.
BUT ...
HEH HEH...
HEH...
HEH HEH.
HA HA!

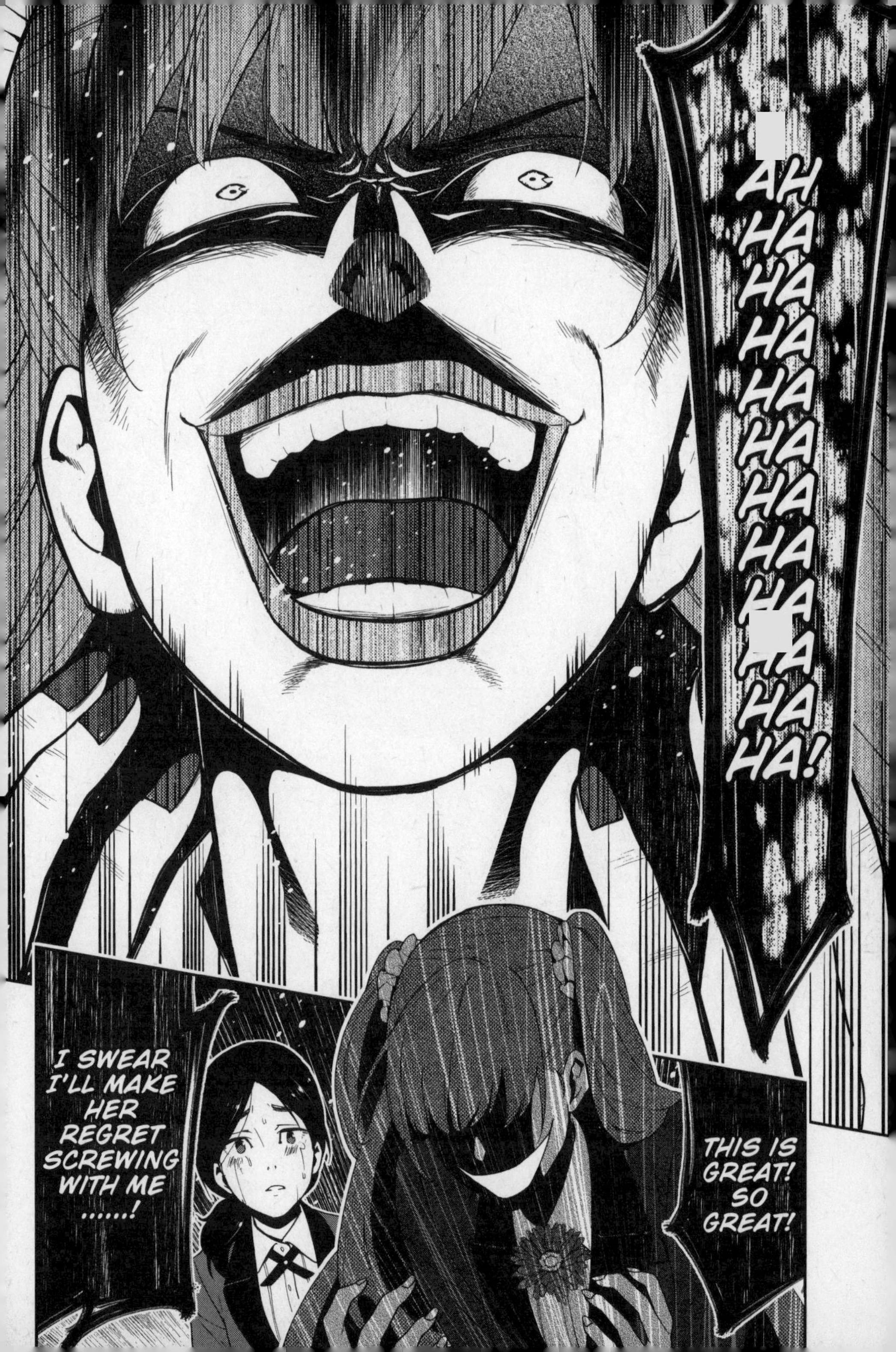
AH HA HA HA HA HA HA HA HA HA HA HA!
THIS IS GREAT! SO GREAT!
I SWEAR I'LL MAKE HER REGRET SCREWING WITH ME ......!

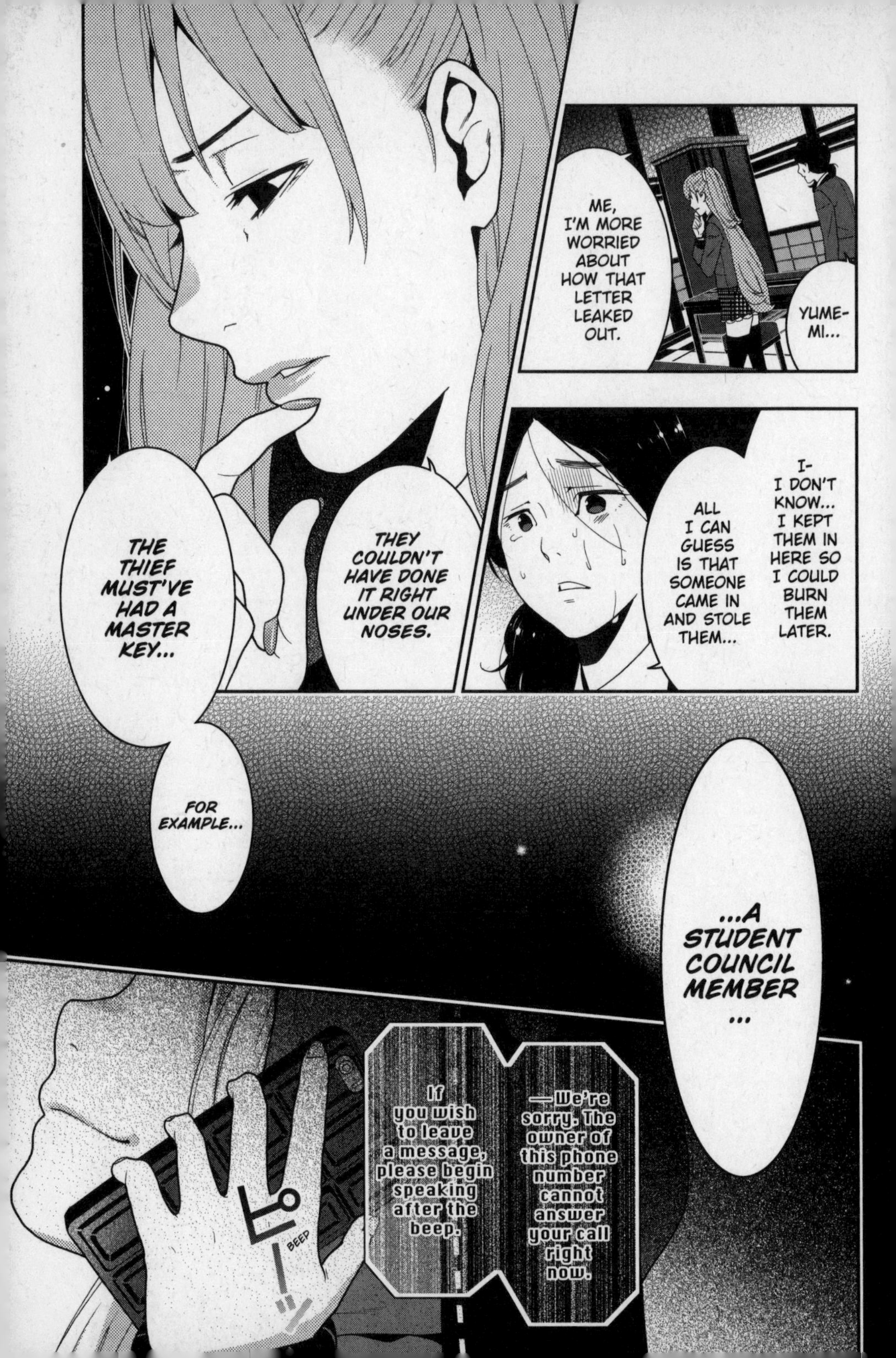
YUME-MI...
ME, I'M MORE WORRIED ABOUT HOW THAT LETTER LEAKED OUT.
I- I DON'T KNOW... I KEPT THEM IN HERE SO I COULD BURN THEM LATER.
ALL I CAN GUESS IS THAT SOMEONE CAME IN AND STOLE THEM...
THEY COULDN'T HAVE DONE IT RIGHT UNDER OUR NOSES.
THE THIEF MUST'VE HAD A MASTER KEY...
FOR EXAMPLE...
...A STUDENT COUNCIL MEMBER...
—We're sorry. The owner of this phone number cannot answer your call right now.
If you wish to leave a message, please begin speaking after the beep.
BEEP

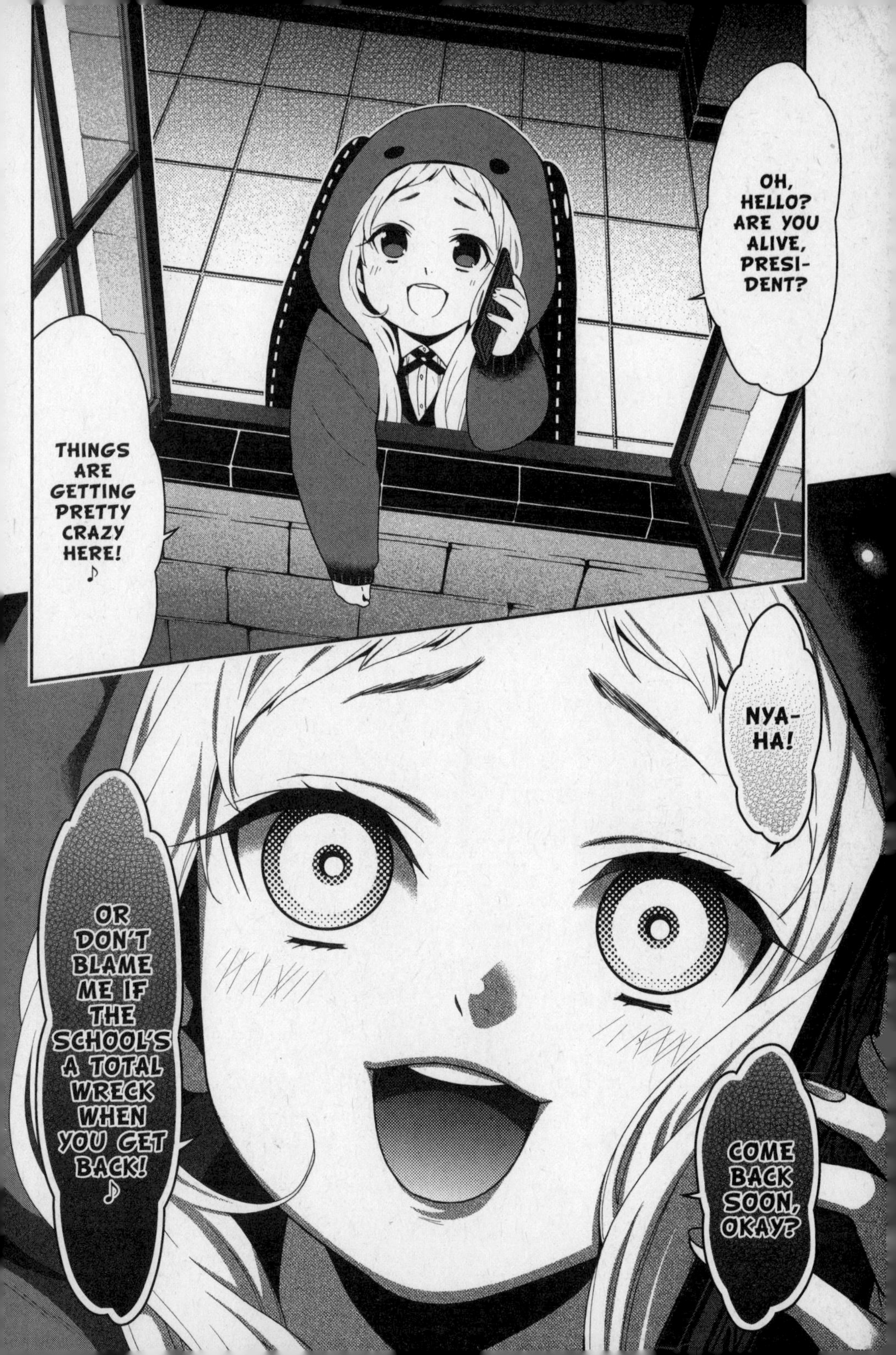
OH, HELLO? ARE YOU ALIVE, PRESI- DENT?
THINGS ARE GETTING PRETTY CRAZY HERE! ♪
NYA- HA!
COME BACK SOON, OKAY?
OR DON'T BLAME ME IF THE SCHOOL'S A TOTAL WRECK WHEN YOU GET BACK! ♪

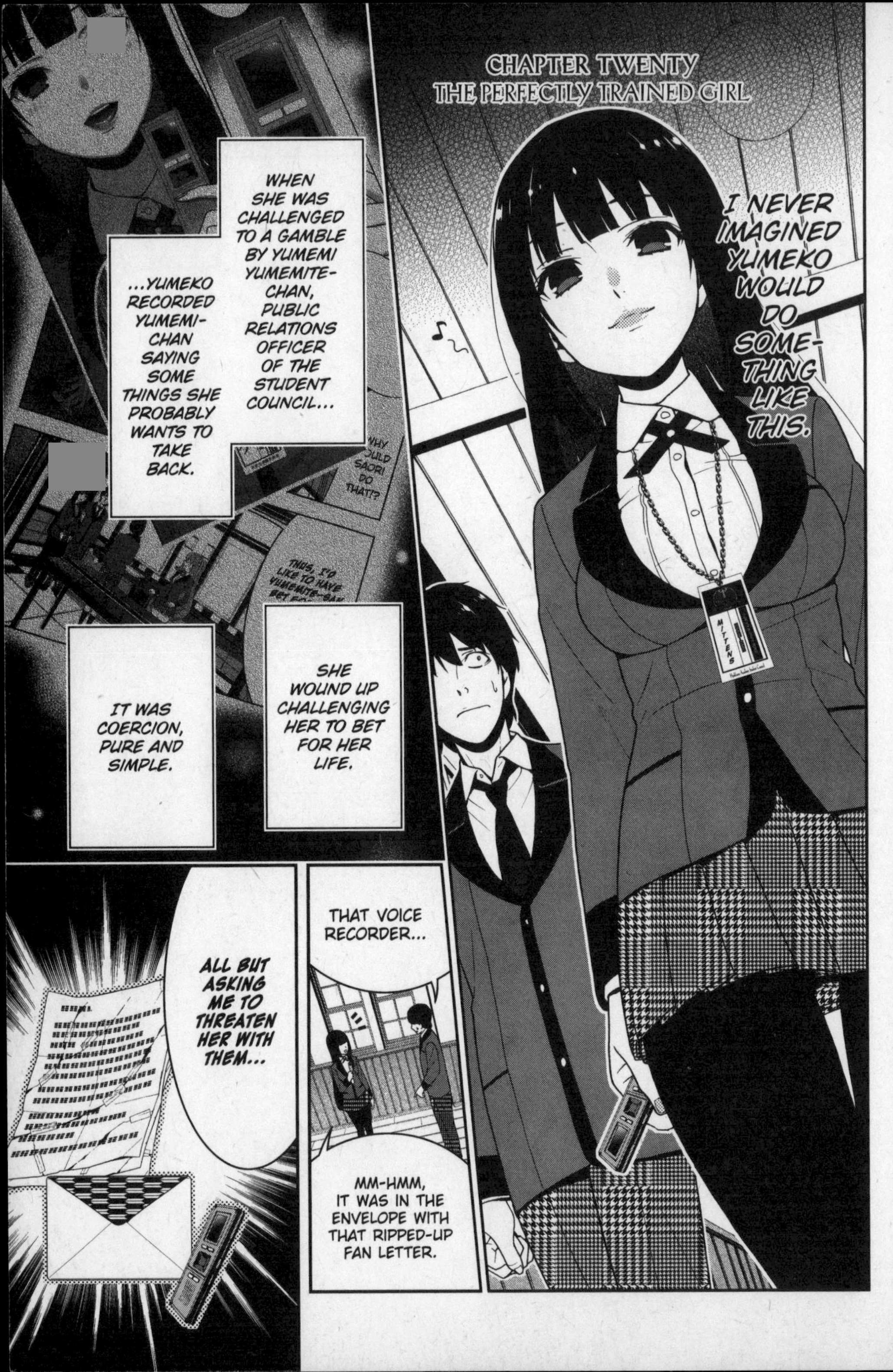
CHAPTER TWENTY
THE PERFECTLY TRAINED GIRL
I NEVER IMAGINED YUMEKO WOULD DO SOMETHING LIKE THIS.
WHEN SHE WAS CHALLENGED TO A GAMBLE BY YUMEMI YUMEMITE-CHAN, PUBLIC RELATIONS OFFICER OF THE STUDENT COUNCIL...
...YUMEKO RECORDED YUMEMI-CHAN SAYING SOME THINGS SHE PROBABLY WANTS TO TAKE BACK.
WHY WOULD SAORI DO THAT!?
SHE WOUND UP CHALLENGING HER TO BET FOR HER LIFE.
IT WAS COERCION, PURE AND SIMPLE.
THAT VOICE RECORDER...
MM-HMM, IT WAS IN THE ENVELOPE WITH THAT RIPPED-UP FAN LETTER.
ALL BUT ASKING ME TO THREATEN HER WITH THEM...

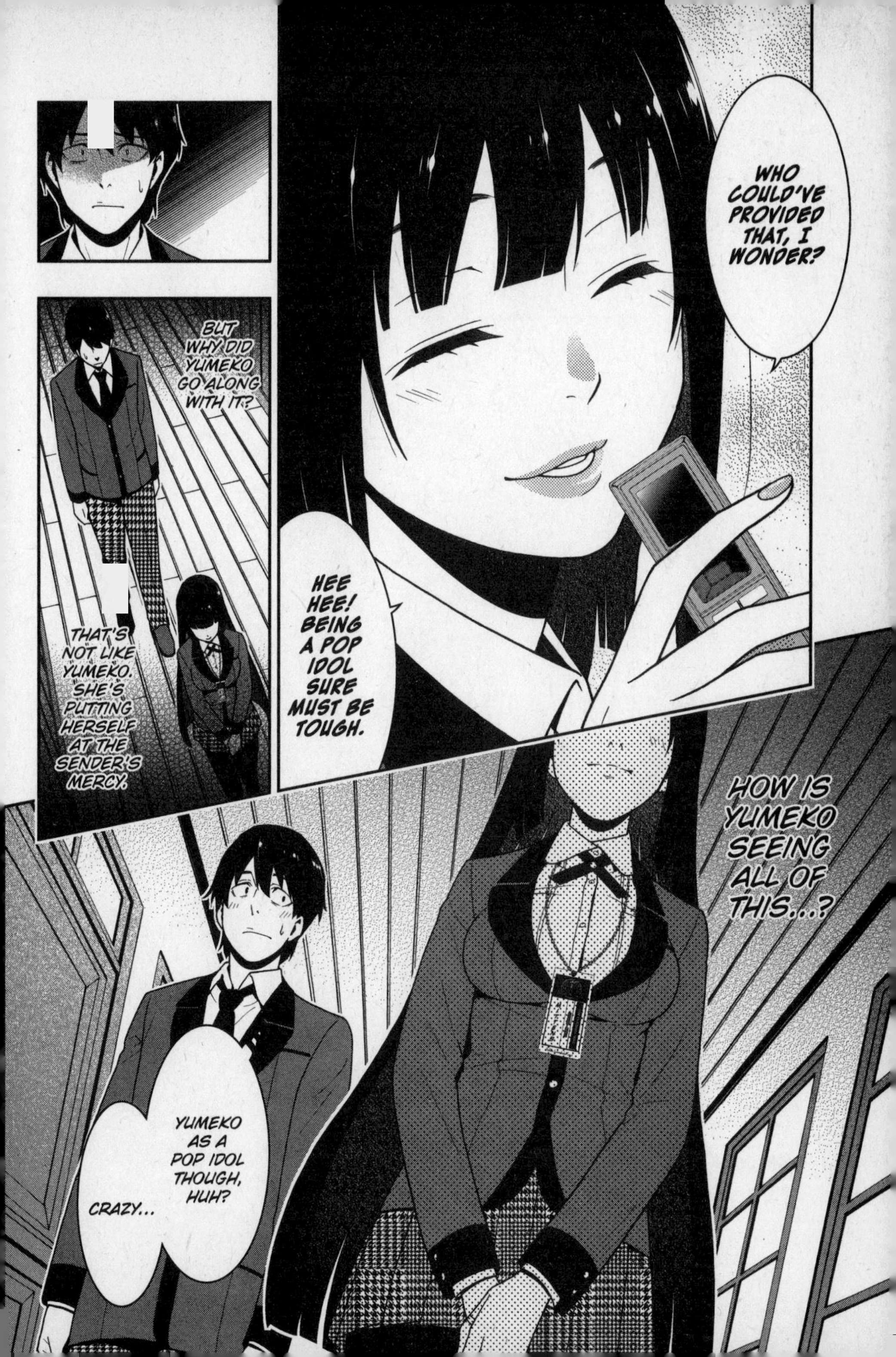
WHO COULD'VE PROVIDED THAT, I WONDER?
HEE HEE! BEING A POP IDOL SURE MUST BE TOUGH.
BUT WHY DID YUMEKO GO ALONG WITH IT?
THAT'S NOT LIKE YUMEKO. SHE'S PUTTING HERSELF AT THE SENDER'S MERCY.
HOW IS YUMEKO SEEING ALL OF THIS...?
YUMEKO AS A POP IDOL THOUGH, HUH?
CRAZY...

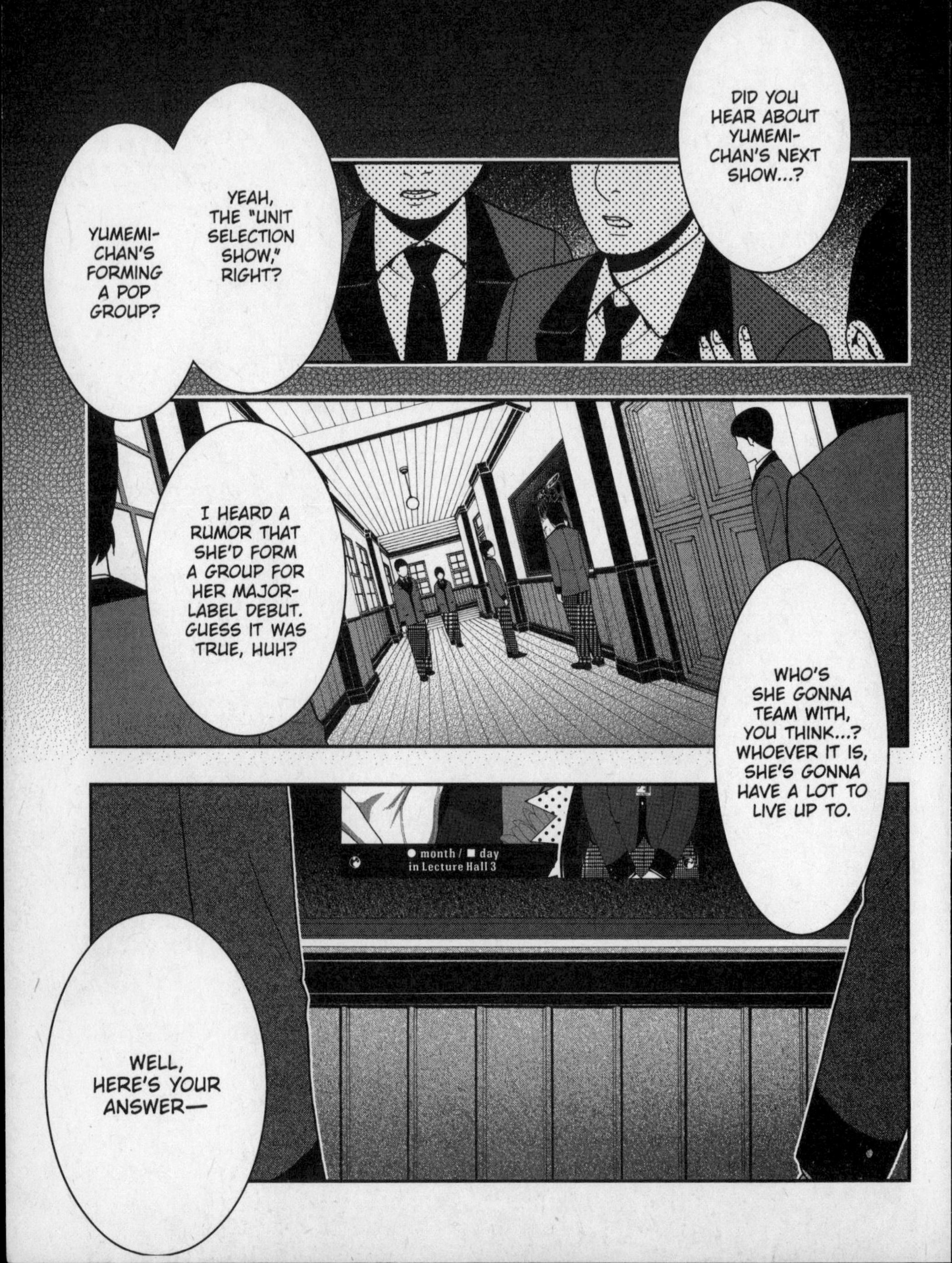

DID YOU HEAR ABOUT YUMEMI-CHAN'S NEXT SHOW...?
YEAH, THE "UNIT SELECTION SHOW," RIGHT?
YUMEMI-CHAN'S FORMING A POP GROUP?
I HEARD A RUMOR THAT SHE'D FORM A GROUP FOR HER MAJOR-LABEL DEBUT. GUESS IT WAS TRUE, HUH?
WHO'S SHE GONNA TEAM WITH, YOU THINK...? WHOEVER IT IS, SHE'S GONNA HAVE A LOT TO LIVE UP TO.
● month / ■ day in Lecture Hall 3
WELL, HERE'S YOUR ANSWER—

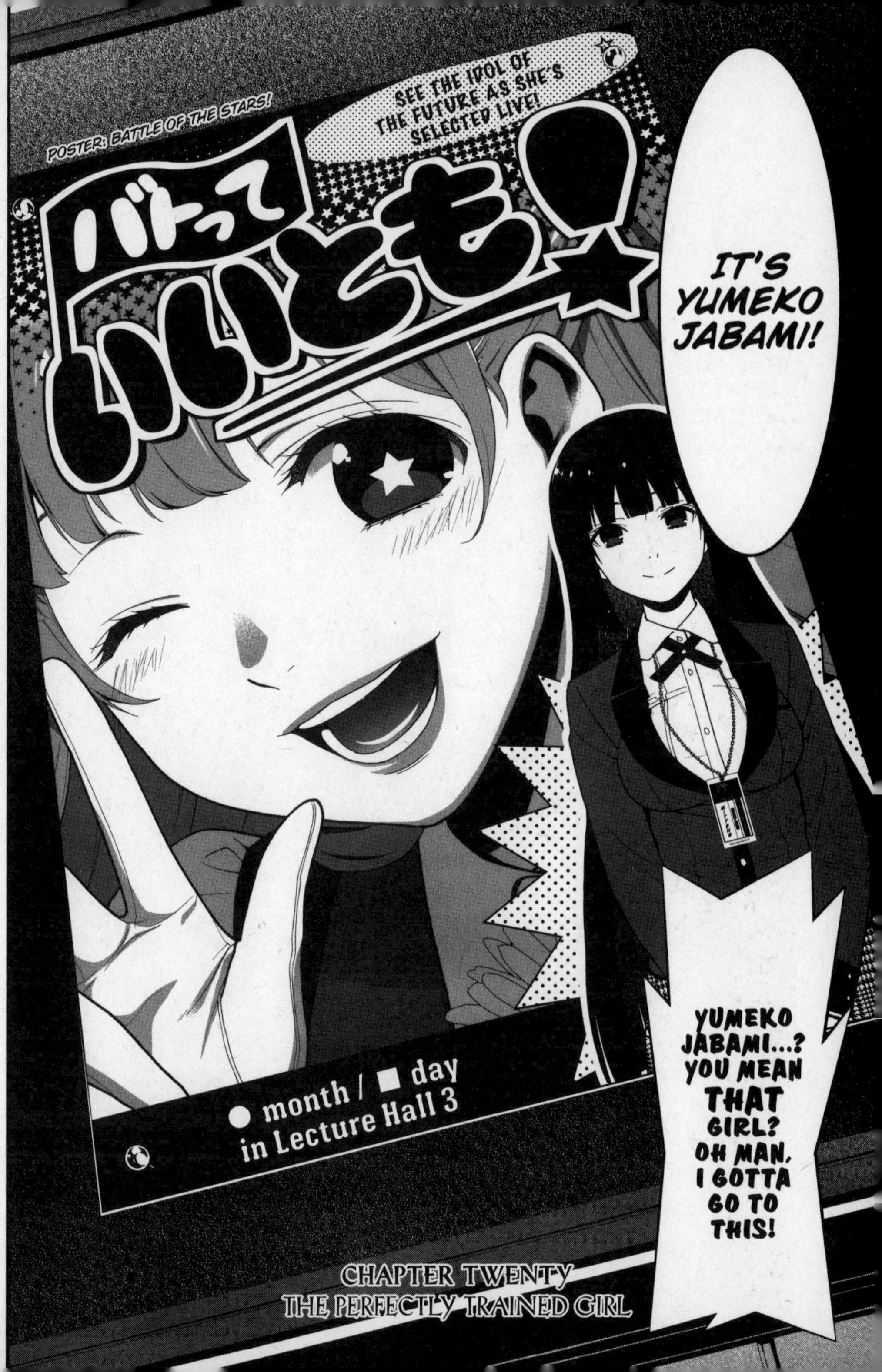
POSTER: BATTLE OF THE STARS!
SEE THE IDOL OF THE FUTURE AS SHE'S SELECTED LIVE!
バトってハいとも!★
● month / ■ day
in Lecture Hall 3
IT'S YUMEKO JABAMI!
YUMEKO JABAMI...? YOU MEAN THAT GIRL? OH MAN, I GOTTA GO TO THIS!
CHAPTER TWENTY
THE PERFECTLY TRAINED GIRL

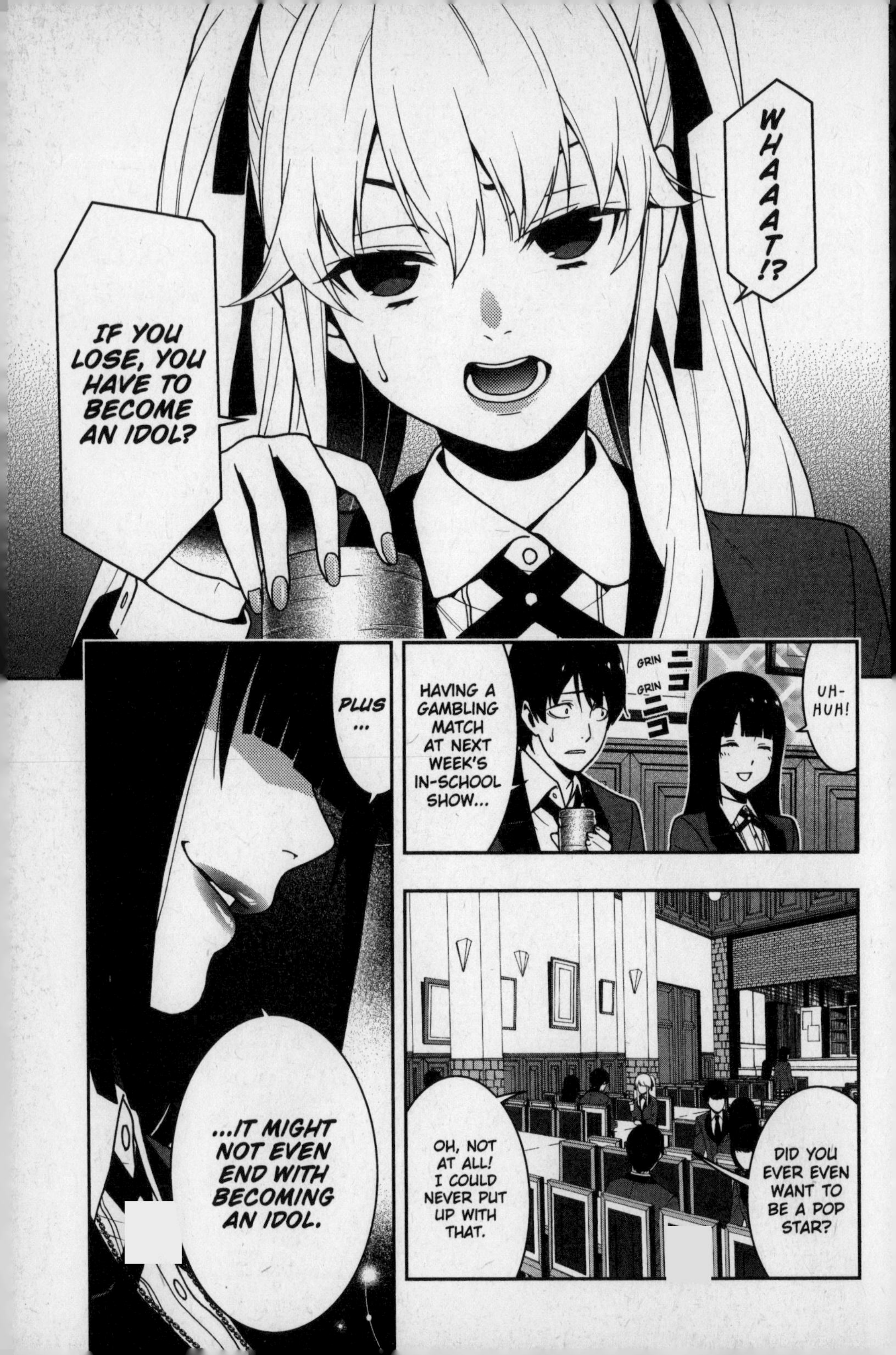
WHAAAT!?
IF YOU LOSE, YOU HAVE TO BECOME AN IDOL?
UH-HUH!
GRIN
GRIN
HAVING A GAMBLING MATCH AT NEXT WEEK'S IN-SCHOOL SHOW...
DID YOU EVER EVEN WANT TO BE A POP STAR?
OH, NOT AT ALL! I COULD NEVER PUT UP WITH THAT.
PLUS...
...IT MIGHT NOT EVEN END WITH BECOMING AN IDOL.

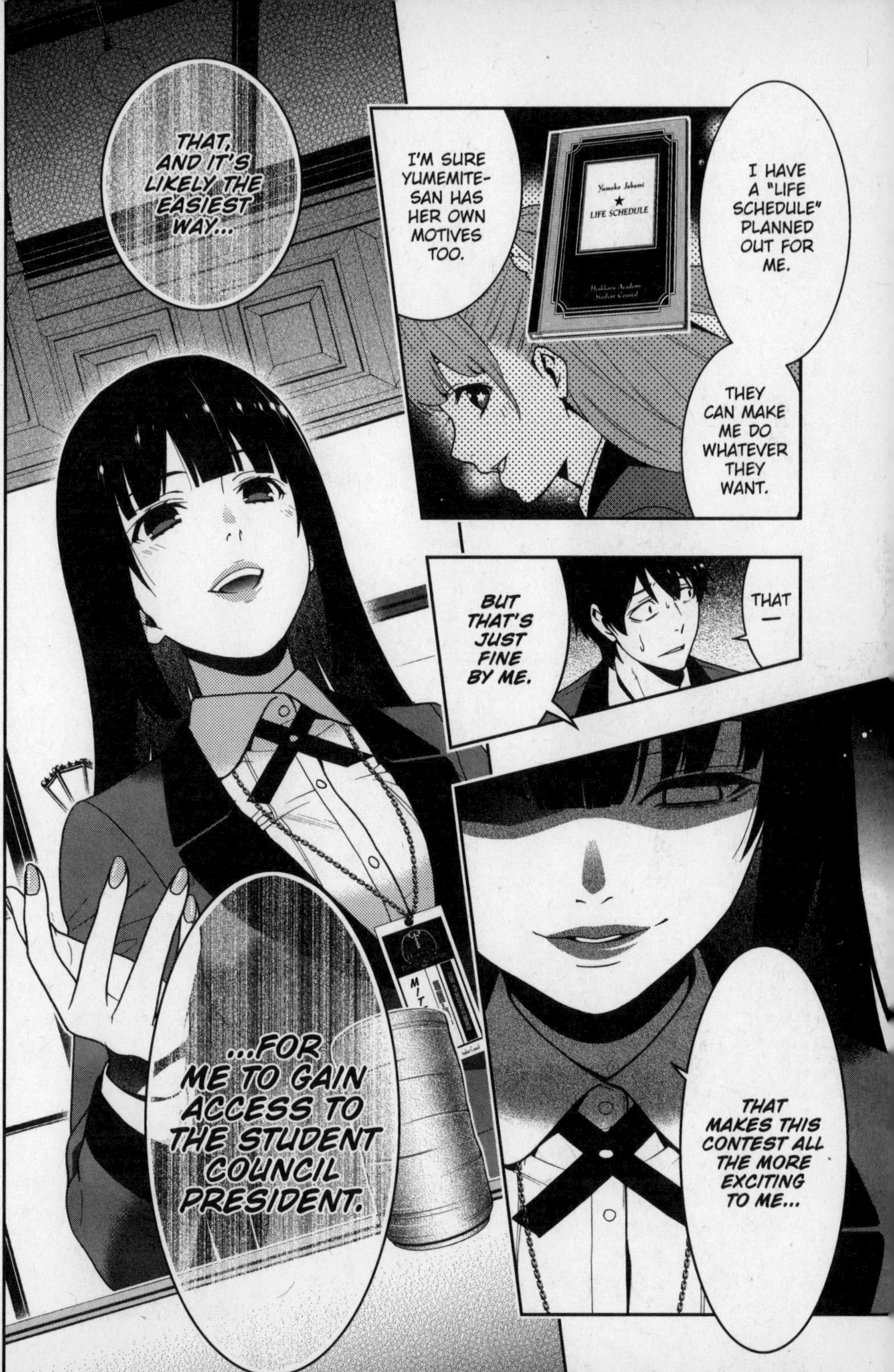
I HAVE A "LIFE SCHEDULE" PLANNED OUT FOR ME.
Yumeko Jabami
LIFE SCHEDULE
THEY CAN MAKE ME DO WHATEVER THEY WANT.
I'M SURE YUMEMITE-SAN HAS HER OWN MOTIVES TOO.
THAT—
BUT THAT'S JUST FINE BY ME.
THAT MAKES THIS CONTEST ALL THE MORE EXCITING TO ME...
THAT, AND IT'S LIKELY THE EASIEST WAY...
...FOR ME TO GAIN ACCESS TO THE STUDENT COUNCIL PRESIDENT.

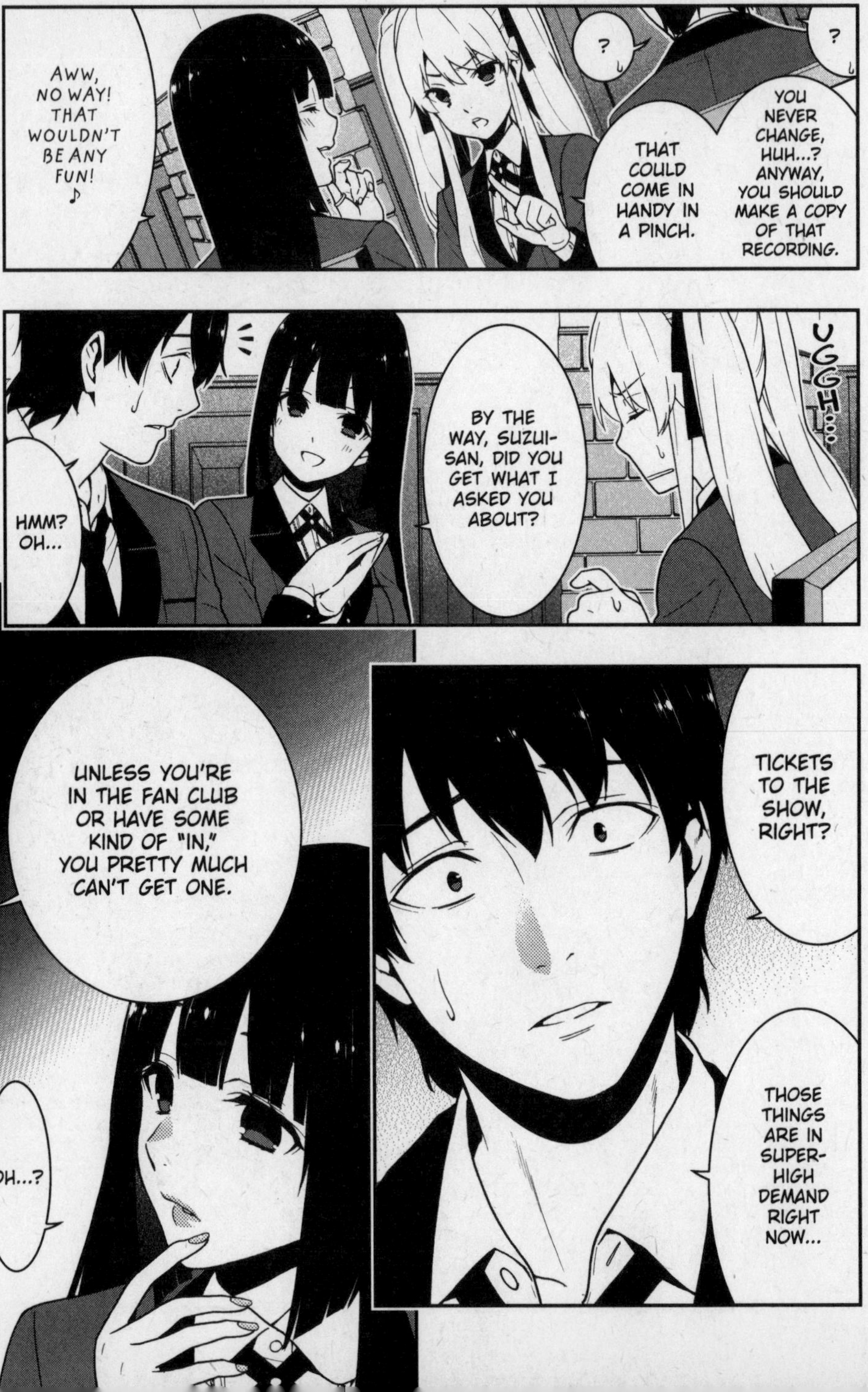
?
?
YOU NEVER CHANGE, HUH...? ANYWAY, YOU SHOULD MAKE A COPY OF THAT RECORDING.
THAT COULD COME IN HANDY IN A PINCH.
AWW, NO WAY! THAT WOULDN'T BE ANY FUN! ♪
UGGH...
BY THE WAY, SUZUI-SAN, DID YOU GET WHAT I ASKED YOU ABOUT?
HMM? OH...
TICKETS TO THE SHOW, RIGHT?
THOSE THINGS ARE IN SUPER-HIGH DEMAND RIGHT NOW...
UNLESS YOU'RE IN THE FAN CLUB OR HAVE SOME KIND OF "IN," YOU PRETTY MUCH CAN'T GET ONE.
OH...?

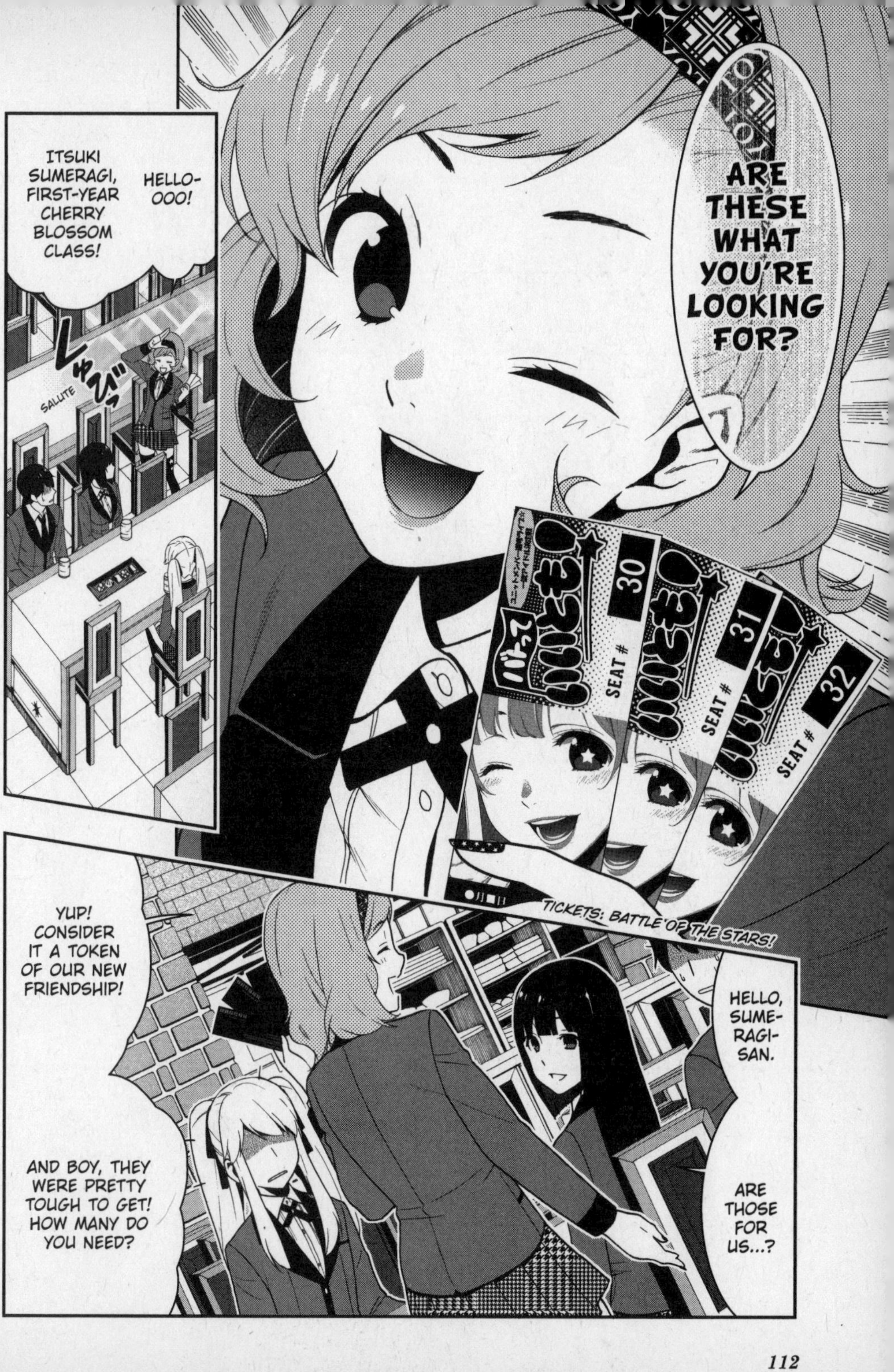
ARE THESE WHAT YOU'RE LOOKING FOR?
SEAT # 30
SEAT # 31
SEAT # 32
TICKETS: BATTLE OF THE STARS!
HELLO-OOO!
ITSUKI SUMERAGI, FIRST-YEAR CHERRY BLOSSOM CLASS!
しゅびっ
SALUTE
HELLO, SUMERAGI-SAN.
ARE THOSE FOR US...?
YUP! CONSIDER IT A TOKEN OF OUR NEW FRIENDSHIP!
AND BOY, THEY WERE PRETTY TOUGH TO GET! HOW MANY DO YOU NEED?

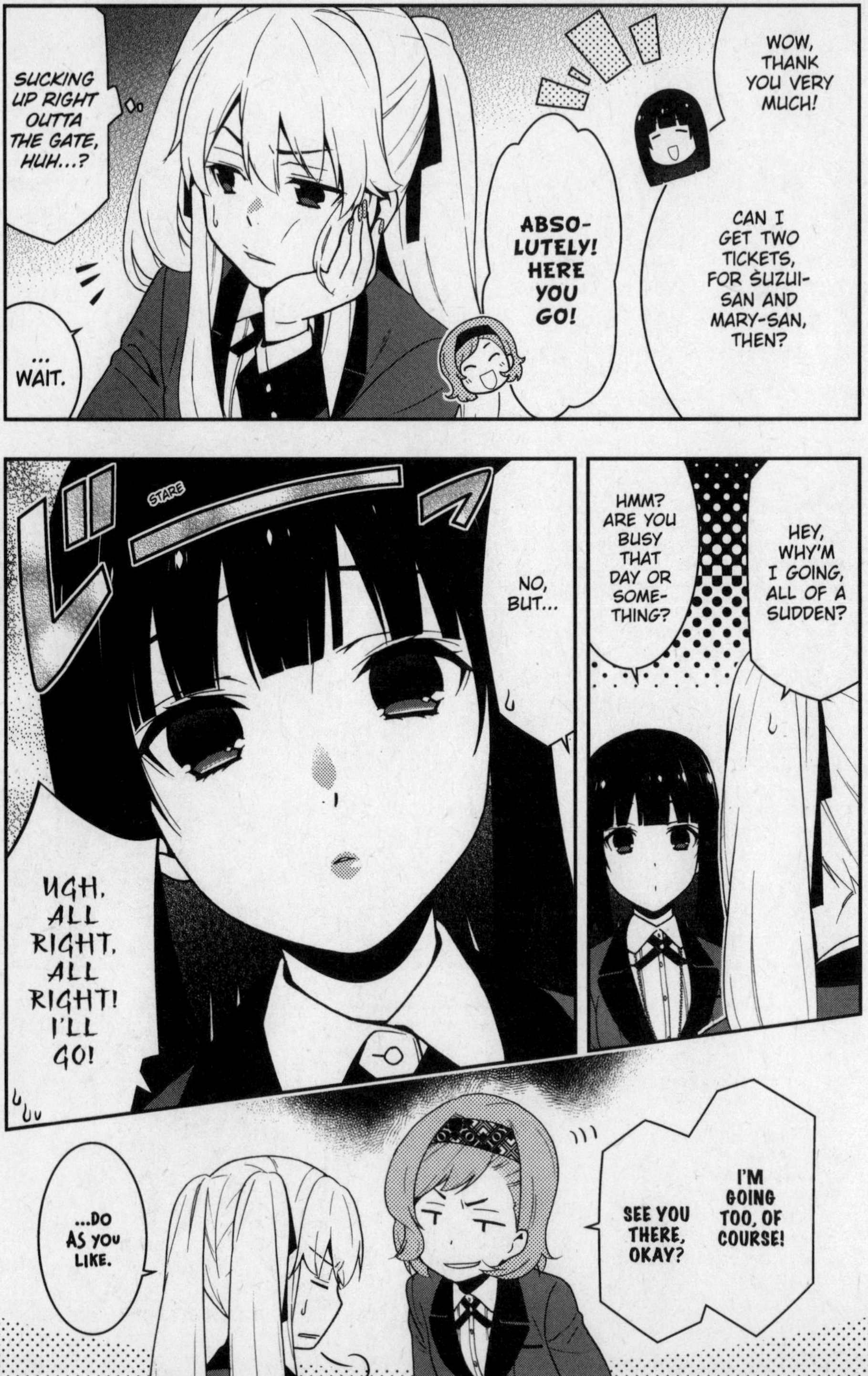
WOW, THANK YOU VERY MUCH!
CAN I GET TWO TICKETS, FOR SUZUI-SAN AND MARY-SAN, THEN?
ABSO-LUTELY! HERE YOU GO!
SUCKING UP RIGHT OUTTA THE GATE, HUH...?
...WAIT.
HEY, WHY'M I GOING, ALL OF A SUDDEN?
HMM? ARE YOU BUSY THAT DAY OR SOME-THING?
NO, BUT...
STARE
UGH. ALL RIGHT. ALL RIGHT! I'LL GO!
I'M GOING TOO, OF COURSE!
SEE YOU THERE, OKAY?
...DO AS YOU LIKE.

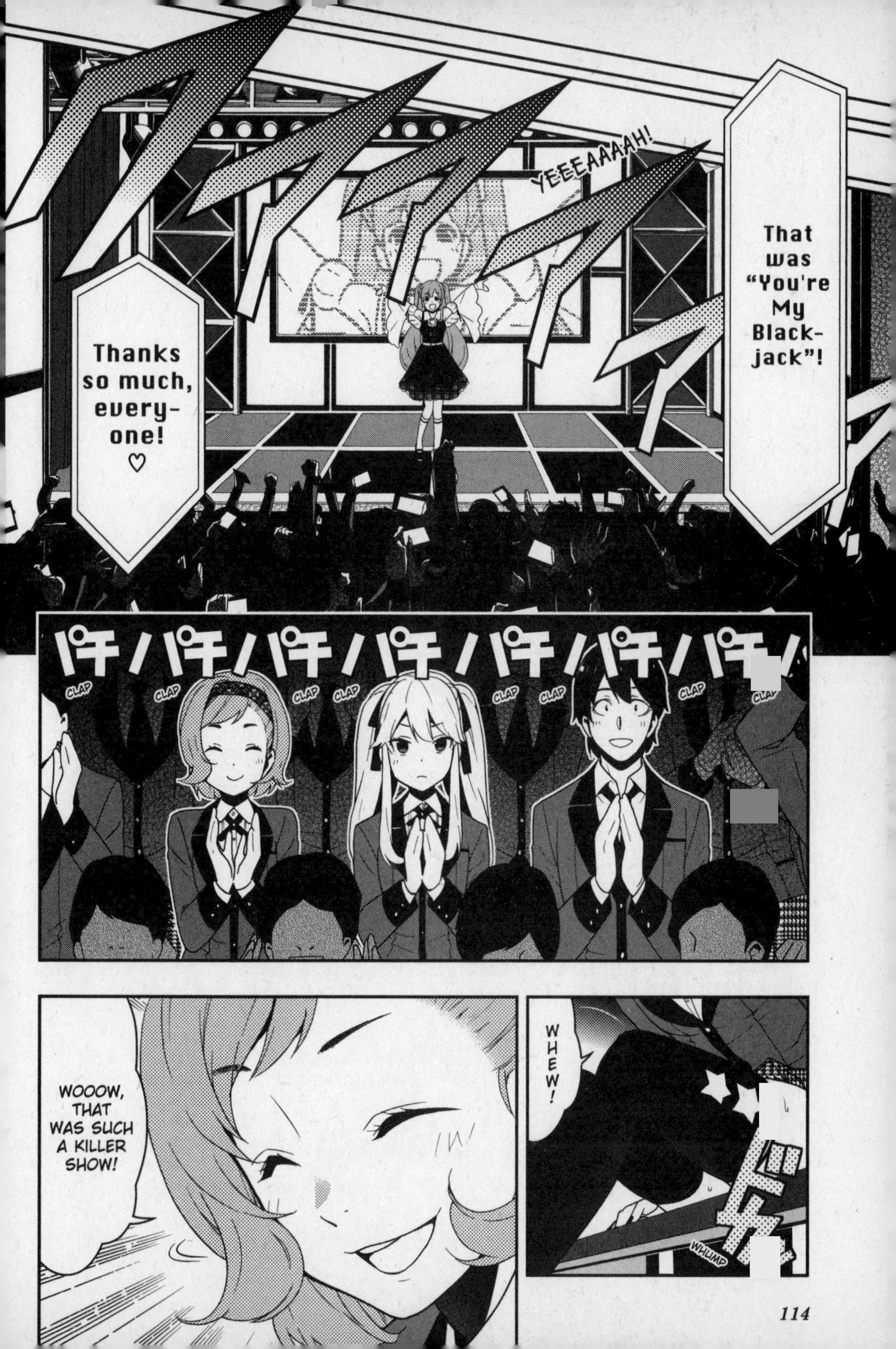
That was "You're My Black-jack"!
YEEEAAAAH!
Thanks so much, every-one! ♡
CLAP
CLAP
CLAP
CLAP
CLAP
CLAP
CLAP
CLAP
WHEW!
WHUMP
WOOOW, THAT WAS SUCH A KILLER SHOW!

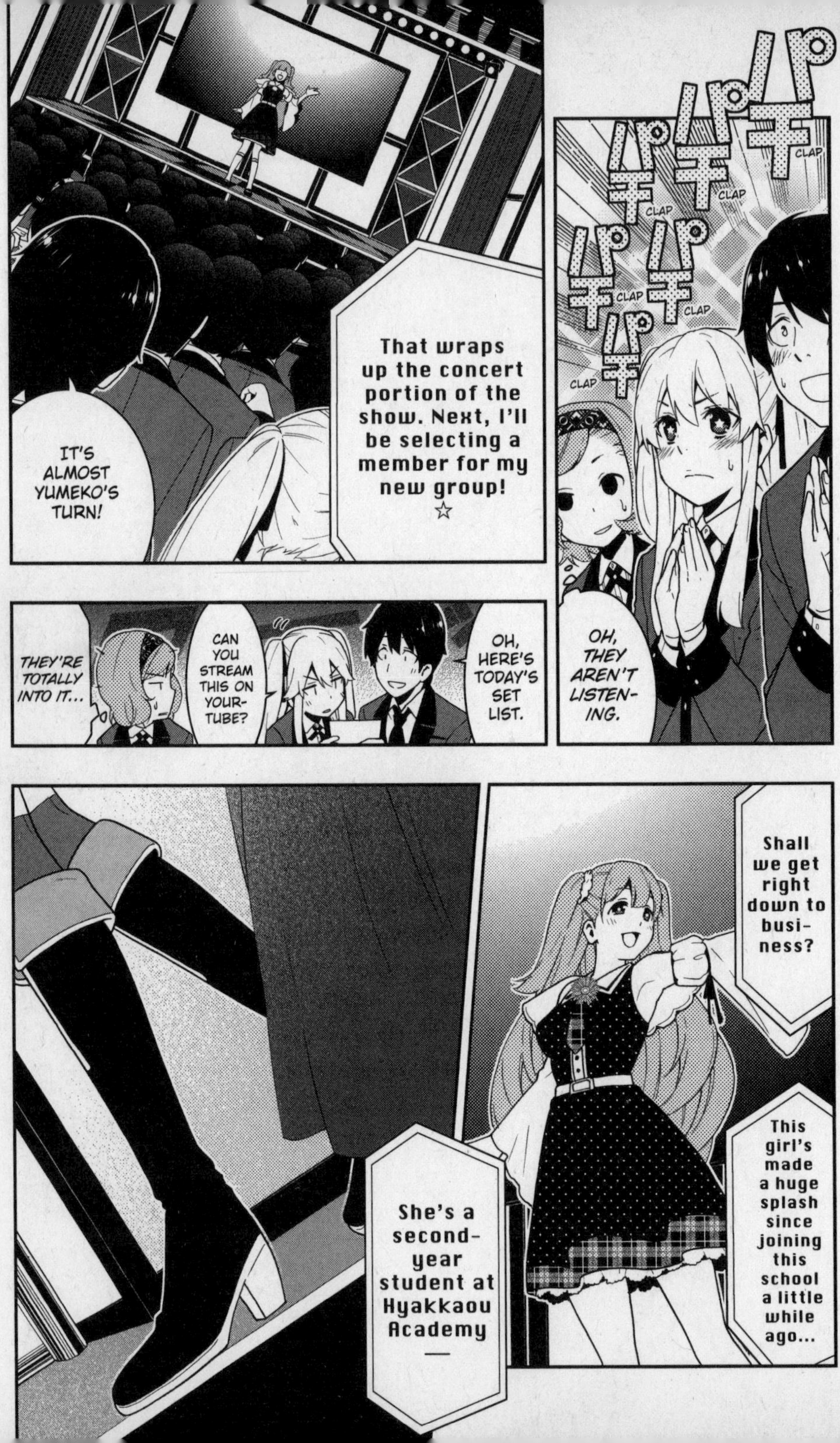
パチパチパチパチ
CLAP CLAP CLAP
パチパチパチ
CLAP CLAP CLAP
OH, THEY AREN'T LISTENING.
That wraps up the concert portion of the show. Next, I'll be selecting a member for my new group! ☆
IT'S ALMOST YUMEKO'S TURN!
OH, HERE'S TODAY'S SET LIST.
CAN YOU STREAM THIS ON YOURTUBE?
THEY'RE TOTALLY INTO IT...
Shall we get right down to business?
This girl's made a huge splash since joining this school a little while ago...
She's a second-year student at Hyakkaou Academy —

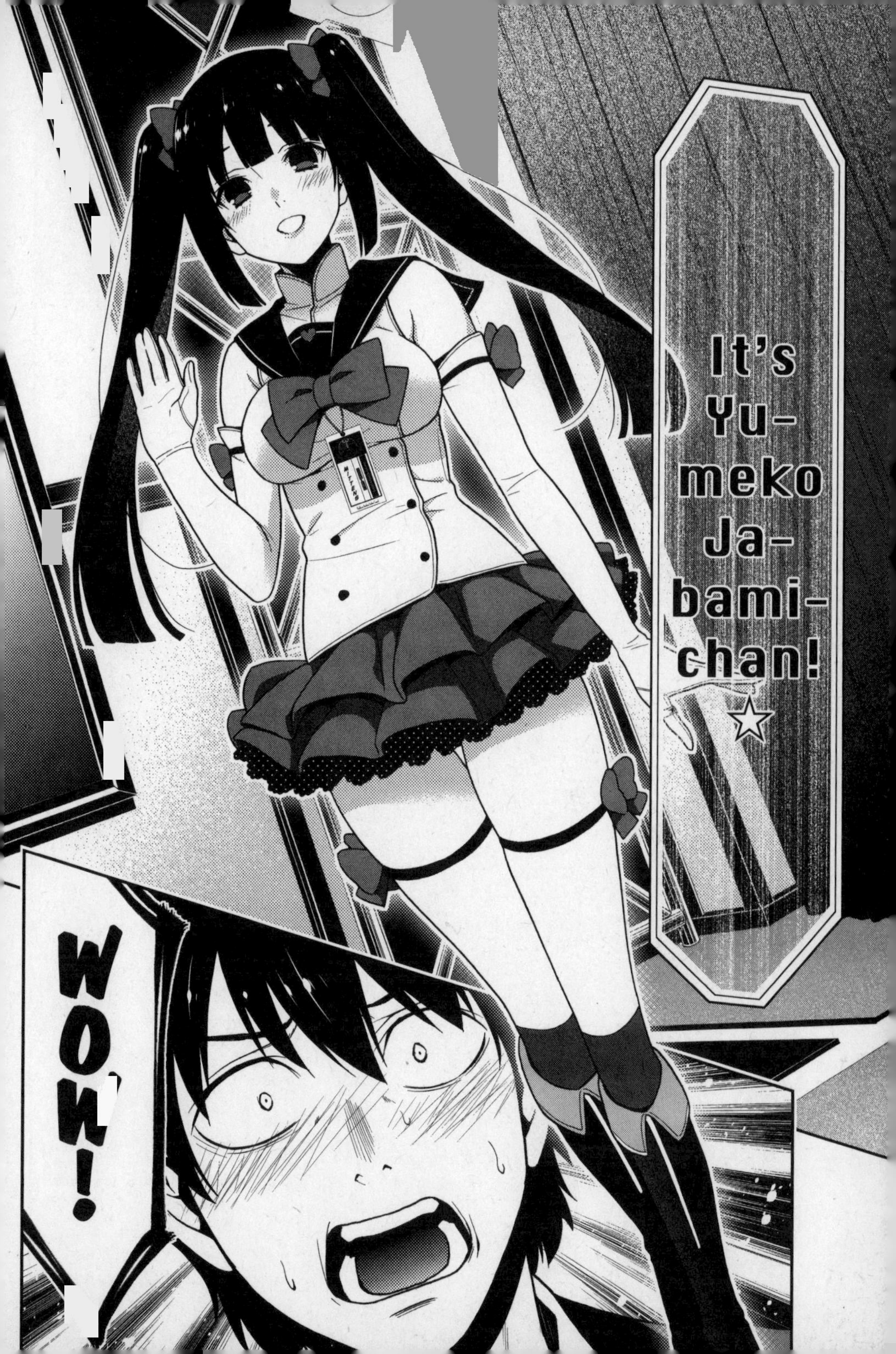
It's Yumeko Jabami-chan! ☆
WOW!

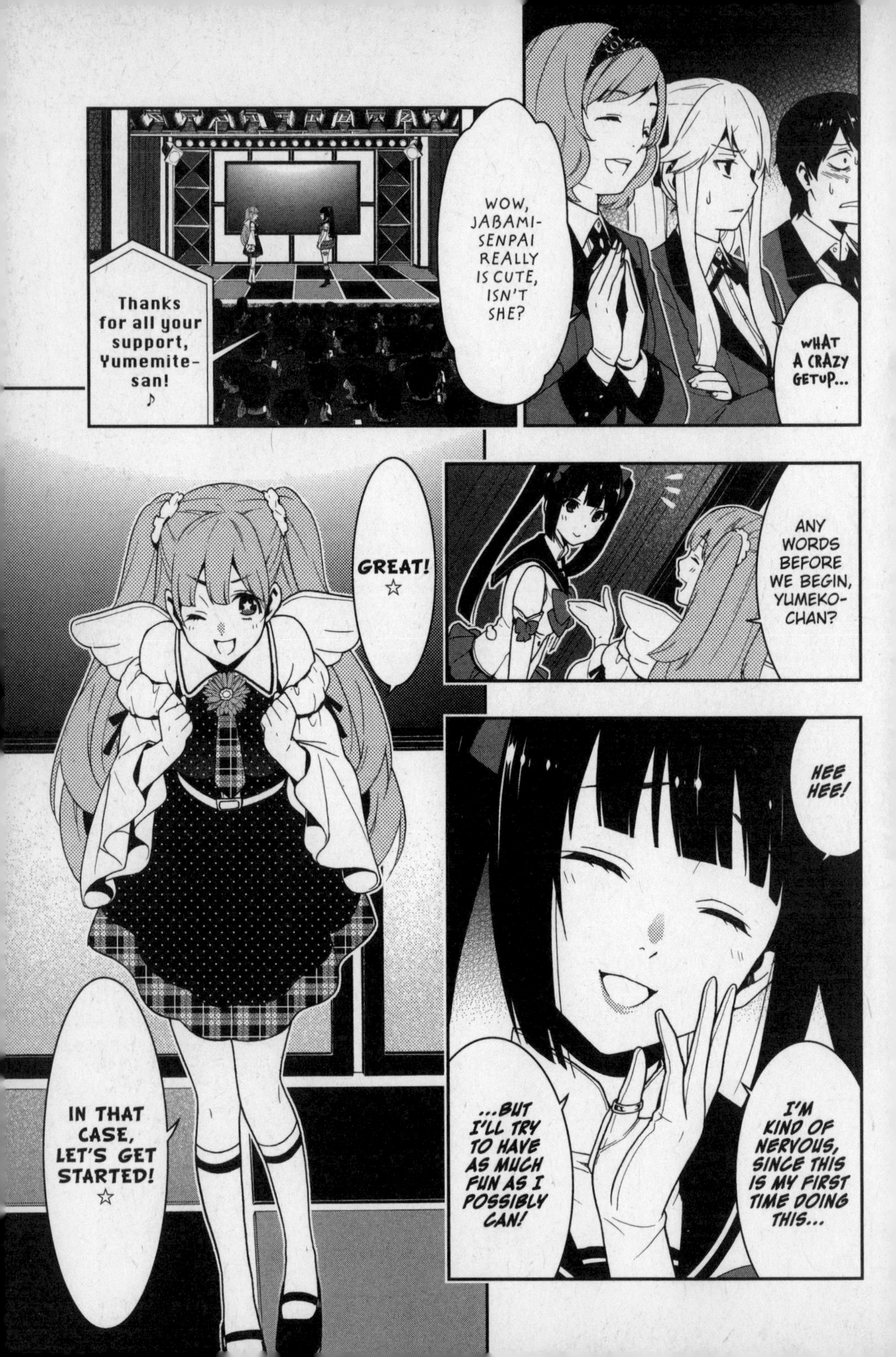
WOW, JABAMI-SENPAI REALLY IS CUTE, ISN'T SHE?
WHAT A CRAZY GETUP...
Thanks for all your support, Yumemite-san! ♪
ANY WORDS BEFORE WE BEGIN, YUMEKO-CHAN?
HEE HEE!
I'M KIND OF NERVOUS, SINCE THIS IS MY FIRST TIME DOING THIS...
...BUT I'LL TRY TO HAVE AS MUCH FUN AS I POSSIBLY CAN!
GREAT! ☆
IN THAT CASE, LET'S GET STARTED! ☆

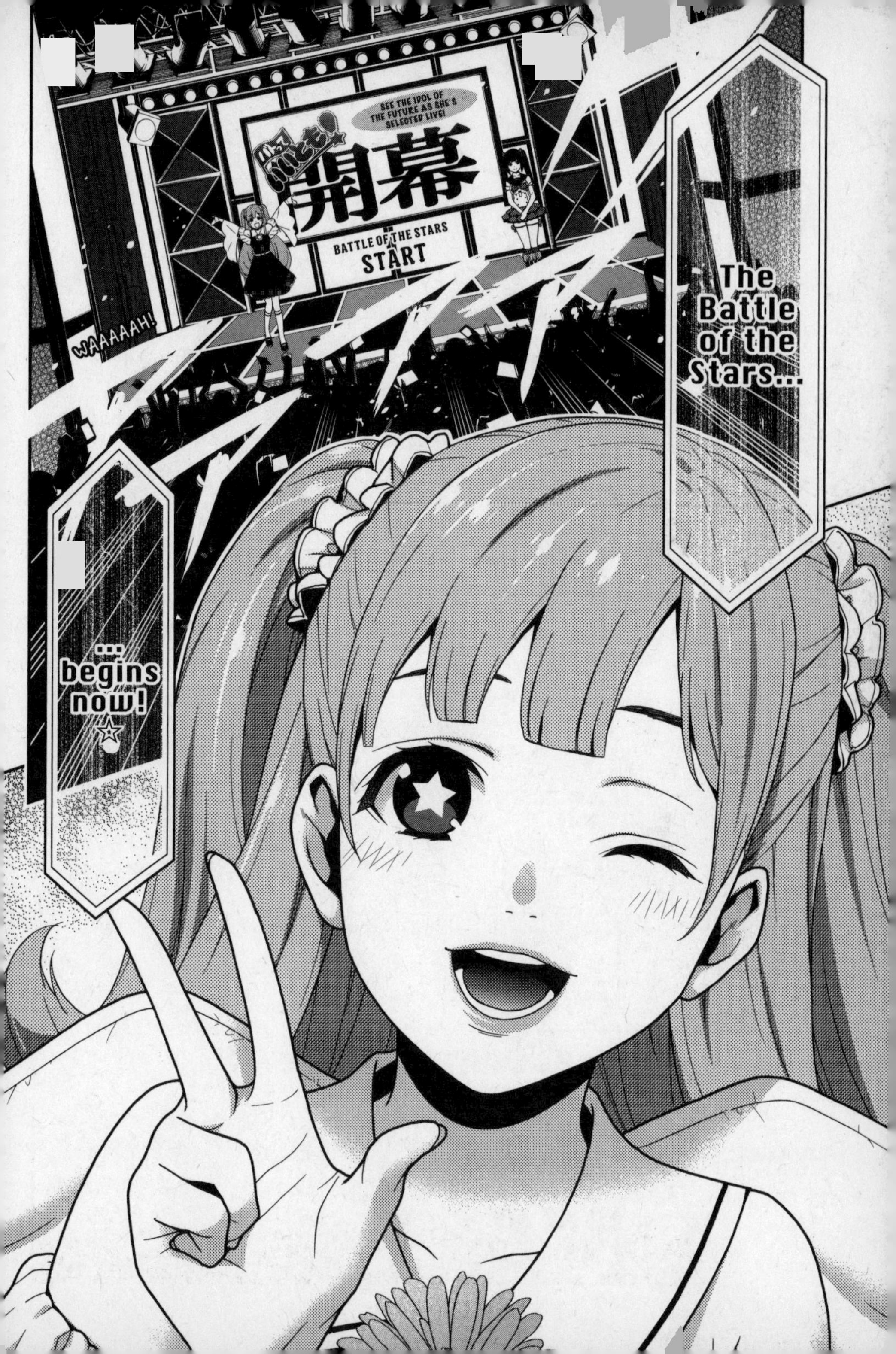
SEE THE IDOL OF THE FUTURE AS SHE'S SELECTED LIVE!
開幕
BATTLE OF THE STARS
START
The Battle of the Stars...
WAAAAAH!
...begins now! ☆

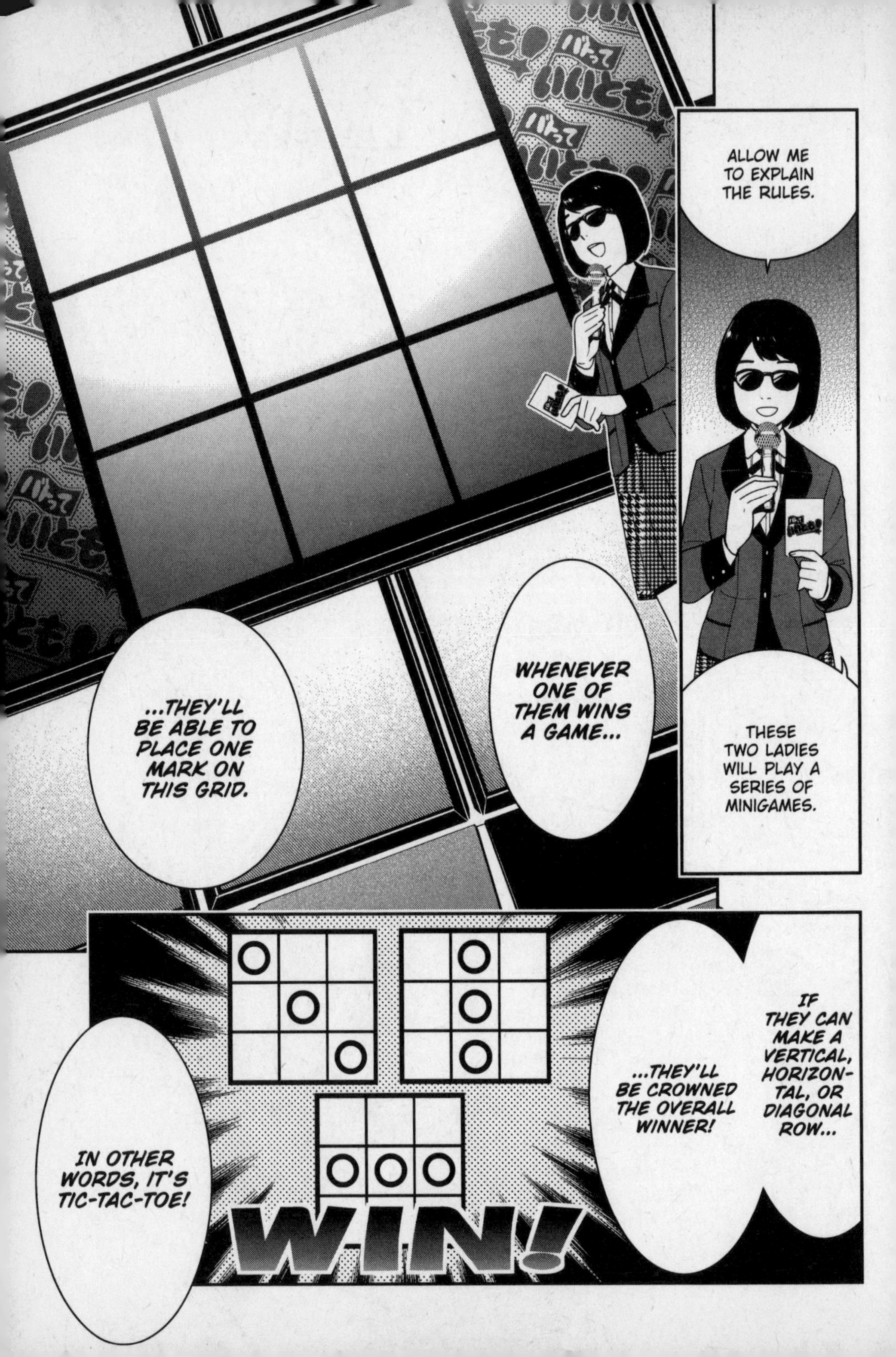
ALLOW ME TO EXPLAIN THE RULES.
THESE TWO LADIES WILL PLAY A SERIES OF MINIGAMES.
WHENEVER ONE OF THEM WINS A GAME...
...THEY'LL BE ABLE TO PLACE ONE MARK ON THIS GRID.
IF THEY CAN MAKE A VERTICAL, HORIZON-TAL, OR DIAGONAL ROW...
...THEY'LL BE CROWNED THE OVERALL WINNER!
WIN!
IN OTHER WORDS, IT'S TIC-TAC-TOE!

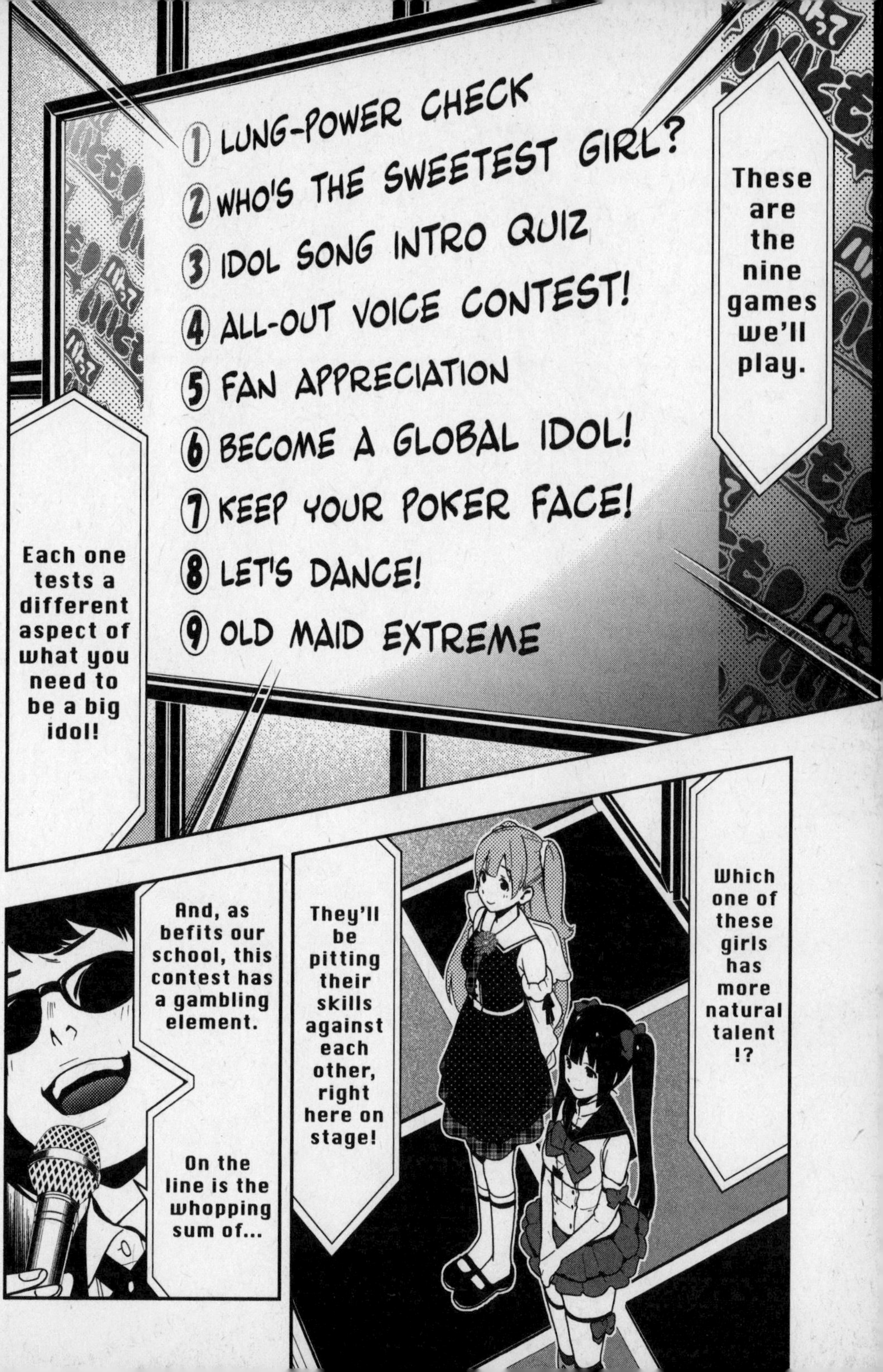
These are the nine games we'll play.
1 LUNG-POWER CHECK
2 WHO'S THE SWEETEST GIRL?
3 IDOL SONG INTRO QUIZ
4 ALL-OUT VOICE CONTEST!
5 FAN APPRECIATION
6 BECOME A GLOBAL IDOL!
7 KEEP YOUR POKER FACE!
8 LET'S DANCE!
9 OLD MAID EXTREME
Each one tests a different aspect of what you need to be a big idol!
Which one of these girls has more natural talent!?
They'll be pitting their skills against each other, right here on stage!
And, as befits our school, this contest has a gambling element.
On the line is the whopping sum of...

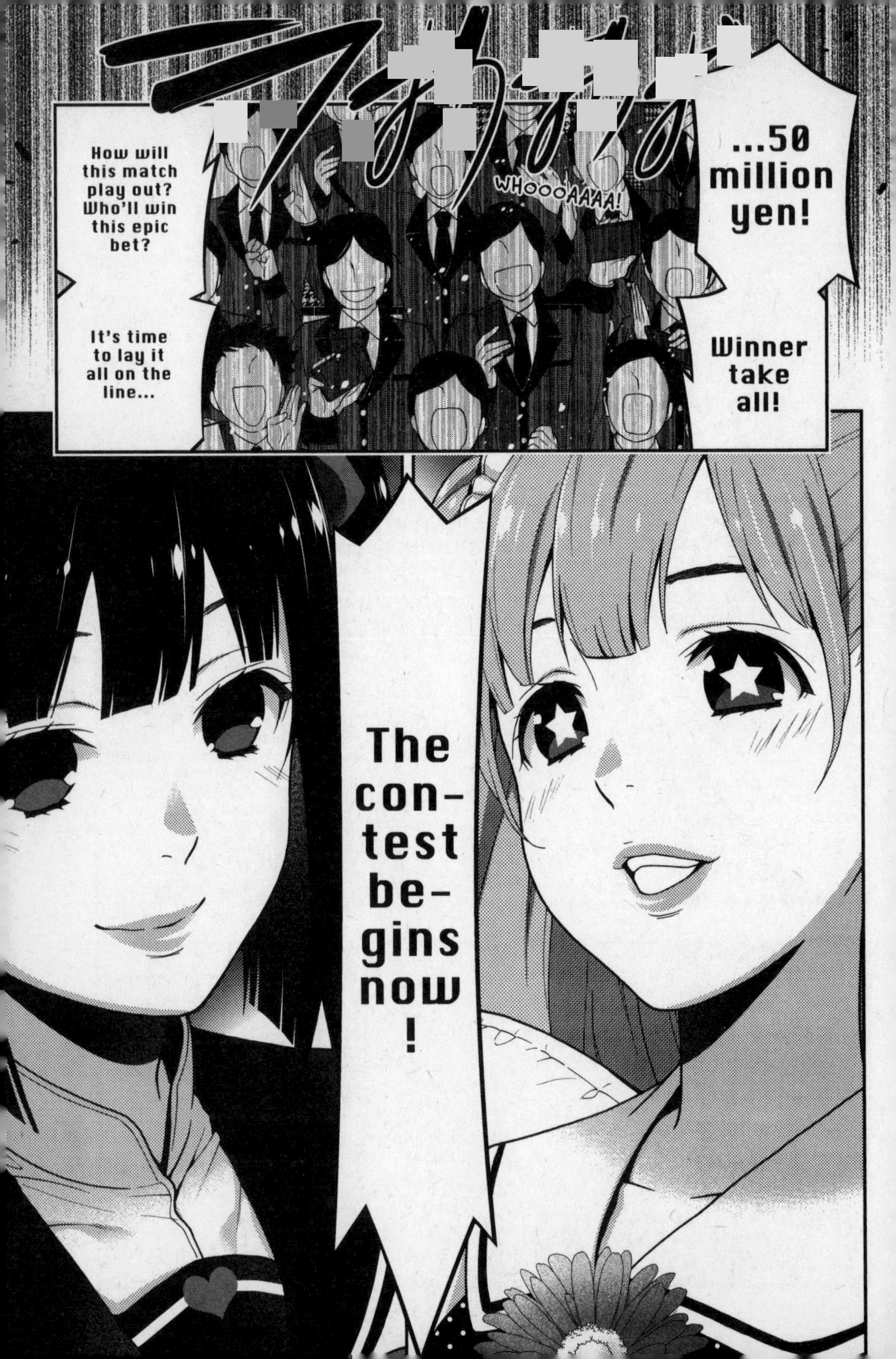
...50 million yen!
Winner take all!
WHOOOAAAA!
How will this match play out? Who'll win this epic bet?
It's time to lay it all on the line...
The con-test be-gins now!

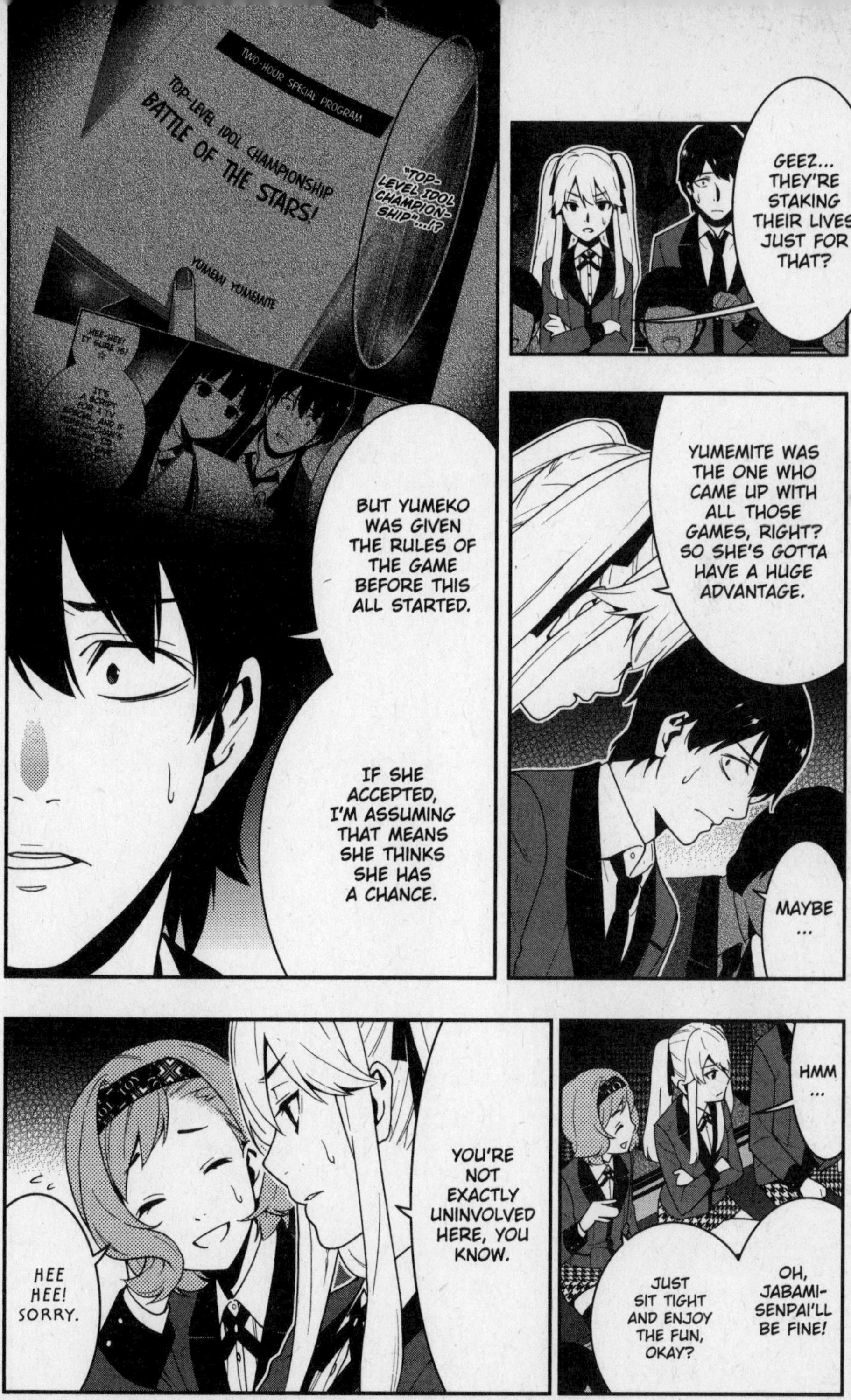
GEEZ... THEY'RE STAKING THEIR LIVES JUST FOR THAT?
YUMEMITE WAS THE ONE WHO CAME UP WITH ALL THOSE GAMES, RIGHT? SO SHE'S GOTTA HAVE A HUGE ADVANTAGE.
MAYBE ...
TWO-HOUR SPECIAL PROGRAM
TOP-LEVEL IDOL CHAMPIONSHIP
BATTLE OF THE STARS!
YUMEMI YUMEMITE
"TOP-LEVEL IDOL CHAMPIONSHIP"...!?
BUT YUMEKO WAS GIVEN THE RULES OF THE GAME BEFORE THIS ALL STARTED.
IF SHE ACCEPTED, I'M ASSUMING THAT MEANS SHE THINKS SHE HAS A CHANCE.
HMM ...
OH, JABAMI-SENPAI'LL BE FINE!
JUST SIT TIGHT AND ENJOY THE FUN, OKAY?
YOU'RE NOT EXACTLY UNINVOLVED HERE, YOU KNOW.
HEE HEE! SORRY.

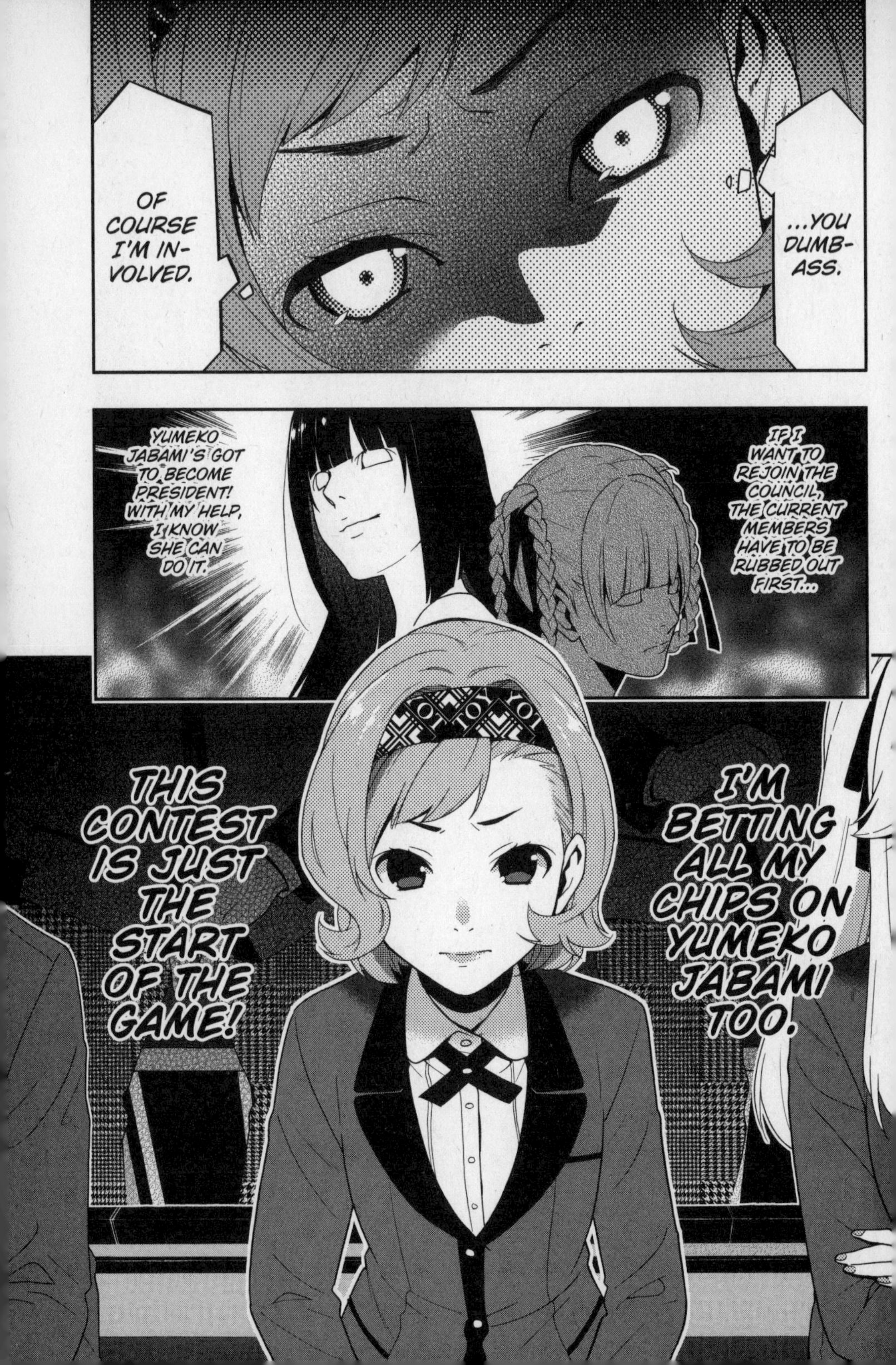
OF COURSE I'M INVOLVED.
...YOU DUMBASS.
YUMEKO JABAMI'S GOT TO BECOME PRESIDENT! WITH MY HELP, I KNOW SHE CAN DO IT.
IF I WANT TO REJOIN THE COUNCIL, THE CURRENT MEMBERS HAVE TO BE RUBBED OUT FIRST...
THIS CONTEST IS JUST THE START OF THE GAME!
I'M BETTING ALL MY CHIPS ON YUMEKO JABAMI TOO.

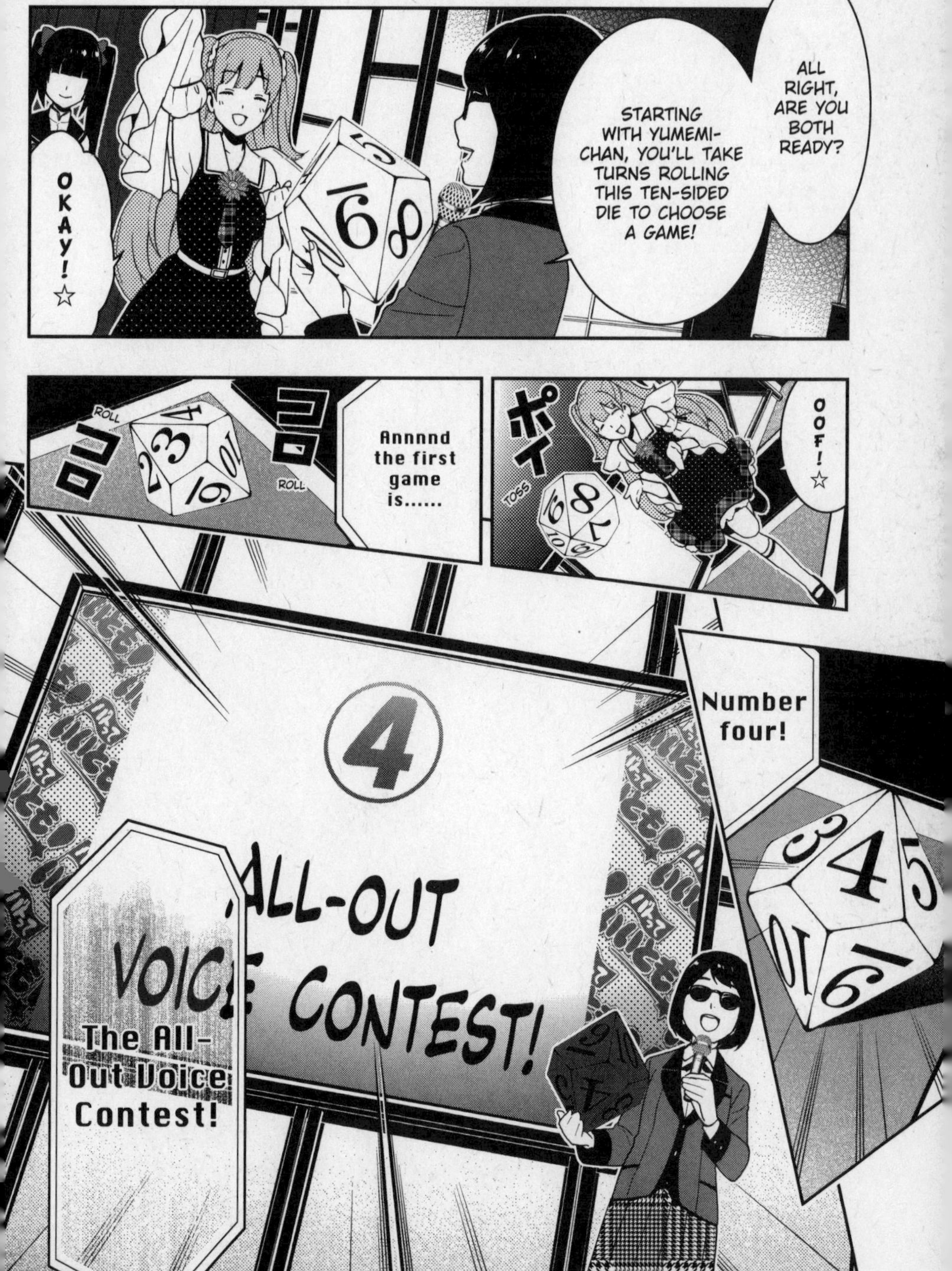
ALL RIGHT, ARE YOU BOTH READY?
STARTING WITH YUMEMI-CHAN, YOU'LL TAKE TURNS ROLLING THIS TEN-SIDED DIE TO CHOOSE A GAME!
OKAY!☆
OOF!☆
ポイ
TOSS
Annnnd the first game is......
コロ
ROLL
コロ
ROLL
Number four!
4
ALL-OUT VOICE CONTEST!
The All-Out Voice Contest!

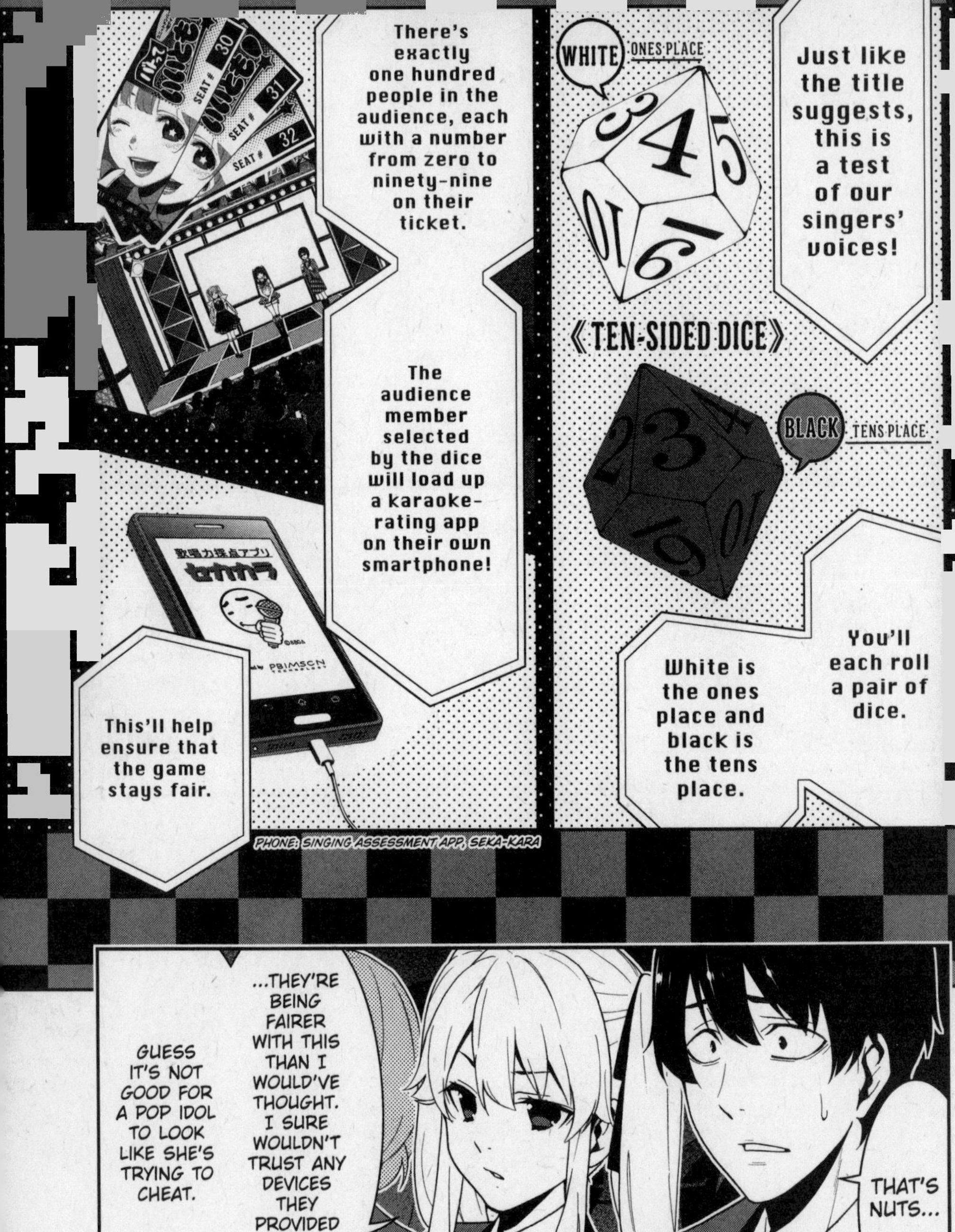
Just like the title suggests, this is a test of our singers' voices!
WHITE
ONES PLACE
《TEN-SIDED DICE》
BLACK
TENS PLACE
You'll each roll a pair of dice.
White is the ones place and black is the tens place.
There's exactly one hundred people in the audience, each with a number from zero to ninety-nine on their ticket.
The audience member selected by the dice will load up a karaoke-rating app on their own smartphone!
This'll help ensure that the game stays fair.
PHONE: SINGING ASSESSMENT APP, SEKA-KARA
THAT'S NUTS...
...THEY'RE BEING FAIRER WITH THIS THAN I WOULD'VE THOUGHT. I SURE WOULDN'T TRUST ANY DEVICES THEY PROVIDED THEMSELVES.
GUESS IT'S NOT GOOD FOR A POP IDOL TO LOOK LIKE SHE'S TRYING TO CHEAT.

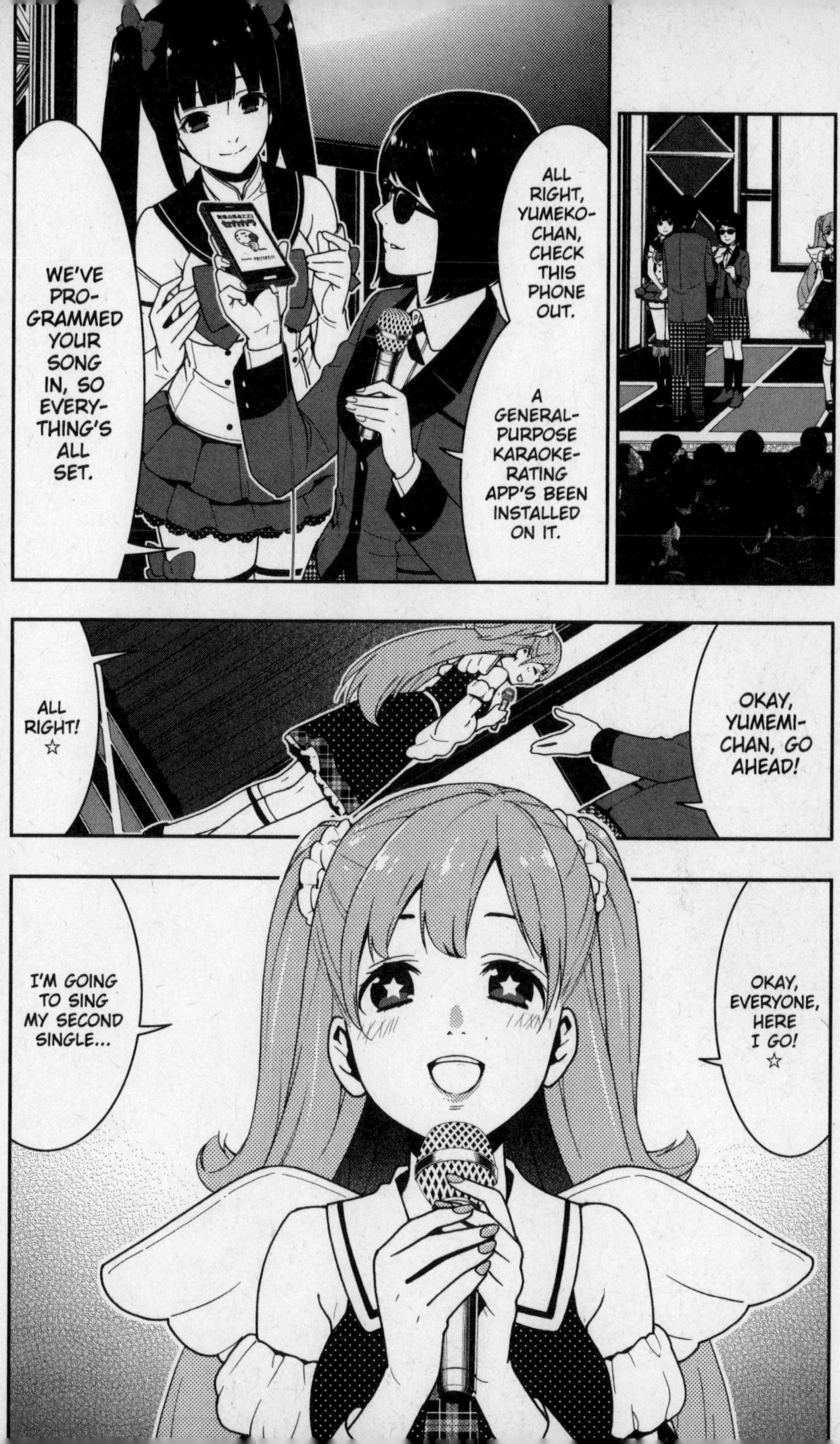
ALL RIGHT, YUMEKO-CHAN, CHECK THIS PHONE OUT.
A GENERAL-PURPOSE KARAOKE-RATING APP'S BEEN INSTALLED ON IT.
WE'VE PROGRAMMED YOUR SONG IN, SO EVERYTHING'S ALL SET.
OKAY, YUMEMI-CHAN, GO AHEAD!
ALL RIGHT! ☆
OKAY, EVERYONE, HERE I GO! ☆
I'M GOING TO SING MY SECOND SINGLE...

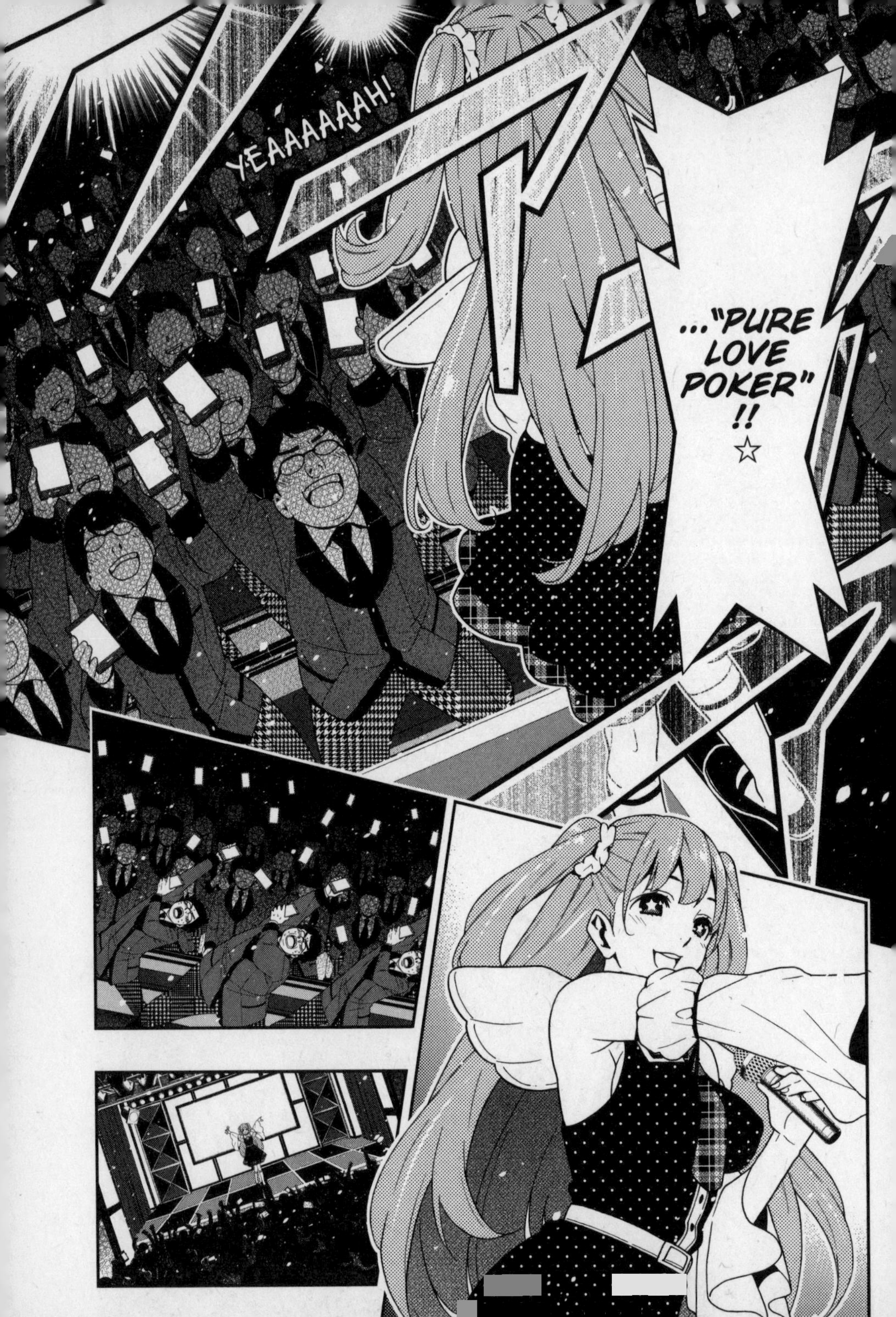
..."PURE LOVE POKER"!! ☆
YEAAAAAAH!

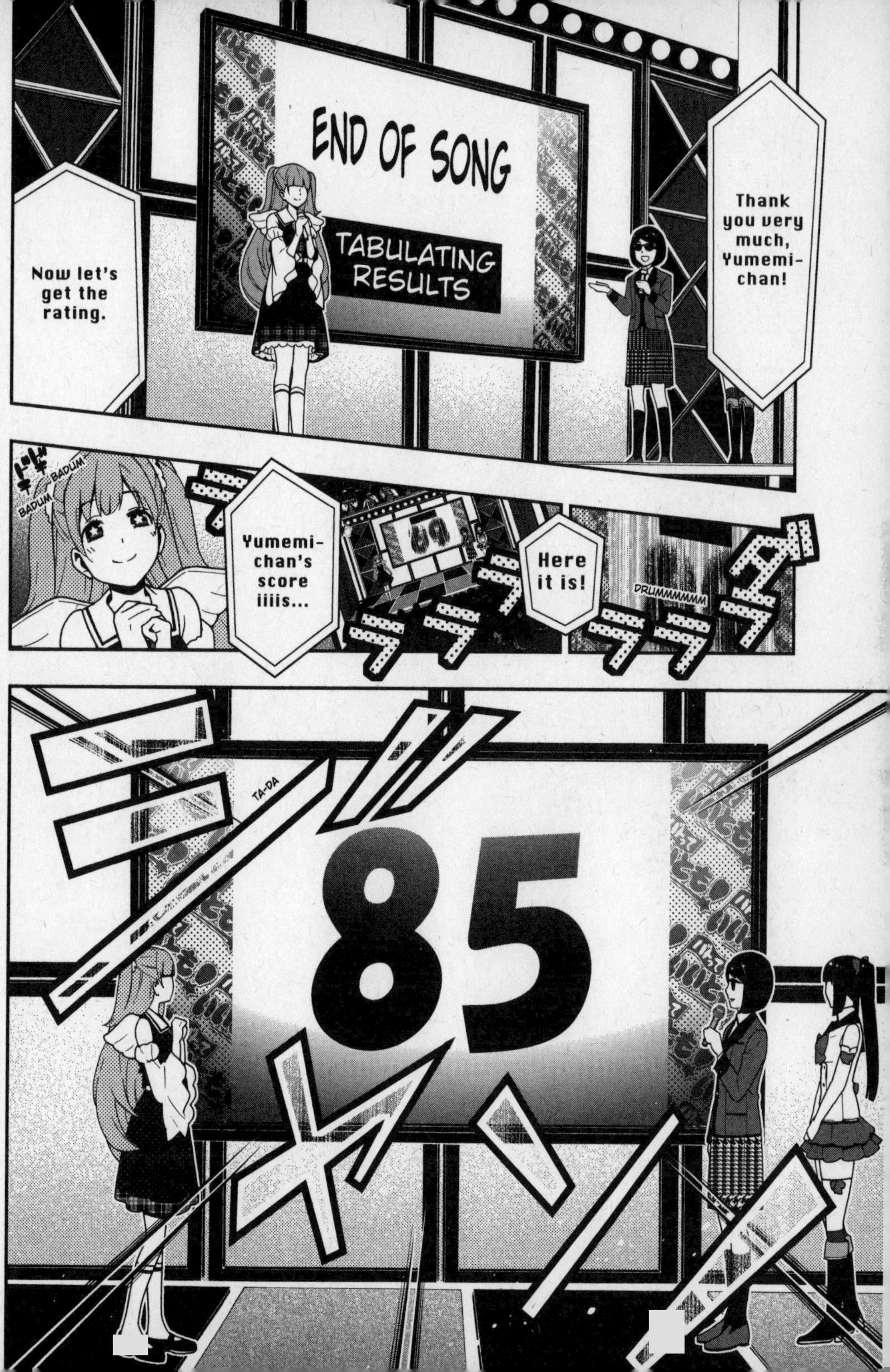
Thank you very much, Yumemi-chan!
END OF SONG
TABULATING RESULTS
Now let's get the rating.
DRUMMMMMMM
Here it is!
Yumemi-chan's score iiiis...
BADLUM BADLUM
TA-DA
85

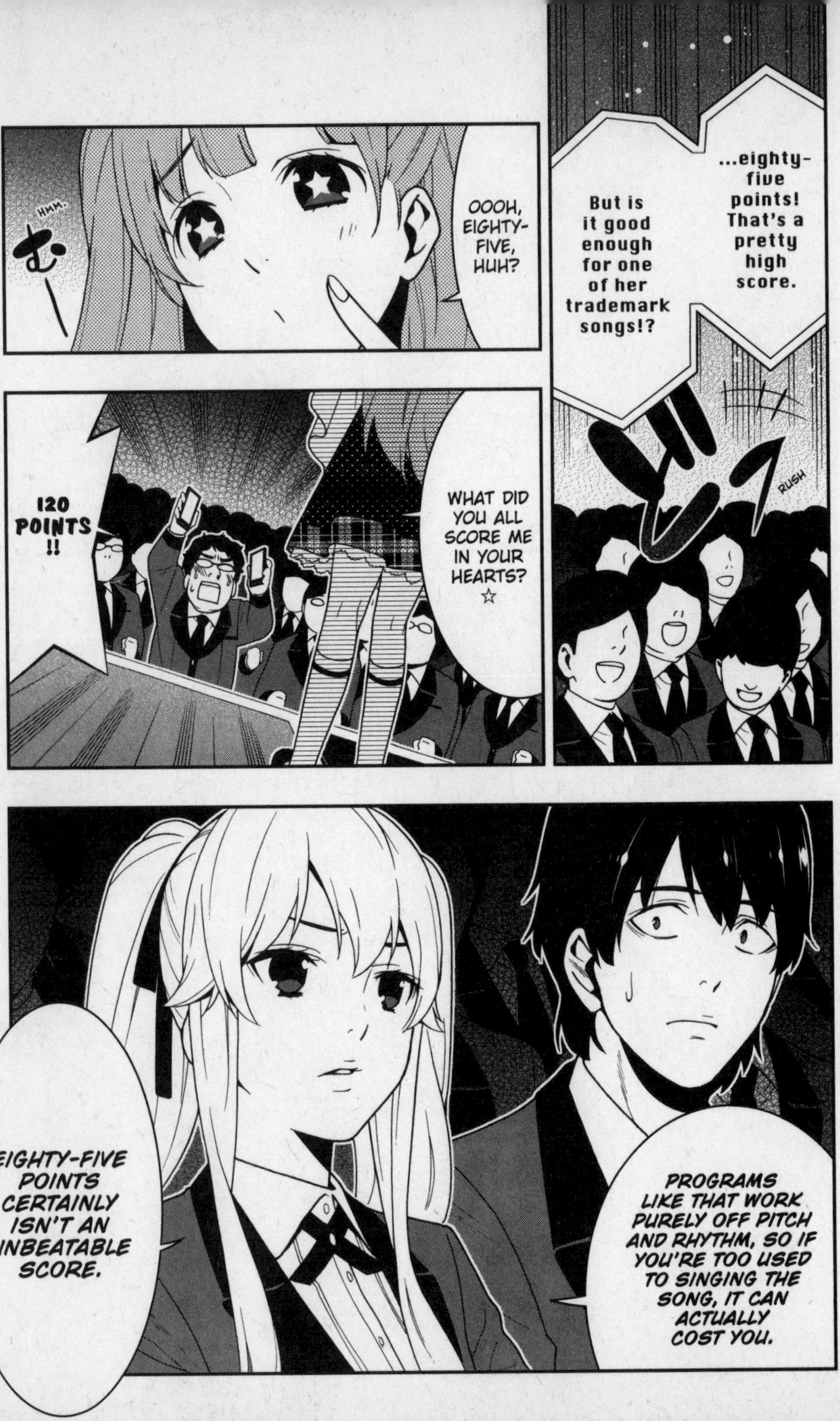
...eighty-five points! That's a pretty high score.
But is it good enough for one of her trademark songs!?
RUSH
OOOH, EIGHTY-FIVE, HUH?
HMM.
WHAT DID YOU ALL SCORE ME IN YOUR HEARTS? ☆
120 POINTS !!
PROGRAMS LIKE THAT WORK PURELY OFF PITCH AND RHYTHM, SO IF YOU'RE TOO USED TO SINGING THE SONG, IT CAN ACTUALLY COST YOU.
EIGHTY-FIVE POINTS CERTAINLY ISN'T AN UNBEATABLE SCORE.

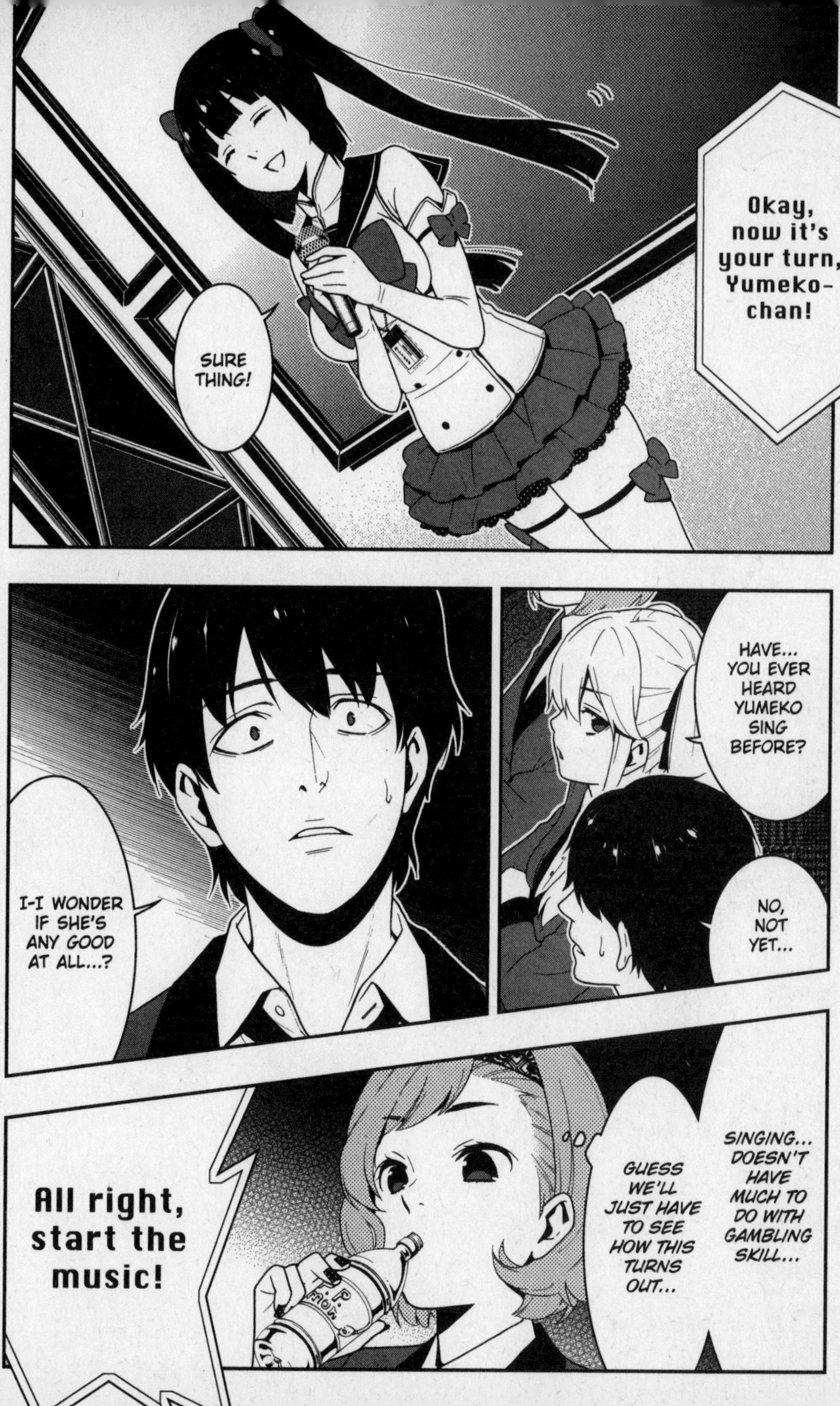
Okay, now it's your turn, Yumeko-chan!
SURE THING!
HAVE... YOU EVER HEARD YUMEKO SING BEFORE?
NO, NOT YET...
I-I WONDER IF SHE'S ANY GOOD AT ALL...?
SINGING... DOESN'T HAVE MUCH TO DO WITH GAMBLING SKILL...
GUESS WE'LL JUST HAVE TO SEE HOW THIS TURNS OUT...
All right, start the music!

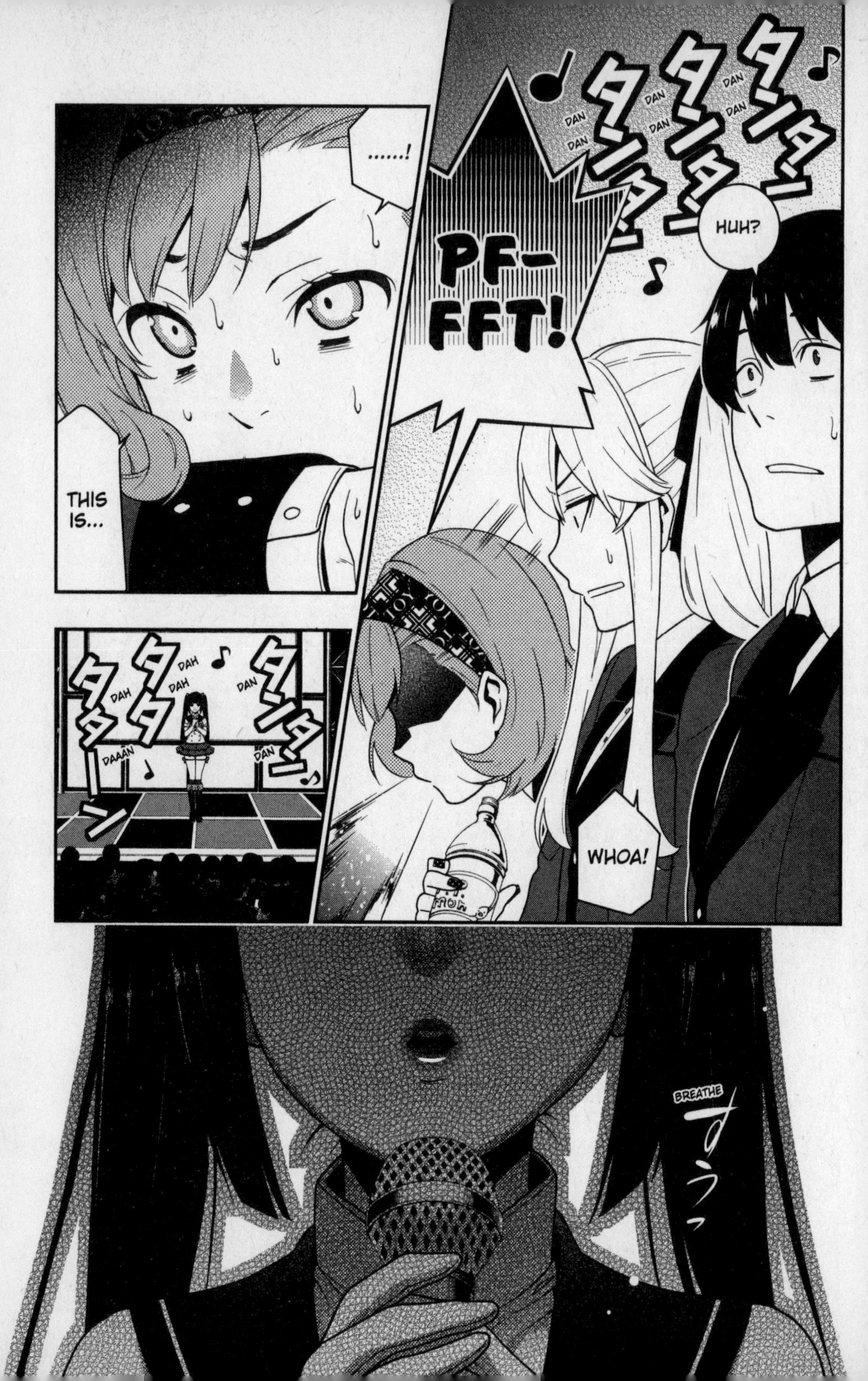
DAN DAN DAN
DAN DAN DAN
HUH?
PF-FFT!
WHOA!
......!
THIS IS...
DAH DAH DAAAN
DAN DAN
BREATHE

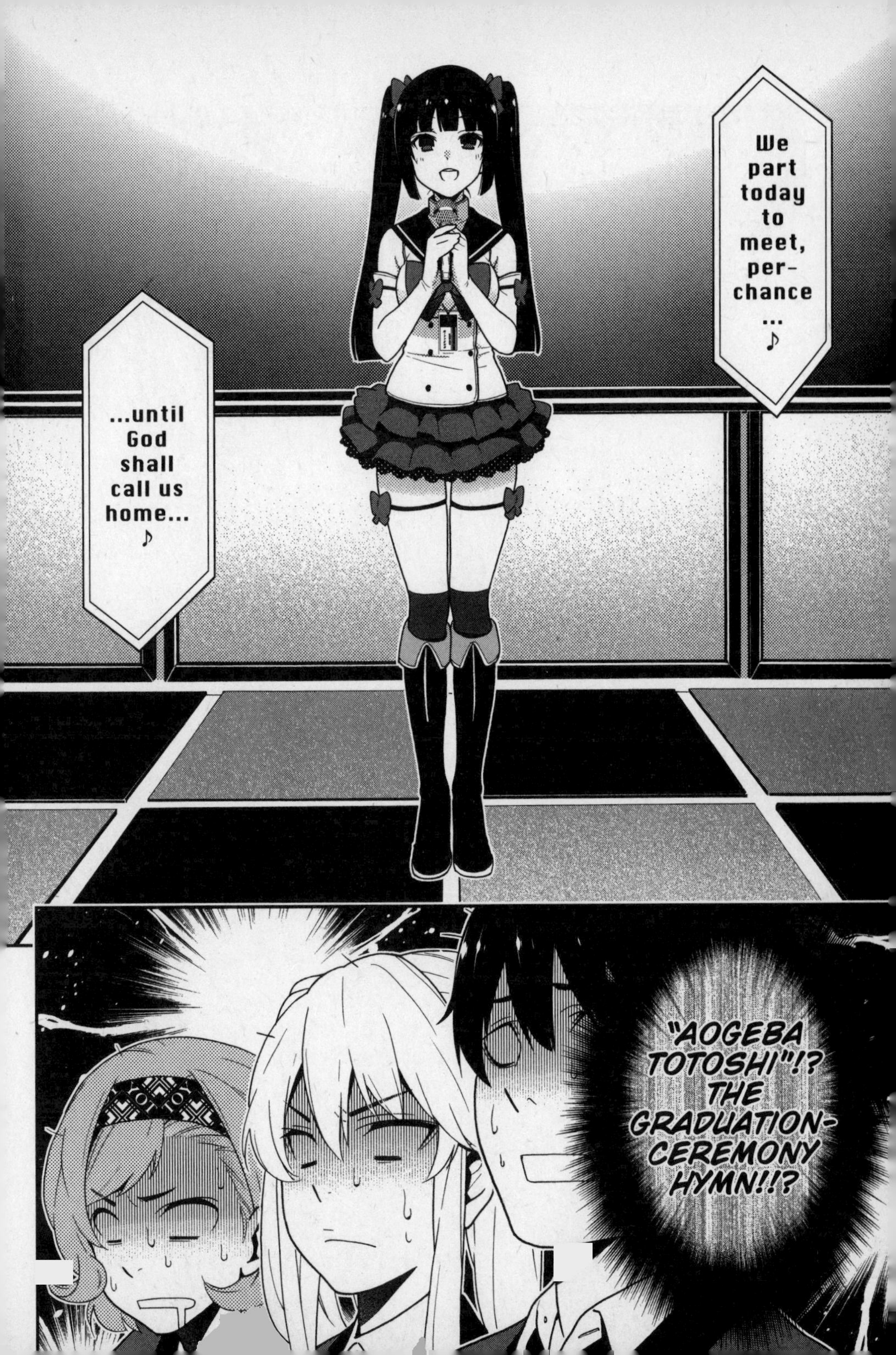
We part today to meet, per-chance ... ♪
...until God shall call us home... ♪
"AOGEBA TOTOSHI"!? THE GRADUATION-CEREMONY HYMN!!?

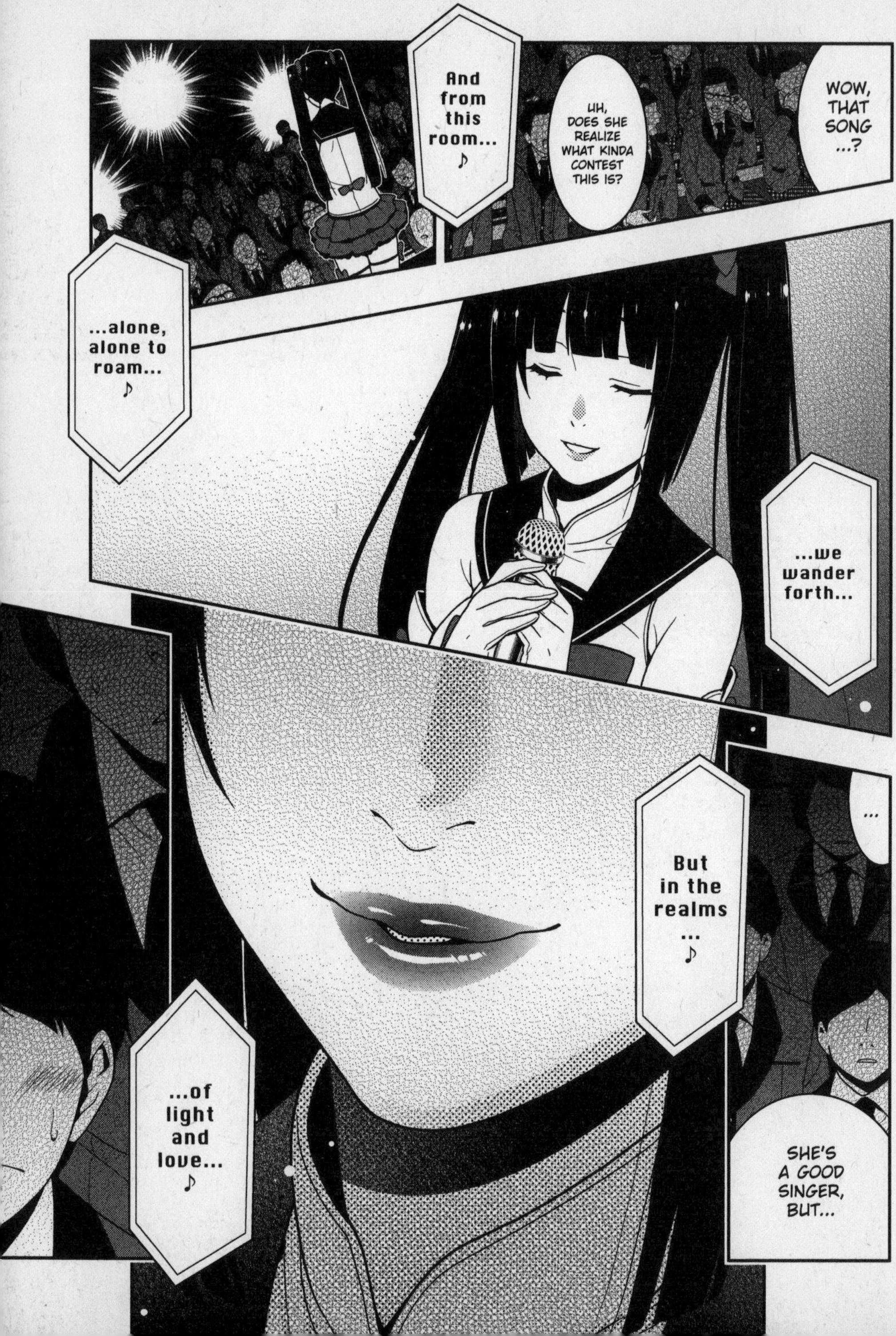
WOW, THAT SONG ...?
UH, DOES SHE REALIZE WHAT KINDA CONTEST THIS IS?
And from this room... ♪
...alone, alone to roam... ♪
...we wander forth...
...
SHE'S A GOOD SINGER, BUT...
But in the realms ... ♪
...of light and love... ♪

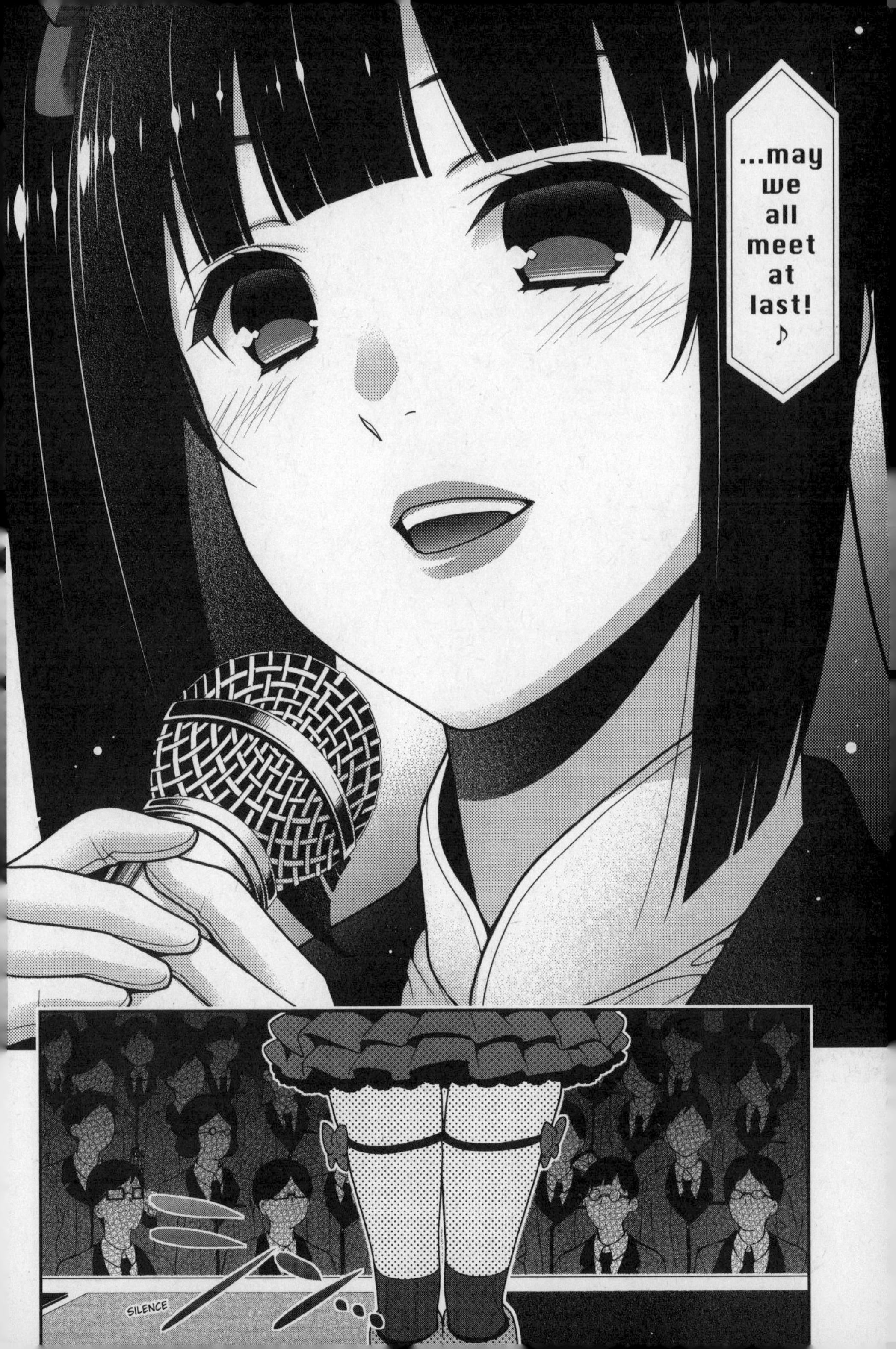
...may we all meet at last! ♪
SILENCE

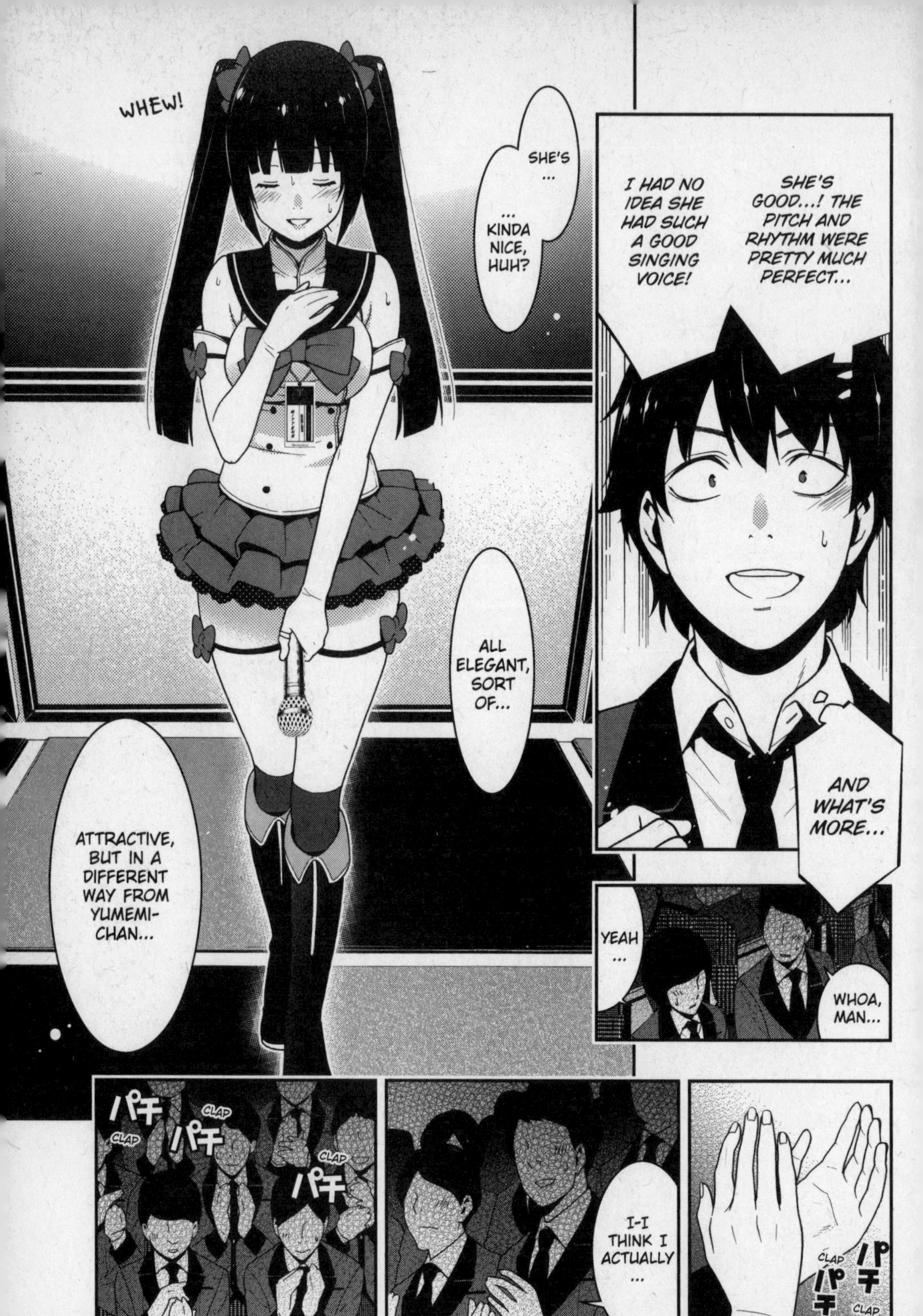
SHE'S GOOD...! THE PITCH AND RHYTHM WERE PRETTY MUCH PERFECT...
I HAD NO IDEA SHE HAD SUCH A GOOD SINGING VOICE!
AND WHAT'S MORE...
WHOA, MAN...
YEAH...
SHE'S... ...KINDA NICE, HUH?
WHEW!
ALL ELEGANT, SORT OF...
ATTRACTIVE, BUT IN A DIFFERENT WAY FROM YUMEMI-CHAN...
パチ CLAP
パチ CLAP
I-I THINK I ACTUALLY...
パチ CLAP
パチ CLAP
パチ CLAP
パチ CLAP

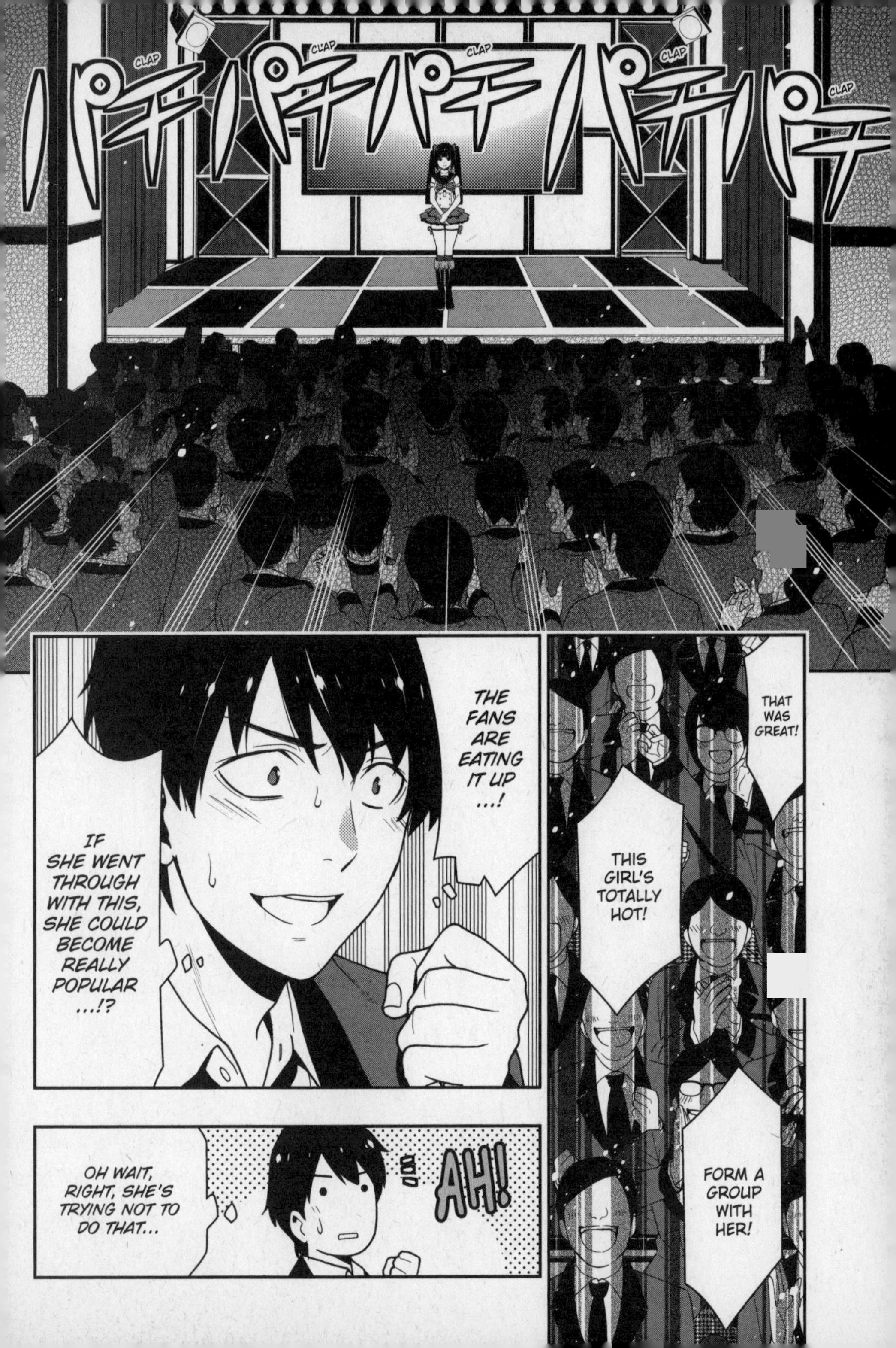
CLAP
CLAP
CLAP
CLAP
CLAP
THAT WAS GREAT!
THIS GIRL'S TOTALLY HOT!
FORM A GROUP WITH HER!
THE FANS ARE EATING IT UP ...!
IF SHE WENT THROUGH WITH THIS, SHE COULD BECOME REALLY POPULAR ...!?
AH!
OH WAIT, RIGHT, SHE'S TRYING NOT TO DO THAT...

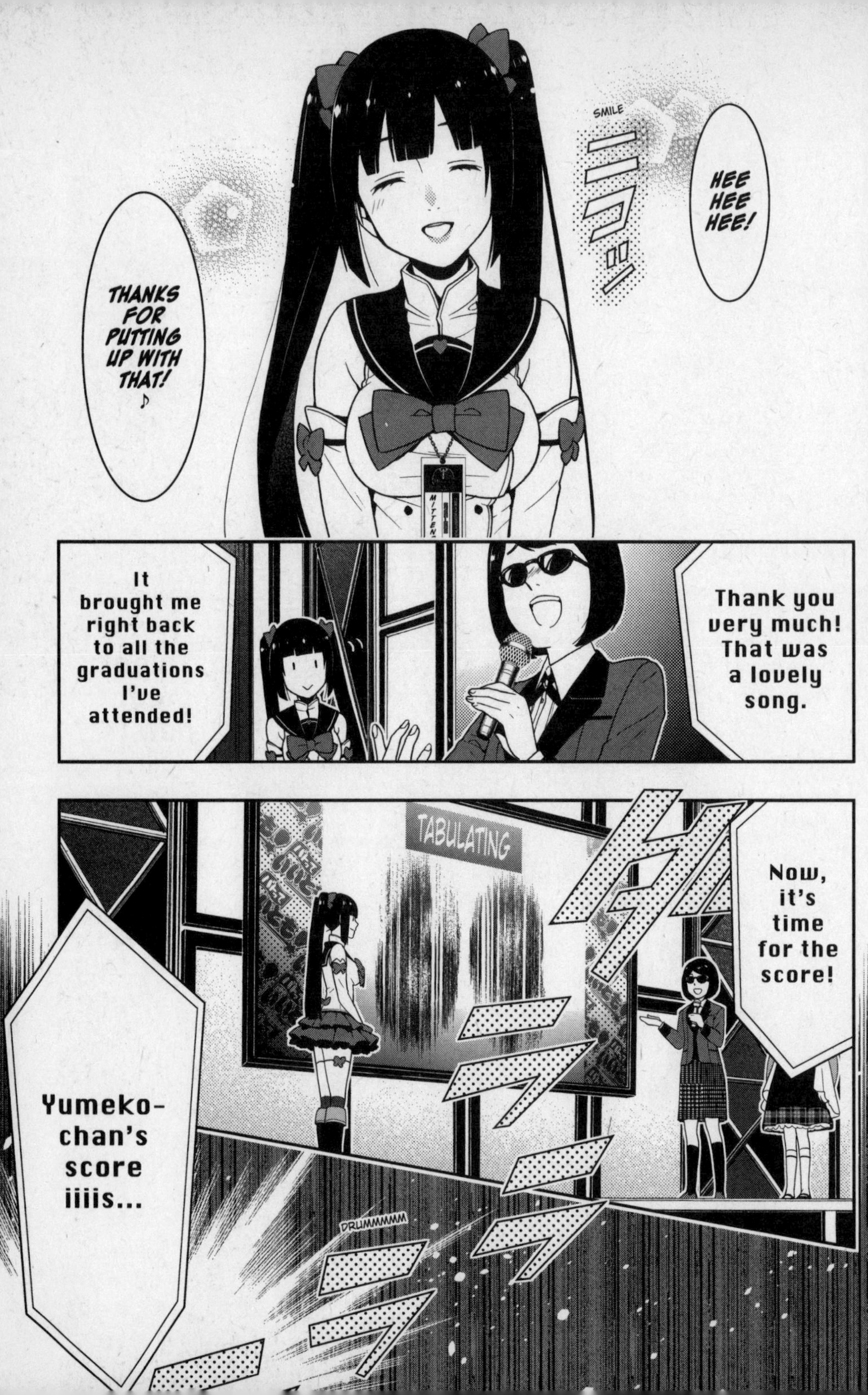
SMILE
HEE HEE HEE!
THANKS FOR PUTTING UP WITH THAT! ♪
Thank you very much! That was a lovely song.
It brought me right back to all the graduations I've attended!
TABULATING
Now, it's time for the score!
Yumeko-chan's score iiiis...
DRUMMMMM

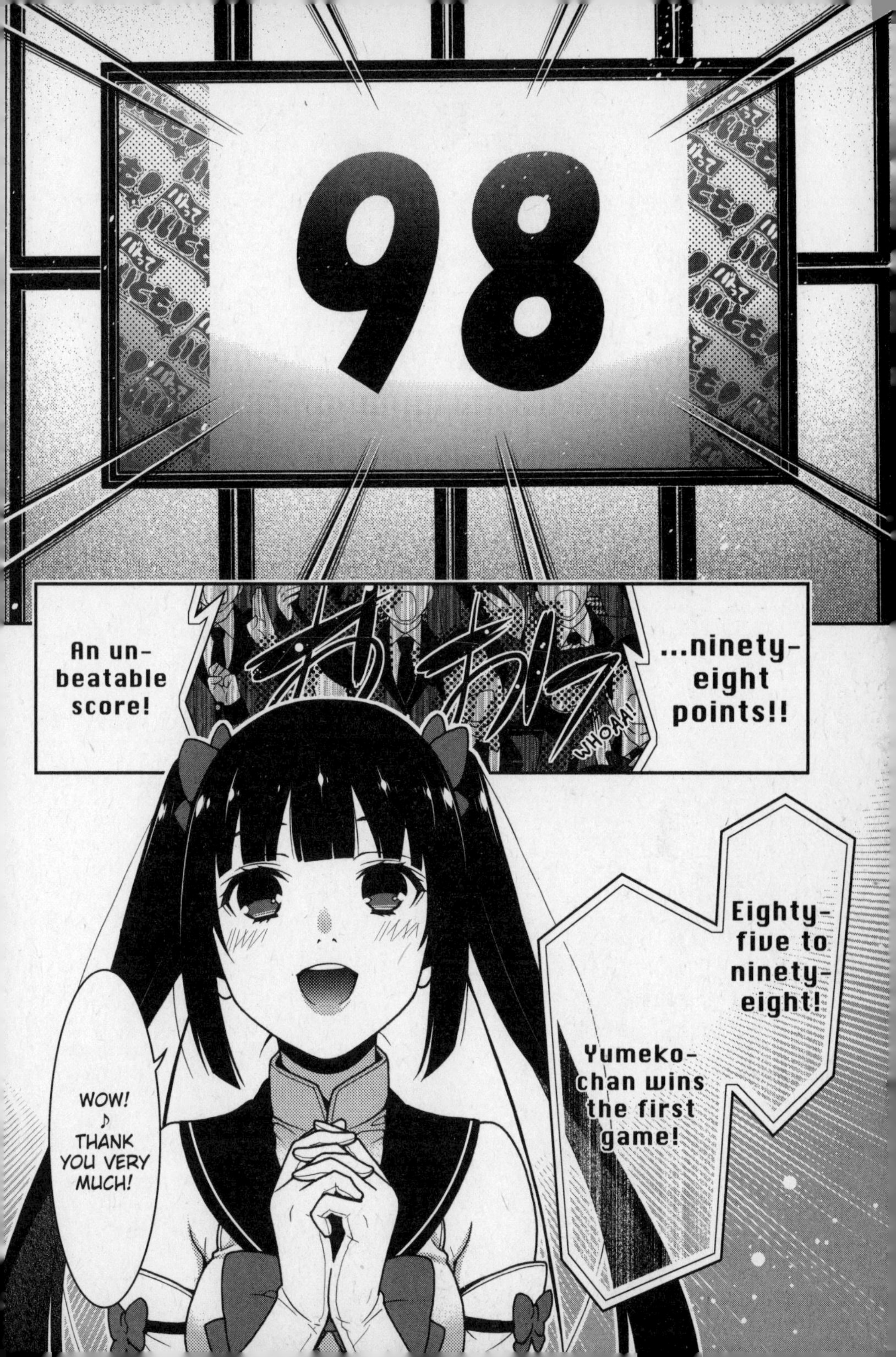
98
...ninety-eight points!!
WHOAA!
An un-beatable score!
Eighty-five to ninety-eight!
Yumeko-chan wins the first game!
WOW! ♪ THANK YOU VERY MUCH!

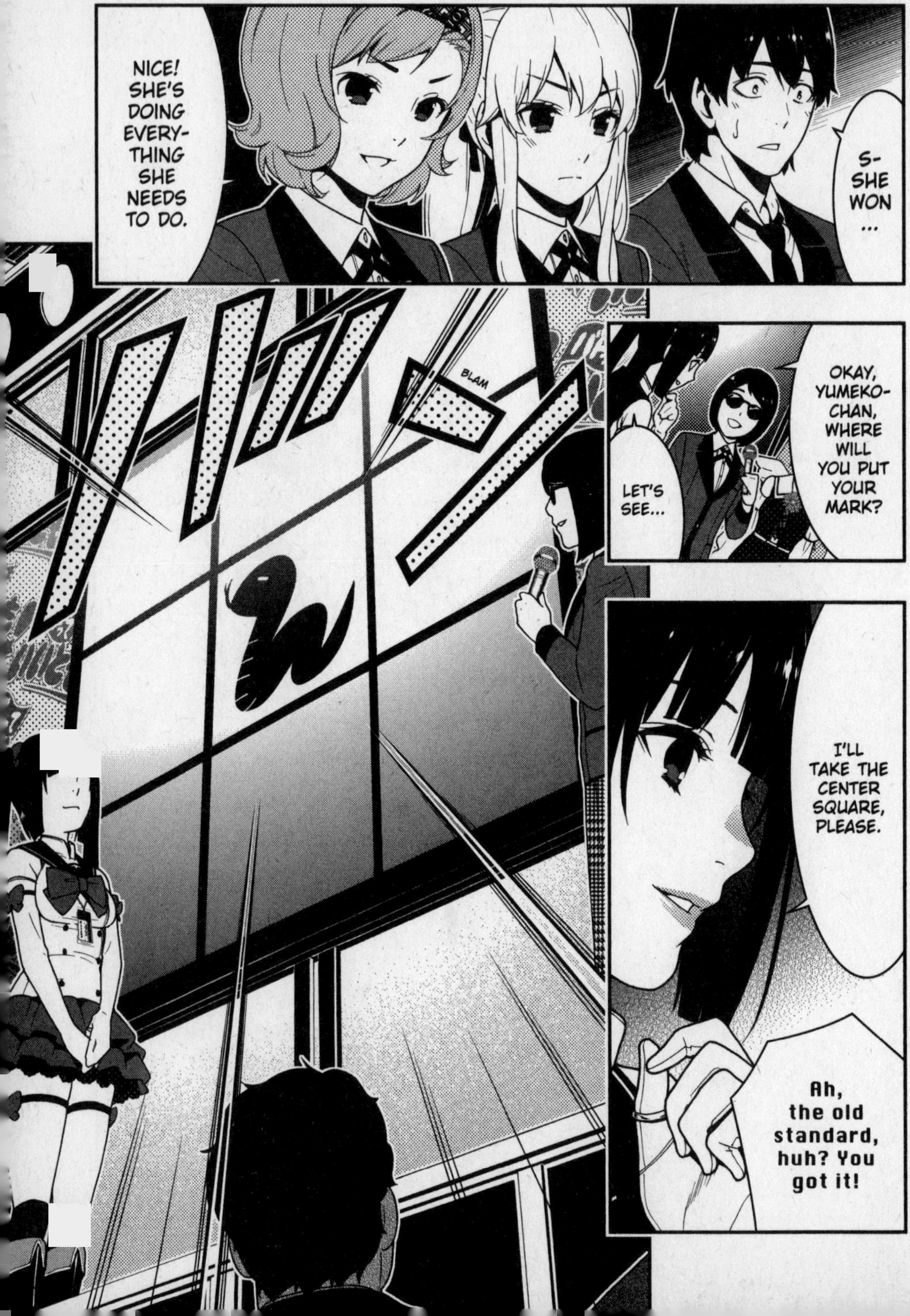
S-SHE WON...
NICE! SHE'S DOING EVERY-THING SHE NEEDS TO DO.
OKAY, YUMEKO-CHAN, WHERE WILL YOU PUT YOUR MARK?
LET'S SEE...
I'LL TAKE THE CENTER SQUARE, PLEASE.
Ah, the old standard, huh? You got it!
BLAM

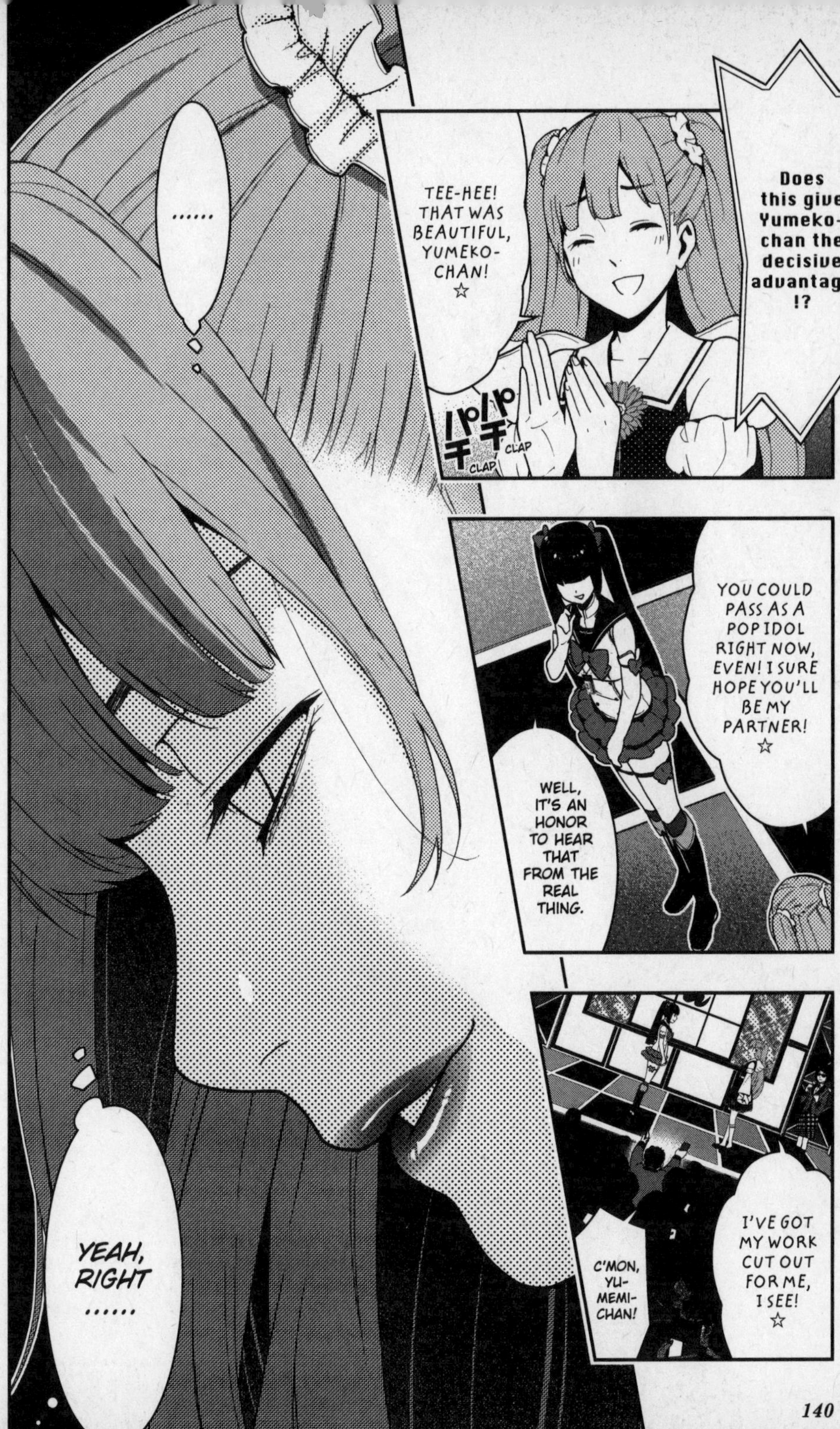
Does this give Yumeko-chan the decisive advantage!?
TEE-HEE! THAT WAS BEAUTIFUL, YUMEKO-CHAN! ☆
パチパチ
CLAP CLAP
YOU COULD PASS AS A POP IDOL RIGHT NOW, EVEN! I SURE HOPE YOU'LL BE MY PARTNER! ☆
WELL, IT'S AN HONOR TO HEAR THAT FROM THE REAL THING.
I'VE GOT MY WORK CUT OUT FOR ME, I SEE! ☆
C'MON, YUMEMI-CHAN!
......
YEAH, RIGHT ......

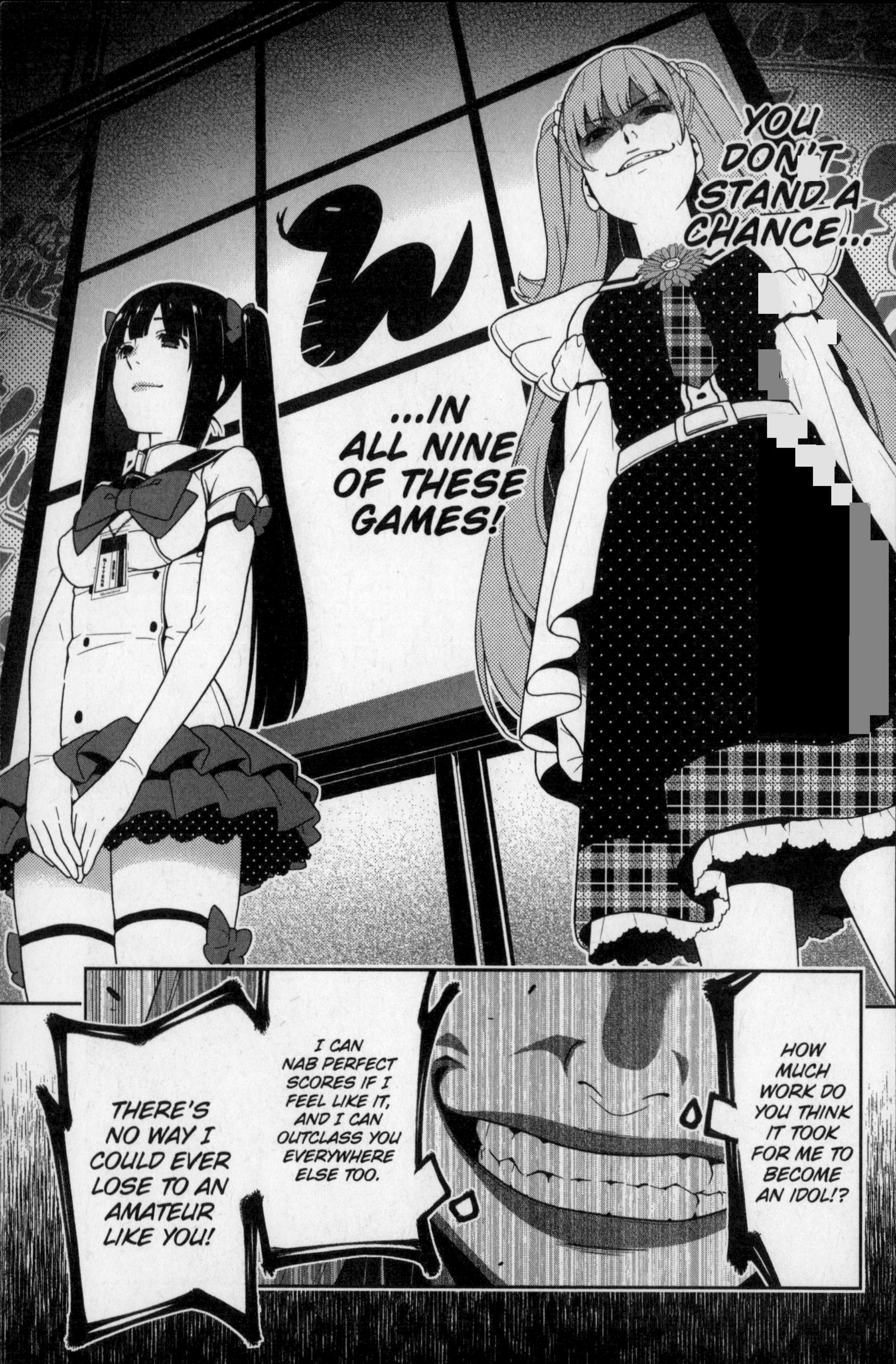
YOU DON'T STAND A CHANCE...
...IN ALL NINE OF THESE GAMES!
HOW MUCH WORK DO YOU THINK IT TOOK FOR ME TO BECOME AN IDOL!?
I CAN NAB PERFECT SCORES IF I FEEL LIKE IT, AND I CAN OUTCLASS YOU EVERYWHERE ELSE TOO.
THERE'S NO WAY I COULD EVER LOSE TO AN AMATEUR LIKE YOU!

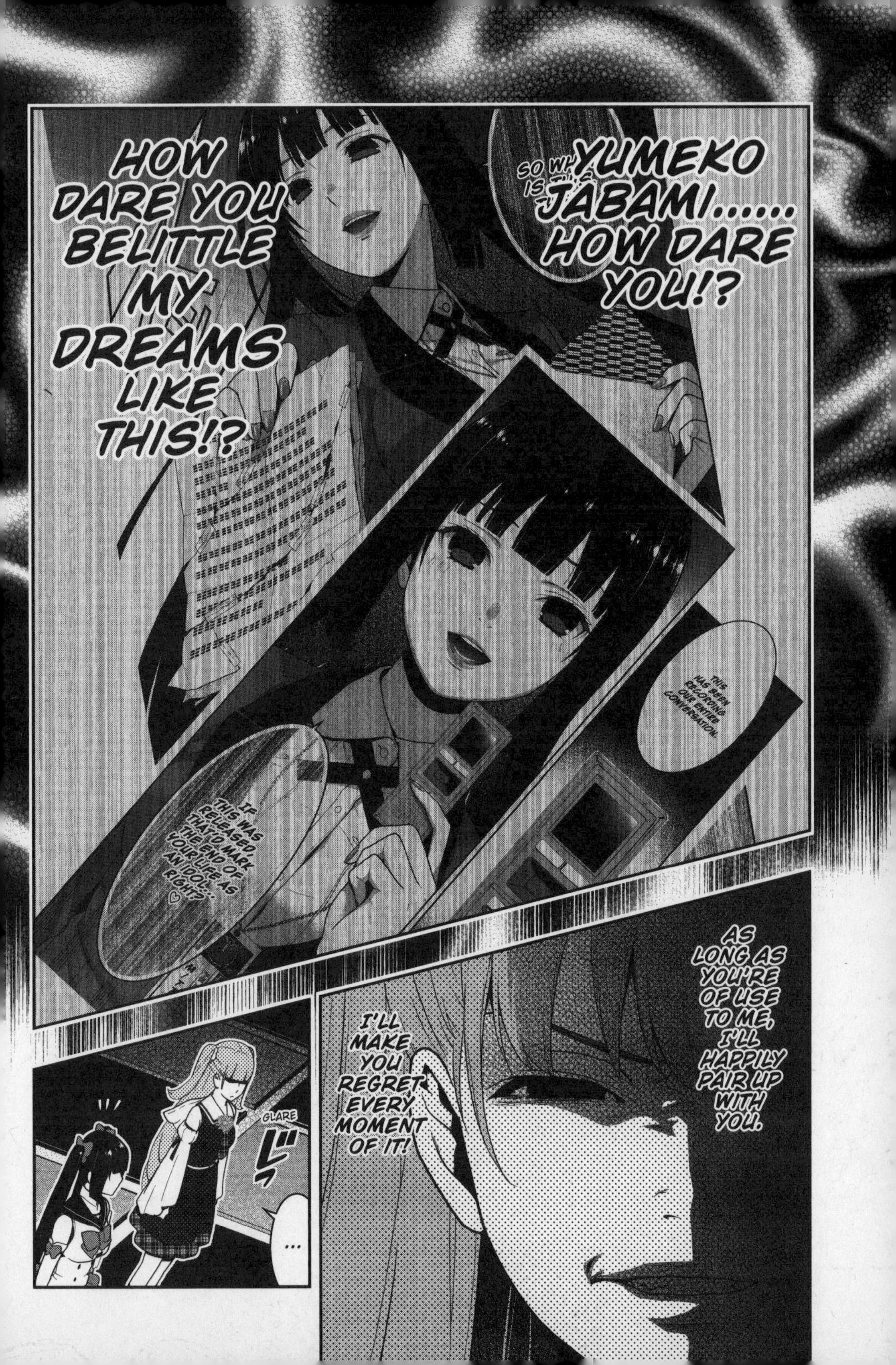
YUMEKO JABAMI...... HOW DARE YOU!?
HOW DARE YOU BELITTLE MY DREAMS LIKE THIS!?
THIS HAS BEEN RECORDING OUR ENTIRE CONVERSATION.
IF THIS WAS RELEASED, THAT'D MARK THE END OF YOUR LIFE AS AN IDOL... RIGHT? ♡
AS LONG AS YOU'RE OF USE TO ME, I'LL HAPPILY PAIR UP WITH YOU.
I'LL MAKE YOU REGRET EVERY MOMENT OF IT!
GLARE
ジッ
...

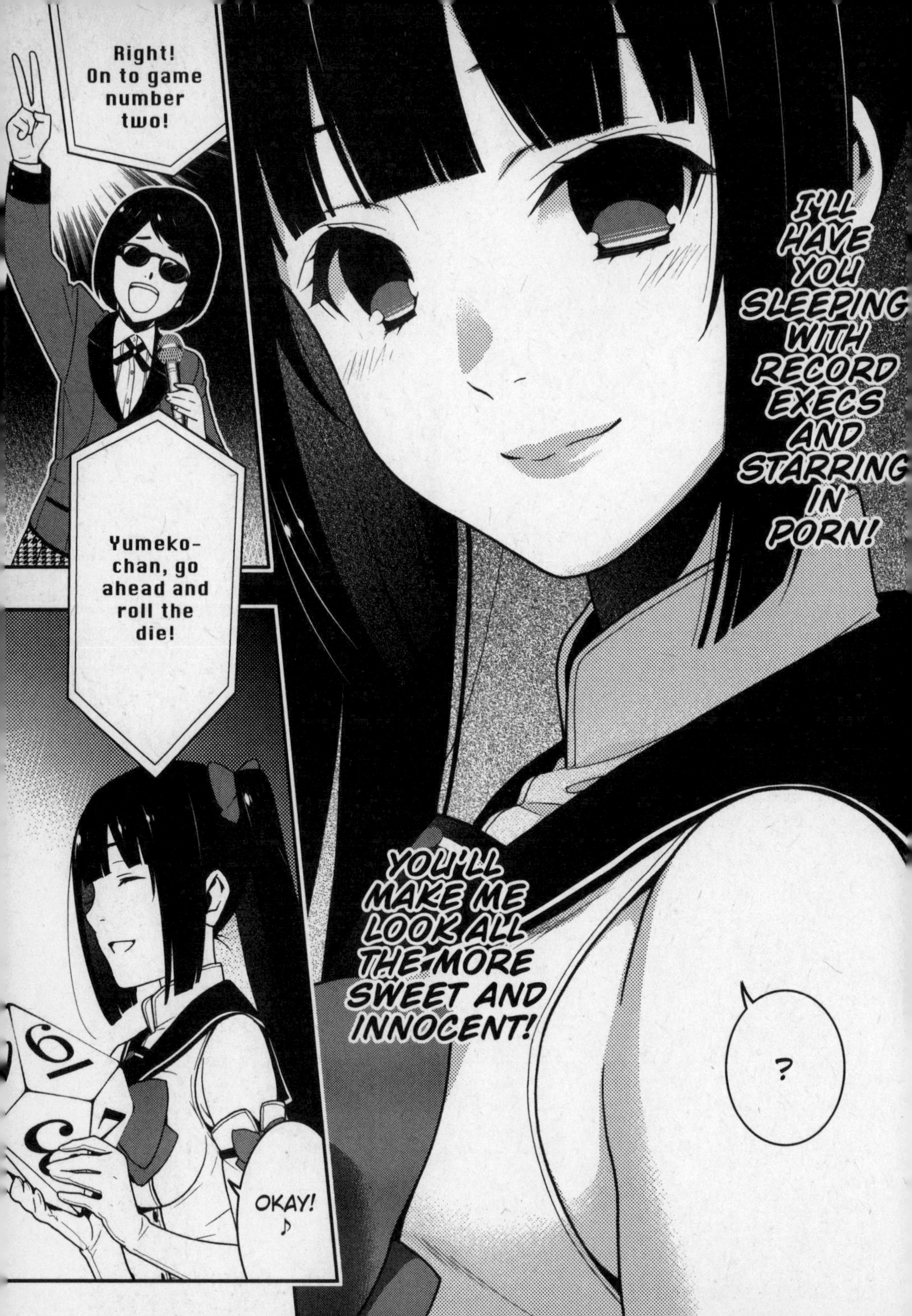

I'LL HAVE YOU SLEEPING WITH RECORD EXECS AND STARRING IN PORN!
YOU'LL MAKE ME LOOK ALL THE MORE SWEET AND INNOCENT!
?
Right! On to game number two!
Yumeko-chan, go ahead and roll the die!
OKAY! ♪

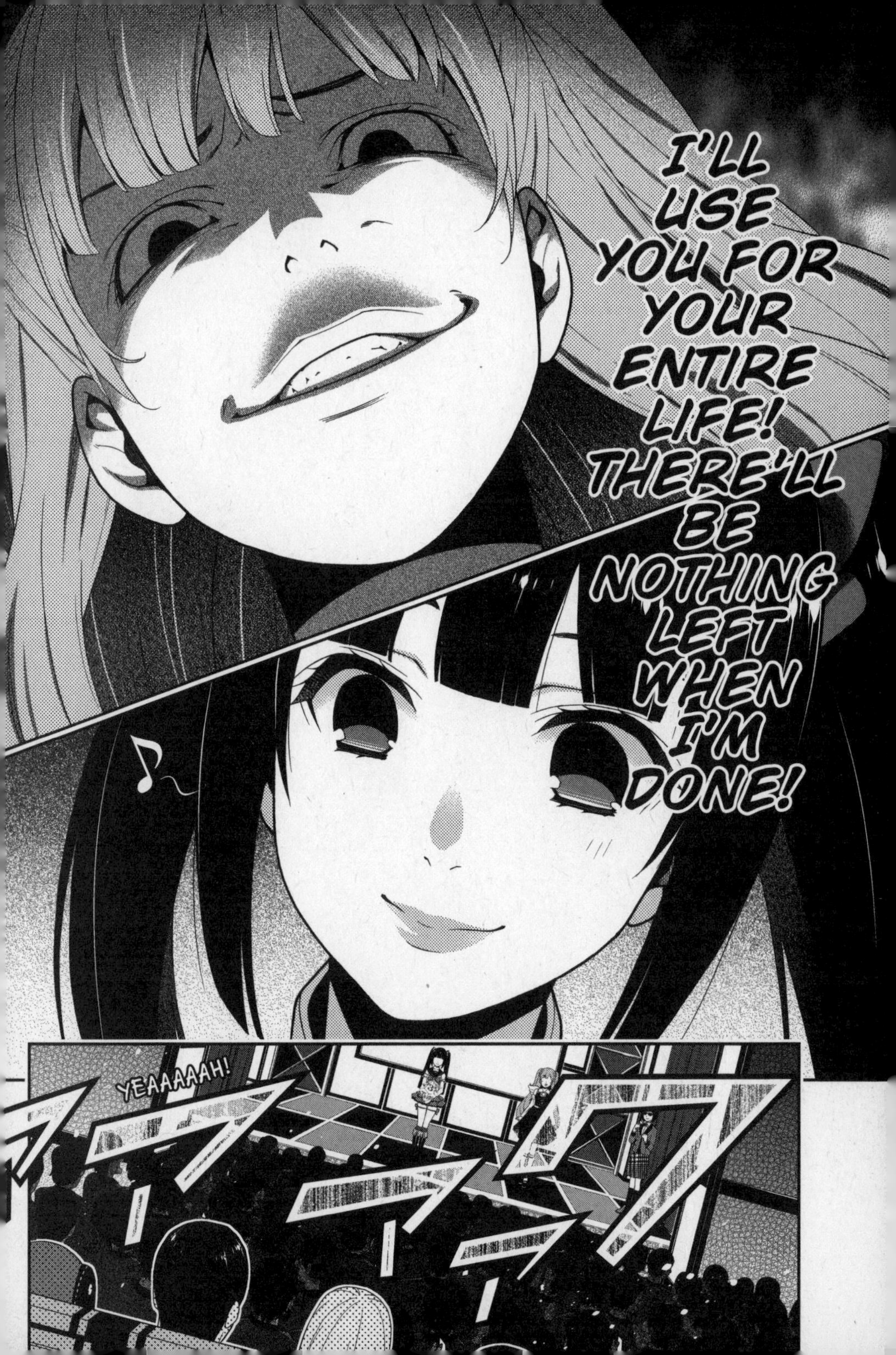
I'LL USE YOU FOR YOUR ENTIRE LIFE! THERE'LL BE NOTHING LEFT WHEN I'M DONE!
YEAAAAAH!

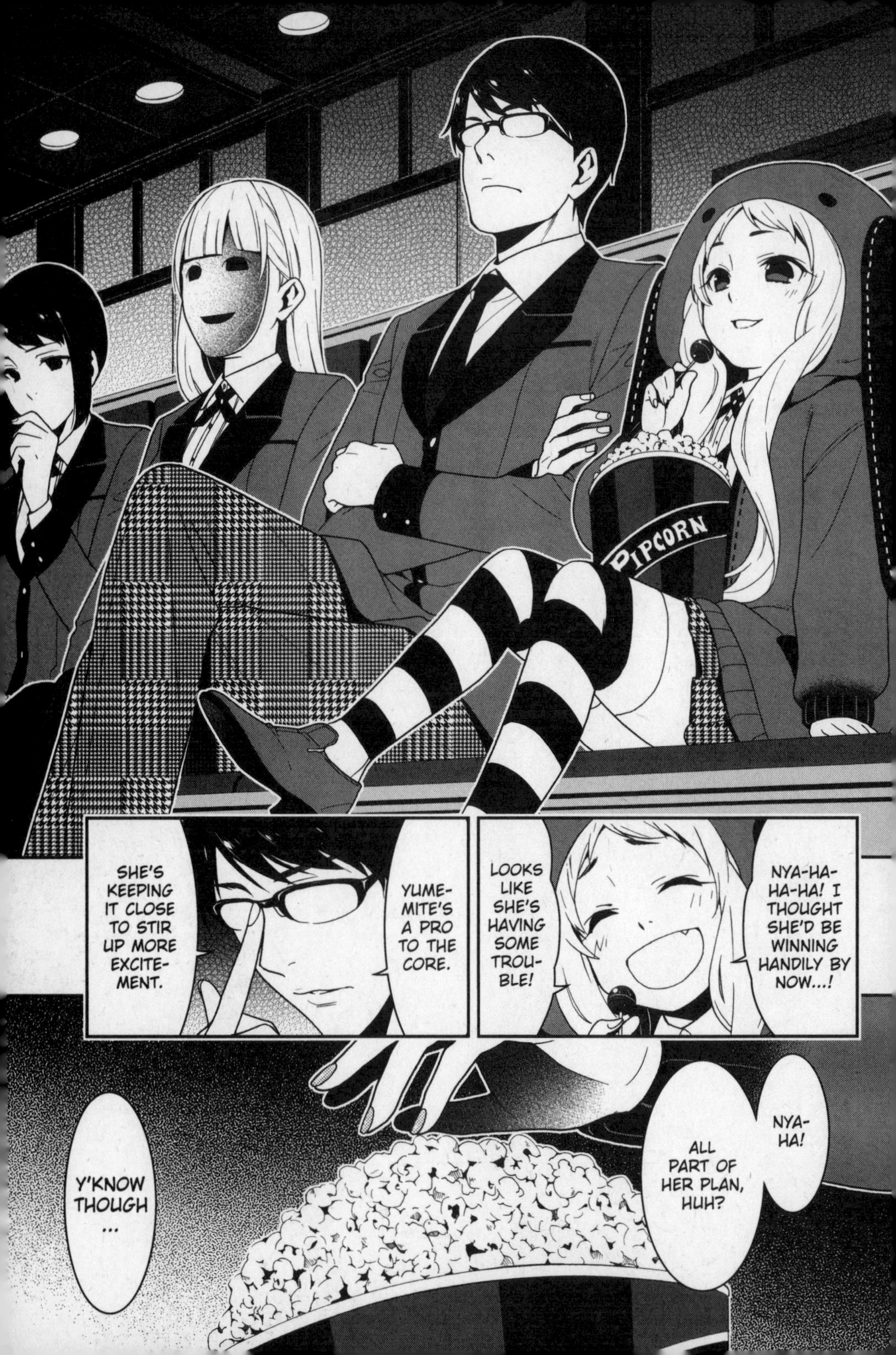
PIPCORN
NYA-HA-HA-HA! I THOUGHT SHE'D BE WINNING HANDILY BY NOW...!
LOOKS LIKE SHE'S HAVING SOME TROUBLE!
YUME-MITE'S A PRO TO THE CORE.
SHE'S KEEPING IT CLOSE TO STIR UP MORE EXCITE-MENT.
NYA-HA!
ALL PART OF HER PLAN, HUH?
Y'KNOW THOUGH...

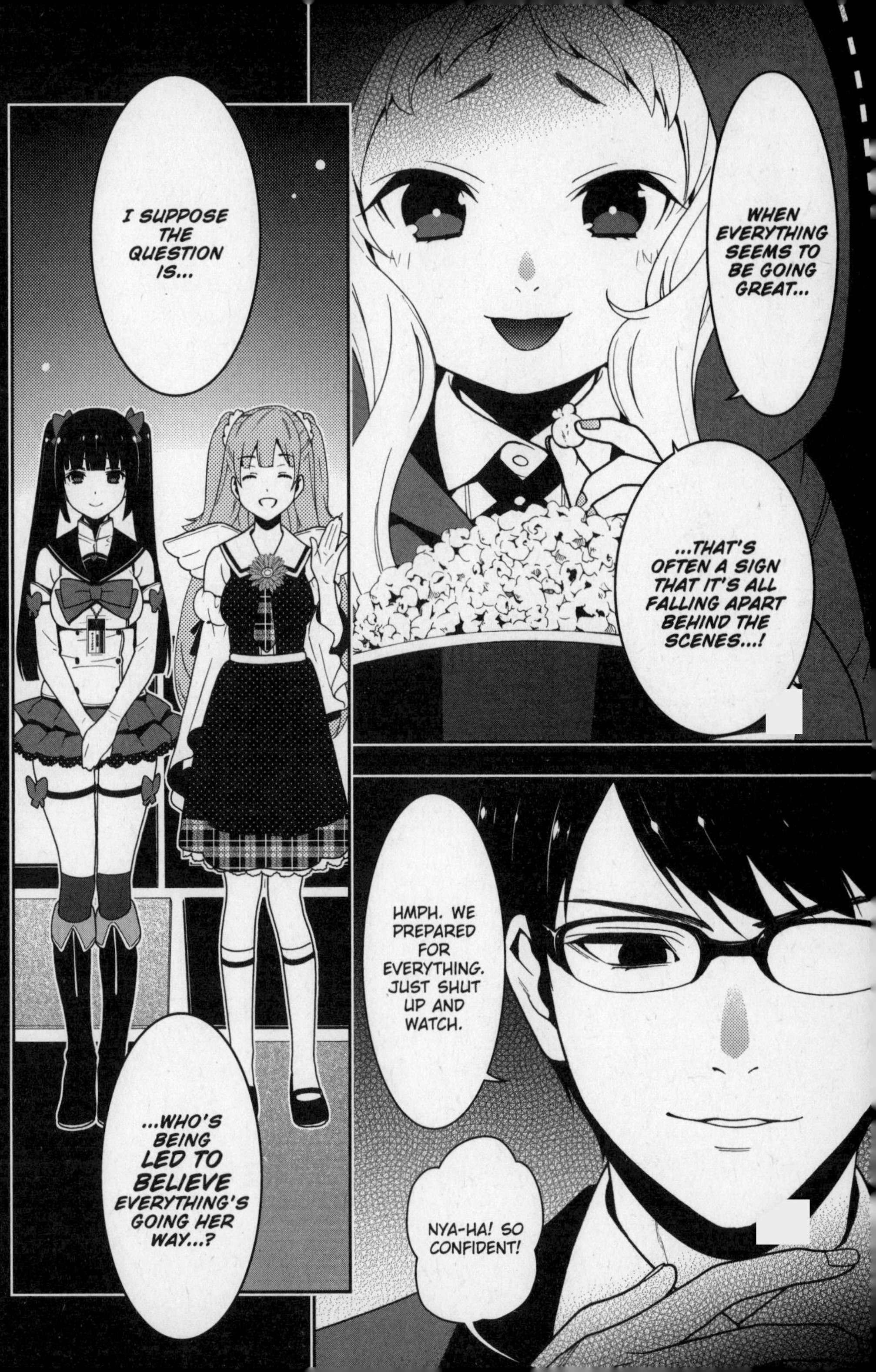
WHEN EVERYTHING SEEMS TO BE GOING GREAT...
...THAT'S OFTEN A SIGN THAT IT'S ALL FALLING APART BEHIND THE SCENES...!
HMPH. WE PREPARED FOR EVERYTHING. JUST SHUT UP AND WATCH.
NYA-HA! SO CONFIDENT!
I SUPPOSE THE QUESTION IS...
...WHO'S BEING **LED TO BELIEVE** EVERYTHING'S GOING HER WAY...?

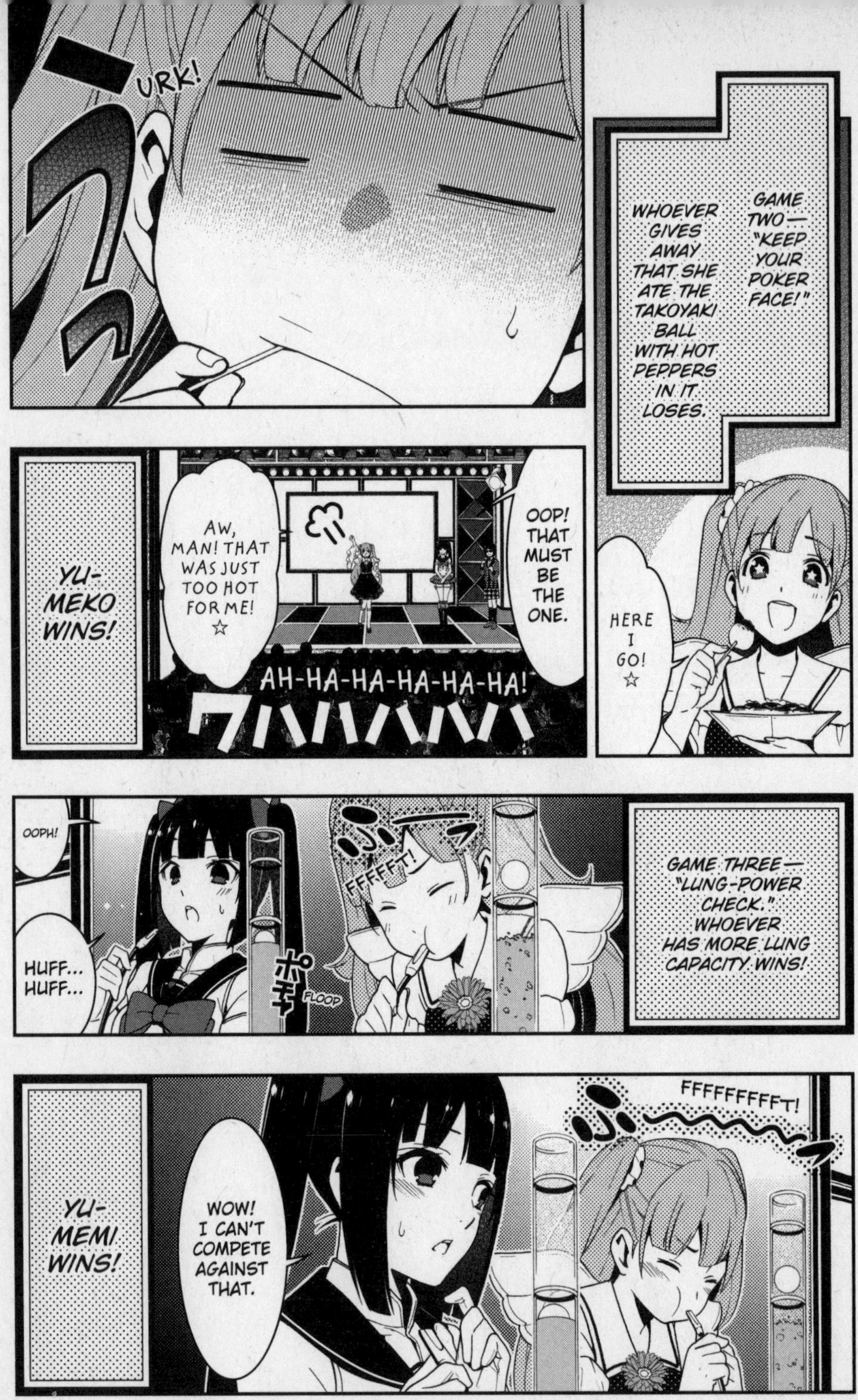
GAME TWO— "KEEP YOUR POKER FACE!"
WHOEVER GIVES AWAY THAT SHE ATE THE TAKOYAKI BALL WITH HOT PEPPERS IN IT LOSES.
HERE I GO! ☆
URK!
OOP! THAT MUST BE THE ONE.
AW, MAN! THAT WAS JUST TOO HOT FOR ME! ☆
AH-HA-HA-HA-HA-HA!
YU-MEKO WINS!
GAME THREE— "LUNG-POWER CHECK." WHOEVER HAS MORE LUNG CAPACITY WINS!
FFFFFFT!
FLOOP
OOPH!
HUFF... HUFF...
FFFFFFFFFT!
WOW! I CAN'T COMPETE AGAINST THAT.
YU-MEMI WINS!

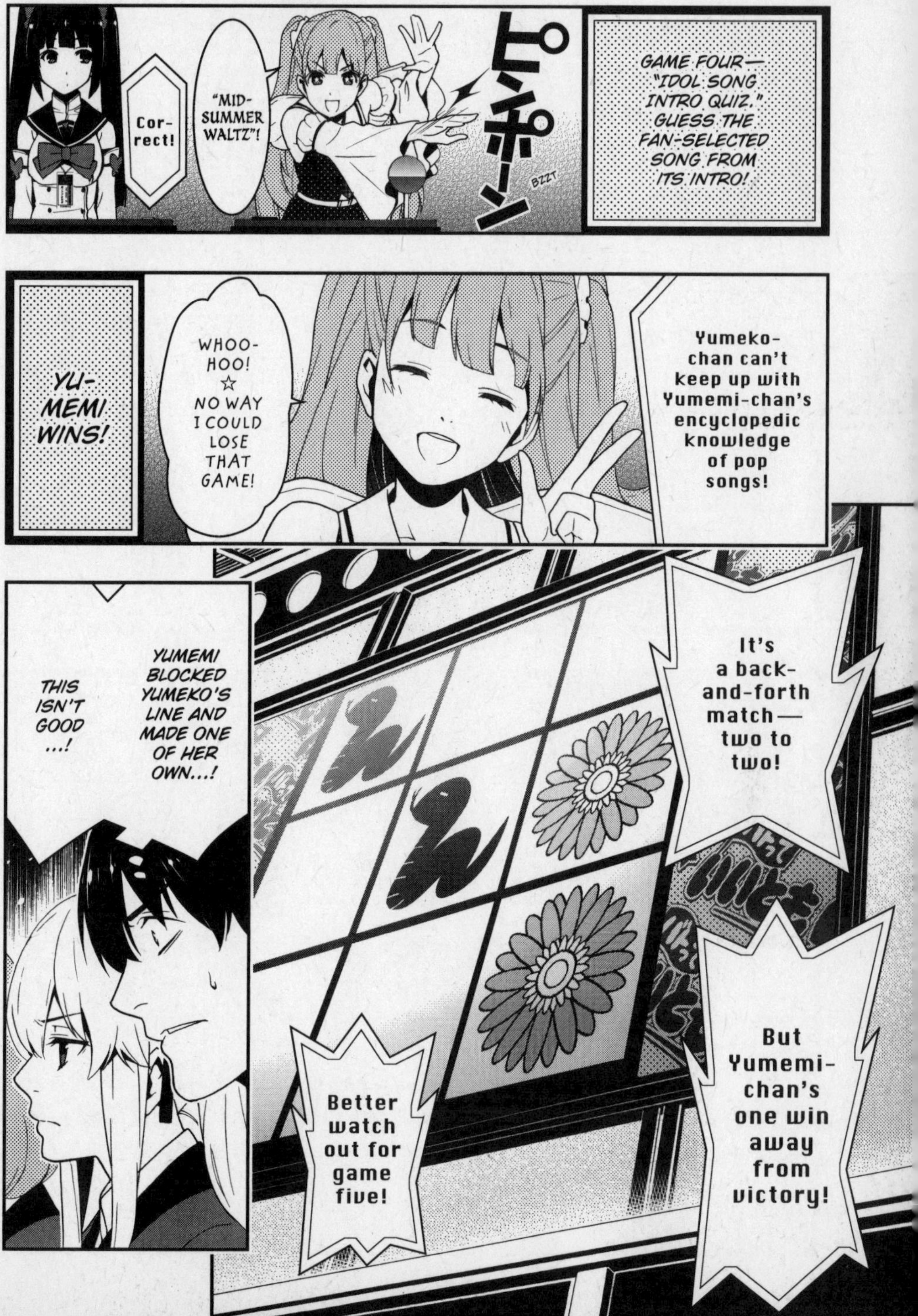
GAME FOUR—"IDOL SONG INTRO QUIZ." GUESS THE FAN-SELECTED SONG FROM ITS INTRO!
ピンポーン
BZZT
"MID-SUMMER WALTZ"!
Cor-rect!
Yumeko-chan can't keep up with Yumemi-chan's encyclopedic knowledge of pop songs!
WHOO-HOO! ☆ NO WAY I COULD LOSE THAT GAME!
YU-MEMI WINS!
It's a back-and-forth match—two to two!
But Yumemi-chan's one win away from victory!
Better watch out for game five!
YUMEMI BLOCKED YUMEKO'S LINE AND MADE ONE OF HER OWN...!
THIS ISN'T GOOD ...!

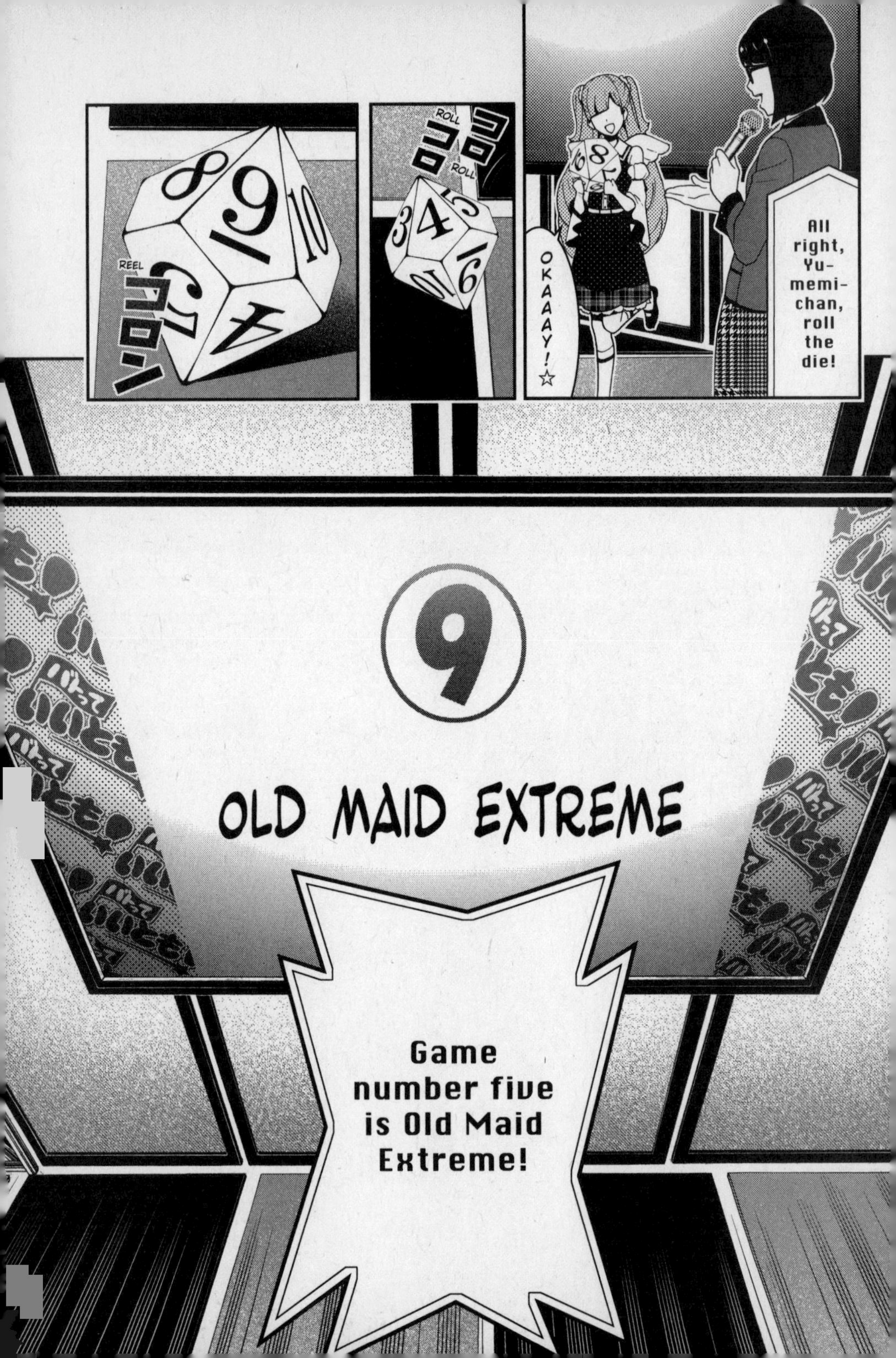
All right, Yumemi-chan, roll the die!
OKAAAAY!☆
ROLL
ROLL
REEL
9
OLD MAID EXTREME
Game number five is Old Maid Extreme!

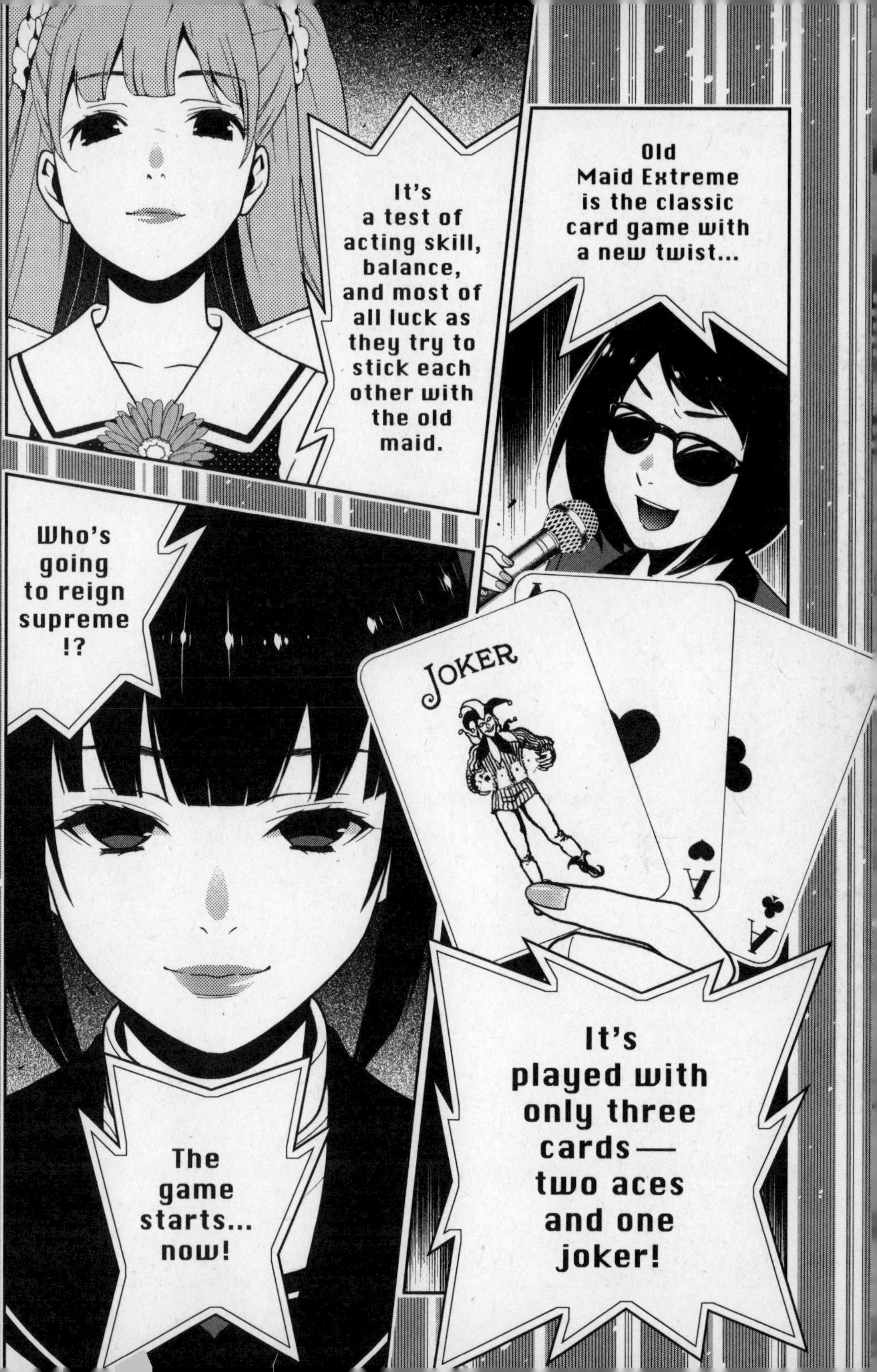
Old Maid Extreme is the classic card game with a new twist...
It's played with only three cards— two aces and one joker!
JOKER
It's a test of acting skill, balance, and most of all luck as they try to stick each other with the old maid.
Who's going to reign supreme !?
The game starts... now!

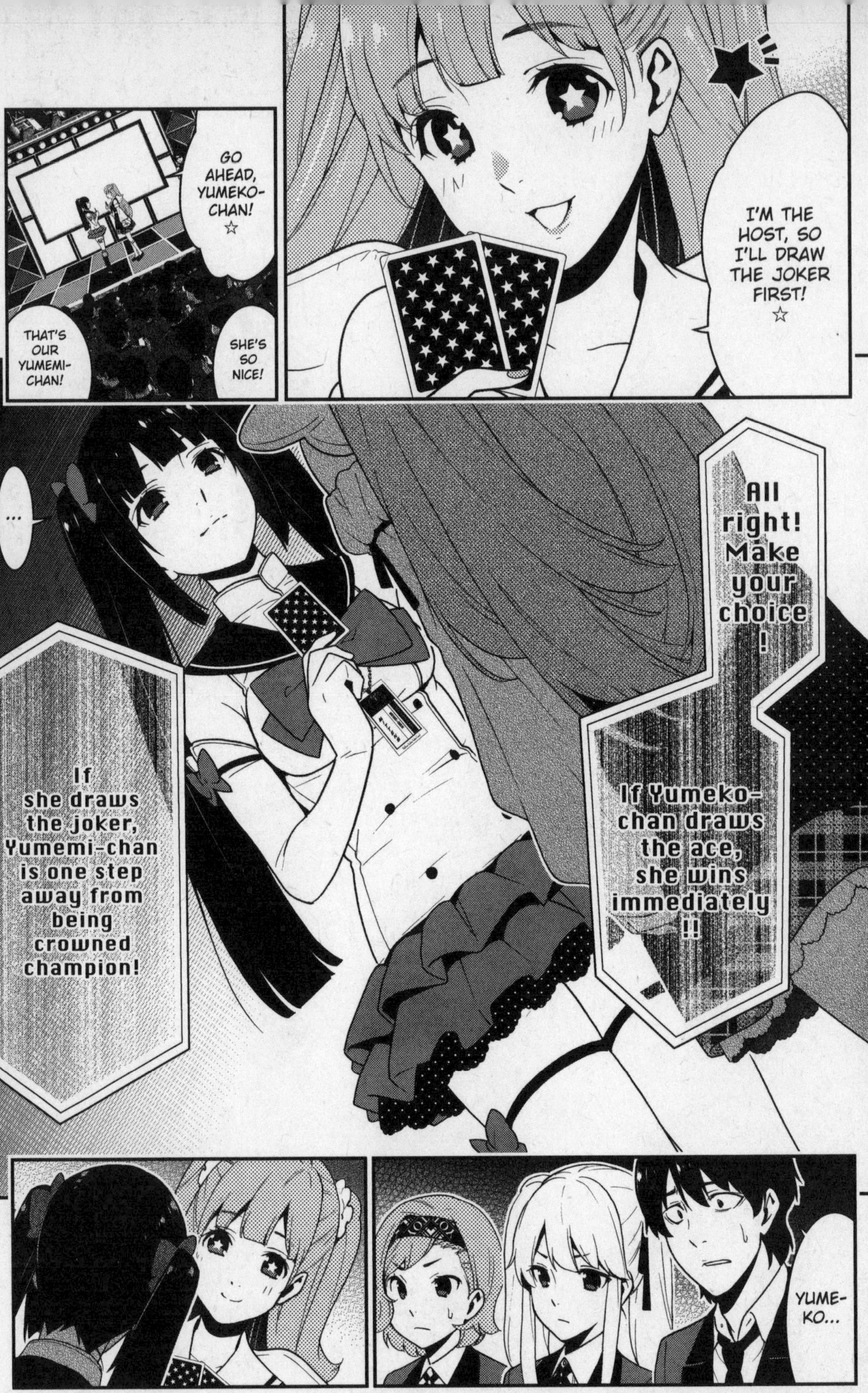
I'M THE HOST, SO I'LL DRAW THE JOKER FIRST! ☆
GO AHEAD, YUMEKO-CHAN! ☆
SHE'S SO NICE!
THAT'S OUR YUMEMI-CHAN!
All right! Make your choice!
If Yumeko-chan draws the ace, she wins immediately!!
If she draws the joker, Yumemi-chan is one step away from being crowned champion!
...
YUME-KO...

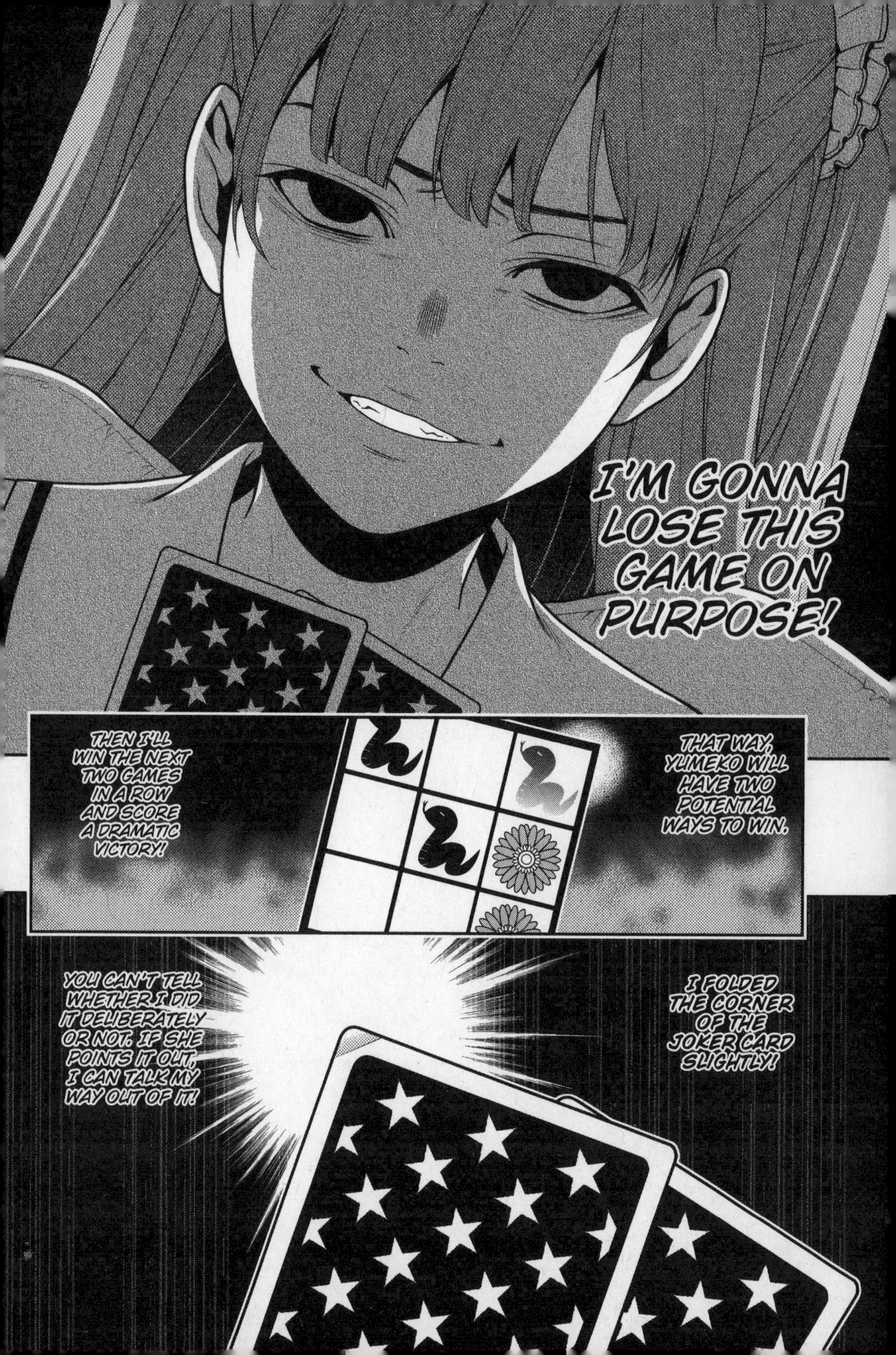
I'M GONNA LOSE THIS GAME ON PURPOSE!
THAT WAY, YUMEKO WILL HAVE TWO POTENTIAL WAYS TO WIN.
THEN I'LL WIN THE NEXT TWO GAMES IN A ROW AND SCORE A DRAMATIC VICTORY!
I FOLDED THE CORNER OF THE JOKER CARD SLIGHTLY!
YOU CAN'T TELL WHETHER I DID IT DELIBERATELY OR NOT. IF SHE POINTS IT OUT, I CAN TALK MY WAY OUT OF IT!

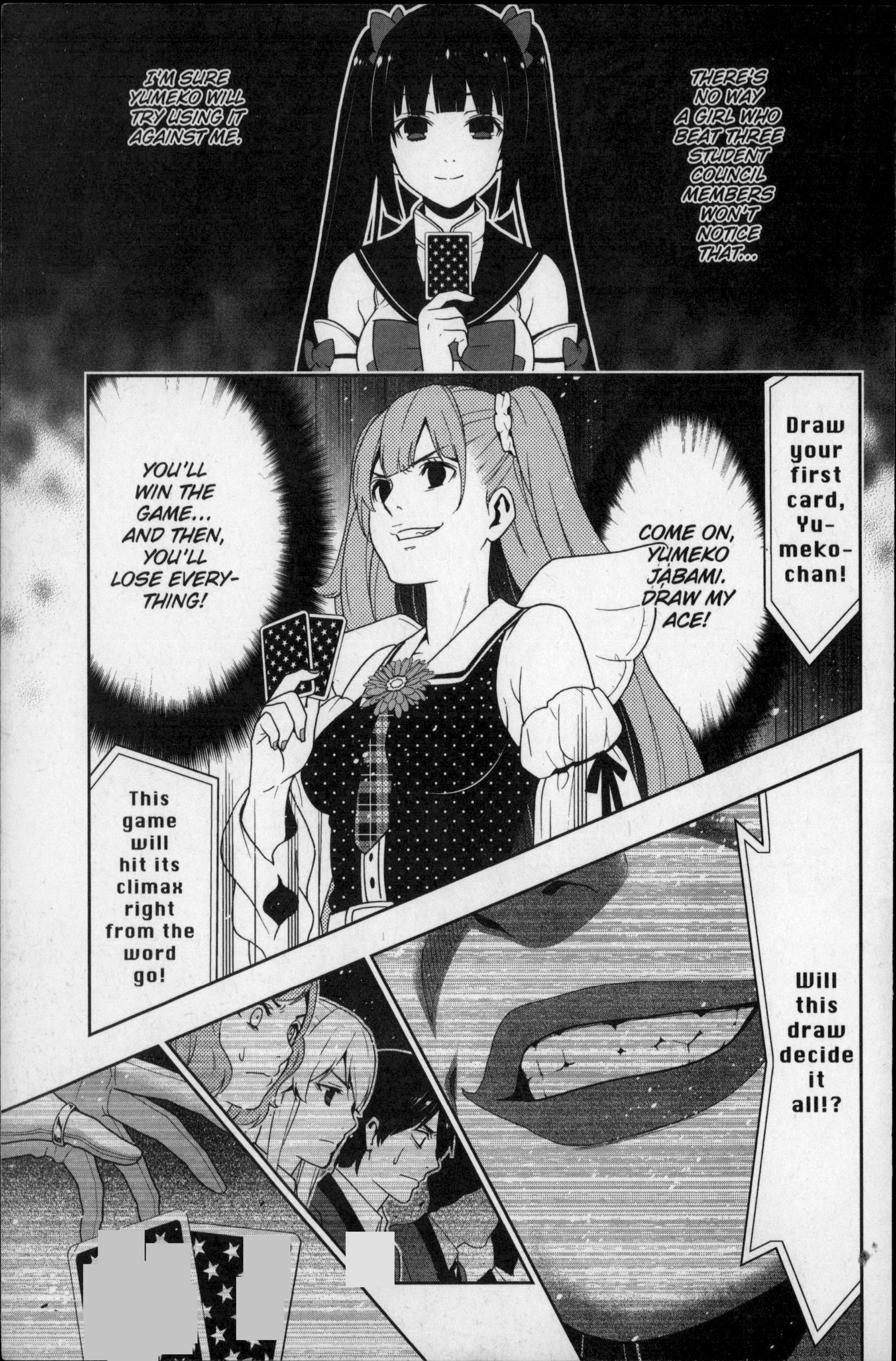
THERE'S NO WAY A GIRL WHO BEAT THREE STUDENT COUNCIL MEMBERS WON'T NOTICE THAT...
I'M SURE YUMEKO WILL TRY USING IT AGAINST ME.
Draw your first card, Yumeko-chan!
COME ON, YUMEKO JABAMI. DRAW MY ACE!
YOU'LL WIN THE GAME... AND THEN, YOU'LL LOSE EVERYTHING!
This game will hit its climax right from the word go!
Will this draw decide it all!?

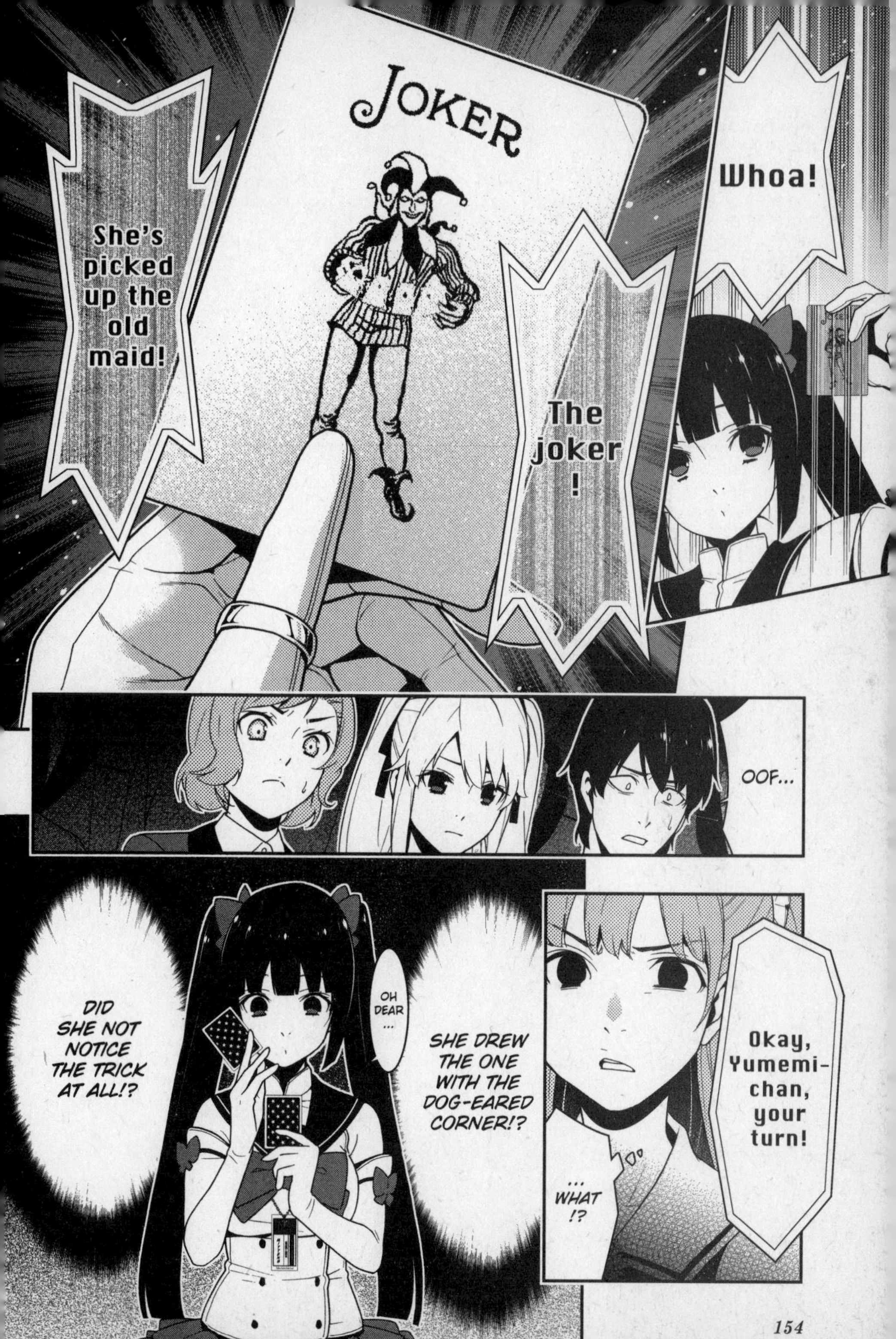
Whoa!
The joker!
JOKER
She's picked up the old maid!
OOF...
Okay, Yumemi-chan, your turn!
...WHAT!?
SHE DREW THE ONE WITH THE DOG-EARED CORNER!?
OH DEAR...
DID SHE NOT NOTICE THE TRICK AT ALL!?

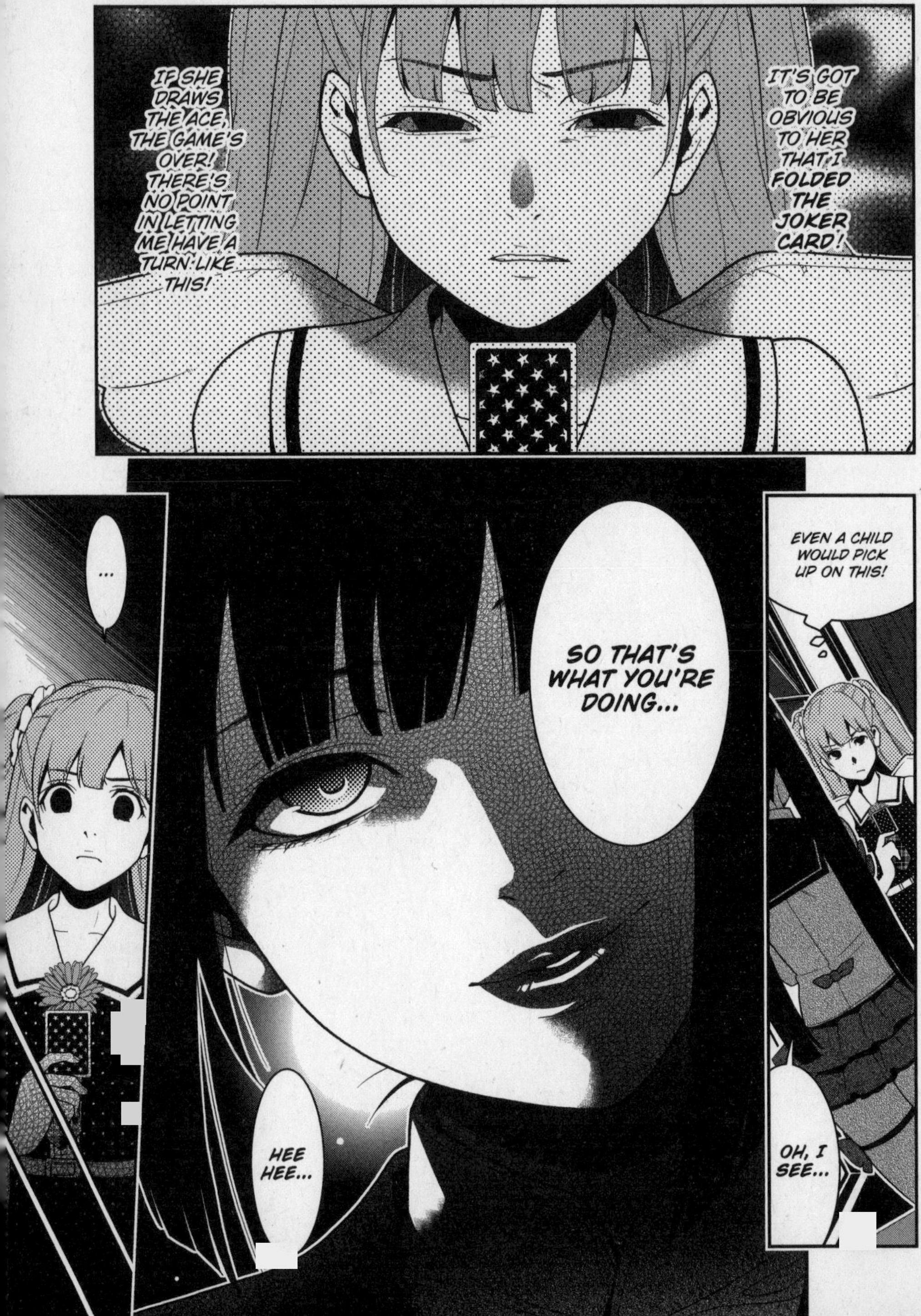
IT'S GOT TO BE OBVIOUS TO HER THAT I FOLDED THE JOKER CARD!
IF SHE DRAWS THE ACE, THE GAME'S OVER! THERE'S NO POINT IN LETTING ME HAVE A TURN LIKE THIS!
EVEN A CHILD WOULD PICK UP ON THIS!
OH, I SEE...
SO THAT'S WHAT YOU'RE DOING...
HEE HEE...
...

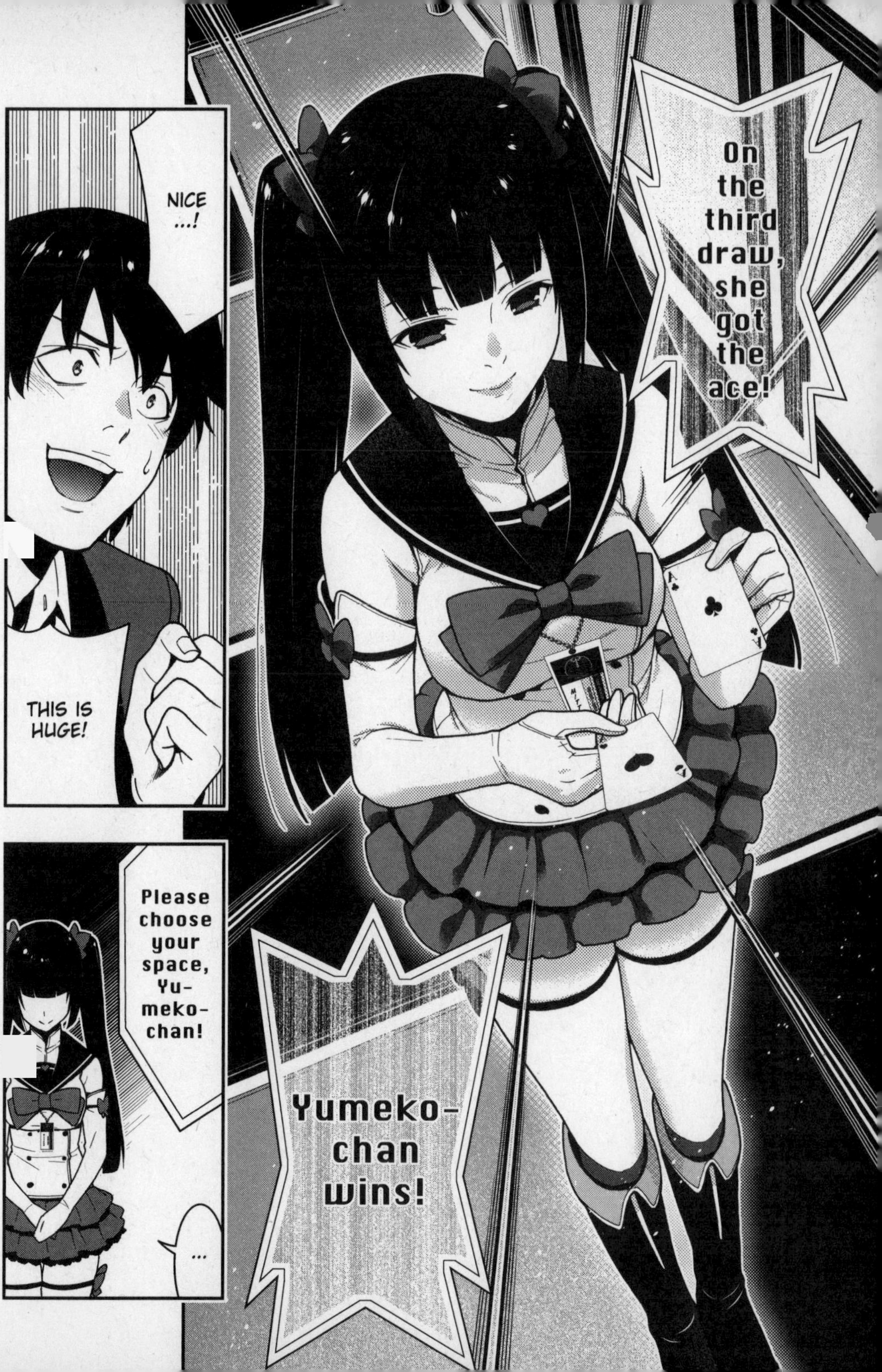
On the third draw, she got the ace!
Yumeko-chan wins!
NICE ...!
THIS IS HUGE!
Please choose your space, Yu-meko-chan!
...

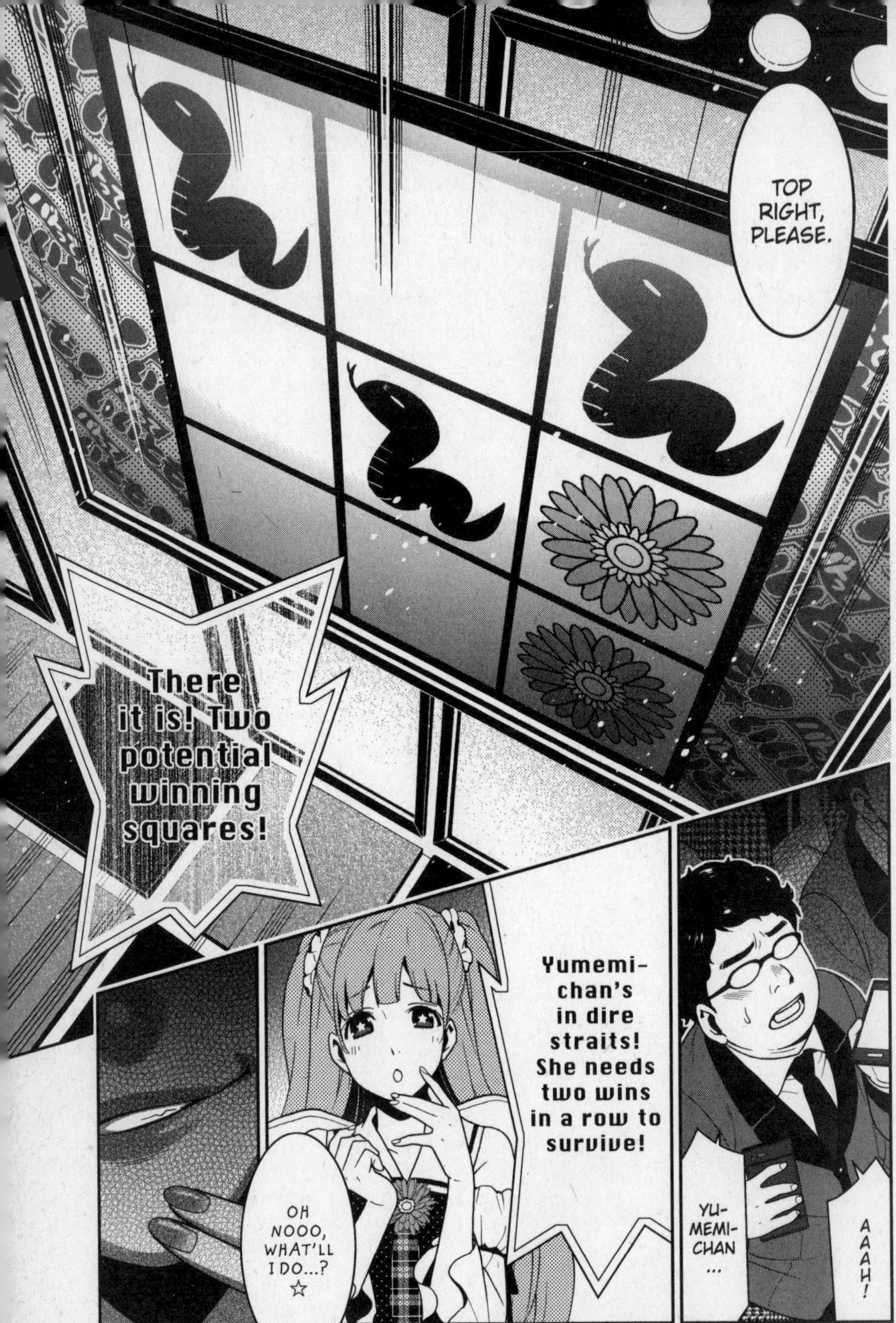
TOP RIGHT, PLEASE.
There it is! Two potential winning squares!
AAAH!
YU-MEMI-CHAN...
Yumemi-chan's in dire straits! She needs two wins in a row to survive!
OH NOOO, WHAT'LL I DO...? ☆

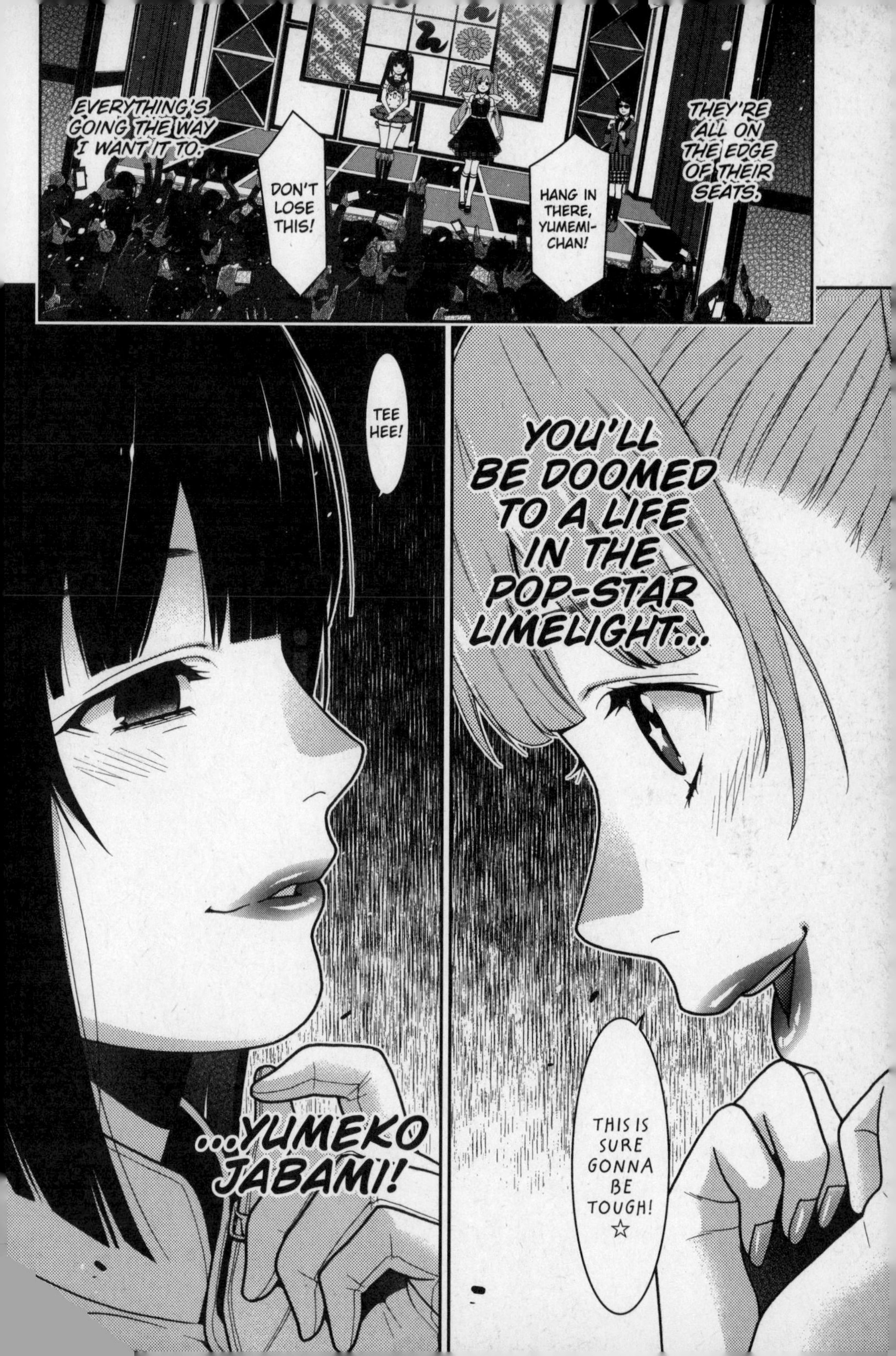
THEY'RE ALL ON THE EDGE OF THEIR SEATS.
HANG IN THERE, YUMEMI-CHAN!
DON'T LOSE THIS!
EVERYTHING'S GOING THE WAY I WANT IT TO.
YOU'LL BE DOOMED TO A LIFE IN THE POP-STAR LIMELIGHT...
THIS IS SURE GONNA BE TOUGH! ☆
TEE HEE!
...YUMEKO JABAMI!

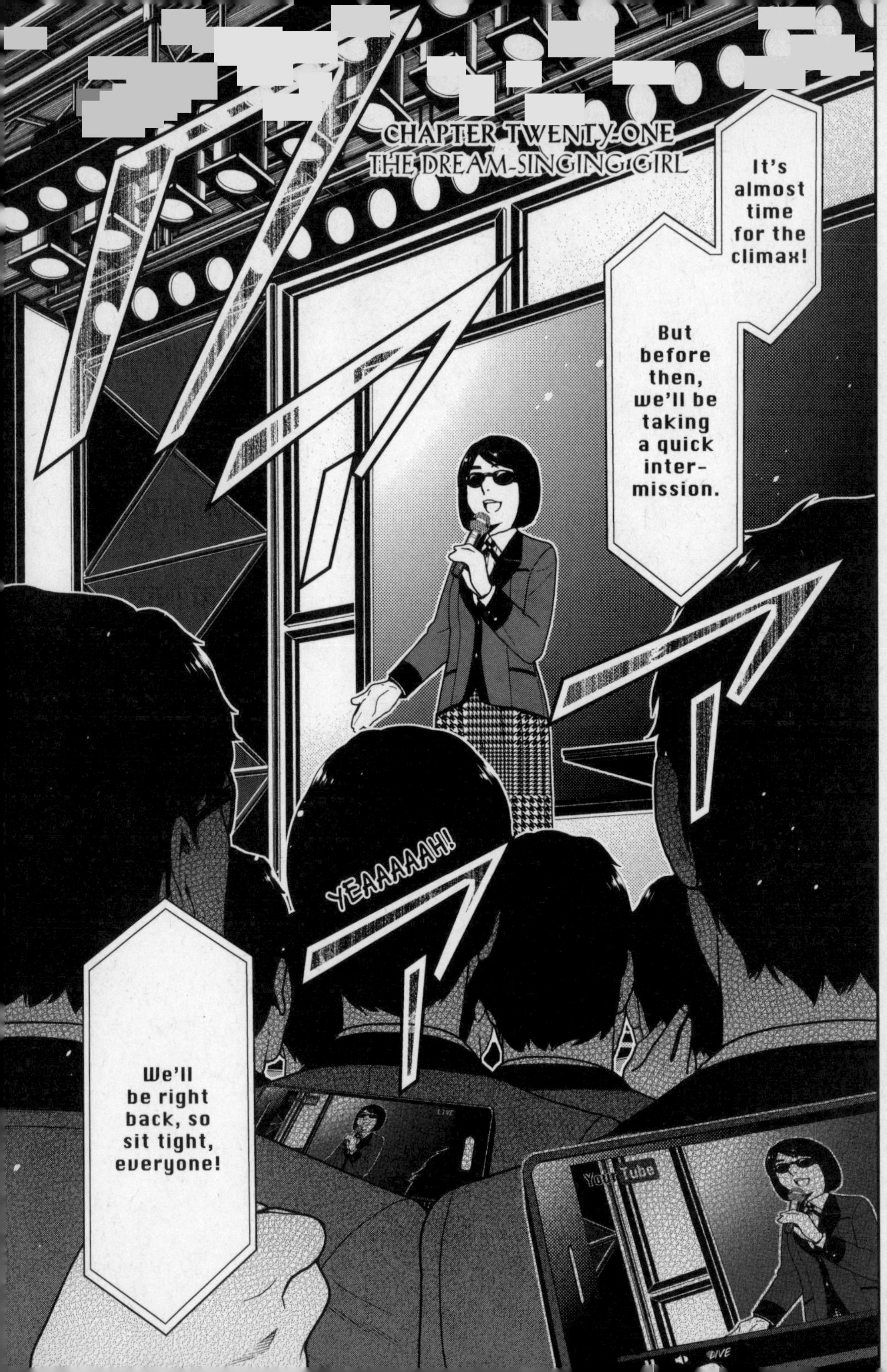
CHAPTER TWENTY-ONE
THE DREAM-SINGING GIRL
It's almost time for the climax!
But before then, we'll be taking a quick inter-mission.
YEAAAAAH!
We'll be right back, so sit tight, everyone!
LIVE
YouTube
LIVE

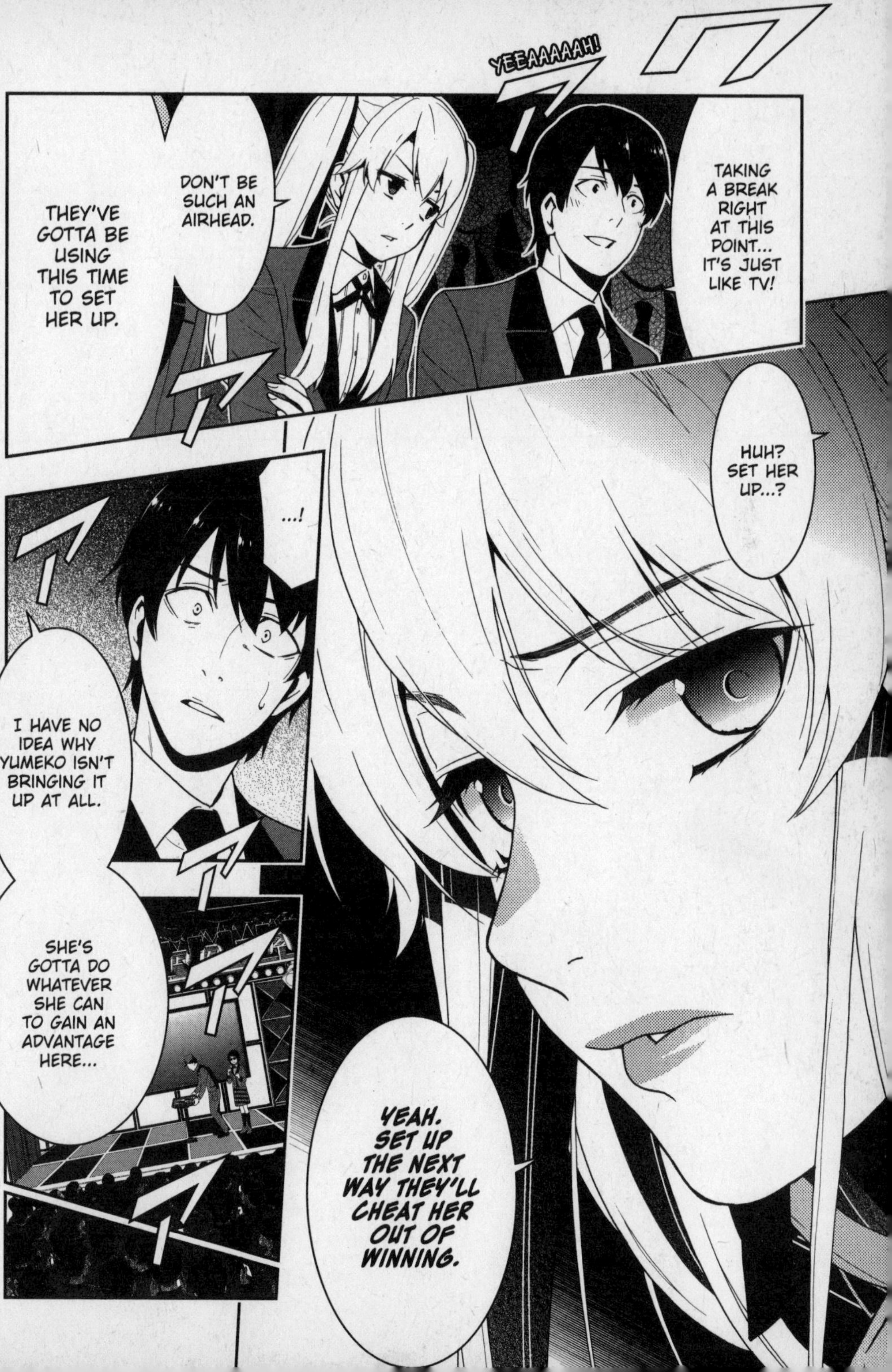
YEEAAAAAH!
TAKING A BREAK RIGHT AT THIS POINT... IT'S JUST LIKE TV!
DON'T BE SUCH AN AIRHEAD.
THEY'VE GOTTA BE USING THIS TIME TO SET HER UP.
HUH? SET HER UP...?
...!
I HAVE NO IDEA WHY YUMEKO ISN'T BRINGING IT UP AT ALL.
SHE'S GOTTA DO WHATEVER SHE CAN TO GAIN AN ADVANTAGE HERE...
YEAH. SET UP THE NEXT WAY THEY'LL CHEAT HER OUT OF WINNING.

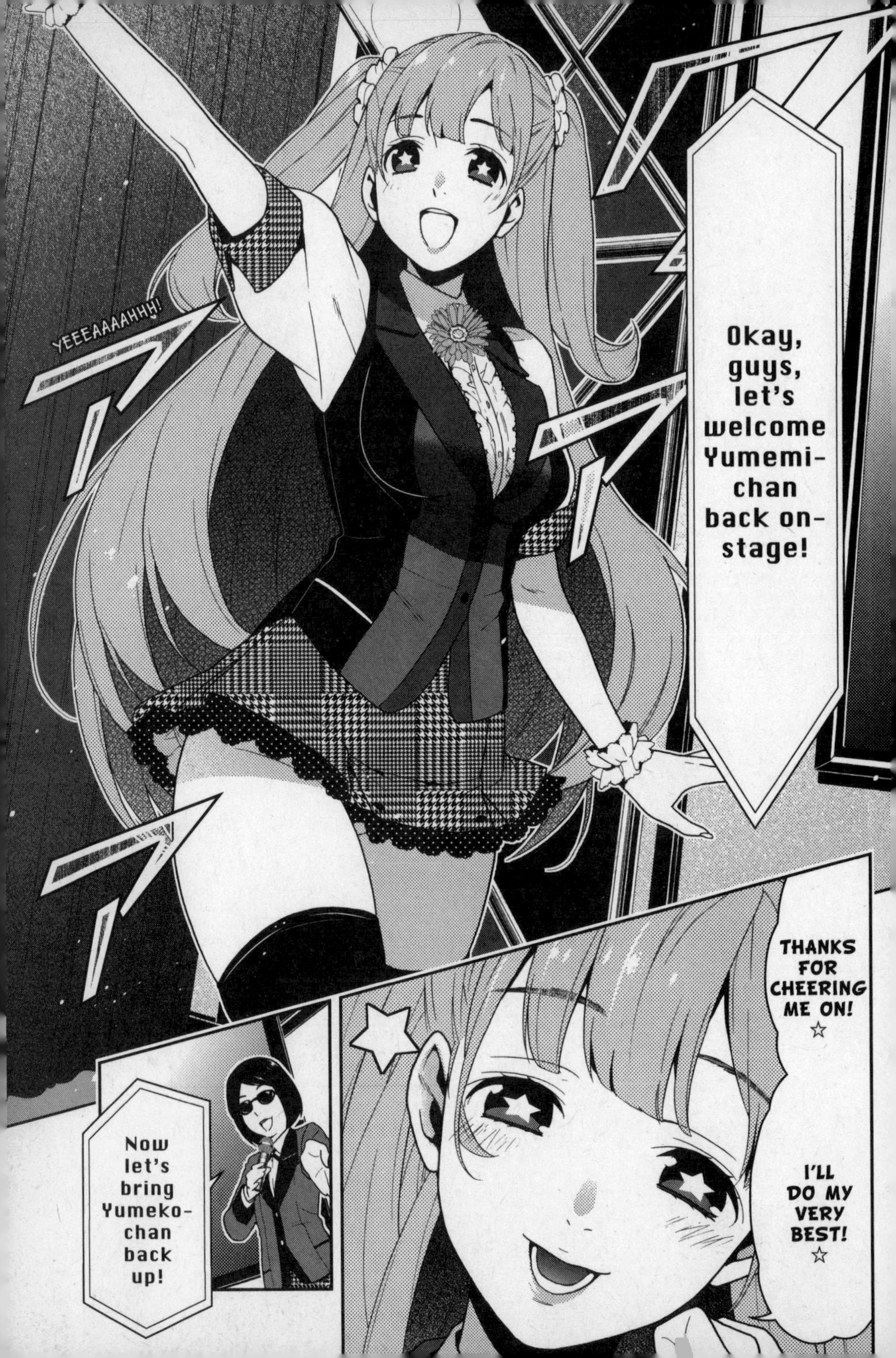
Okay, guys, let's welcome Yumemi-chan back on-stage!
YEEEAAAAHHH!
THANKS FOR CHEERING ME ON! ☆
I'LL DO MY VERY BEST! ☆
Now let's bring Yumeko-chan back up!

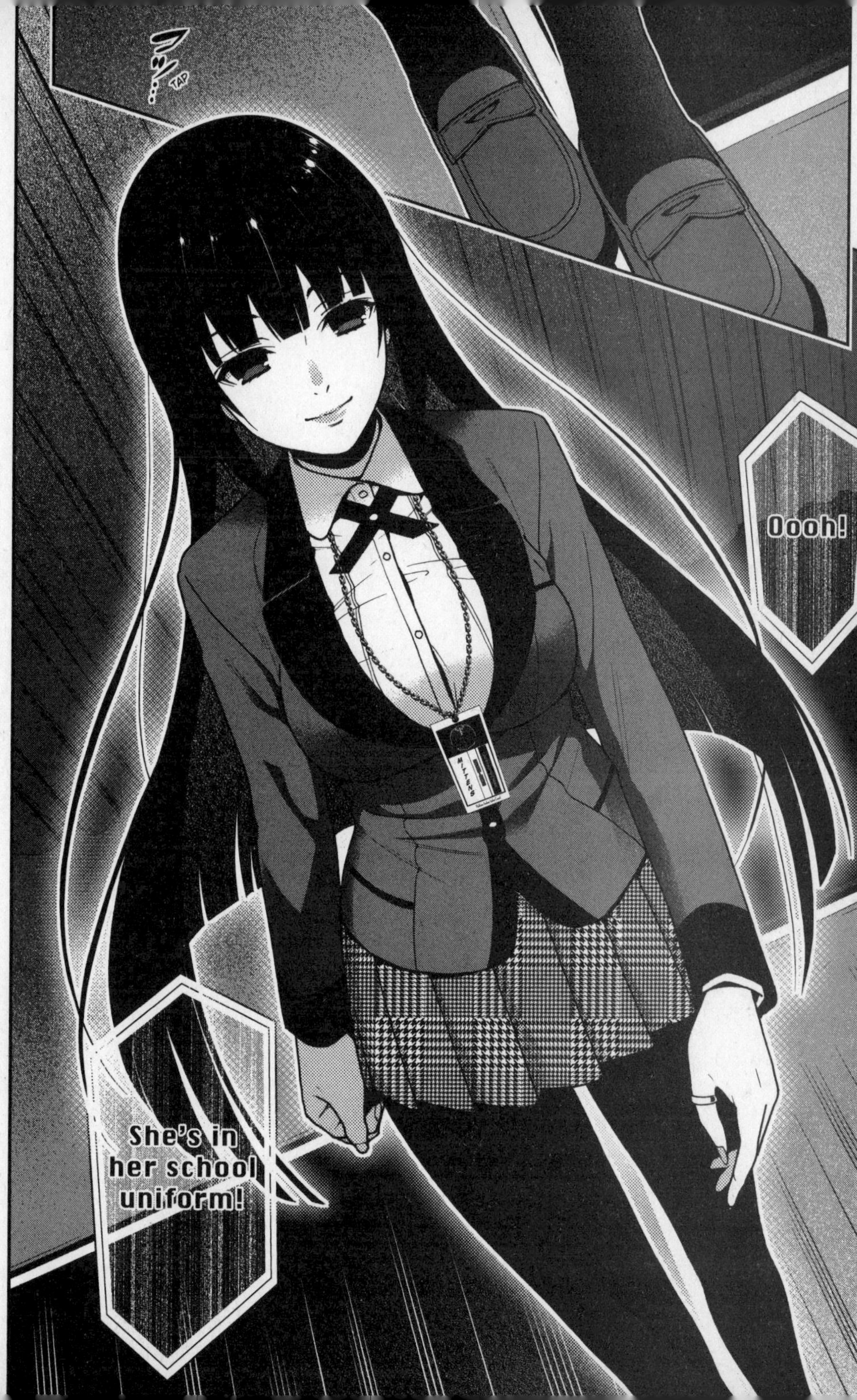
TAP
Oooh!
She's in her school uniform!

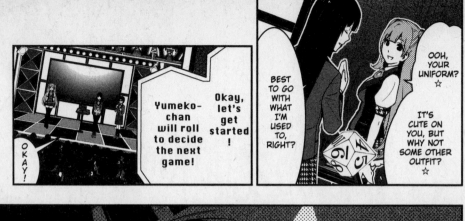

OOH, YOUR UNIFORM? ☆

IT'S CUTE ON YOU, BUT WHY NOT SOME OTHER OUTFIT? ☆

BEST TO GO WITH WHAT I'M USED TO, RIGHT?

Okay, let's get started!

Yumeko-chan will roll to decide the next game!

OKAY!

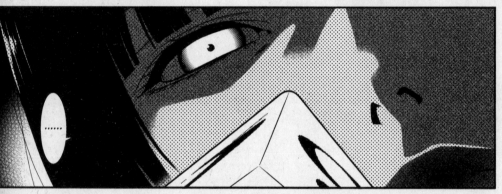

......

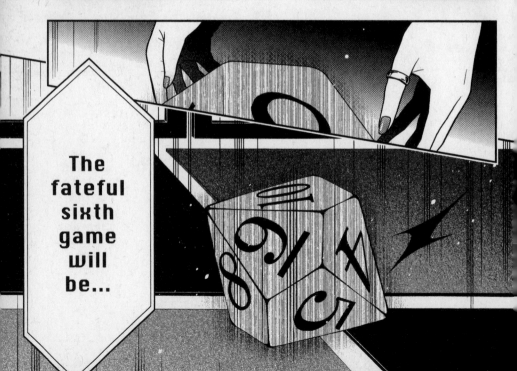

The fateful sixth game will be...

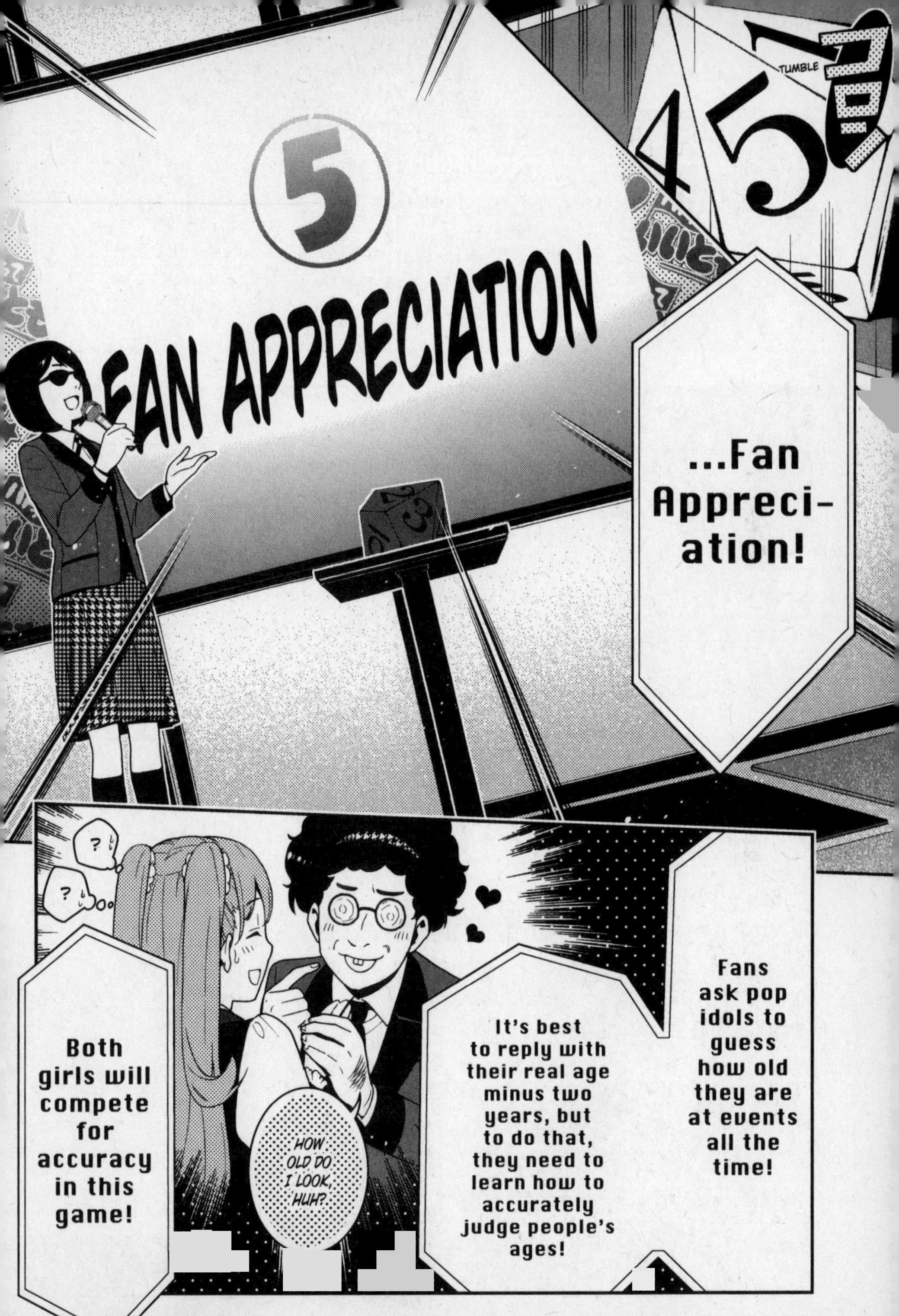
TUMBLE
5
FAN APPRECIATION
...Fan Appreci-ation!
Fans ask pop idols to guess how old they are at events all the time!
It's best to reply with their real age minus two years, but to do that, they need to learn how to accurately judge people's ages!
HOW OLD DO I LOOK, HUH?
Both girls will compete for accuracy in this game!

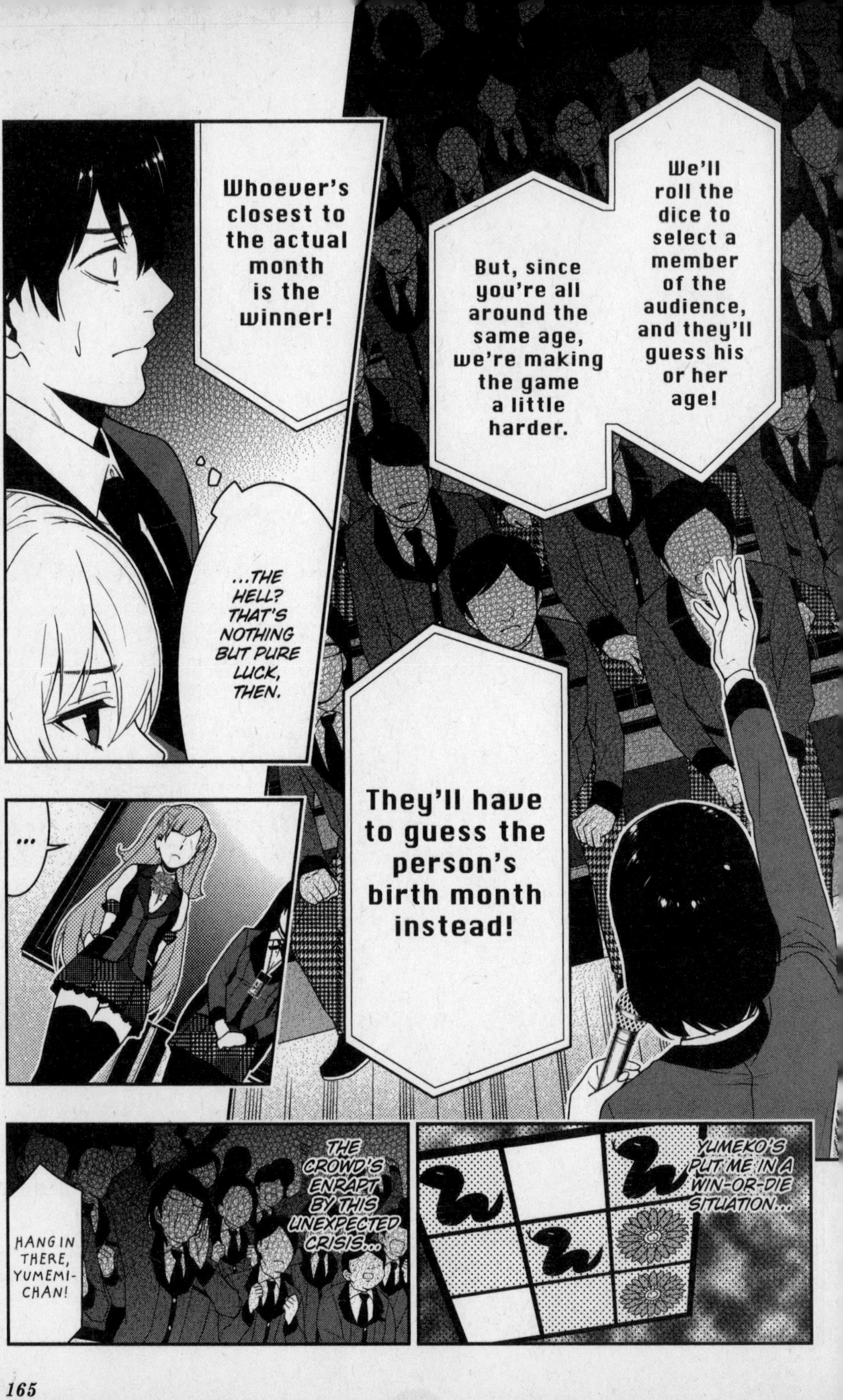
We'll roll the dice to select a member of the audience, and they'll guess his or her age!
But, since you're all around the same age, we're making the game a little harder.
They'll have to guess the person's birth month instead!
Whoever's closest to the actual month is the winner!
...THE HELL? THAT'S NOTHING BUT PURE LUCK, THEN.
...
YUMEKO'S PUT ME IN A WIN-OR-DIE SITUATION...
THE CROWD'S ENRAPT BY THIS UNEXPECTED CRISIS...
HANG IN THERE, YUMEMI-CHAN!

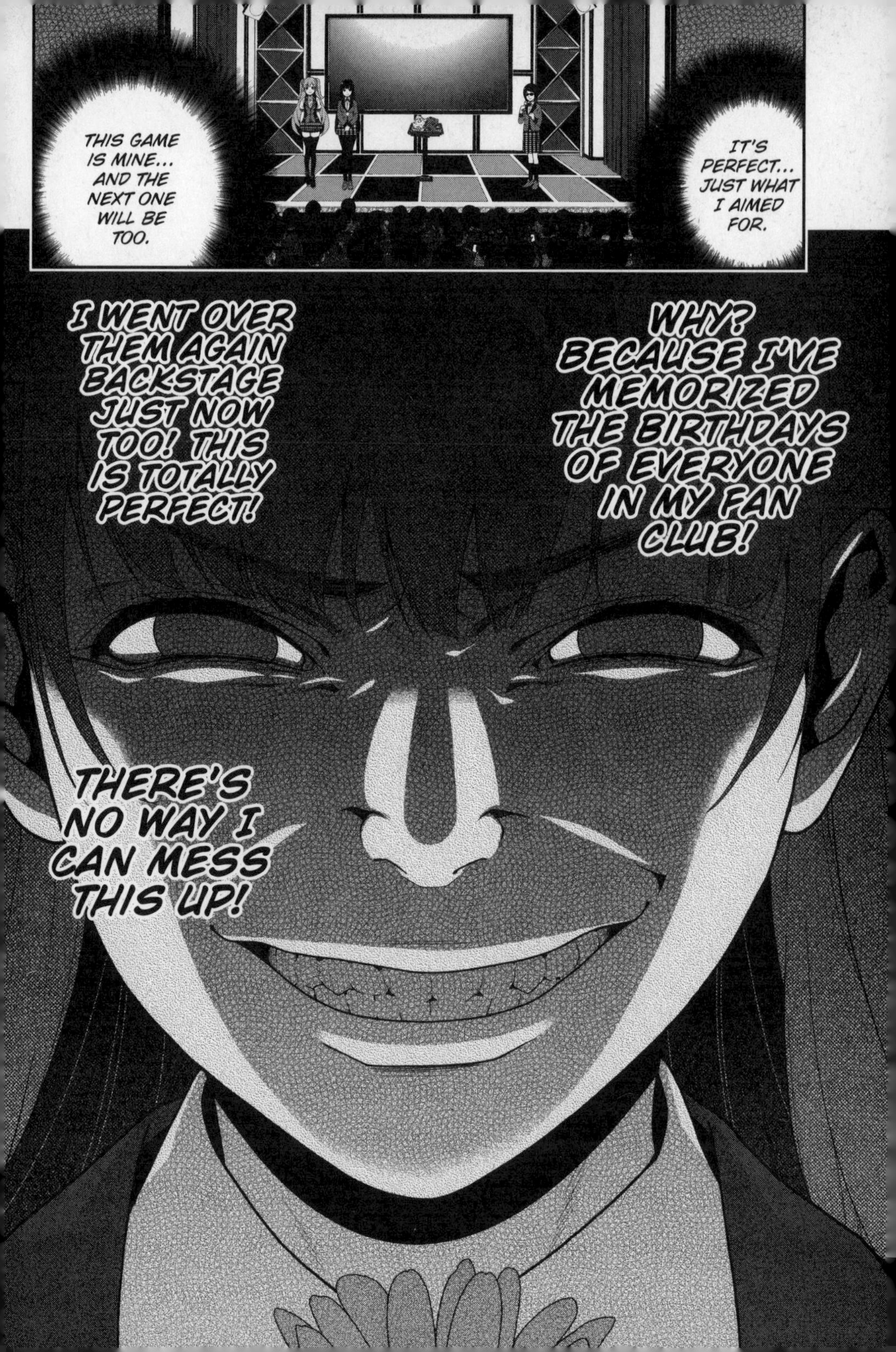
IT'S PERFECT... JUST WHAT I AIMED FOR.
THIS GAME IS MINE... AND THE NEXT ONE WILL BE TOO.
WHY? BECAUSE I'VE MEMORIZED THE BIRTHDAYS OF EVERYONE IN MY FAN CLUB!
I WENT OVER THEM AGAIN BACKSTAGE JUST NOW TOO! THIS IS TOTALLY PERFECT!
THERE'S NO WAY I CAN MESS THIS UP!

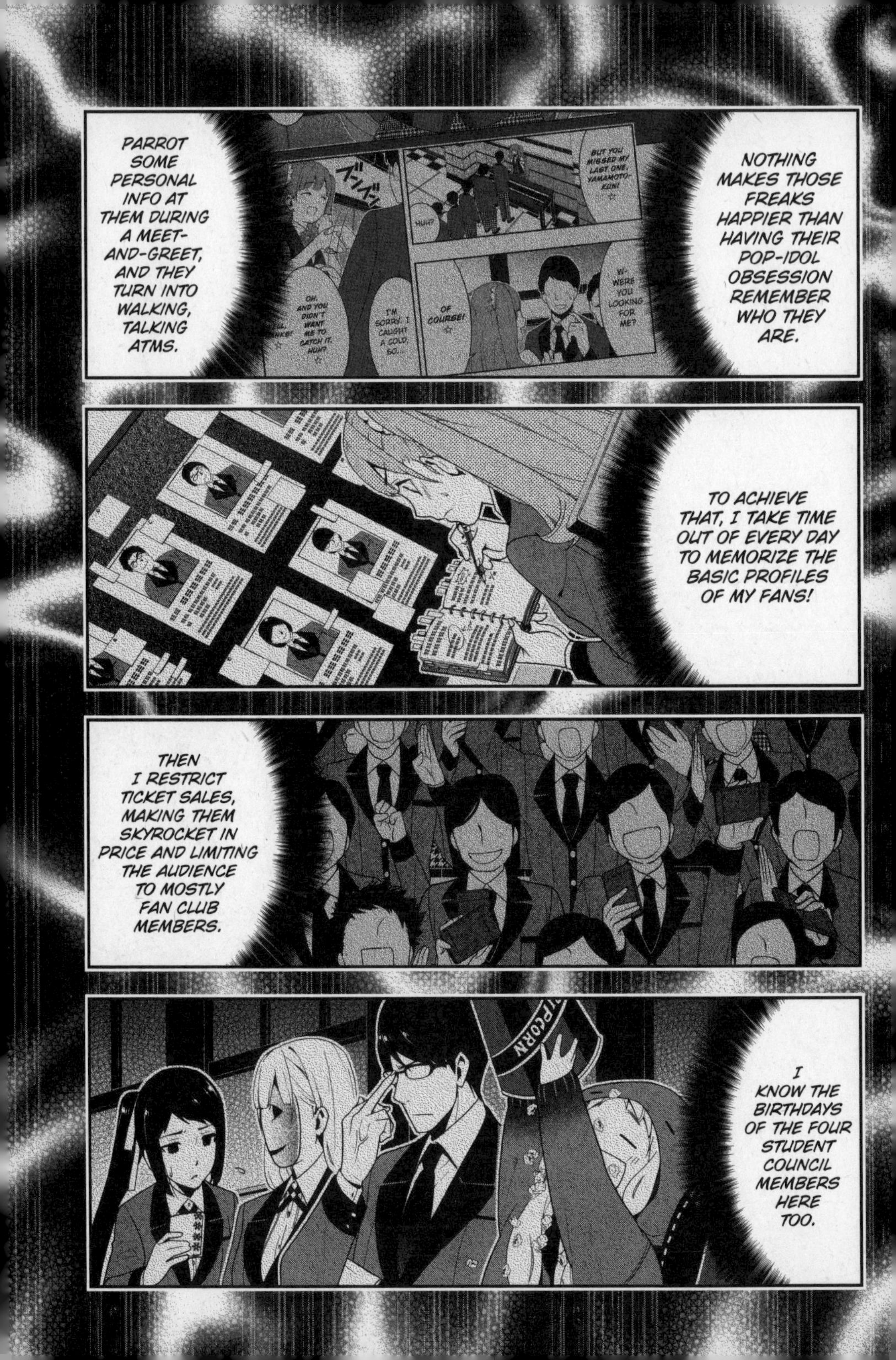
NOTHING MAKES THOSE FREAKS HAPPIER THAN HAVING THEIR POP-IDOL OBSESSION REMEMBER WHO THEY ARE.
BUT YOU MISSED MY LAST ONE, YAMAMOTO-KUN! ☆
HUH?
W-WERE YOU LOOKING FOR ME?
OF COURSE! ☆
I'M SORRY. I CAUGHT A COLD, SO...
OH, AND YOU DIDN'T WANT ME TO CATCH IT, HUH? ☆
PARROT SOME PERSONAL INFO AT THEM DURING A MEET-AND-GREET, AND THEY TURN INTO WALKING, TALKING ATMS.
TO ACHIEVE THAT, I TAKE TIME OUT OF EVERY DAY TO MEMORIZE THE BASIC PROFILES OF MY FANS!
THEN I RESTRICT TICKET SALES, MAKING THEM SKYROCKET IN PRICE AND LIMITING THE AUDIENCE TO MOSTLY FAN CLUB MEMBERS.
I KNOW THE BIRTHDAYS OF THE FOUR STUDENT COUNCIL MEMBERS HERE TOO.

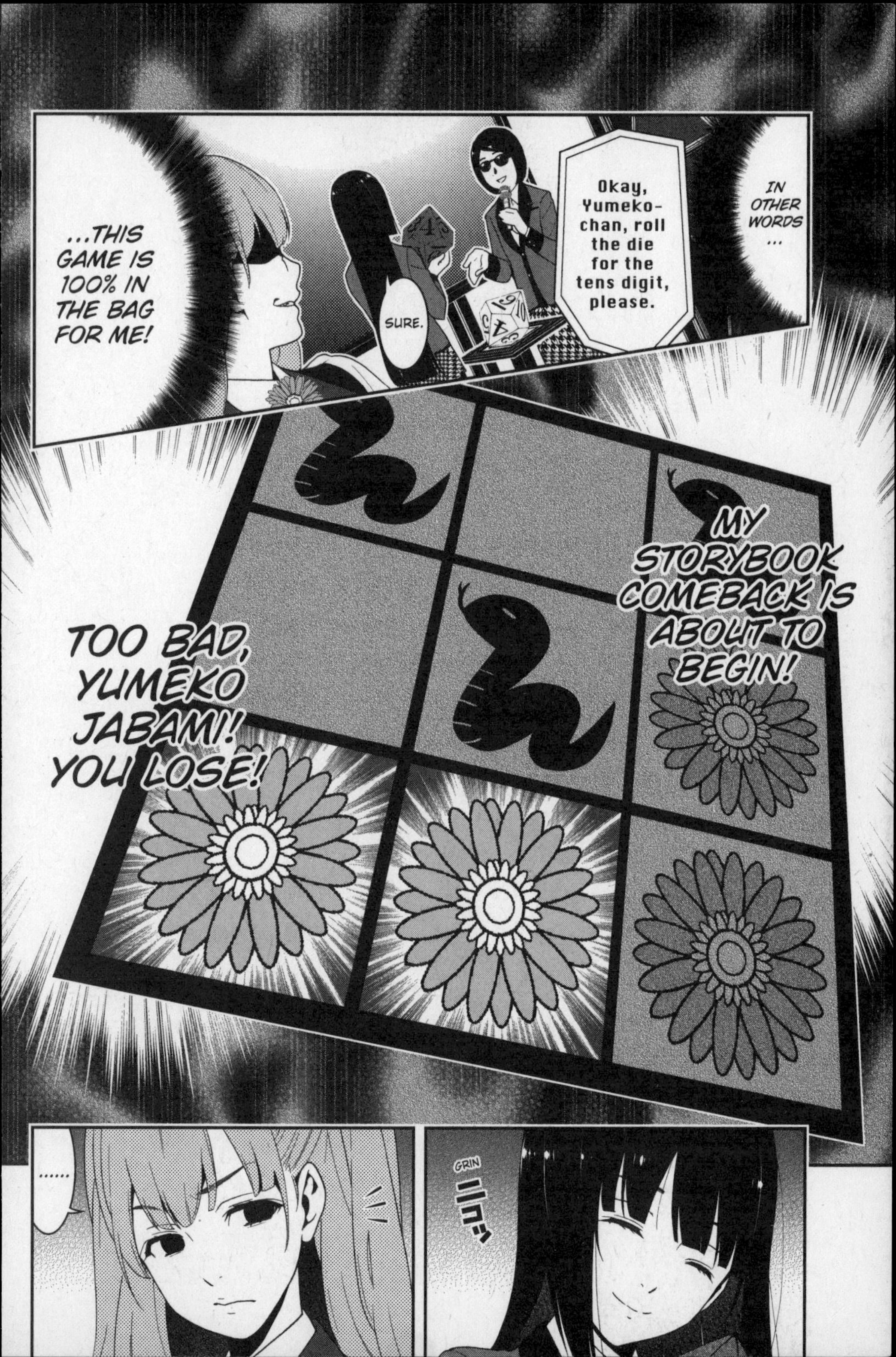
IN OTHER WORDS...
Okay, Yumeko-chan, roll the die for the tens digit, please.
SURE.
...THIS GAME IS 100% IN THE BAG FOR ME!
MY STORYBOOK COMEBACK IS ABOUT TO BEGIN!
TOO BAD, YUMEKO JABAMI! YOU LOSE!
GRIN
ニコッ
......

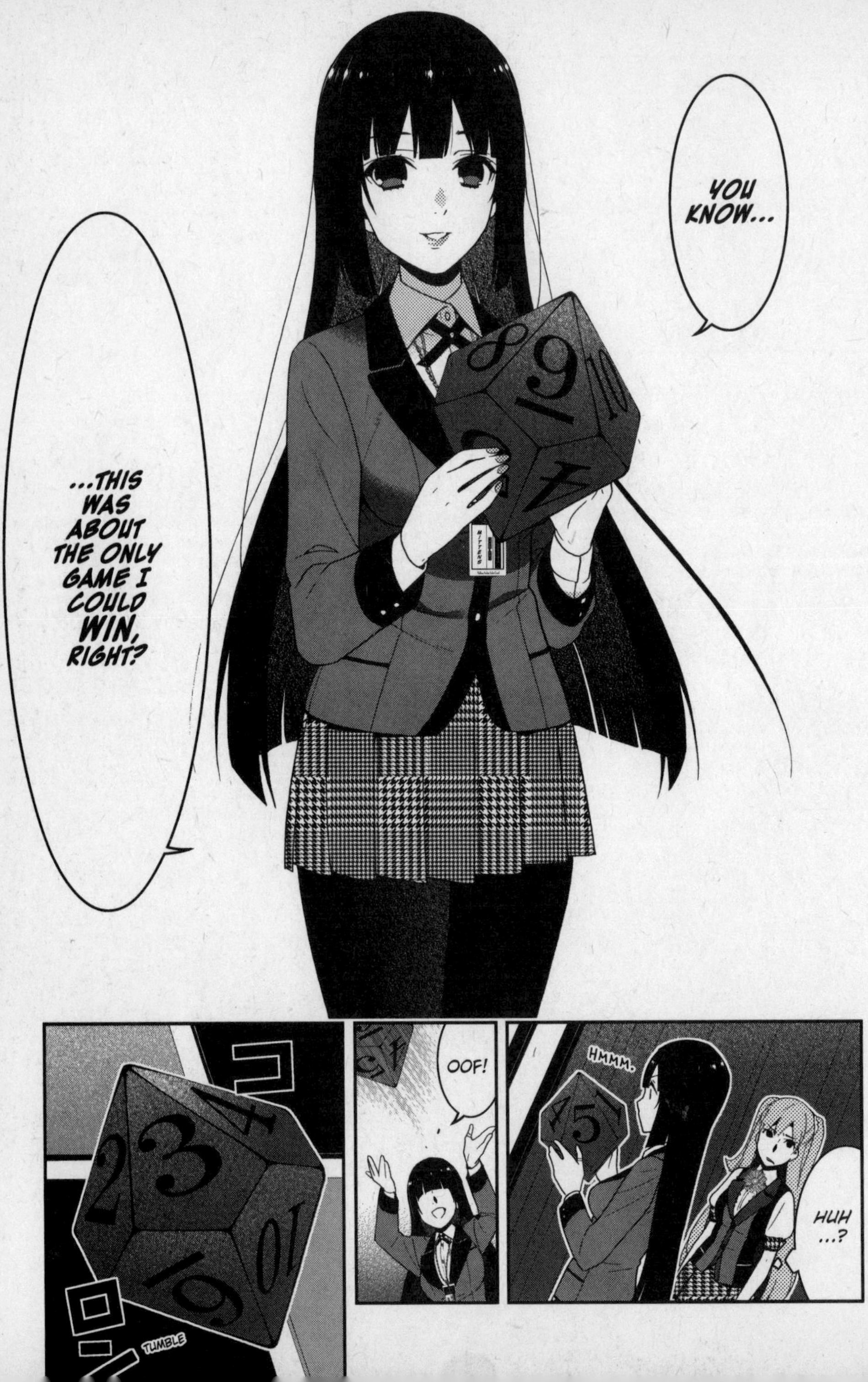
YOU KNOW...
...THIS WAS ABOUT THE ONLY GAME I COULD WIN, RIGHT?
HMMM.
HUH ...?
OOF!
TUMBLE

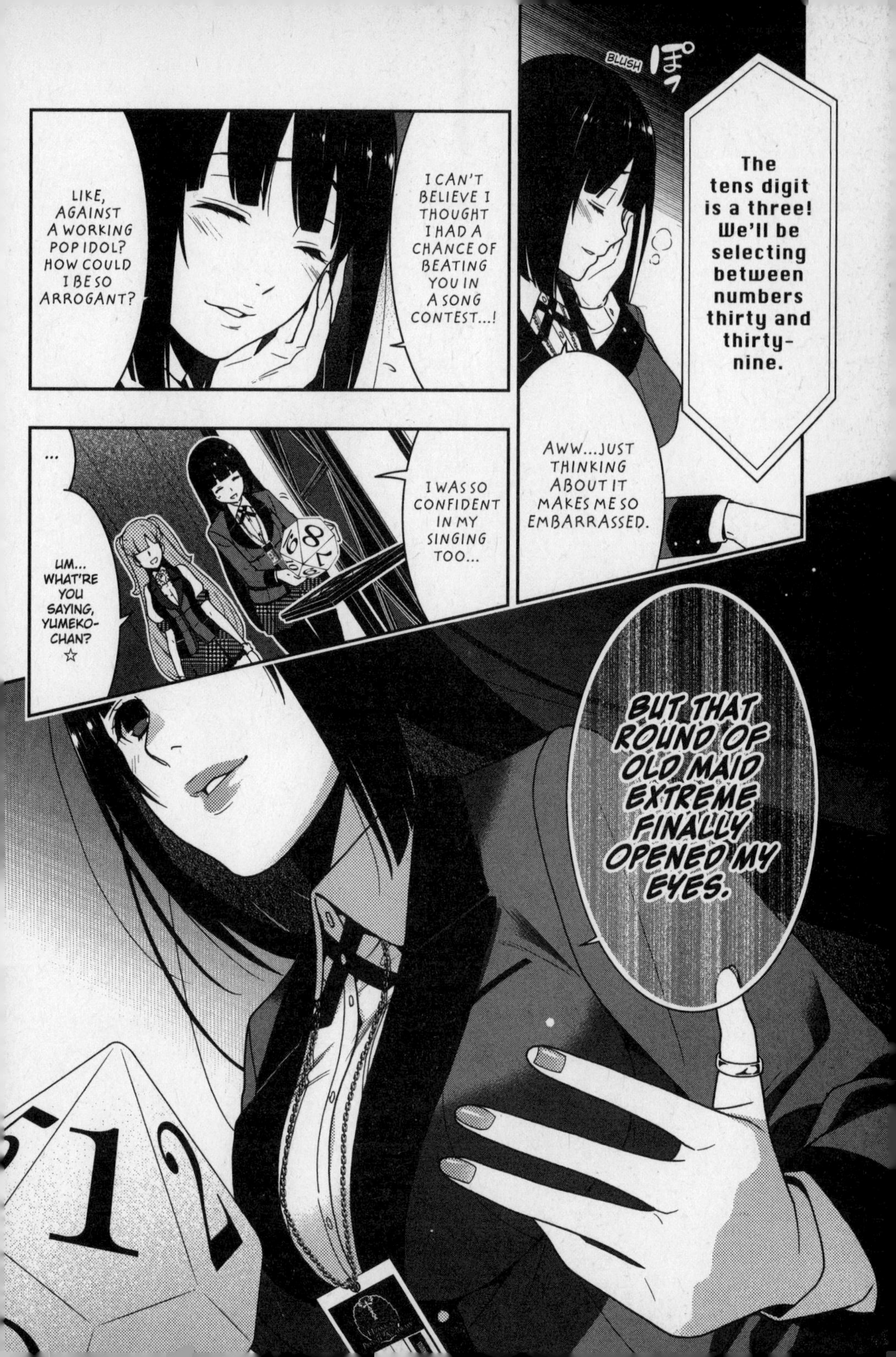

BLUSH
ぽっ
The tens digit is a three! We'll be selecting between numbers thirty and thirty-nine.
AWW...JUST THINKING ABOUT IT MAKES ME SO EMBARRASSED.
I CAN'T BELIEVE I THOUGHT I HAD A CHANCE OF BEATING YOU IN A SONG CONTEST...!
LIKE, AGAINST A WORKING POP IDOL? HOW COULD I BE SO ARROGANT?
I WAS SO CONFIDENT IN MY SINGING TOO...
...
UM... WHAT'RE YOU SAYING, YUMEKO-CHAN? ☆
BUT THAT ROUND OF OLD MAID EXTREME FINALLY OPENED MY EYES.

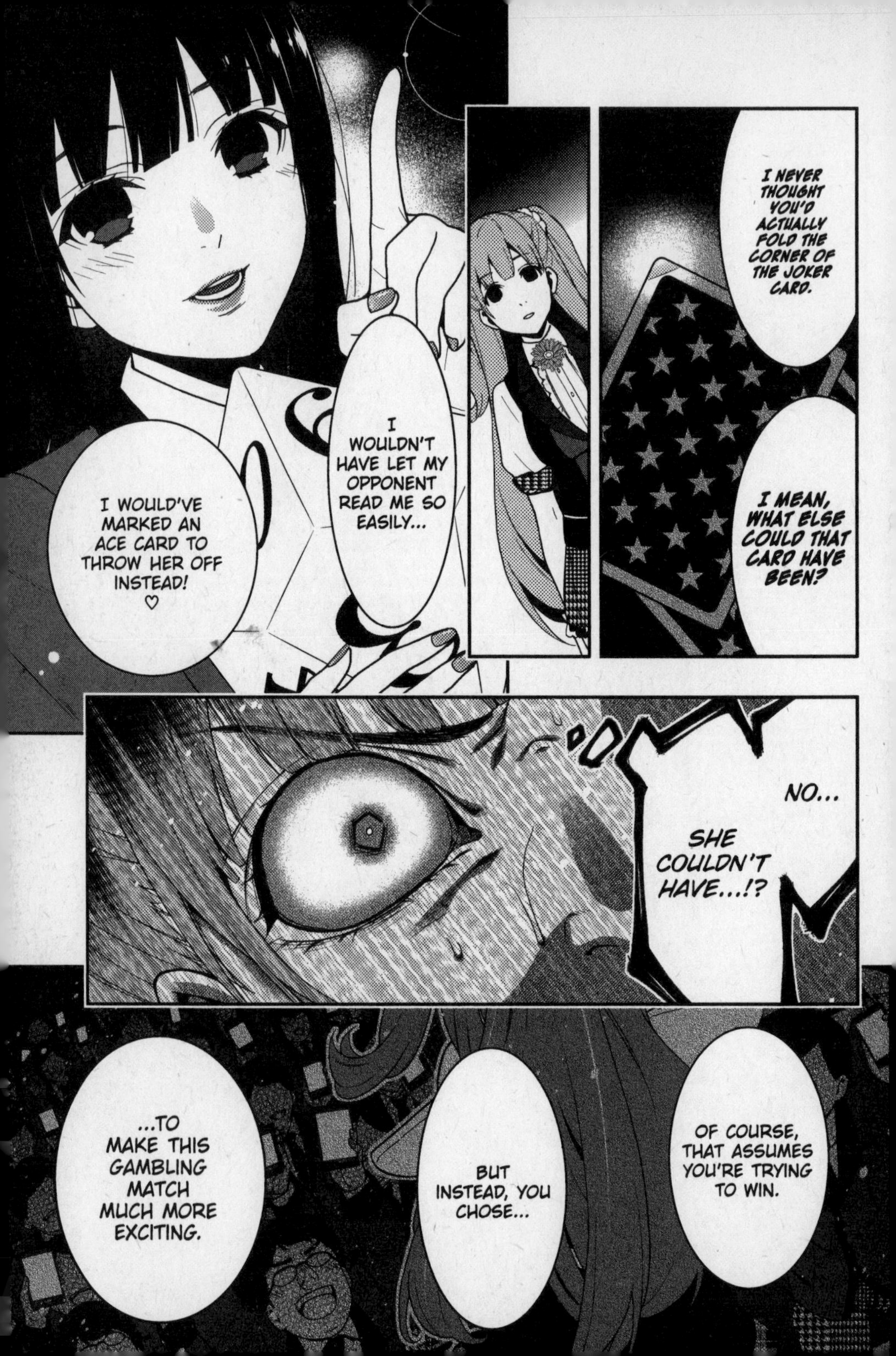
I NEVER THOUGHT YOU'D ACTUALLY FOLD THE CORNER OF THE JOKER CARD.
I MEAN, WHAT ELSE COULD THAT CARD HAVE BEEN?
I WOULDN'T HAVE LET MY OPPONENT READ ME SO EASILY...
I WOULD'VE MARKED AN ACE CARD TO THROW HER OFF INSTEAD! ♡
NO...
SHE COULDN'T HAVE...!?
OF COURSE, THAT ASSUMES YOU'RE TRYING TO WIN.
BUT INSTEAD, YOU CHOSE...
...TO MAKE THIS GAMBLING MATCH MUCH MORE EXCITING.

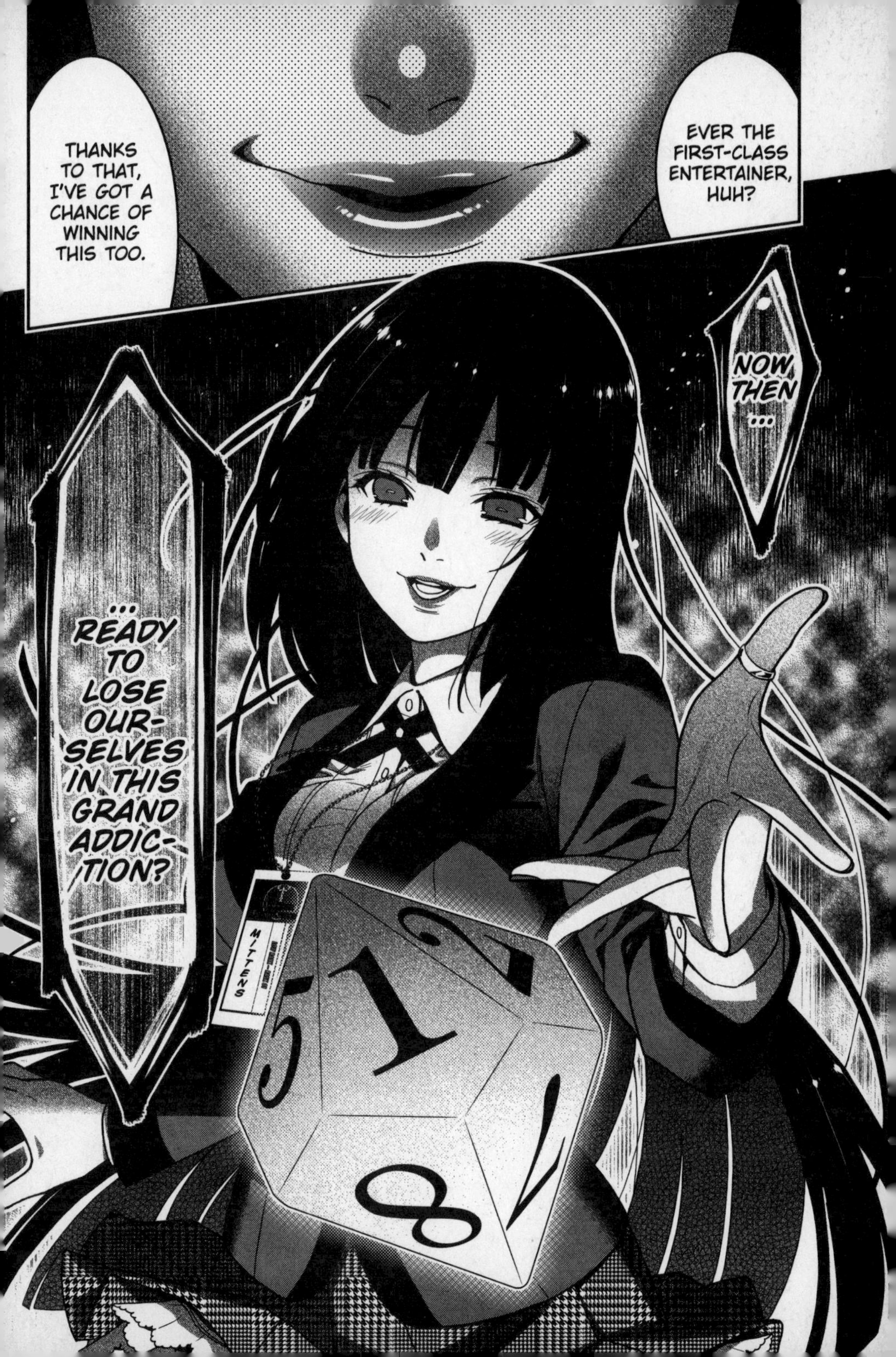
EVER THE FIRST-CLASS ENTERTAINER, HUH?
THANKS TO THAT, I'VE GOT A CHANCE OF WINNING THIS TOO.
NOW THEN ...
... READY TO LOSE OURSELVES IN THIS GRAND ADDICTION?
MITTENS

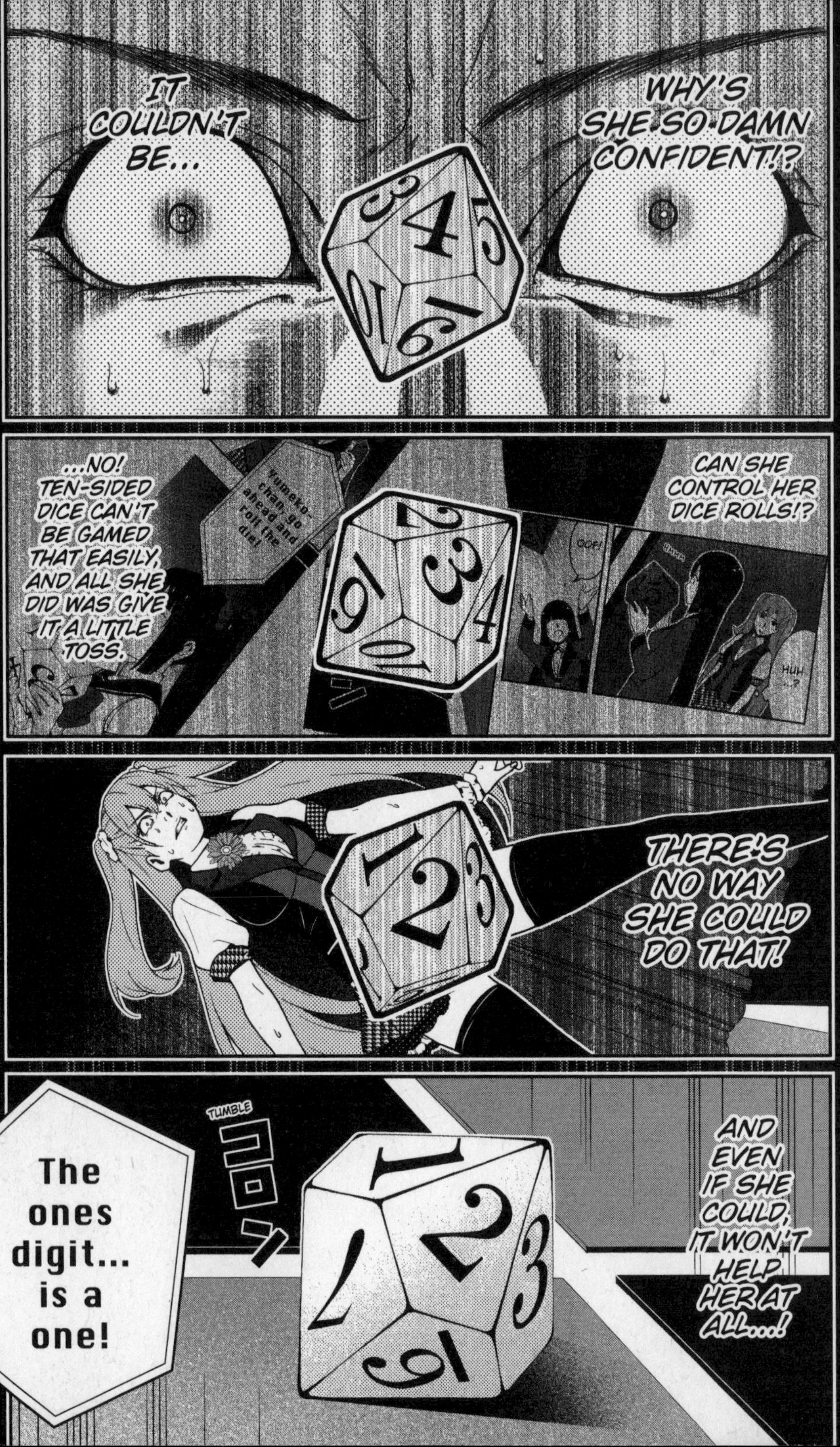
WHY'S SHE SO DAMN CONFIDENT!?
IT COULDN'T BE...
CAN SHE CONTROL HER DICE ROLLS!?
HUH ...?
HMMM
OOF!
...NO! TEN-SIDED DICE CAN'T BE GAMED THAT EASILY, AND ALL SHE DID WAS GIVE IT A LITTLE TOSS.
Yumeko-chan, go ahead and roll the die!
THERE'S NO WAY SHE COULD DO THAT!
AND EVEN IF SHE COULD, IT WON'T HELP HER AT ALL...!
TUMBLE
The ones digit... is a one!

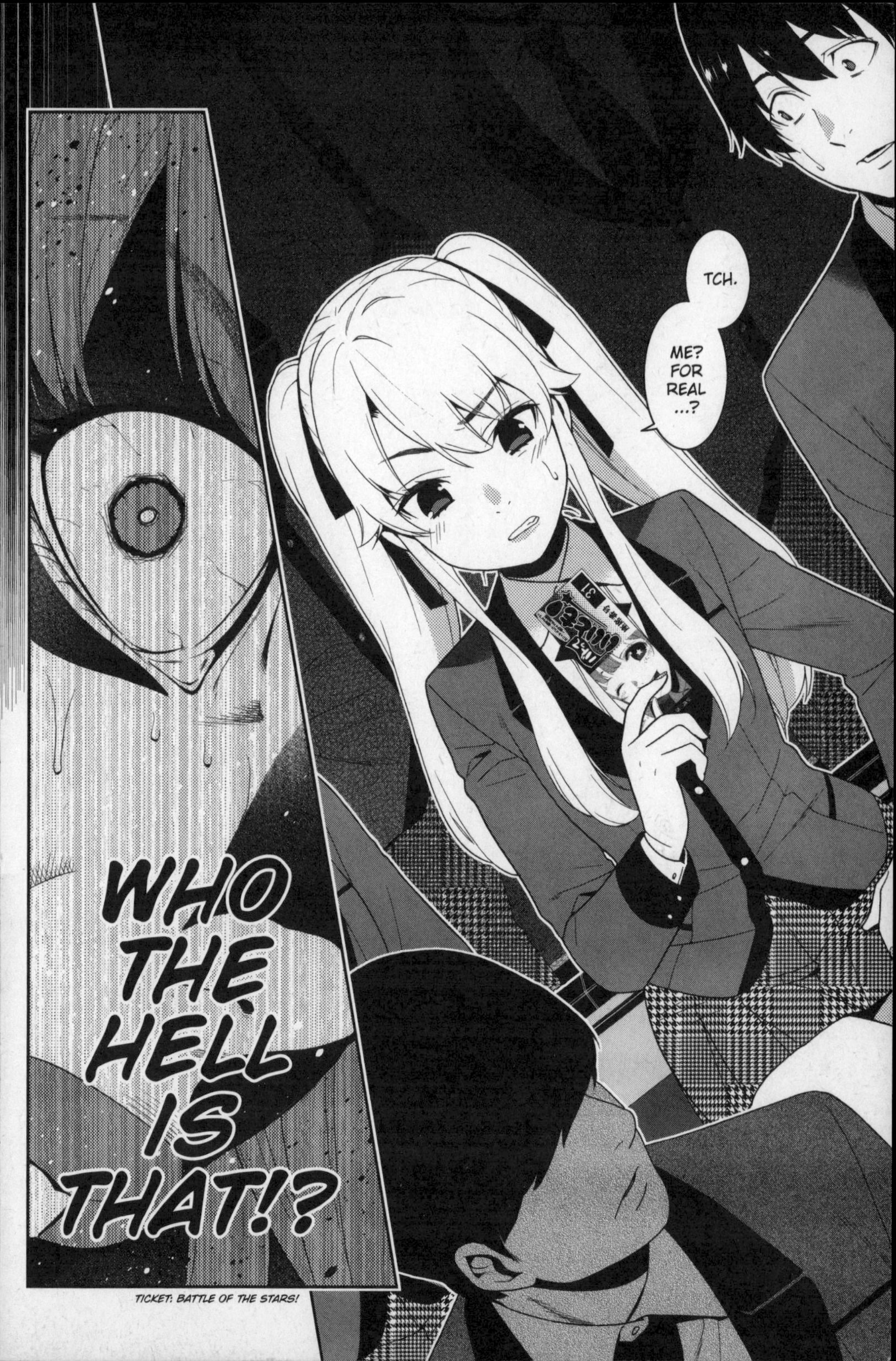
TCH.
ME? FOR REAL ...?
WHO THE HELL IS THAT!?
TICKET: BATTLE OF THE STARS!

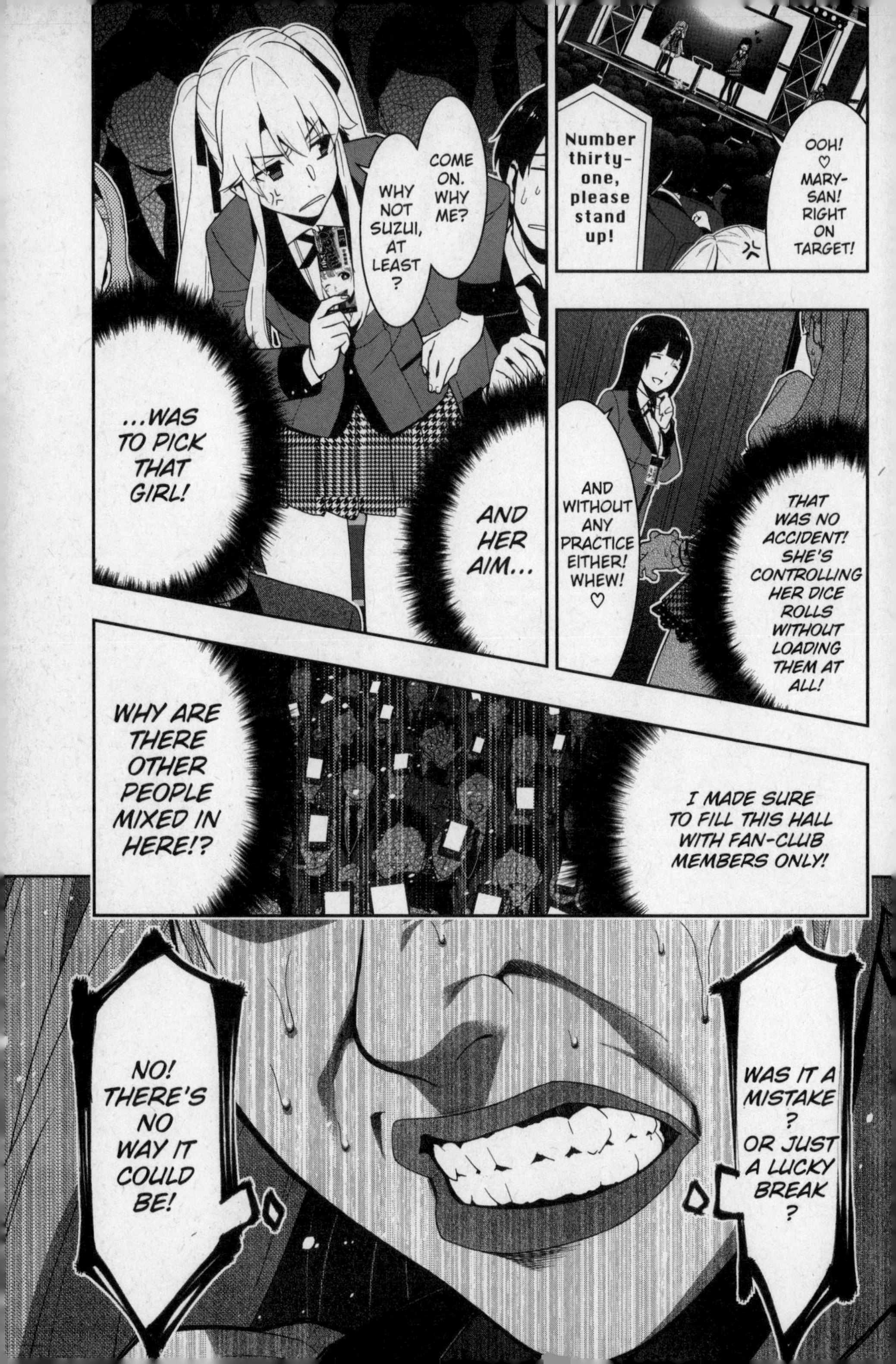
OOH! ♡ MARY-SAN! RIGHT ON TARGET!
Number thirty-one, please stand up!
THAT WAS NO ACCIDENT! SHE'S CONTROLLING HER DICE ROLLS WITHOUT LOADING THEM AT ALL!
AND WITHOUT ANY PRACTICE EITHER! WHEW! ♡
COME ON. WHY ME?
WHY NOT SUZUI, AT LEAST?
AND HER AIM...
...WAS TO PICK THAT GIRL!
I MADE SURE TO FILL THIS HALL WITH FAN-CLUB MEMBERS ONLY!
WHY ARE THERE OTHER PEOPLE MIXED IN HERE!?
WAS IT A MISTAKE? OR JUST A LUCKY BREAK?
NO! THERE'S NO WAY IT COULD BE!

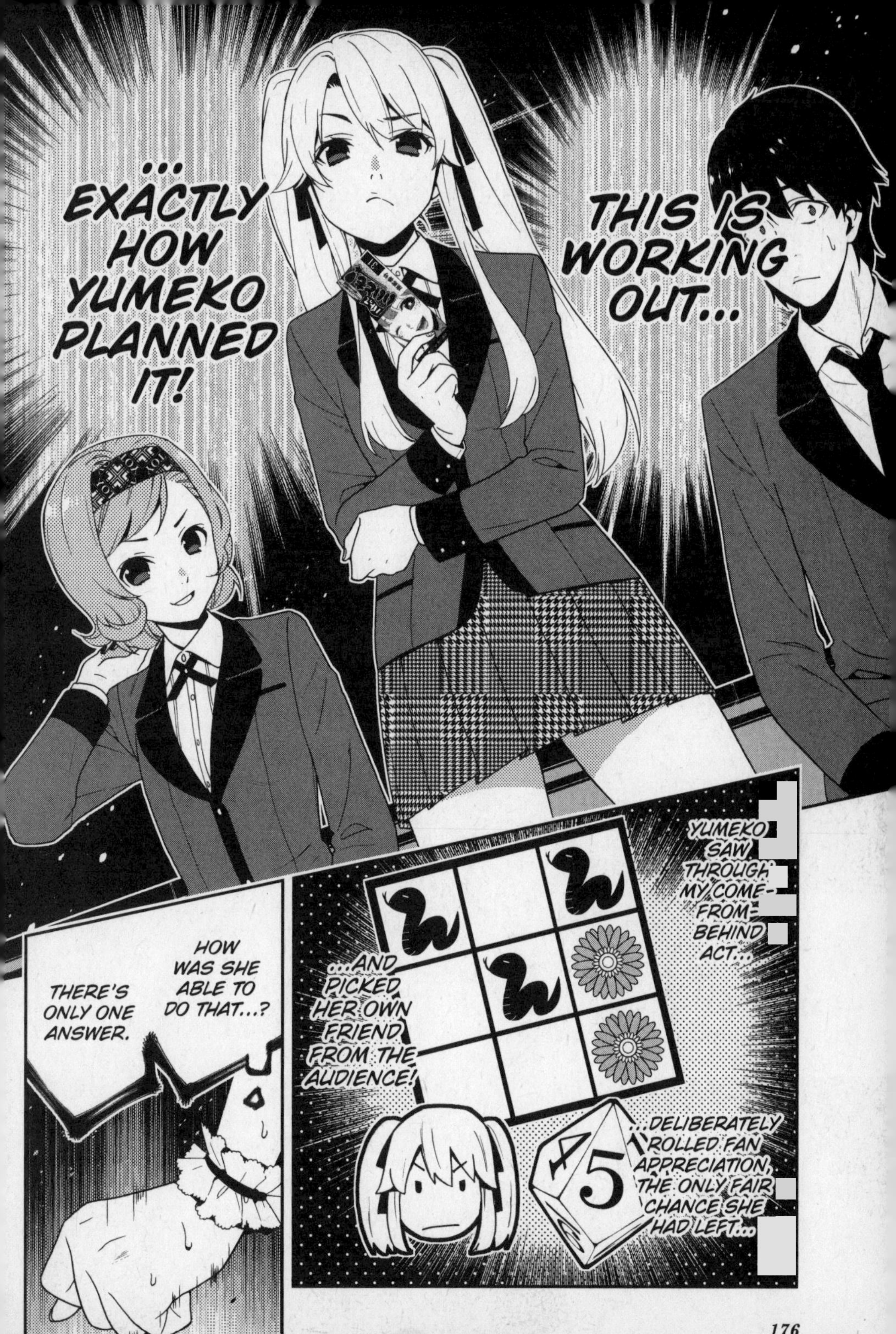
THIS IS WORKING OUT…
…EXACTLY HOW YUMEKO PLANNED IT!
YUMEKO SAW THROUGH MY COME-FROM-BEHIND ACT…
…DELIBERATELY ROLLED FAN APPRECIATION, THE ONLY FAIR CHANCE SHE HAD LEFT…
…AND PICKED HER OWN FRIEND FROM THE AUDIENCE!
HOW WAS SHE ABLE TO DO THAT…?
THERE'S ONLY ONE ANSWER.

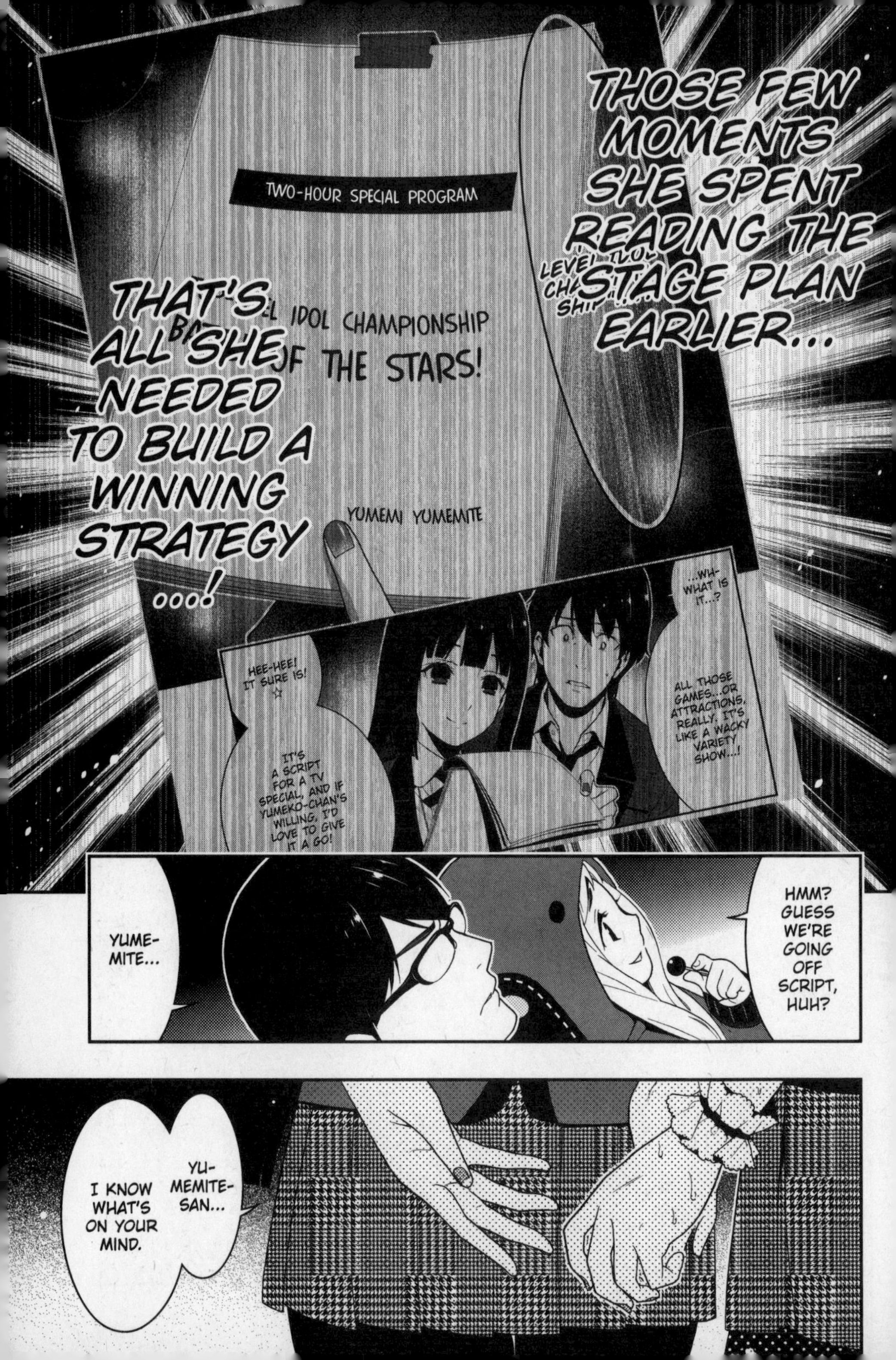
THOSE FEW MOMENTS SHE SPENT READING THE STAGE PLAN EARLIER...
TWO-HOUR SPECIAL PROGRAM
IDOL CHAMPIONSHIP
THE STARS!
YUMEMI YUMEMITE
THAT'S ALL SHE NEEDED TO BUILD A WINNING STRATEGY...!
...WH-WHAT IS IT...?
ALL THOSE GAMES...OR ATTRACTIONS, REALLY. IT'S LIKE A WACKY VARIETY SHOW...!
HEE-HEE! IT SURE IS! ☆
IT'S A SCRIPT FOR A TV SPECIAL, AND IF YUMEKO-CHAN'S WILLING, I'D LOVE TO GIVE IT A GO!
HMM? GUESS WE'RE GOING OFF SCRIPT, HUH?
YUME-MITE...
YU-MEMITE-SAN...
I KNOW WHAT'S ON YOUR MIND.

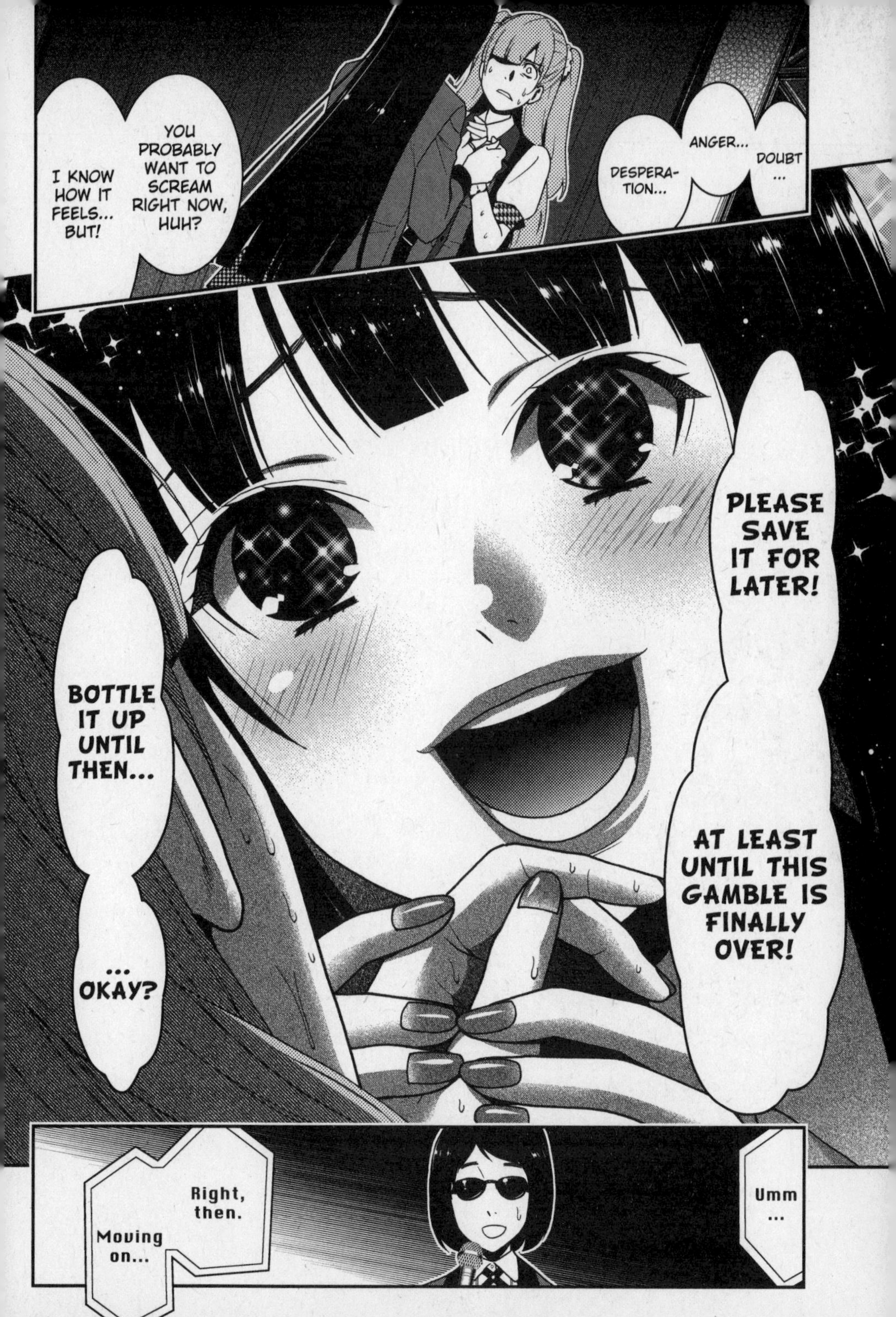
ANGER... DOUBT... DESPERATION...
YOU PROBABLY WANT TO SCREAM RIGHT NOW, HUH?
I KNOW HOW IT FEELS... BUT!
PLEASE SAVE IT FOR LATER!
AT LEAST UNTIL THIS GAMBLE IS FINALLY OVER!
BOTTLE IT UP UNTIL THEN...
... OKAY?
Umm ...
Right, then. Moving on...

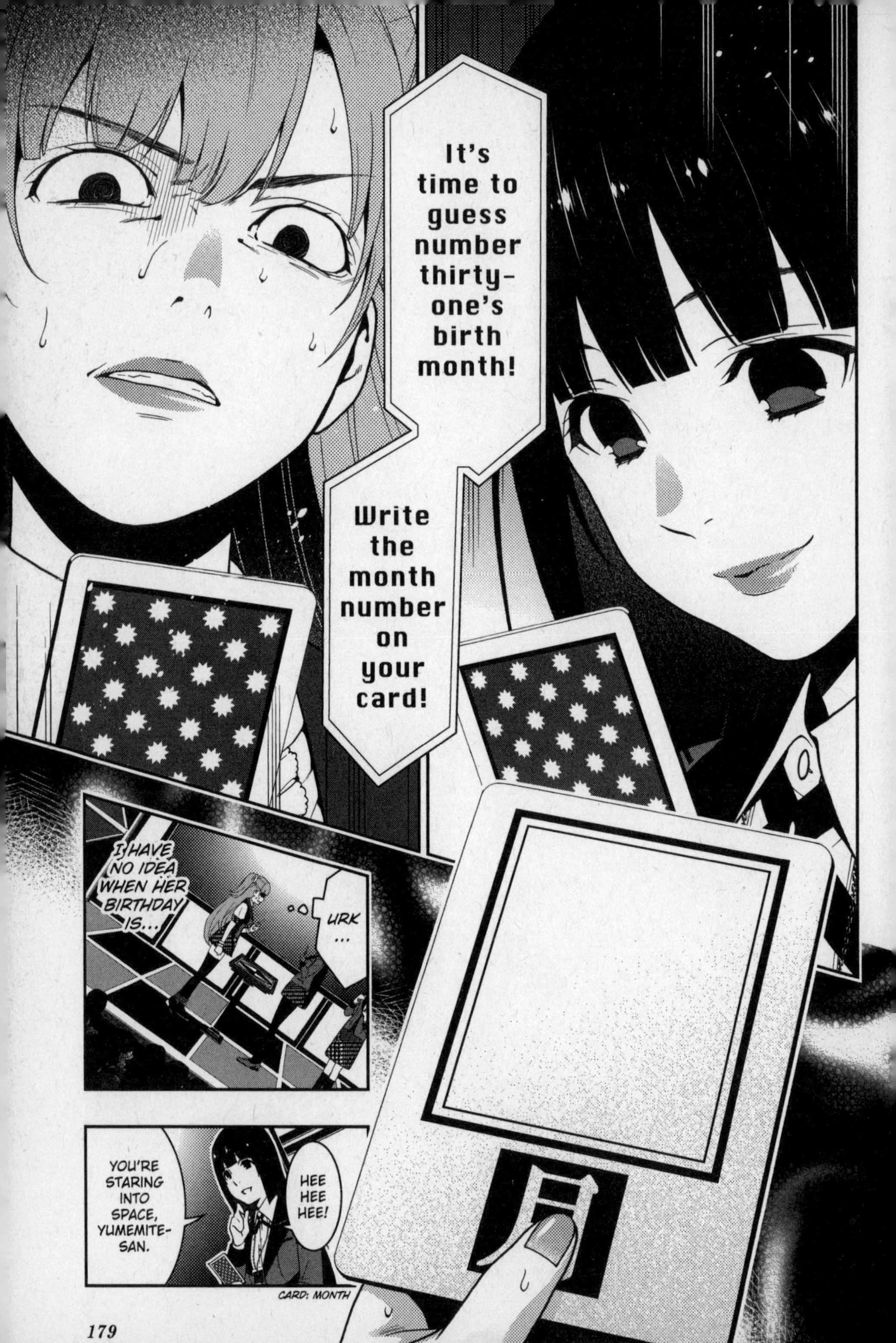
It's time to guess number thirty-one's birth month!
Write the month number on your card!
URK ...
I HAVE NO IDEA WHEN HER BIRTHDAY IS...
HEE HEE HEE!
YOU'RE STARING INTO SPACE, YUMEMITE-SAN.
月
CARD: MONTH

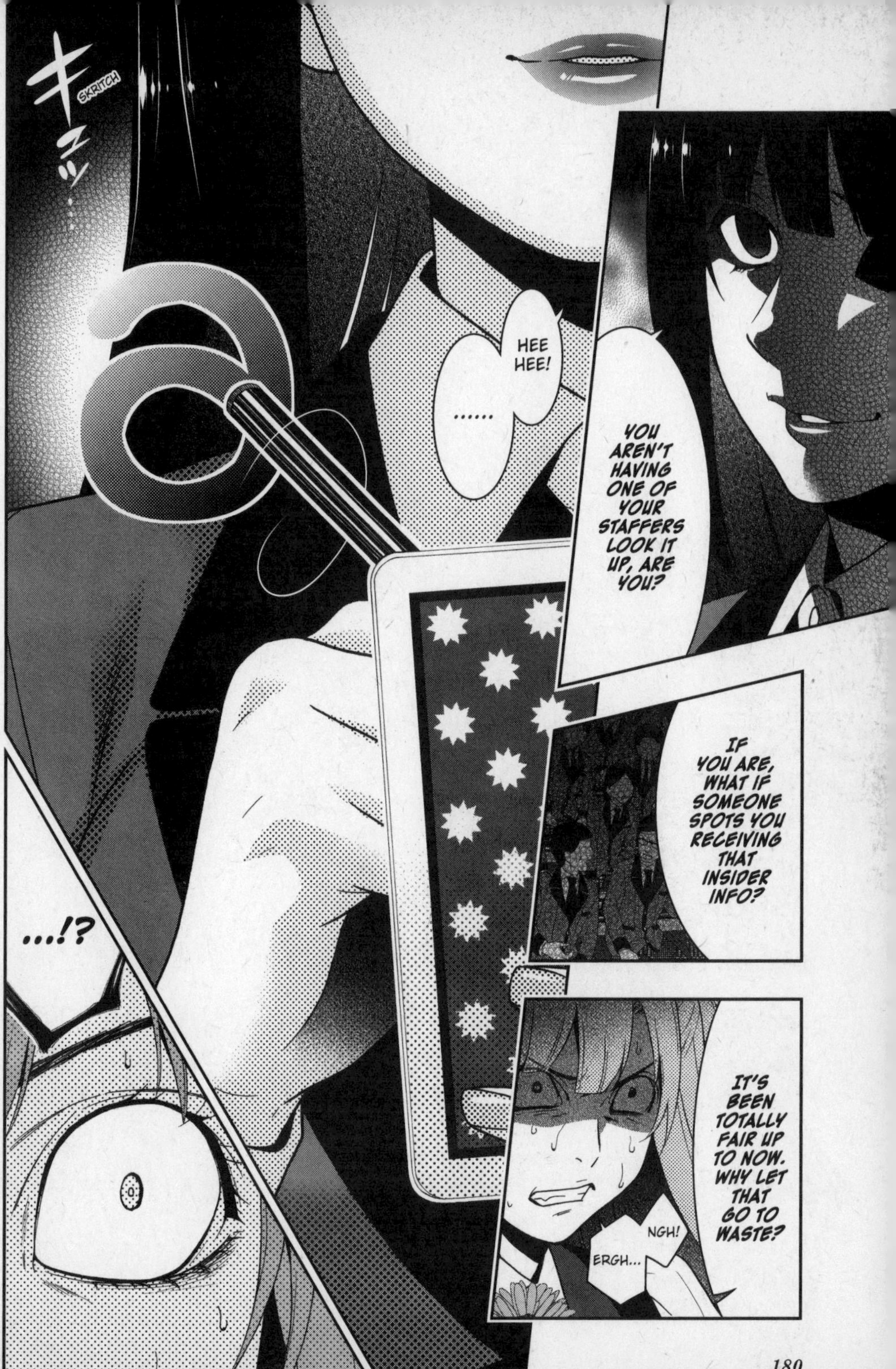
SKRITCH
HEE HEE!
......
YOU AREN'T HAVING ONE OF YOUR STAFFERS LOOK IT UP, ARE YOU?
IF YOU ARE, WHAT IF SOMEONE SPOTS YOU RECEIVING THAT INSIDER INFO?
IT'S BEEN TOTALLY FAIR UP TO NOW. WHY LET THAT GO TO WASTE?
NGH!
ERGH...
...!?

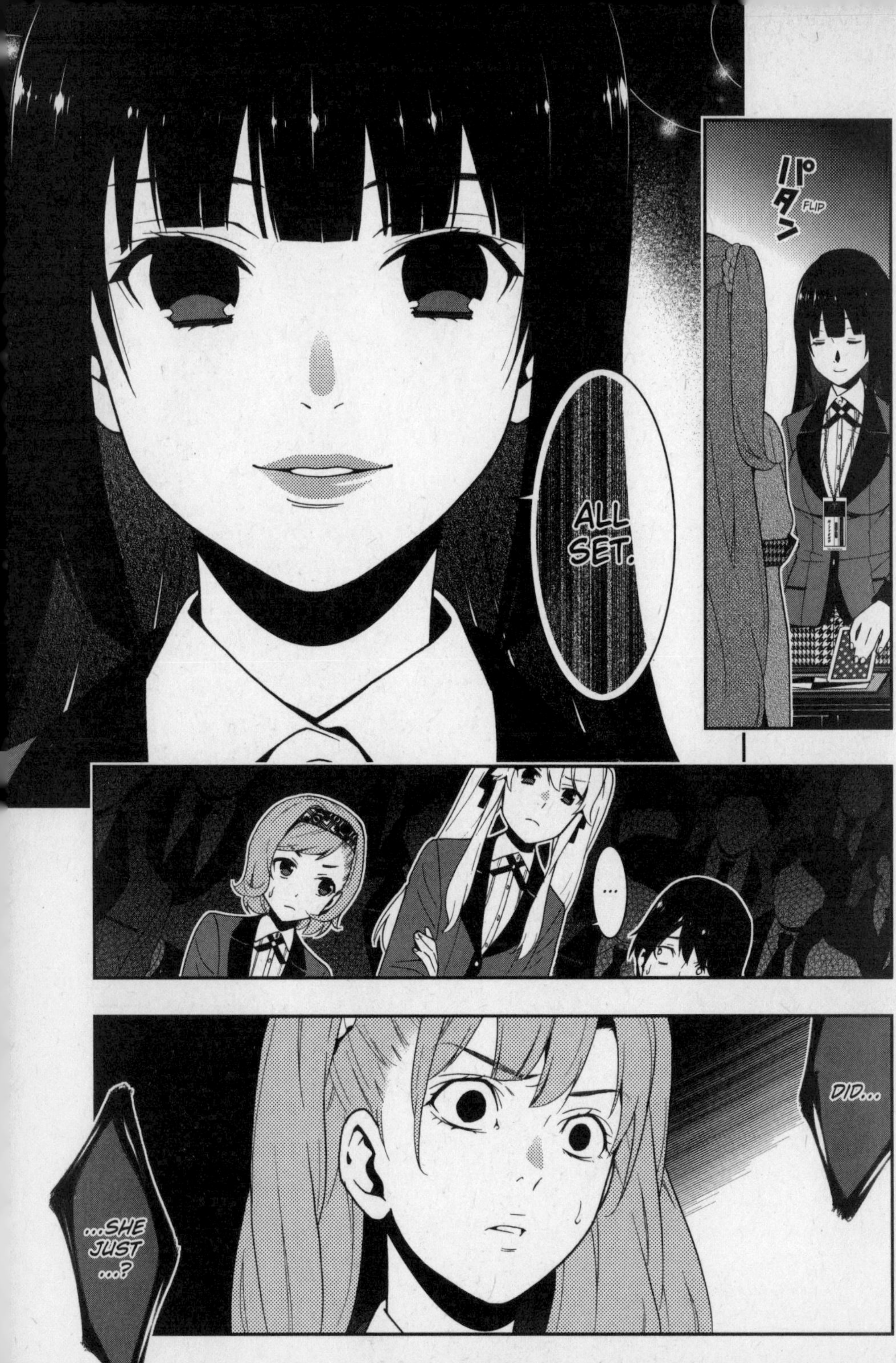
パタン
FLIP
ALL SET.
...
DID...
...SHE JUST ...?

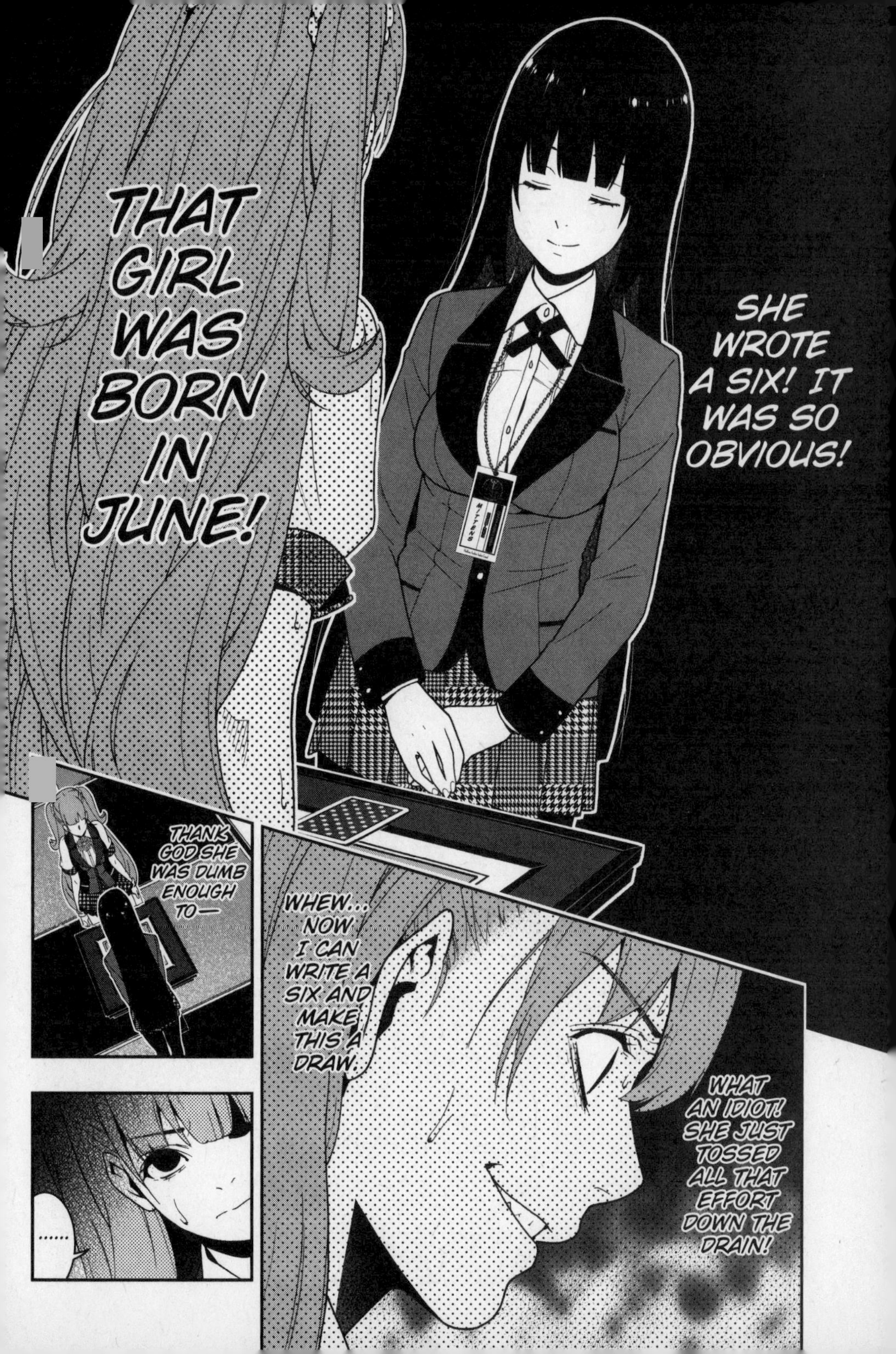
SHE WROTE A SIX! IT WAS SO OBVIOUS!
THAT GIRL WAS BORN IN JUNE!
WHEW... NOW I CAN WRITE A SIX AND MAKE THIS A DRAW.
WHAT AN IDIOT! SHE JUST TOSSED ALL THAT EFFORT DOWN THE DRAIN!
THANK GOD SHE WAS DUMB ENOUGH TO—
......

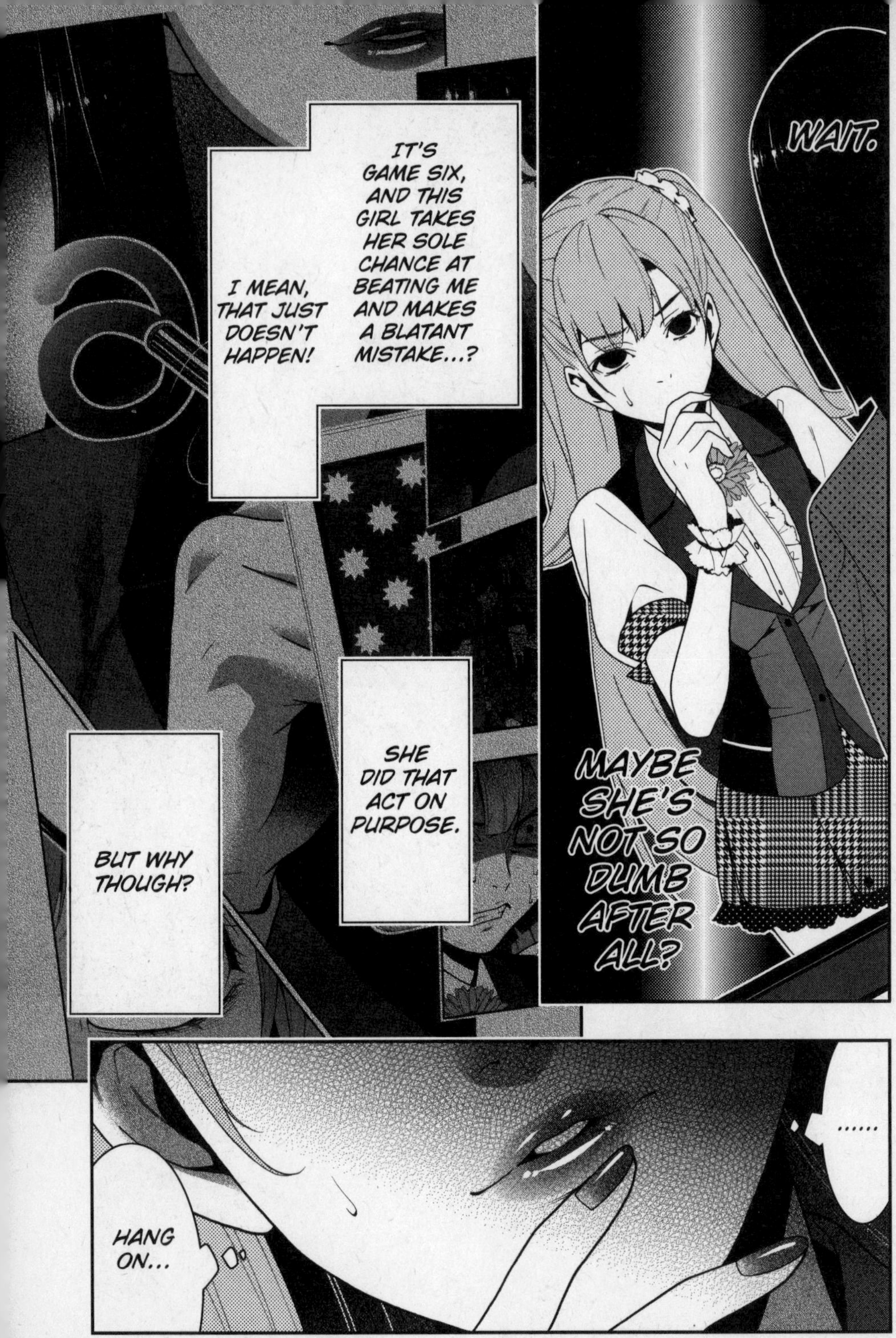
WAIT.
MAYBE SHE'S NOT SO DUMB AFTER ALL?
IT'S GAME SIX, AND THIS GIRL TAKES HER SOLE CHANCE AT BEATING ME AND MAKES A BLATANT MISTAKE...?
I MEAN, THAT JUST DOESN'T HAPPEN!
SHE DID THAT ACT ON PURPOSE.
BUT WHY THOUGH?
......
HANG ON...

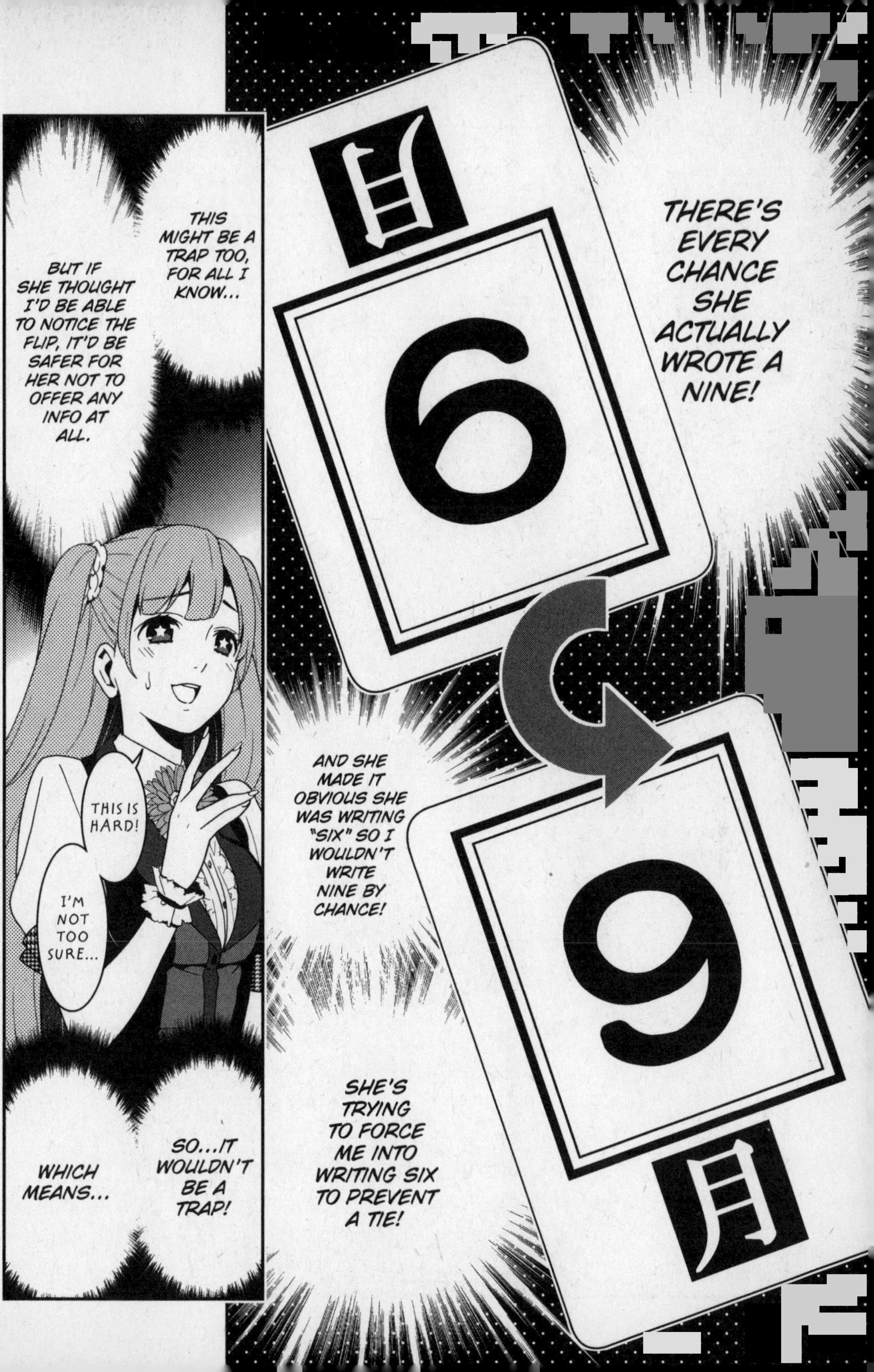
THERE'S EVERY CHANCE SHE ACTUALLY WROTE A NINE!
AND SHE MADE IT OBVIOUS SHE WAS WRITING "SIX" SO I WOULDN'T WRITE NINE BY CHANCE!
SHE'S TRYING TO FORCE ME INTO WRITING SIX TO PREVENT A TIE!
THIS MIGHT BE A TRAP TOO, FOR ALL I KNOW...
BUT IF SHE THOUGHT I'D BE ABLE TO NOTICE THE FLIP, IT'D BE SAFER FOR HER NOT TO OFFER ANY INFO AT ALL.
THIS IS HARD!
I'M NOT TOO SURE...
SO...IT WOULDN'T BE A TRAP!
WHICH MEANS...

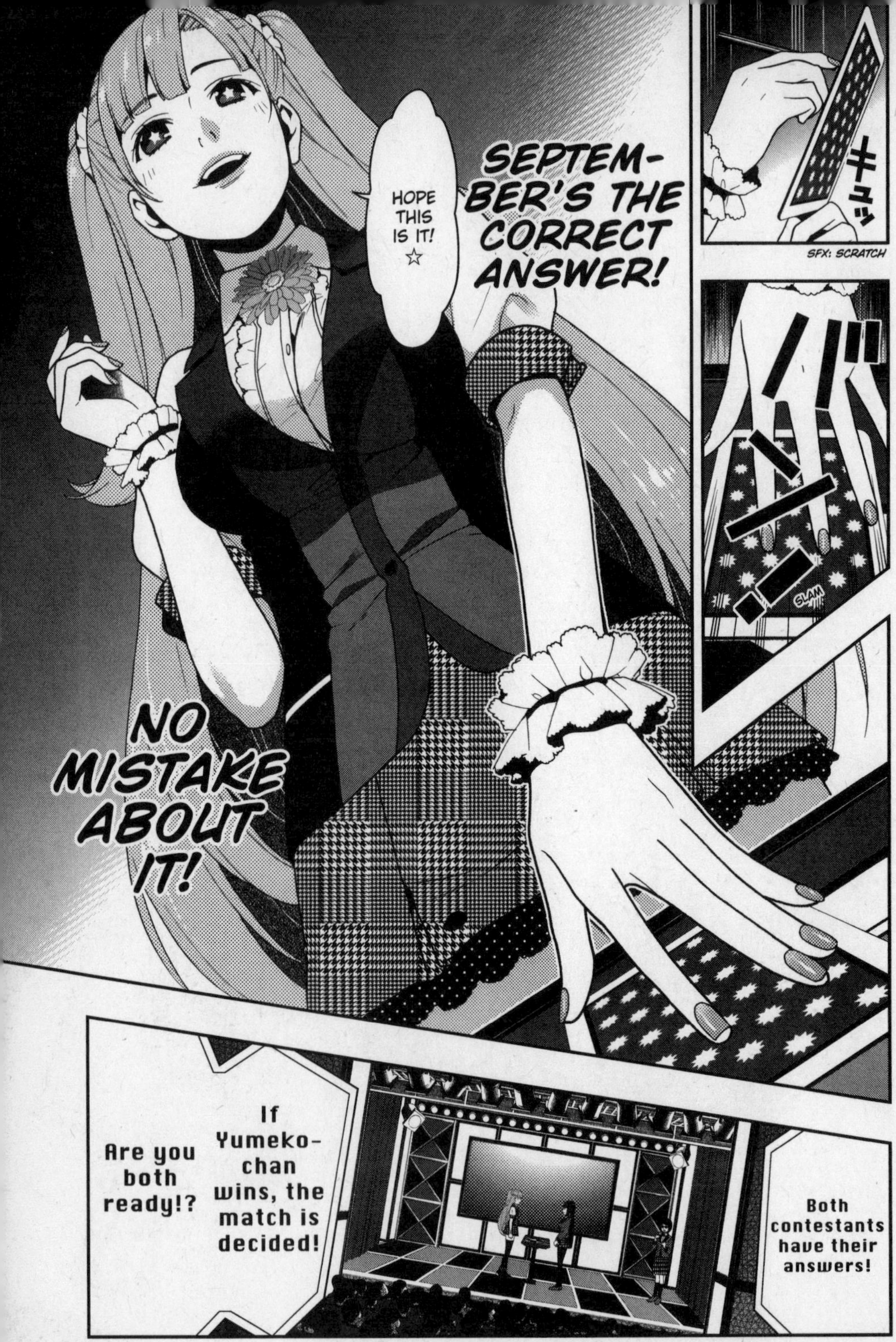
キュッ
SFX: SCRATCH
SLAM
SEPTEMBER'S THE CORRECT ANSWER!
HOPE THIS IS IT! ☆
NO MISTAKE ABOUT IT!
Both contestants have their answers!
If Yumeko-chan wins, the match is decided!
Are you both ready!?

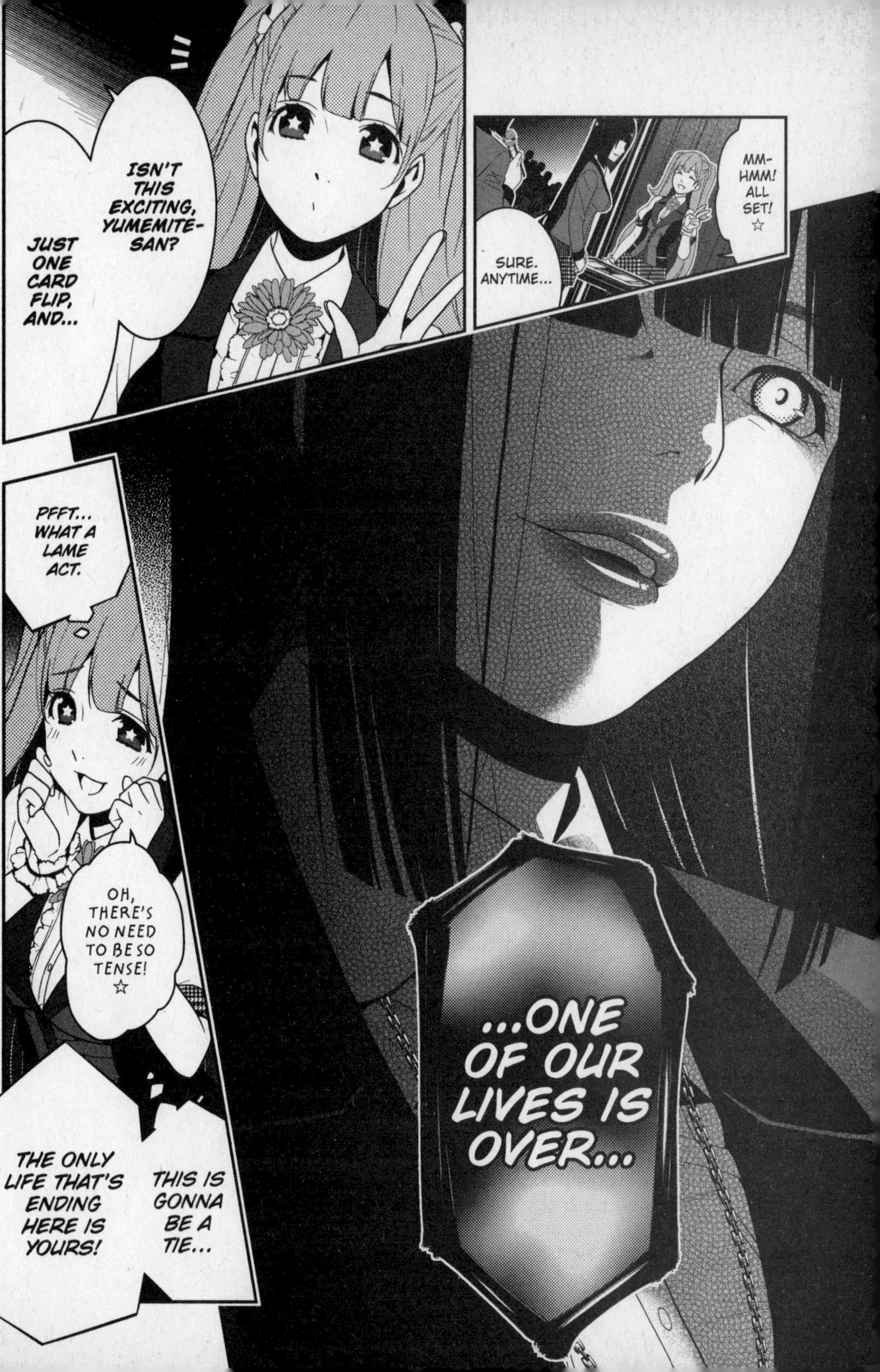
MM-HMM! ALL SET! ☆
SURE. ANYTIME...
ISN'T THIS EXCITING, YUMEMITE-SAN?
JUST ONE CARD FLIP, AND...
...ONE OF OUR LIVES IS OVER...
PFFT... WHAT A LAME ACT.
OH, THERE'S NO NEED TO BE SO TENSE! ☆
THIS IS GONNA BE A TIE...
THE ONLY LIFE THAT'S ENDING HERE IS YOURS!

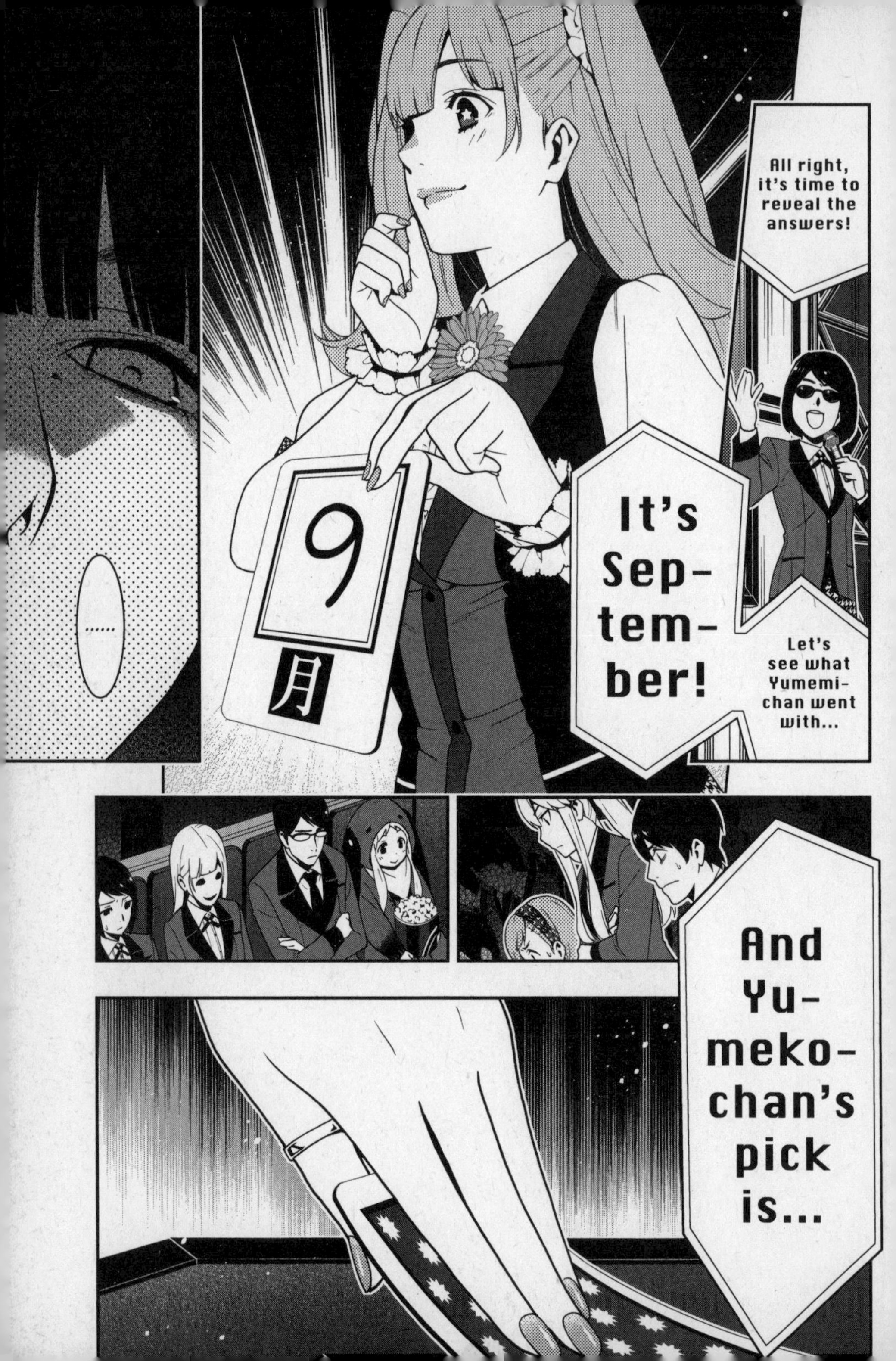
All right, it's time to reveal the answers!
Let's see what Yumemi-chan went with...
It's Sep-tem-ber!
9
月
......
And Yu-meko-chan's pick is...

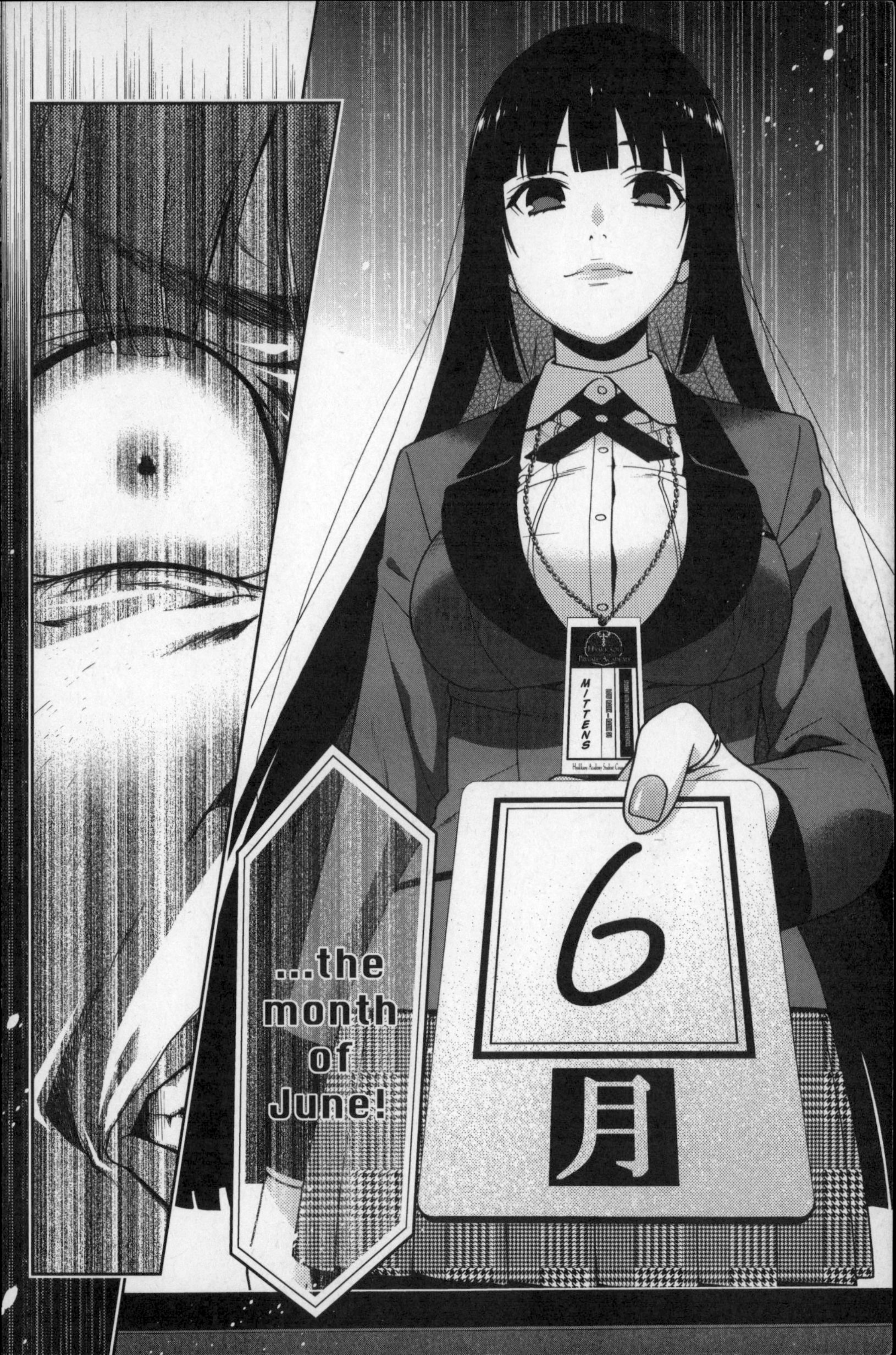
MITTENS
6
月
...the month of June!

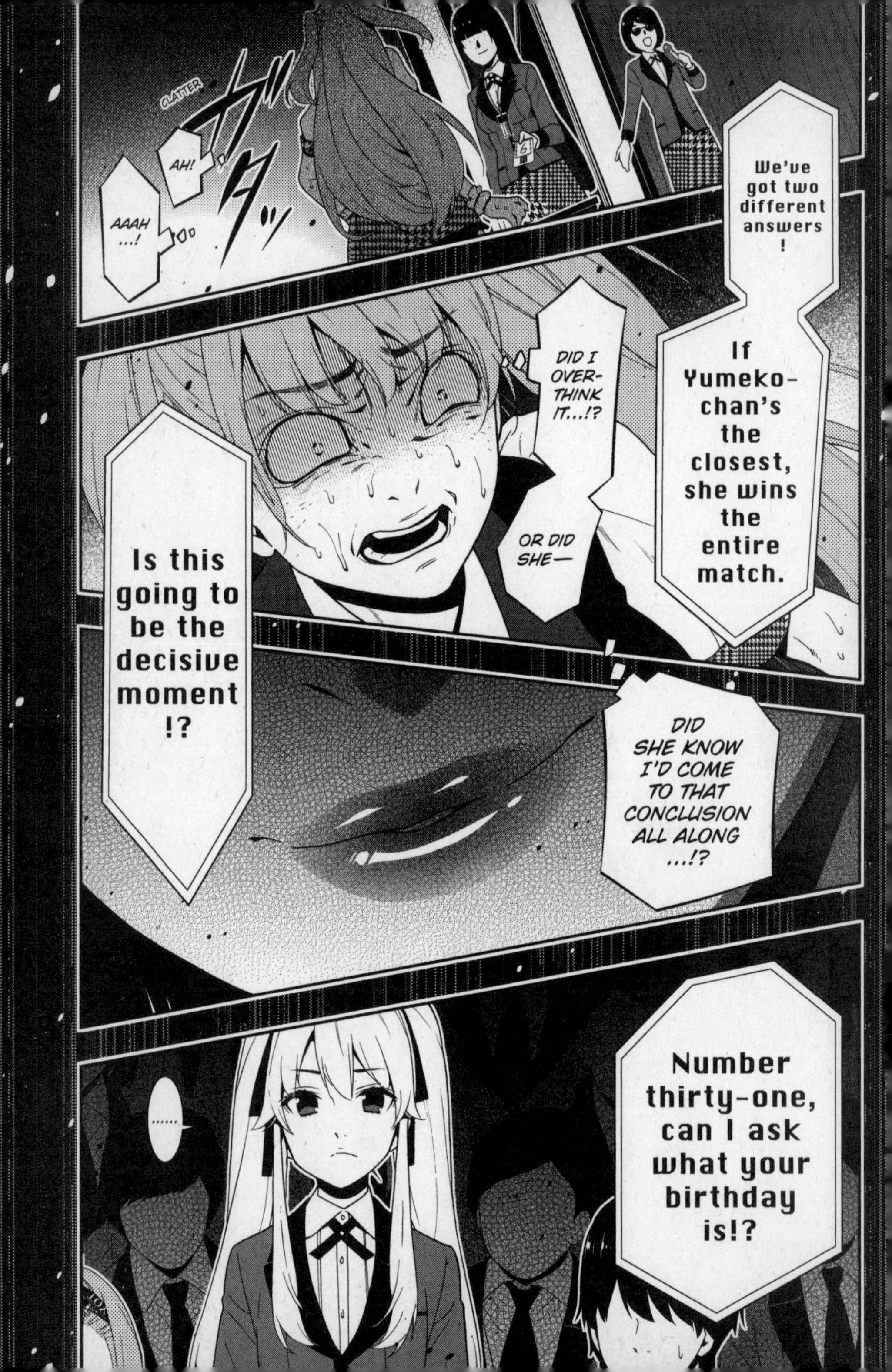
We've got two different answers!
CLATTER
AH!
AAAH ...!
If Yumeko-chan's the closest, she wins the entire match.
DID I OVER-THINK IT...!?
OR DID SHE—
Is this going to be the decisive moment!?
DID SHE KNOW I'D COME TO THAT CONCLUSION ALL ALONG ...!?
Number thirty-one, can I ask what your birthday is!?
......

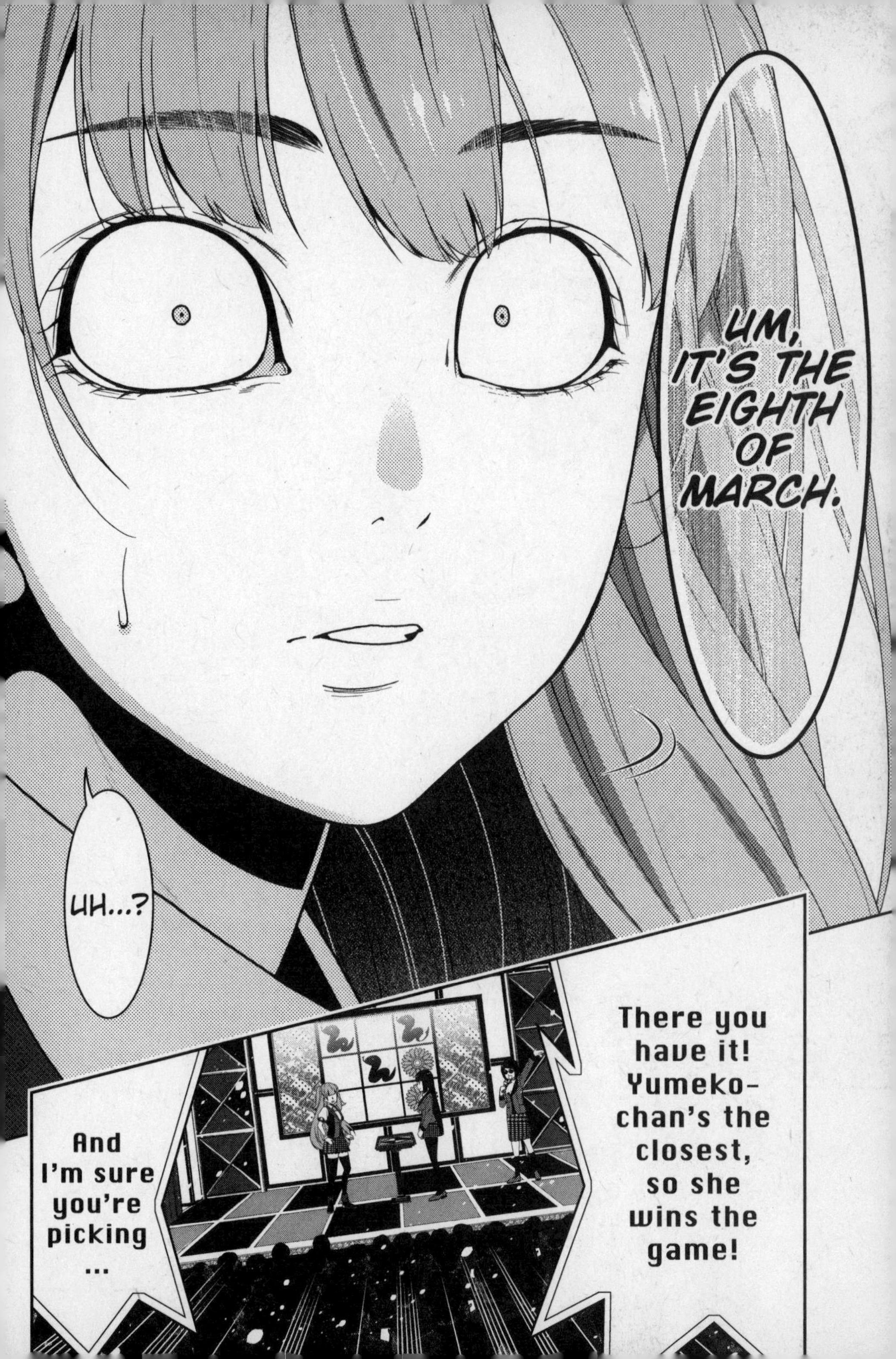
UM, IT'S THE EIGHTH OF MARCH.
UH...?
There you have it! Yumeko-chan's the closest, so she wins the game!
And I'm sure you're picking ...

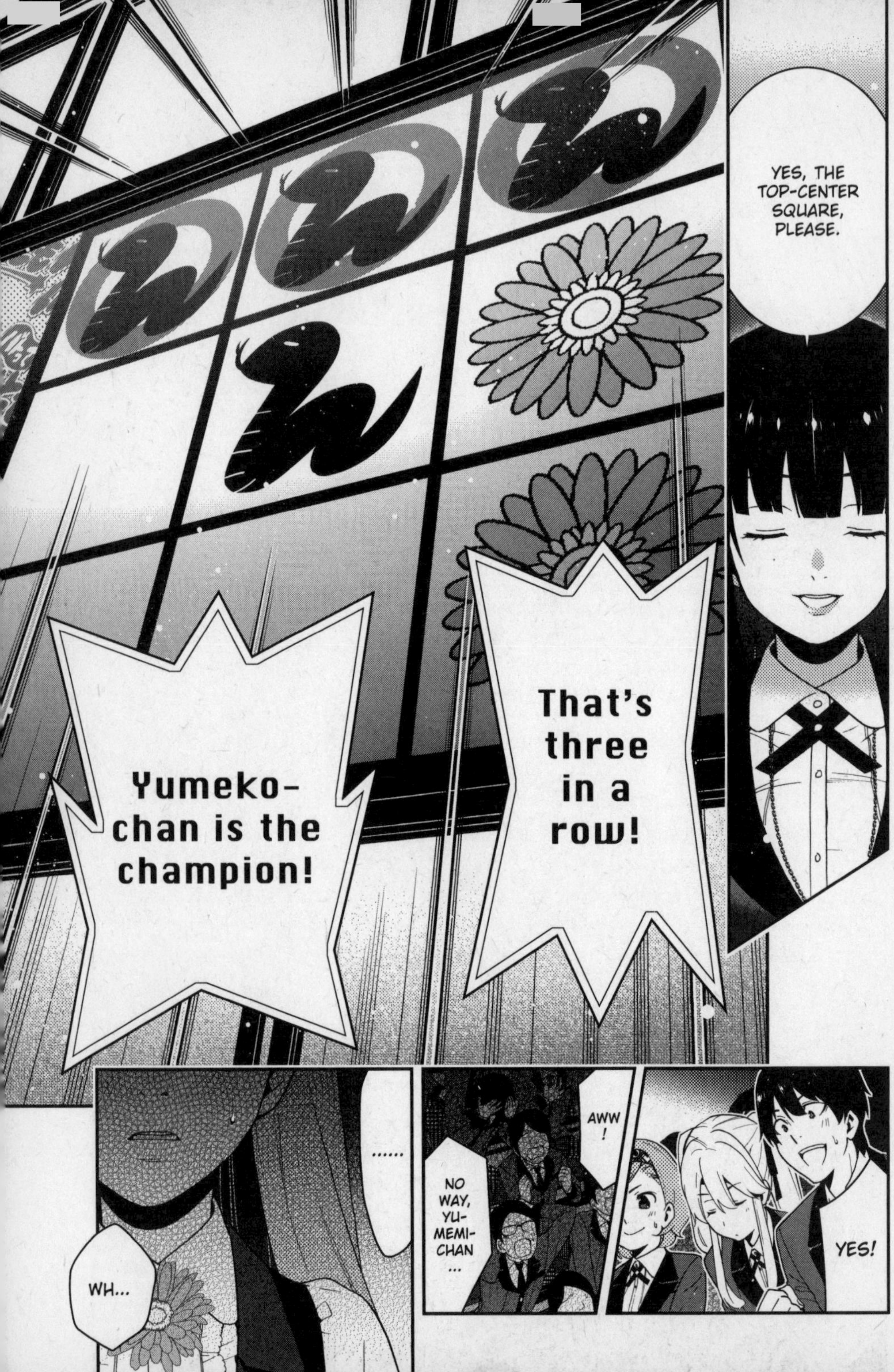
YES, THE TOP-CENTER SQUARE, PLEASE.
That's three in a row!
Yumeko-chan is the champion!
YES!
AWW!
NO WAY, YUMEMI-CHAN...
......
WH...

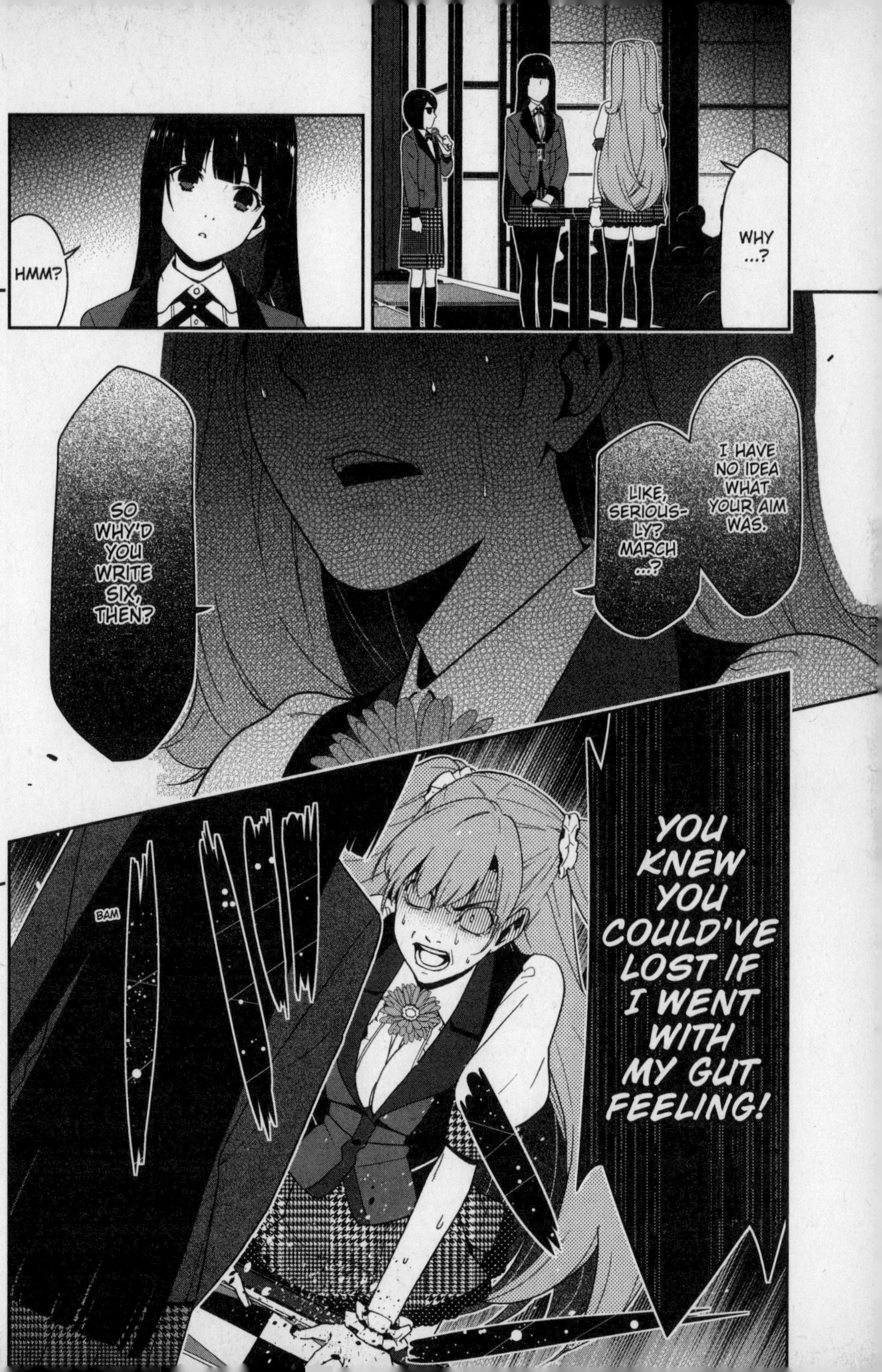
WHY ...?
HMM?
I HAVE NO IDEA WHAT YOUR AIM WAS.
LIKE, SERIOUS-LY? MARCH ...?
SO WHY'D YOU WRITE SIX, THEN?
YOU KNEW YOU COULD'VE LOST IF I WENT WITH MY GUT FEELING!
BAM

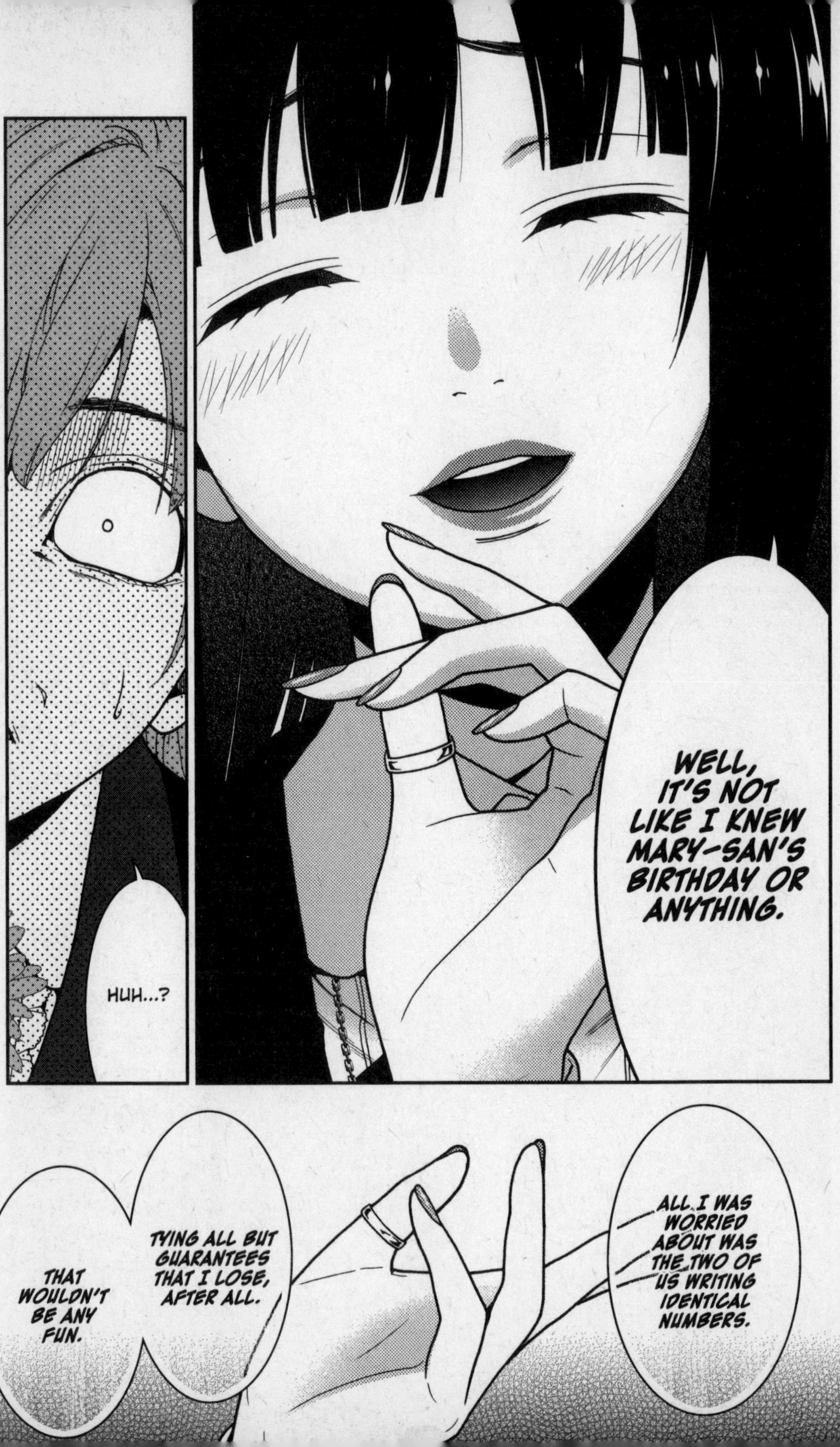
WELL, IT'S NOT LIKE I KNEW MARY-SAN'S BIRTHDAY OR ANYTHING.
HUH...?
ALL I WAS WORRIED ABOUT WAS THE TWO OF US WRITING IDENTICAL NUMBERS.
TYING ALL BUT GUARANTEES THAT I LOSE, AFTER ALL.
THAT WOULDN'T BE ANY FUN.

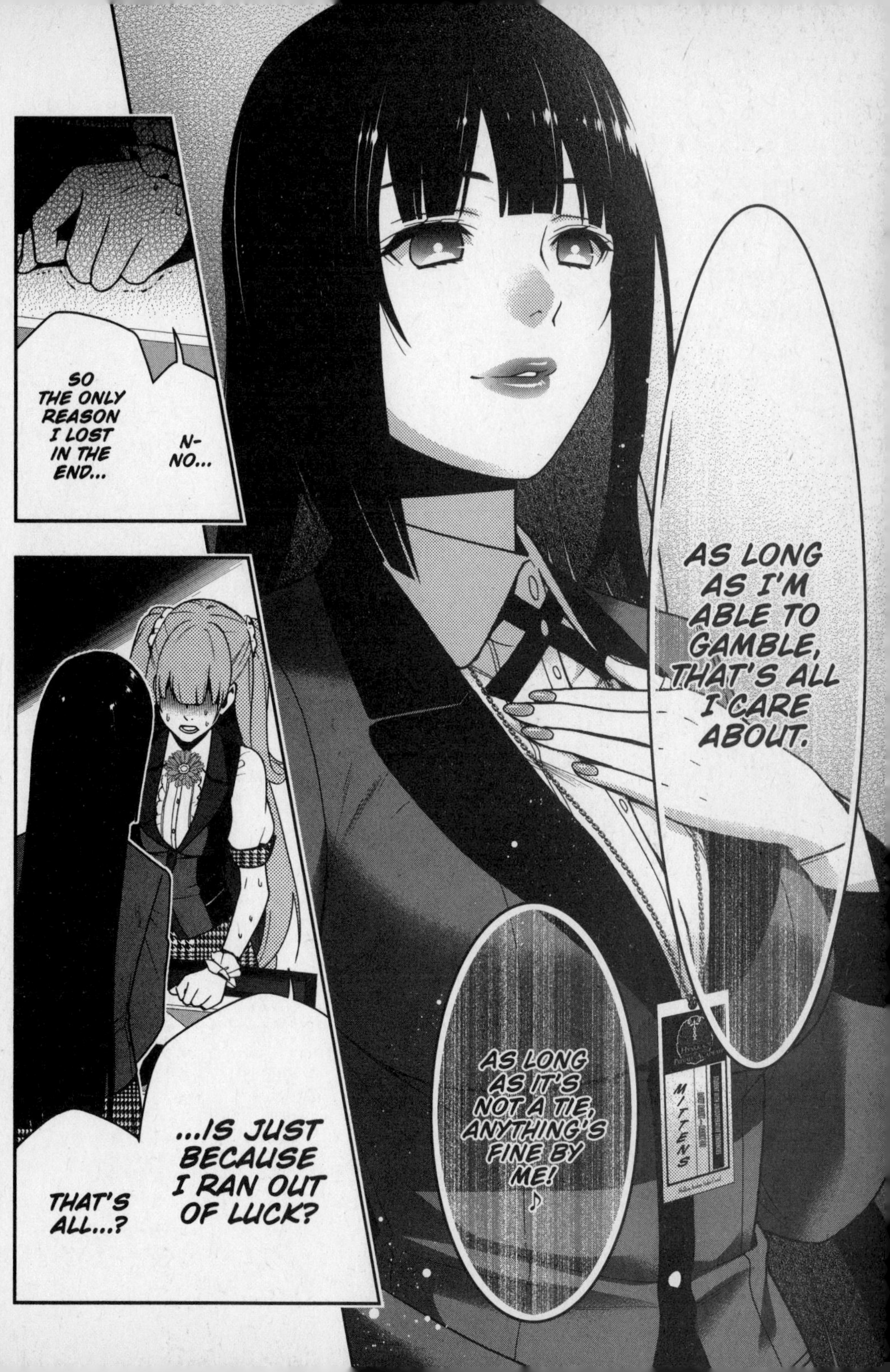
AS LONG AS I'M ABLE TO GAMBLE, THAT'S ALL I CARE ABOUT.
AS LONG AS IT'S NOT A TIE, ANYTHING'S FINE BY ME! ♪
N-NO...
SO THE ONLY REASON I LOST IN THE END...
...IS JUST BECAUSE I RAN OUT OF LUCK?
THAT'S ALL...?

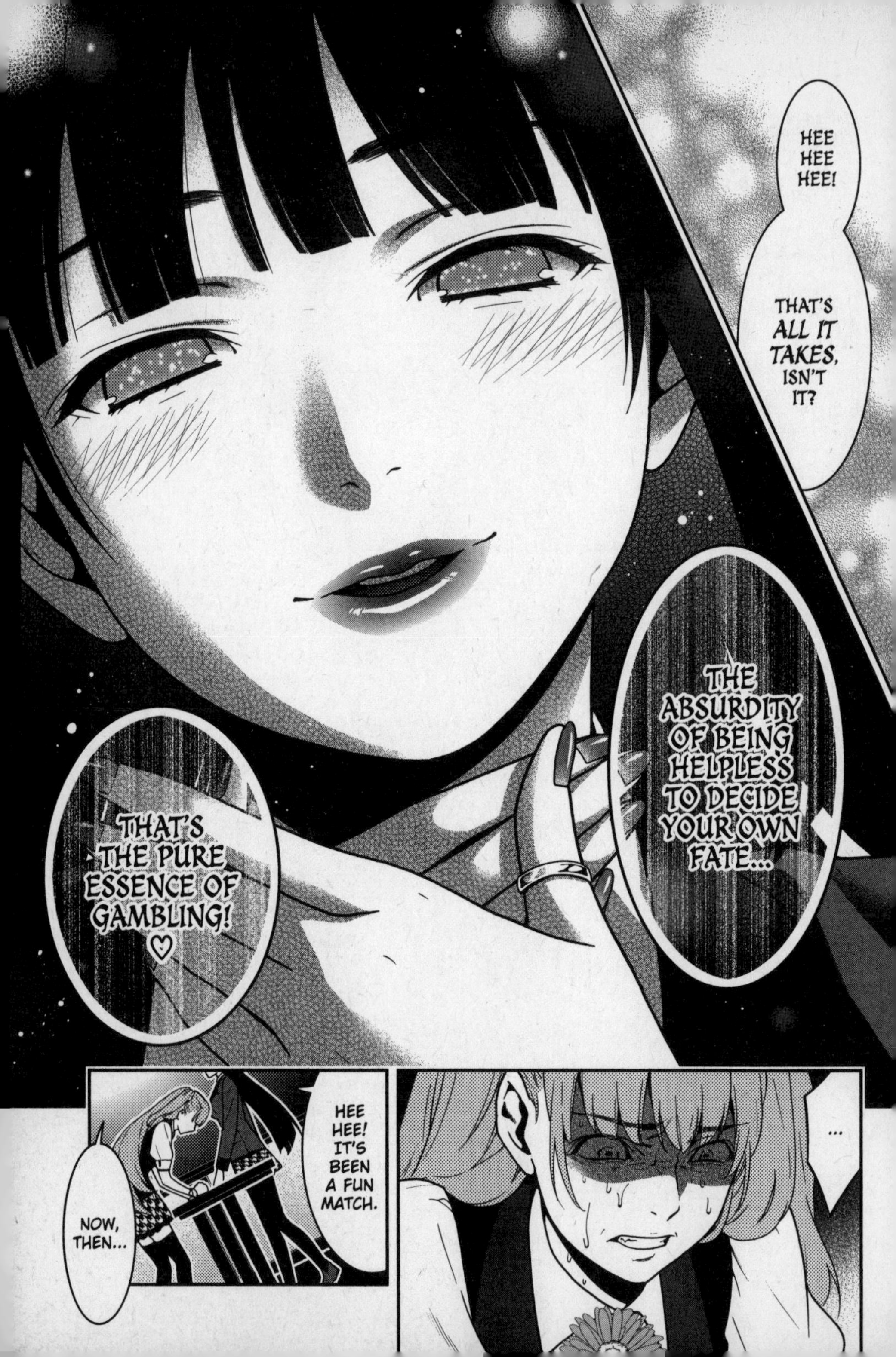
HEE HEE HEE!
THAT'S ALL IT TAKES, ISN'T IT?
THE ABSURDITY OF BEING HELPLESS TO DECIDE YOUR OWN FATE...
THAT'S THE PURE ESSENCE OF GAMBLING! ♡
...
HEE HEE! IT'S BEEN A FUN MATCH.
NOW, THEN...

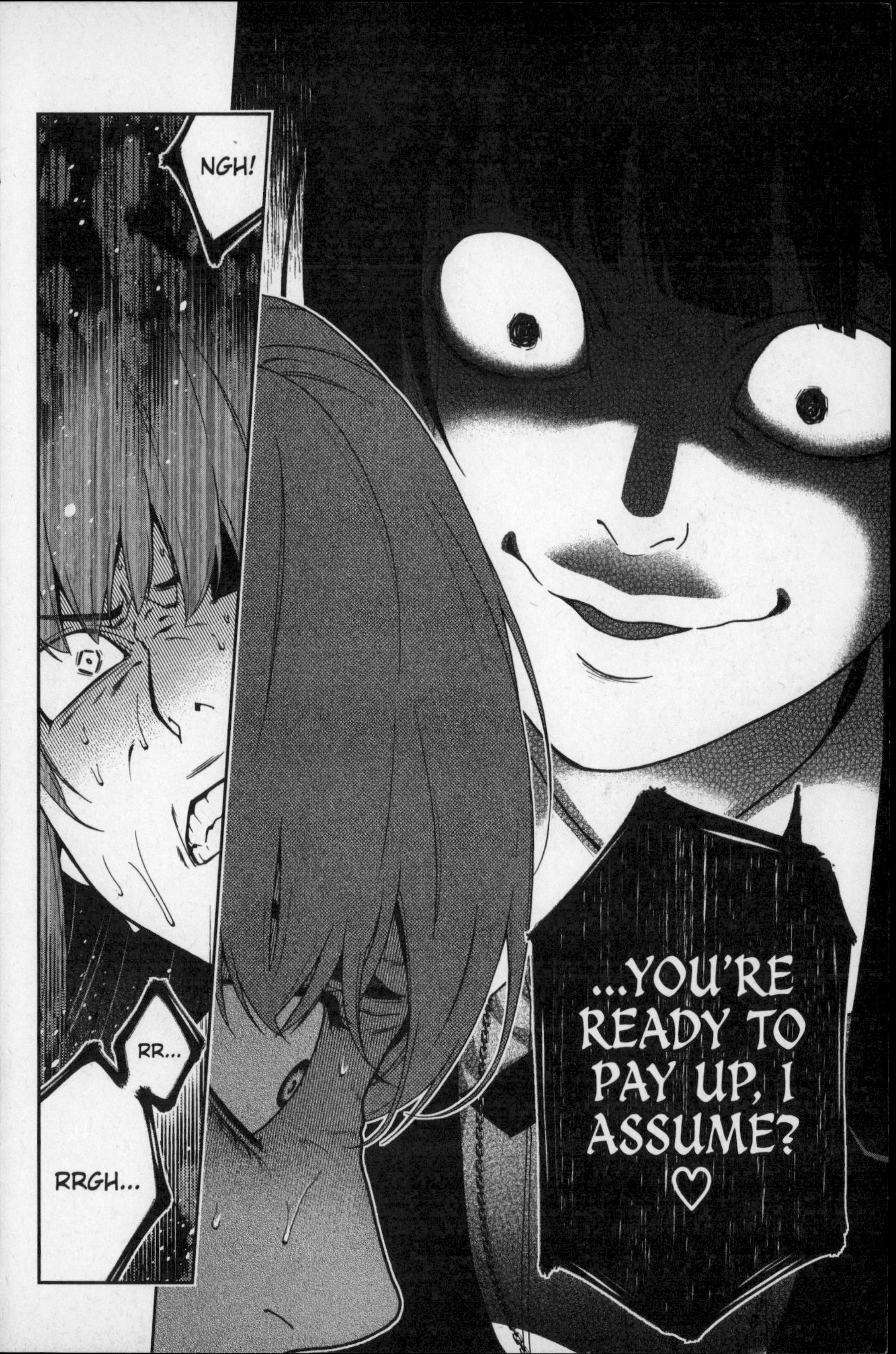
...YOU'RE READY TO PAY UP, I ASSUME? ♡
NGH!
RR...
RRGH...

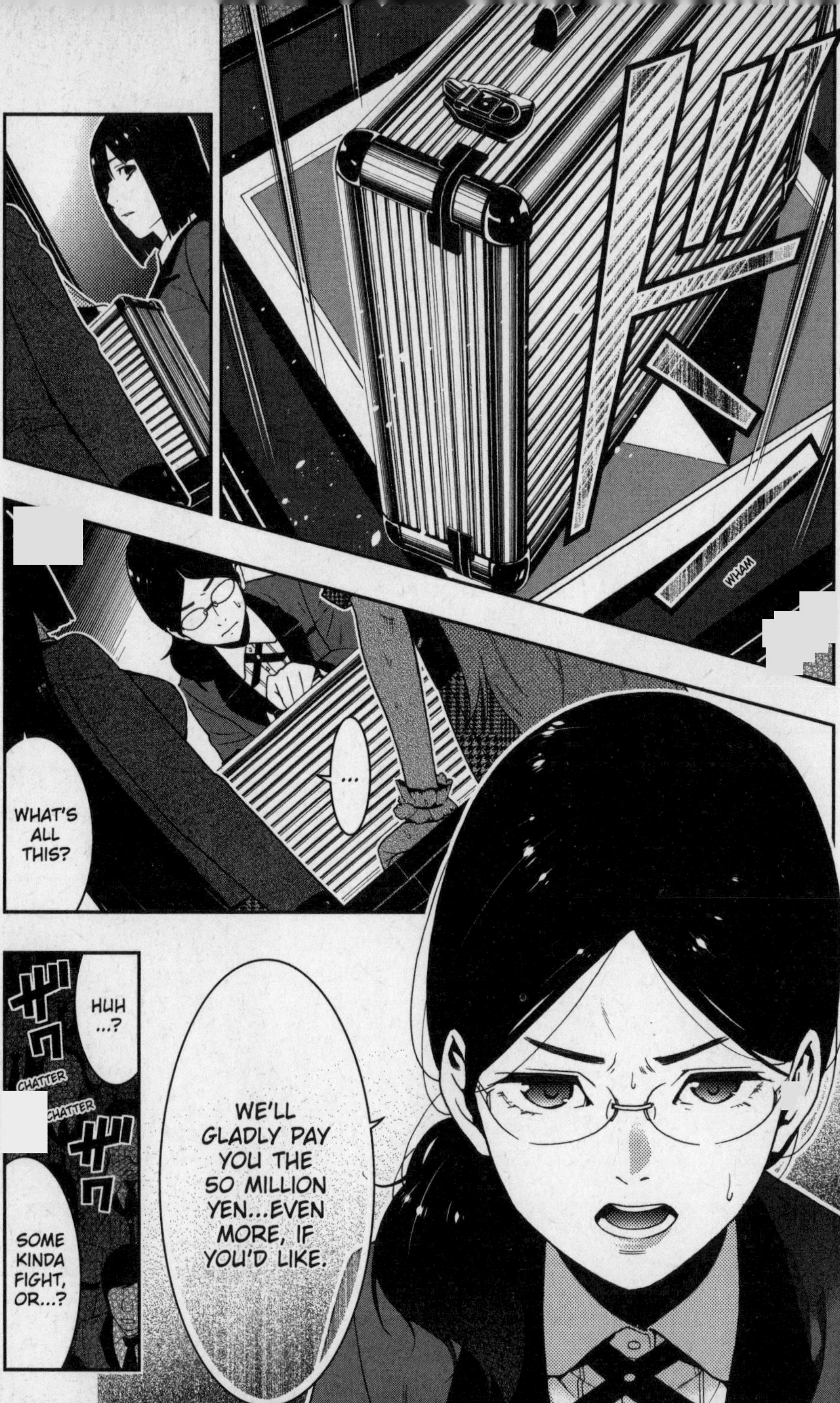
WHAM
...
WHAT'S ALL THIS?
WE'LL GLADLY PAY YOU THE 50 MILLION YEN...EVEN MORE, IF YOU'D LIKE.
HUH ...?
CHATTER
CHATTER
SOME KINDA FIGHT, OR...?

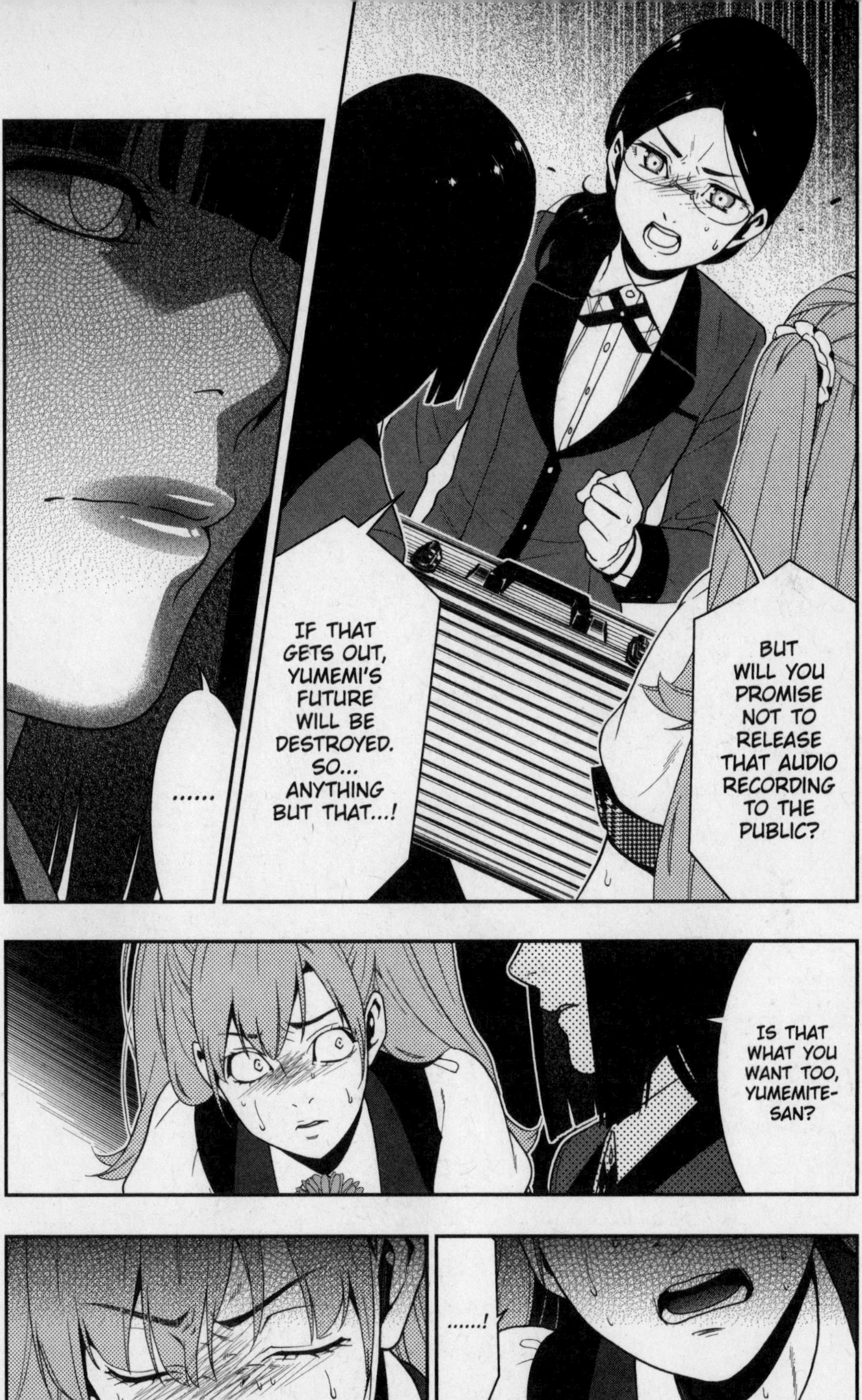
BUT WILL YOU PROMISE NOT TO RELEASE THAT AUDIO RECORDING TO THE PUBLIC?
IF THAT GETS OUT, YUMEMI'S FUTURE WILL BE DESTROYED. SO... ANYTHING BUT THAT...!
......
IS THAT WHAT YOU WANT TOO, YUMEMITE-SAN?
......!

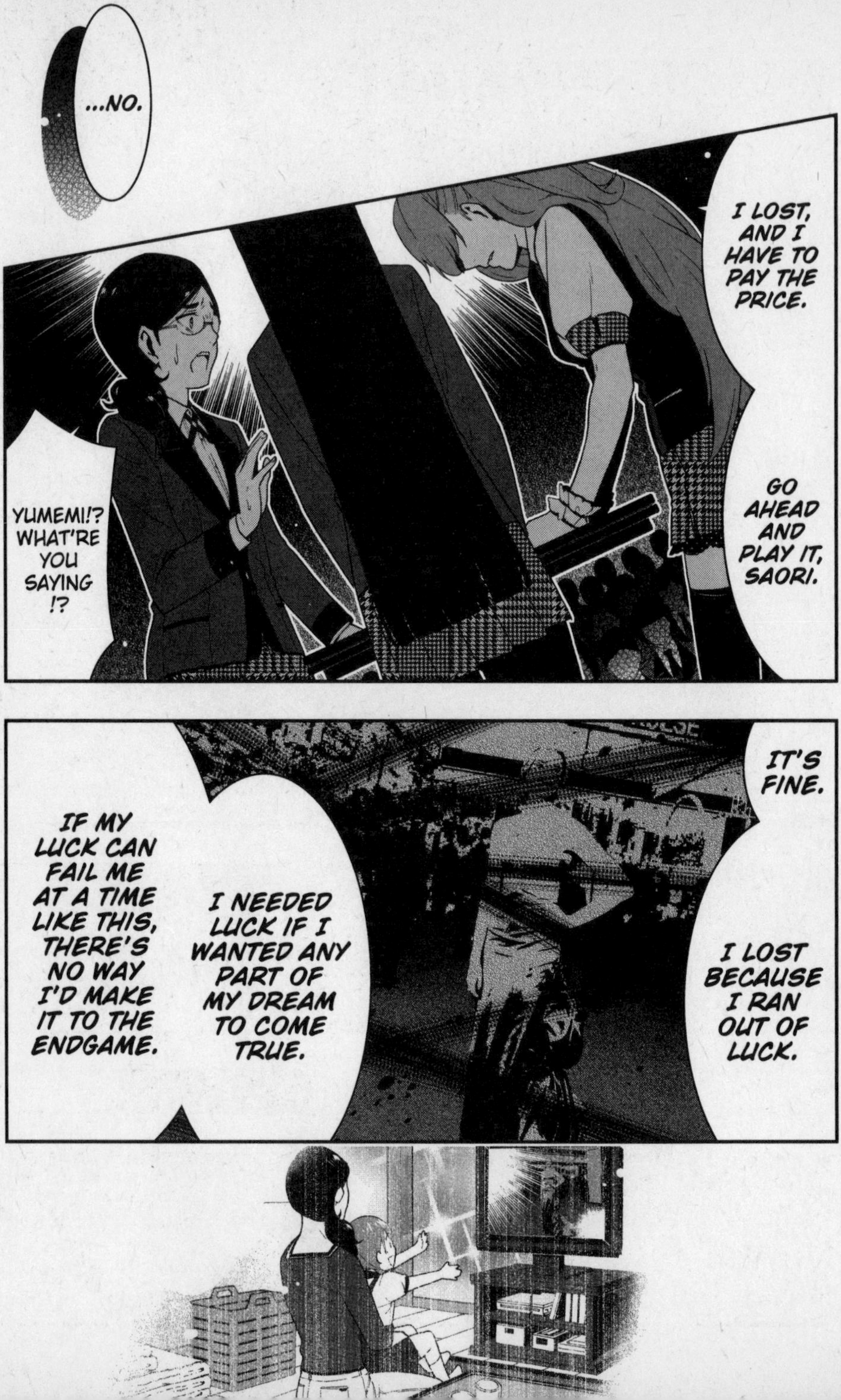
...NO.
I LOST, AND I HAVE TO PAY THE PRICE.
GO AHEAD AND PLAY IT, SAORI.
YUMEMI!? WHAT'RE YOU SAYING!?
IT'S FINE.
I LOST BECAUSE I RAN OUT OF LUCK.
I NEEDED LUCK IF I WANTED ANY PART OF MY DREAM TO COME TRUE.
IF MY LUCK CAN FAIL ME AT A TIME LIKE THIS, THERE'S NO WAY I'D MAKE IT TO THE ENDGAME.

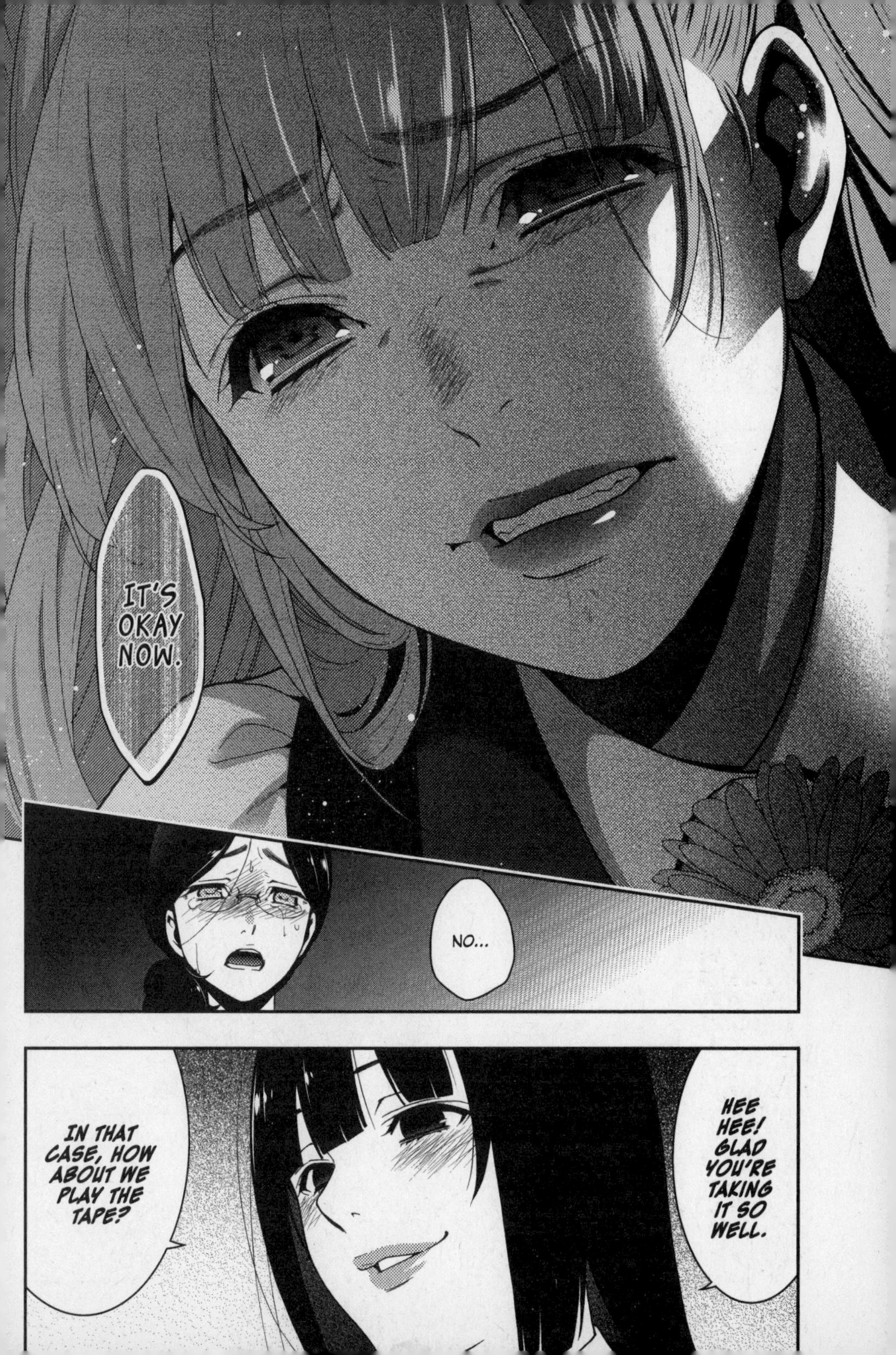
IT'S OKAY NOW.
NO...
HEE HEE! GLAD YOU'RE TAKING IT SO WELL.
IN THAT CASE, HOW ABOUT WE PLAY THE TAPE?

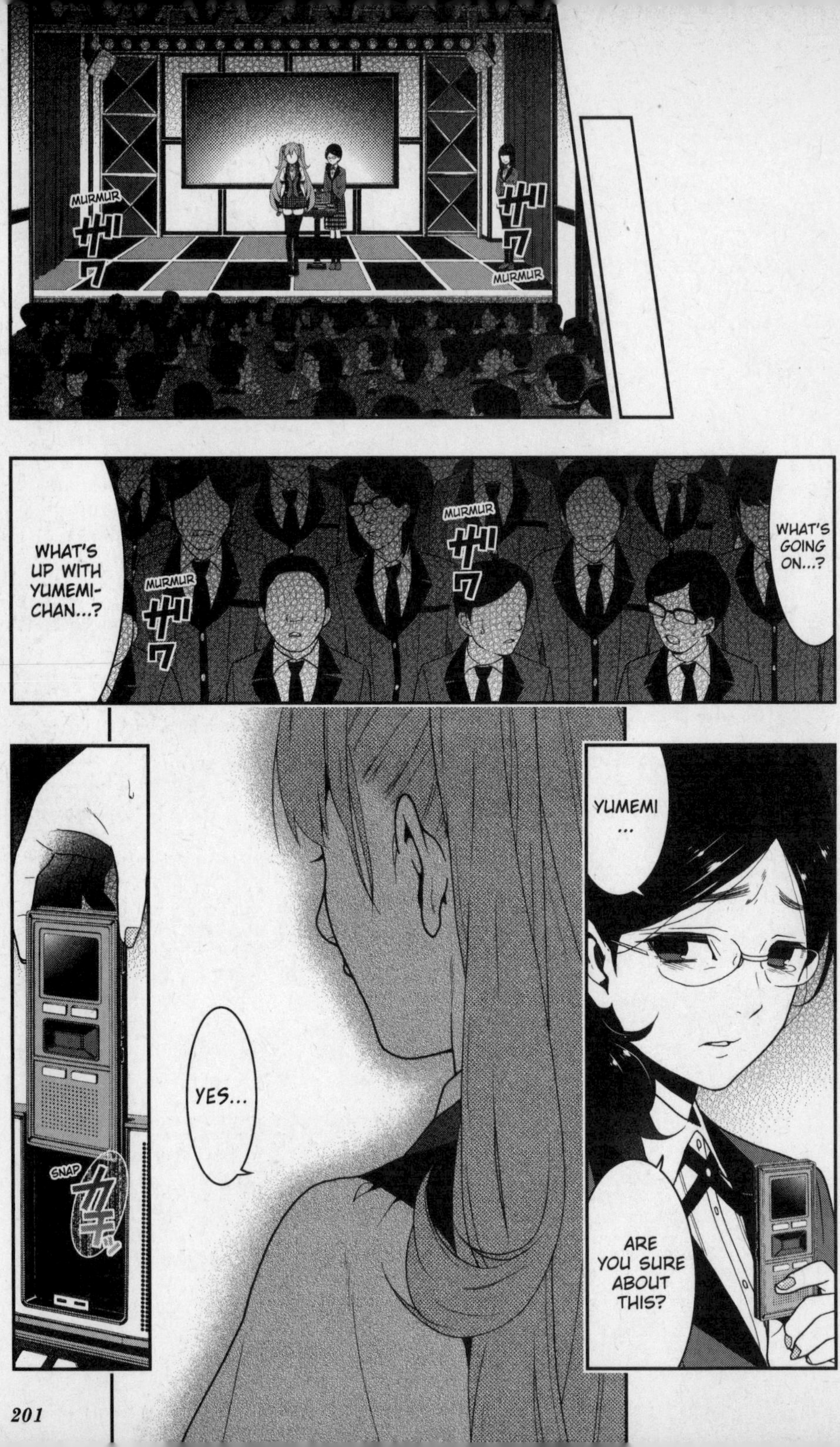
MURMUR
MURMUR
WHAT'S GOING ON...?
MURMUR
MURMUR
WHAT'S UP WITH YUMEMI-CHAN...?
YUMEMI ...
ARE YOU SURE ABOUT THIS?
YES...
SNAP

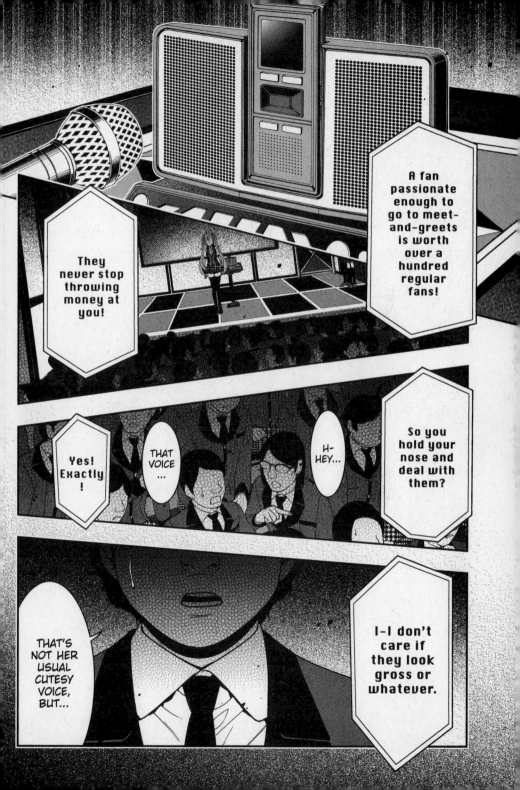

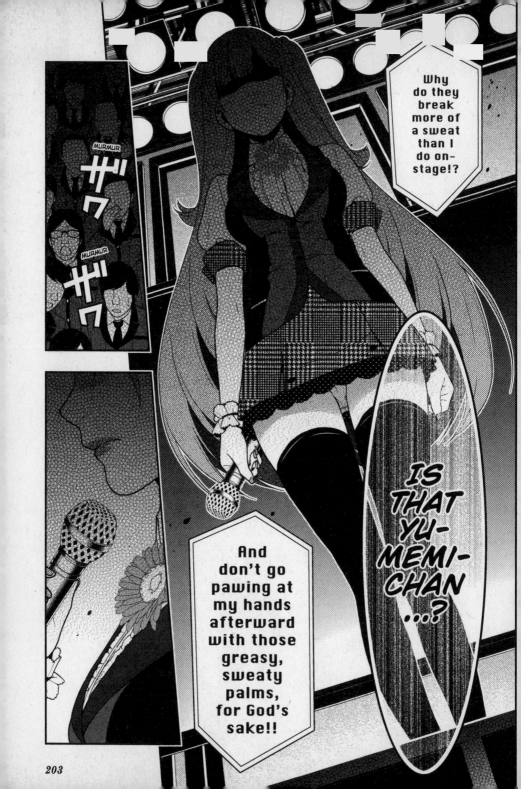

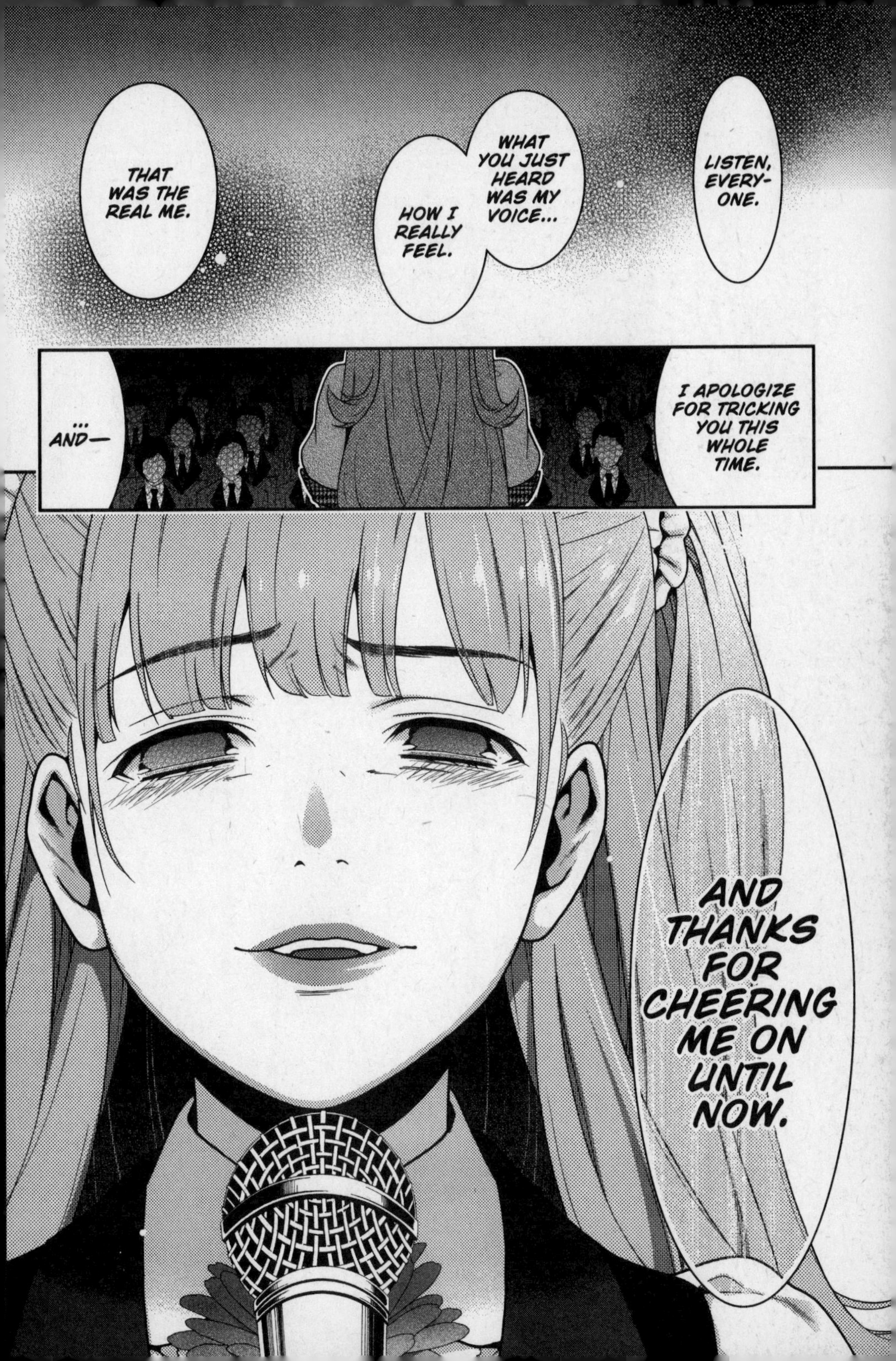
LISTEN, EVERYONE.
WHAT YOU JUST HEARD WAS MY VOICE...
HOW I REALLY FEEL.
THAT WAS THE REAL ME.
I APOLOGIZE FOR TRICKING YOU THIS WHOLE TIME.
...AND—
AND THANKS FOR CHEERING ME ON UNTIL NOW.

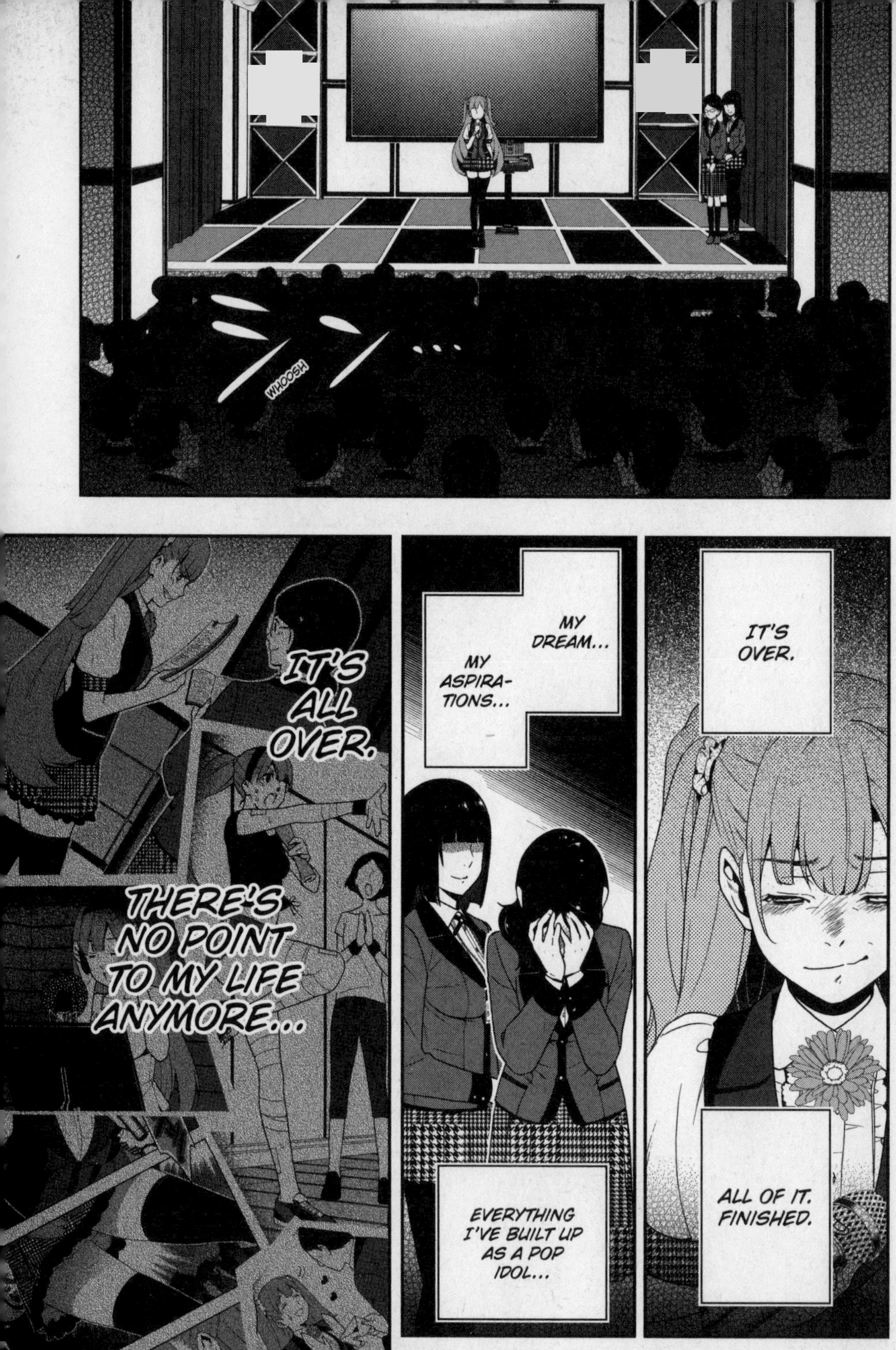
WHOOSH
IT'S OVER.
ALL OF IT. FINISHED.
MY DREAM...
MY ASPIRATIONS...
EVERYTHING I'VE BUILT UP AS A POP IDOL...
IT'S ALL OVER.
THERE'S NO POINT TO MY LIFE ANYMORE...

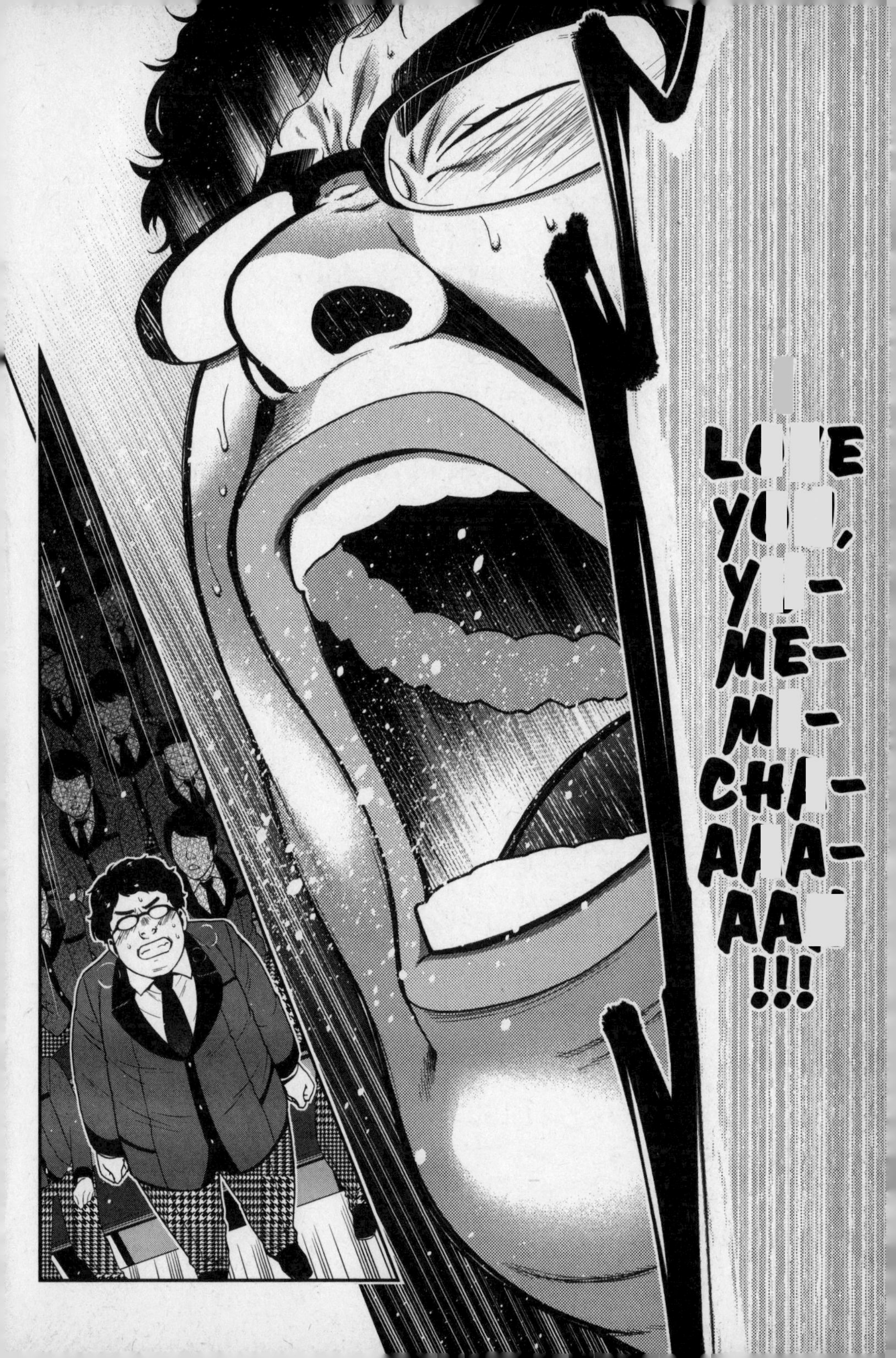

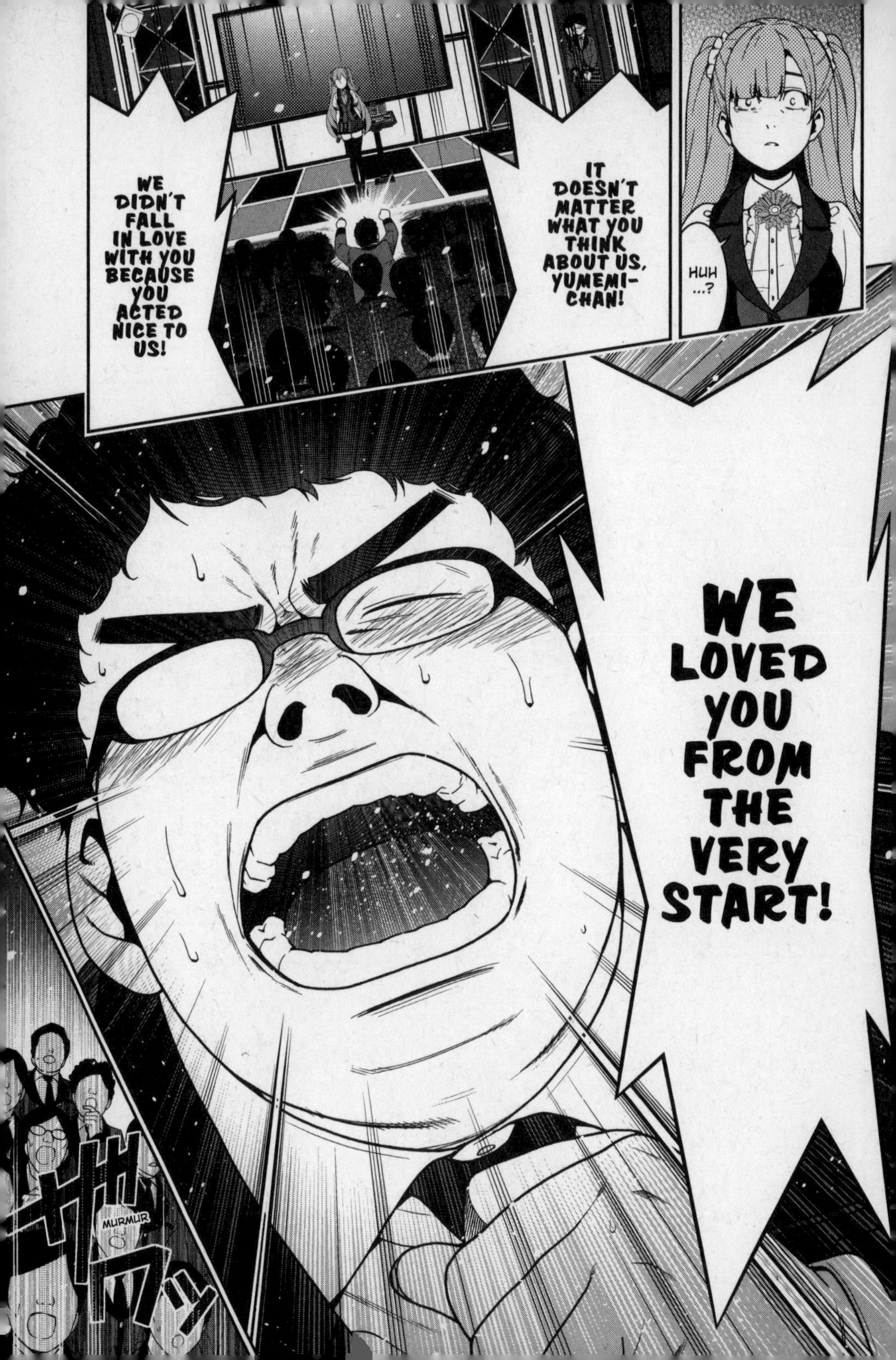
HUH ...?
IT DOESN'T MATTER WHAT YOU THINK ABOUT US, YUMEMI-CHAN!
WE DIDN'T FALL IN LOVE WITH YOU BECAUSE YOU ACTED NICE TO US!
WE LOVED YOU FROM THE VERY START!
MURMUR

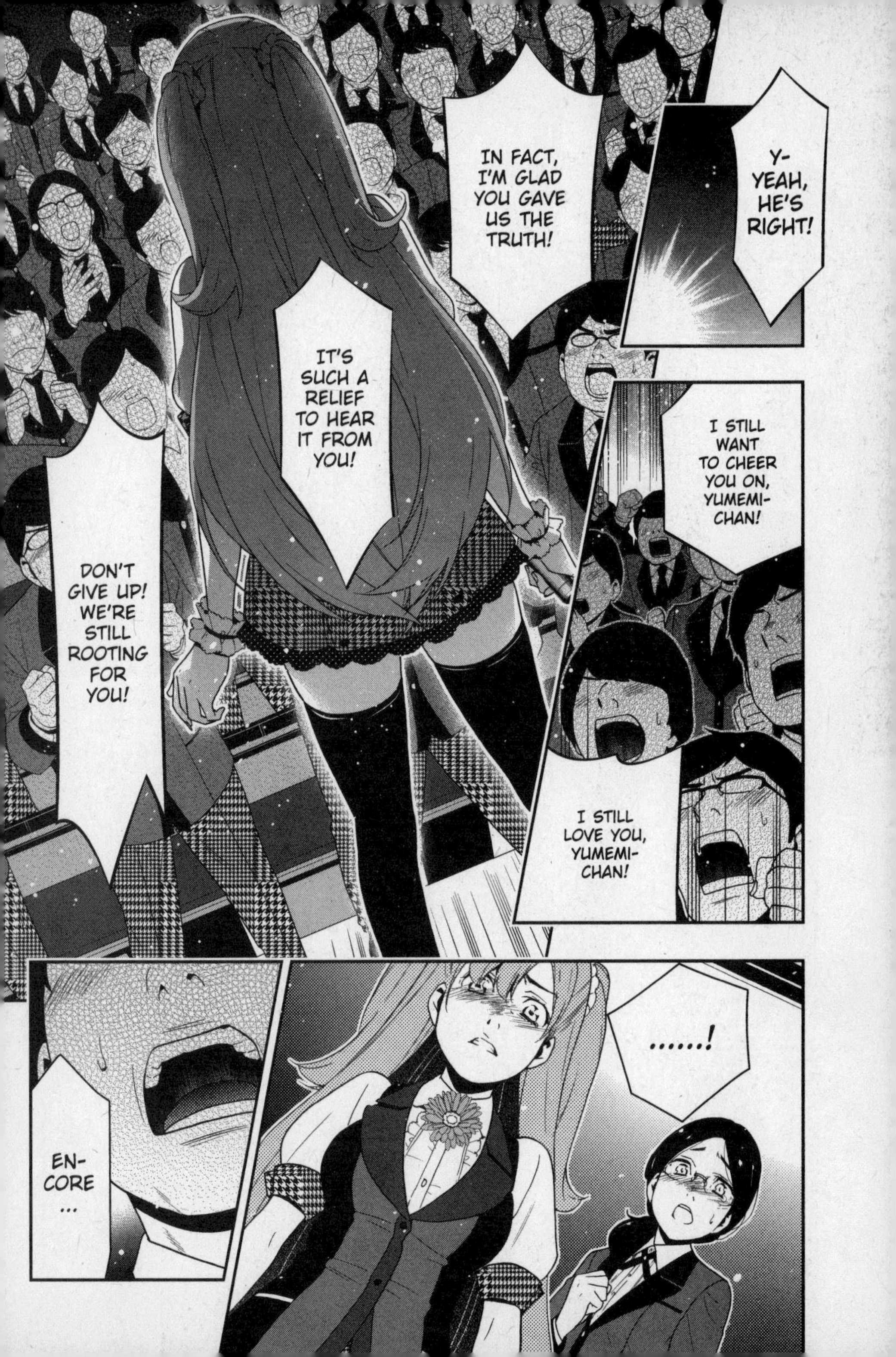
Y-YEAH, HE'S RIGHT!
I STILL WANT TO CHEER YOU ON, YUMEMI-CHAN!
I STILL LOVE YOU, YUMEMI-CHAN!
IN FACT, I'M GLAD YOU GAVE US THE TRUTH!
IT'S SUCH A RELIEF TO HEAR IT FROM YOU!
DON'T GIVE UP! WE'RE STILL ROOTING FOR YOU!
......!
EN-CORE...

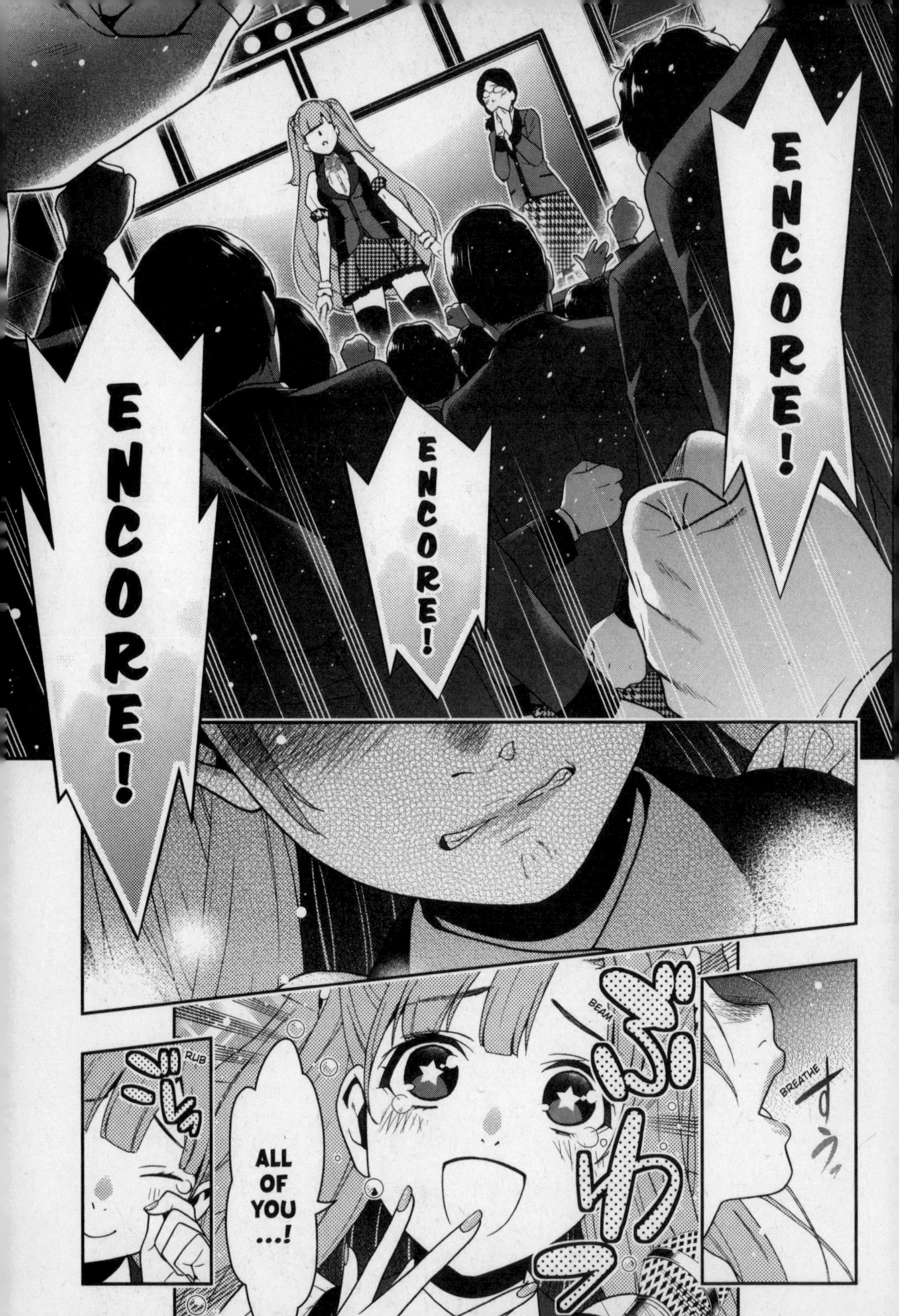
ENCORE!
ENCORE!
ENCORE!
BREATHE
すぅ
BEAM
ぶわっ
ALL OF YOU...!
RUB

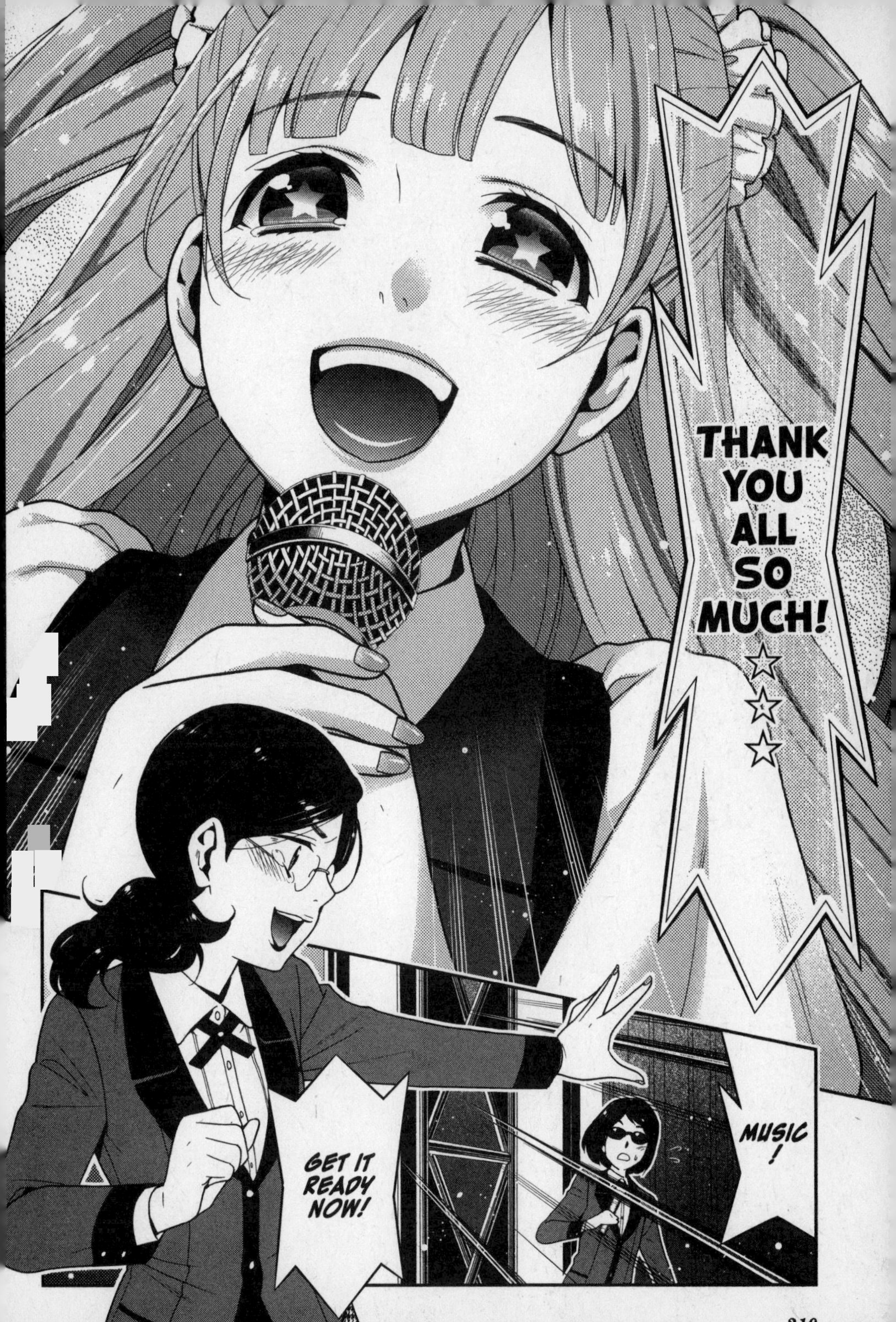
THANK YOU ALL SO MUCH! ☆☆☆
MUSIC!
GET IT READY NOW!

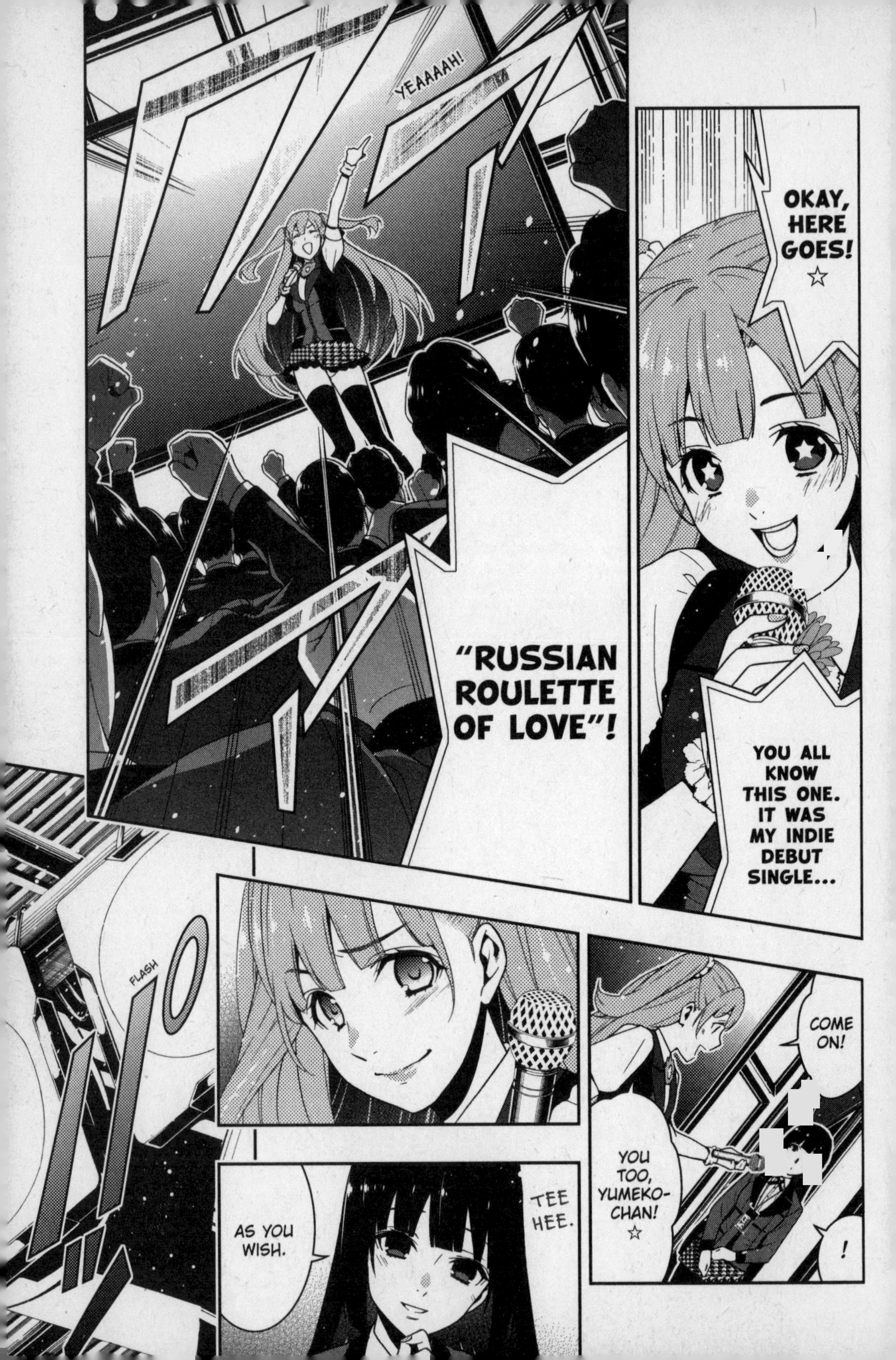
OKAY, HERE GOES! ☆
YOU ALL KNOW THIS ONE. IT WAS MY INDIE DEBUT SINGLE...
"RUSSIAN ROULETTE OF LOVE"!
YEAAAAH!
COME ON!
YOU TOO, YUMEKO-CHAN! ☆
!
FLASH
TEE HEE.
AS YOU WISH.

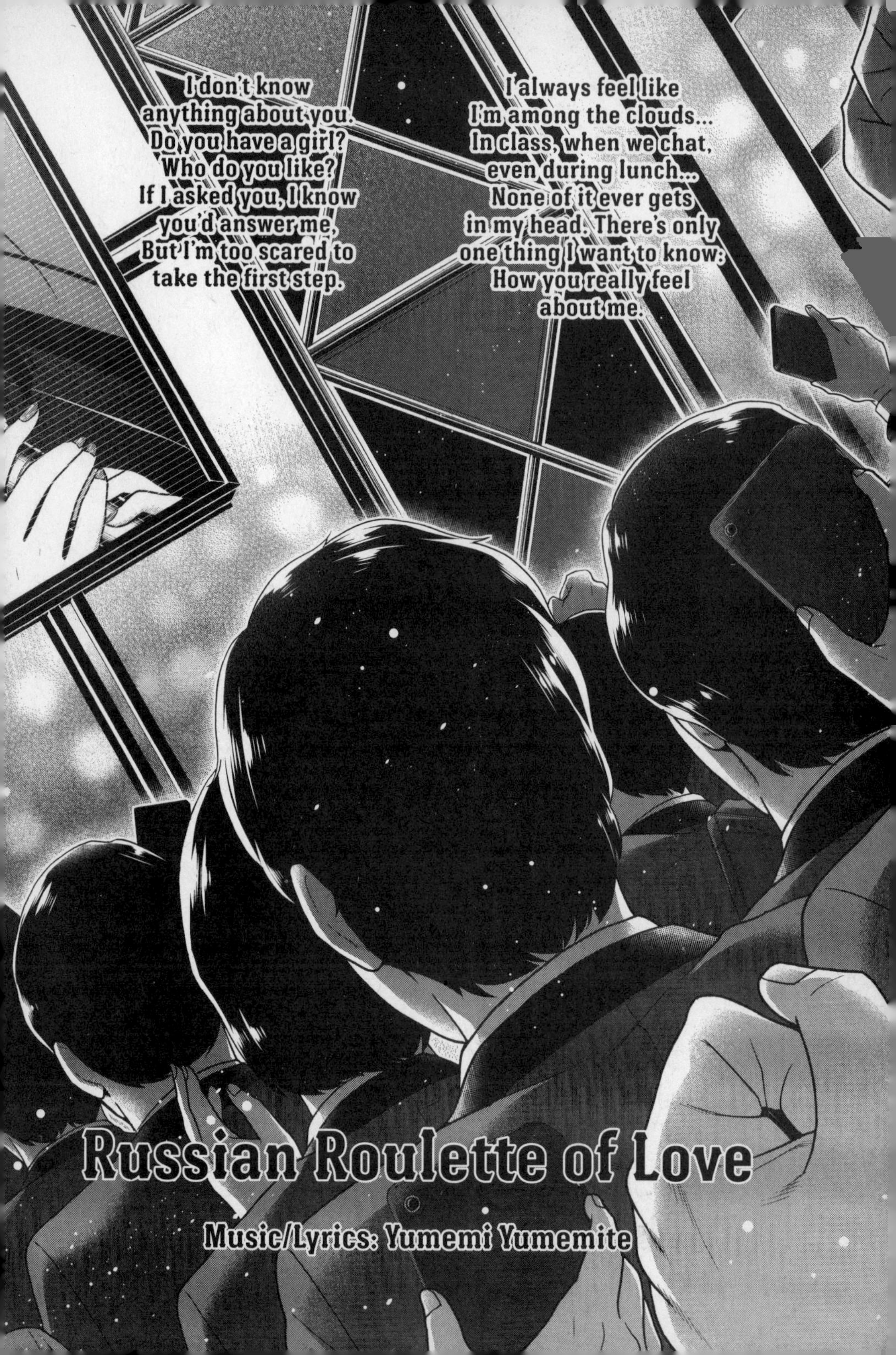
I always feel like I'm among the clouds... In class, when we chat, even during lunch... None of it ever gets in my head. There's only one thing I want to know: How you really feel about me.
I don't know anything about you. Do you have a girl? Who do you like? If I asked you, I know you'd answer me. But I'm too scared to take the first step.
Russian Roulette of Love
Music/Lyrics: Yumemi Yumemite

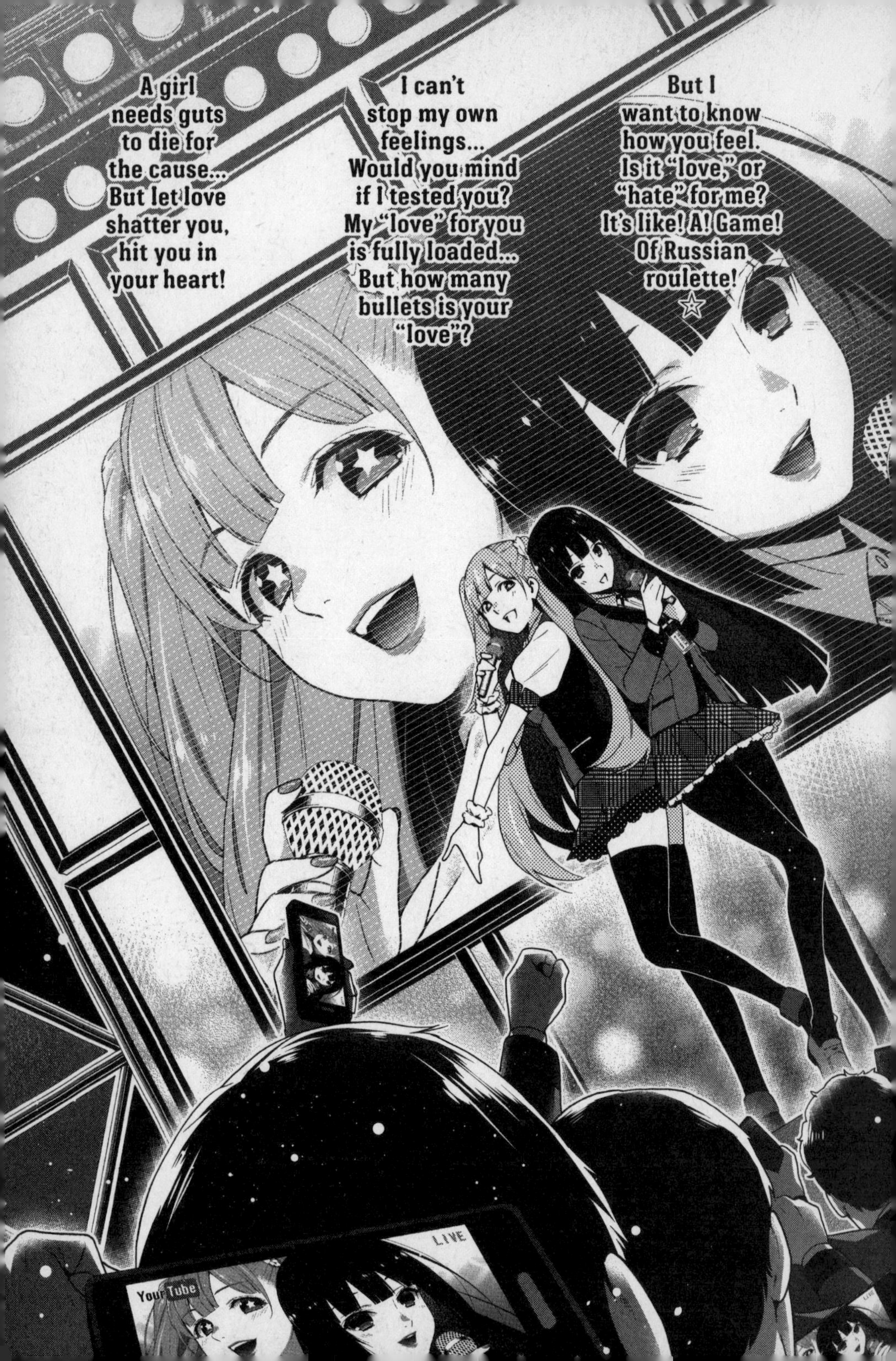
But I want to know how you feel. Is it "love," or "hate" for me? It's like! A! Game! Of Russian roulette! ☆
I can't stop my own feelings... Would you mind if I tested you? My "love" for you is fully loaded... But how many bullets is your "love"?
A girl needs guts to die for the cause... But let love shatter you, hit you in your heart!
LIVE
Your Tube

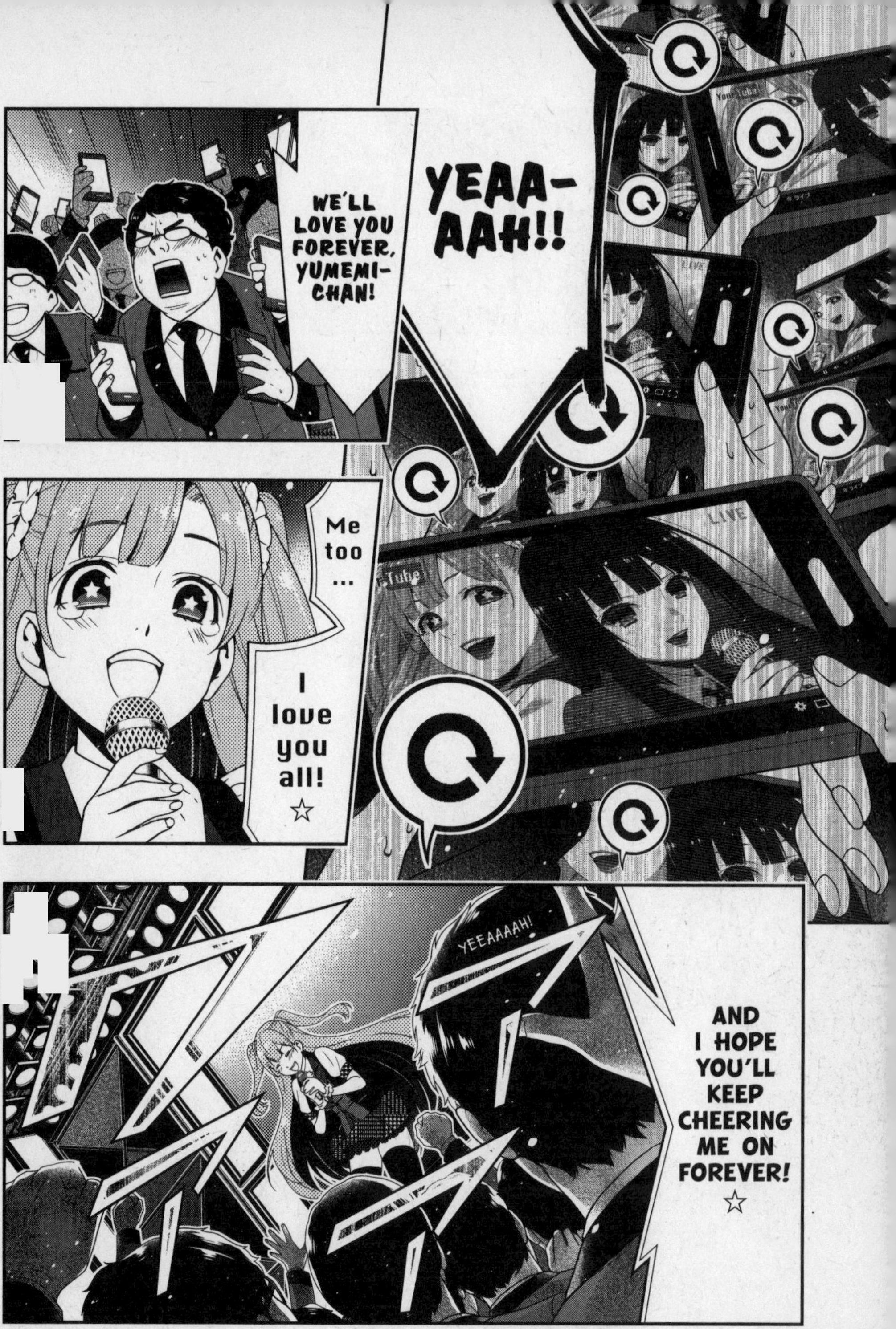
YEAA-AAH!!
WE'LL LOVE YOU FOREVER, YUMEMI-CHAN!
Me too...
I love you all! ☆
YEEAAAAH!
AND I HOPE YOU'LL KEEP CHEERING ME ON FOREVER! ☆

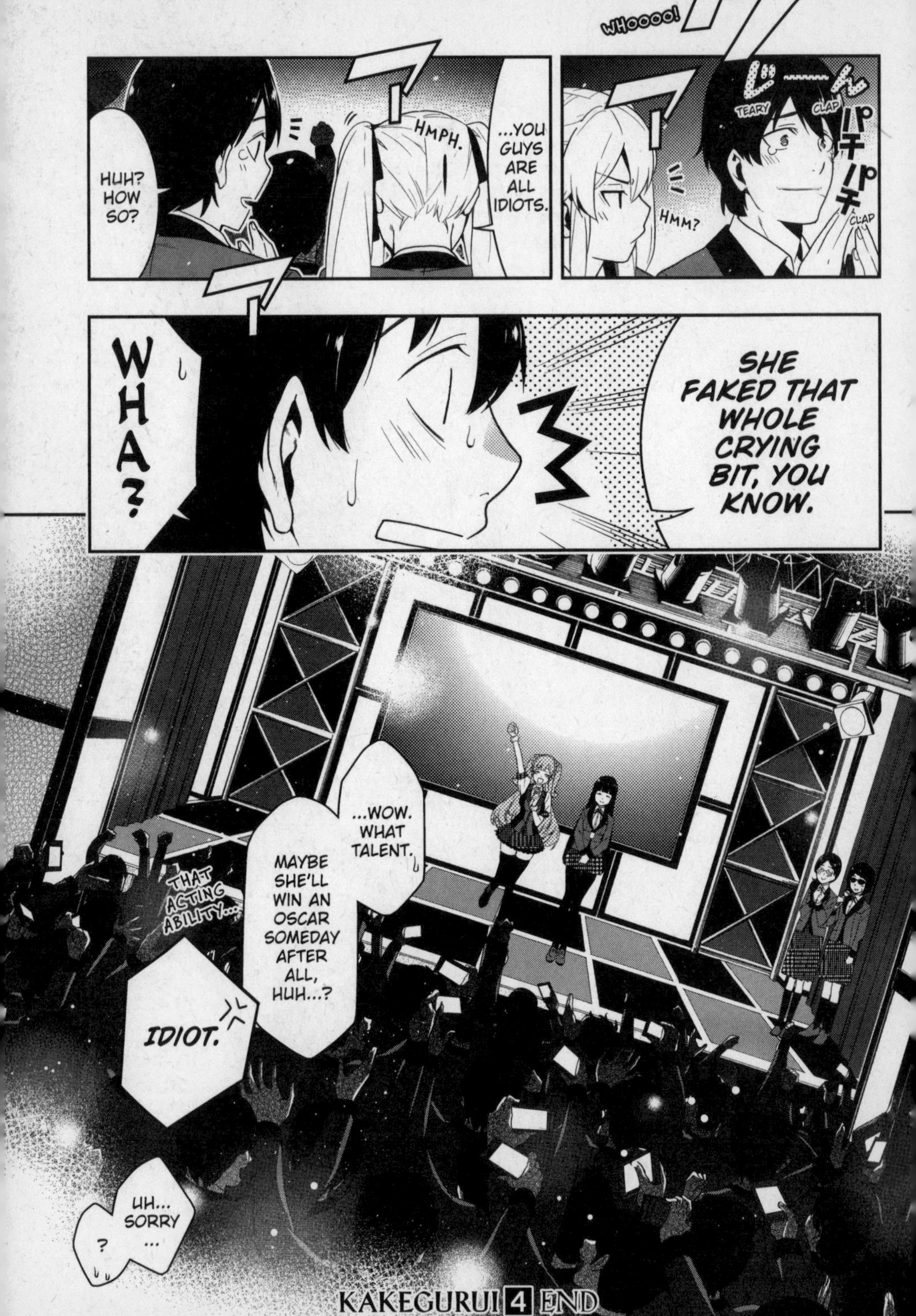
WHOOOO!
じーん
TEARY
パチパチ
CLAP
CLAP
HMM?
...YOU GUYS ARE ALL IDIOTS.
HMPH.
HUH? HOW SO?
SHE FAKED THAT WHOLE CRYING BIT, YOU KNOW.
WHA?
...WOW. WHAT TALENT.
MAYBE SHE'LL WIN AN OSCAR SOMEDAY AFTER ALL, HUH...?
THAT ACTING ABILITY...
IDIOT.
UH... SORRY ...
?

KAKEGURUI 4 END

TIME FOR SOME END-OF-THE-VOLUME BONUS COMICS!

STUDENT COUNCIL MAID CAFÉ PROJECT

*This has no relation to the actual story.

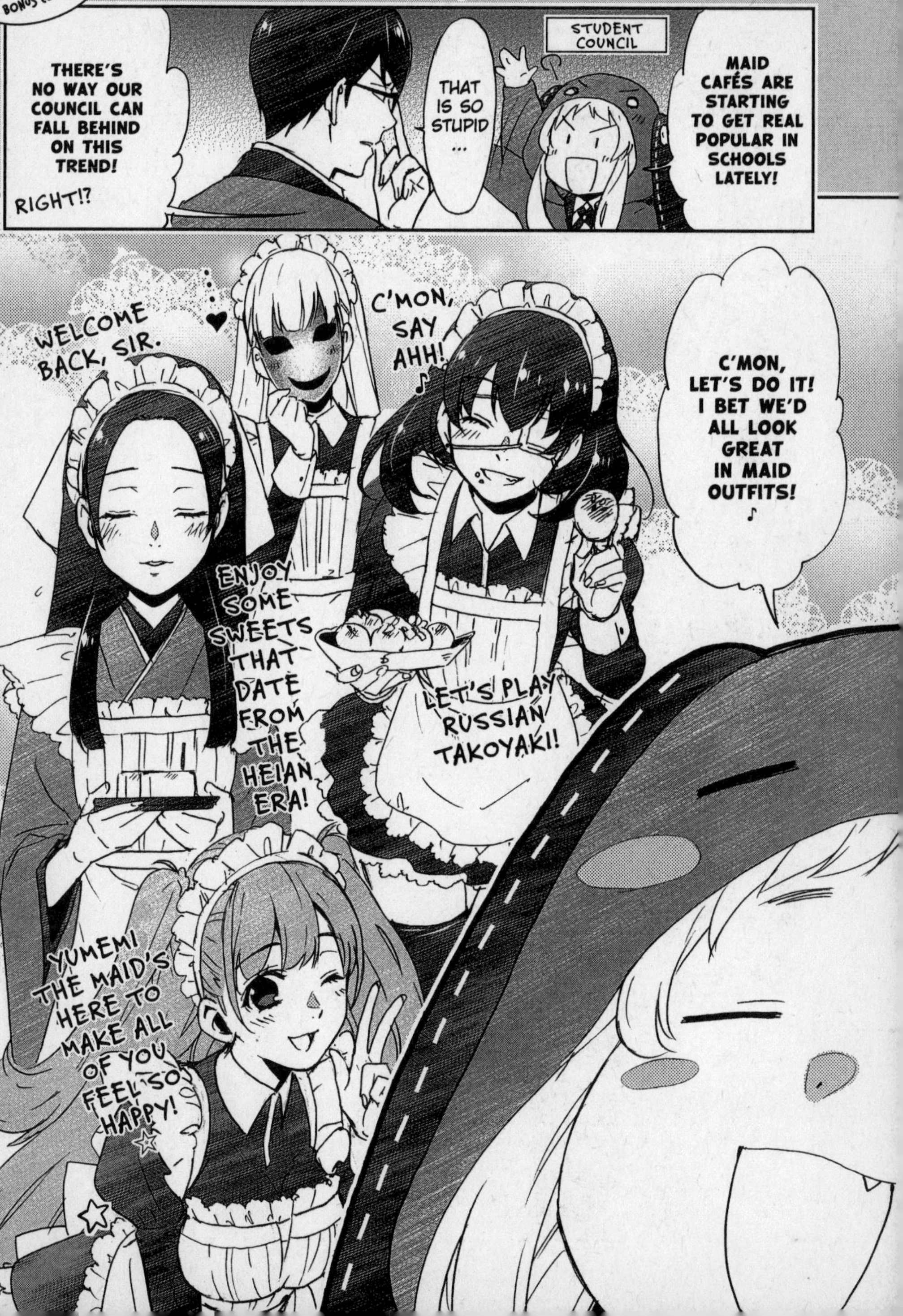
STUDENT COUNCIL
MAID CAFÉS ARE STARTING TO GET REAL POPULAR IN SCHOOLS LATELY!
THAT IS SO STUPID...
THERE'S NO WAY OUR COUNCIL CAN FALL BEHIND ON THIS TREND!
RIGHT!?
C'MON, LET'S DO IT! I BET WE'D ALL LOOK GREAT IN MAID OUTFITS! ♪
C'MON, SAY AHH! ♪
LET'S PLAY RUSSIAN TAKOYAKI!
... ♥
WELCOME BACK, SIR.
ENJOY SOME SWEETS THAT DATE FROM THE HEIAN ERA!
YUMEMI THE MAID'S HERE TO MAKE ALL OF YOU FEEL SO HAPPY! ☆

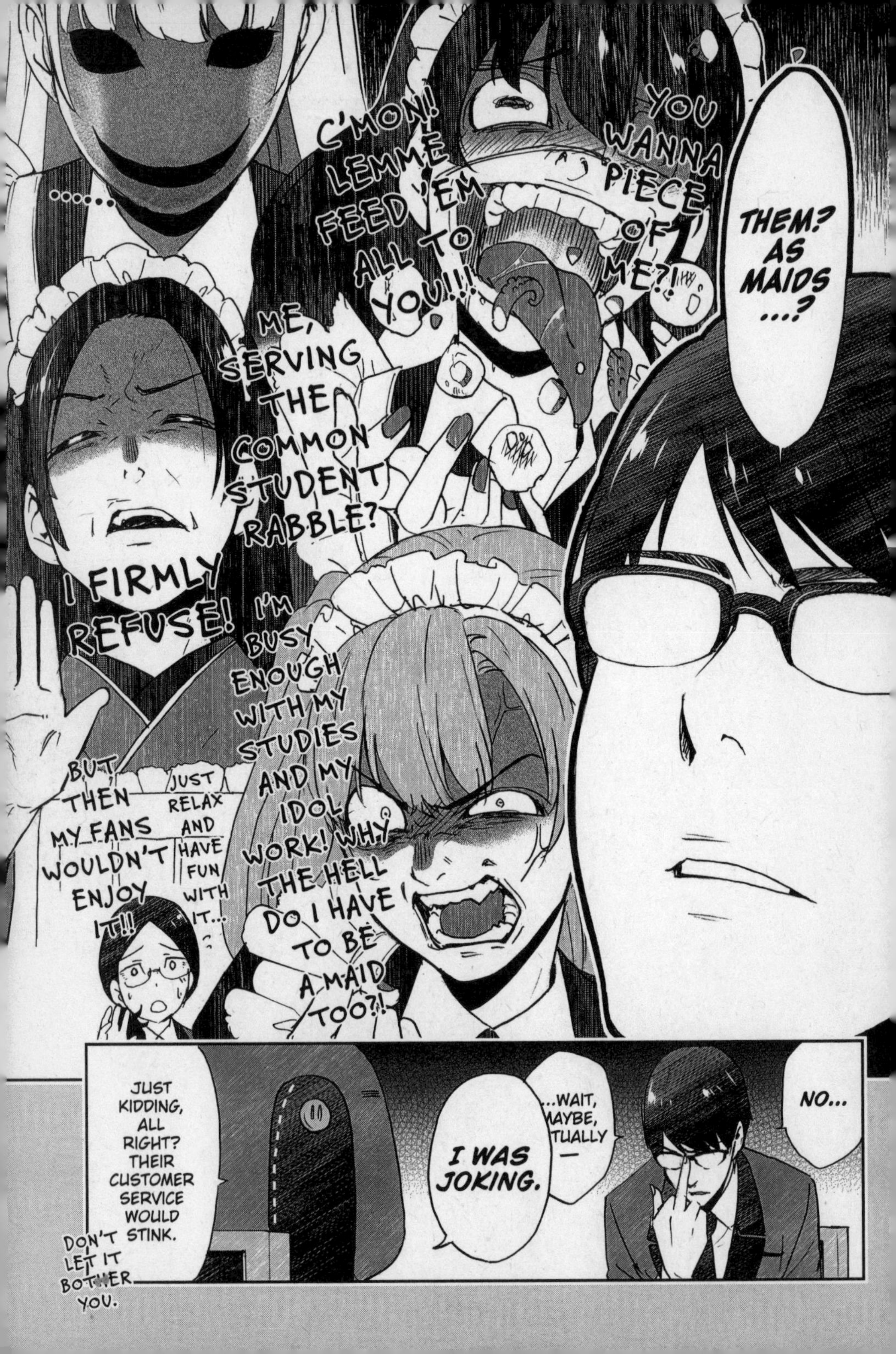
THEM? AS MAIDS...?
YOU WANNA PIECE OF ME?!
C'MON! LEMME FEED 'EM ALL TO YOU!!!
......
ME, SERVING THE COMMON STUDENT RABBLE?
I FIRMLY REFUSE!
I'M BUSY ENOUGH WITH MY STUDIES AND MY IDOL WORK! WHY THE HELL DO I HAVE TO BE A MAID TOO?!
JUST RELAX AND HAVE FUN WITH IT...
BUT THEN MY FANS WOULDN'T ENJOY IT!!
NO...
...WAIT, MAYBE, TUALLY—
I WAS JOKING.
JUST KIDDING, ALL RIGHT? THEIR CUSTOMER SERVICE WOULD STINK.
DON'T LET IT BOTHER YOU.

GAMBLING, THAT IS MY RAISON D'ÊTRE.

Battle of the Stars! was originally a show concept for TV or Internet distribution, one that Yumemi altered a bit to add the gambling element. Maybe she thought it up along with the Mari Productions president and his people. There were a few other games that didn't make it in—a sweets matchup, an English-language battle, and a dance competition. These were all other categories Yumemi could've notched perfect scores in if she wanted to—running these during the show would let her adjust her point scores relative to her opponent, making the results more exciting to watch. The "Fan Appreciation" game isn't strictly like that, but it made the cut because it created interaction with the audience.

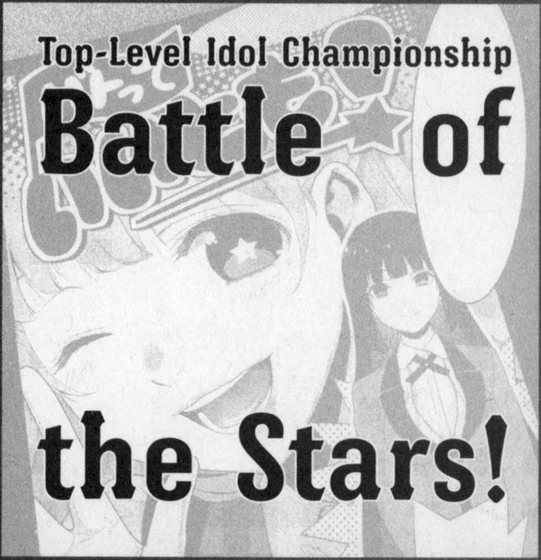

Top-Level Idol Championship
Battle★of the Stars!

Thank you for picking up Volume 4 of *Kakegurui*. Yumemi Yumemite is a very forward-thinking girl, investing all of her talents in the pursuit of her dreams. If it helps her make those dreams come true, there is literally no mountain high enough to stop her. She'll do anything for it—which can sound like a negative thing, but if you look at it another way, it shows how much of a professional attitude she takes toward her career of choice, I think. As an idol, someone whose job it is to sell dreams to her fans, she never lets up for a moment—never reveals a single second of weakness. That might be what being a pro really means in the idol business, the ability to keep providing these dreams that never quite fade. This volume got its start with Yumemi, my vision of what the ultimate idol would be like, as well as the passing thought of what Yumeko would be like as a pop star. It turned out absolutely wonderfully—the art couldn't look any cuter and cooler, and I have Naomura-sensei and his assistants to thank for that. This also goes for our editors—Sasaki-sama, Yumoto-sama—for letting us get away with this silliness, as well as all of our readers and their support. I also have Tanaka and others to mention—thanks to all of you.

The story continues in Volume 5. See you then!

Homura Kawamoto

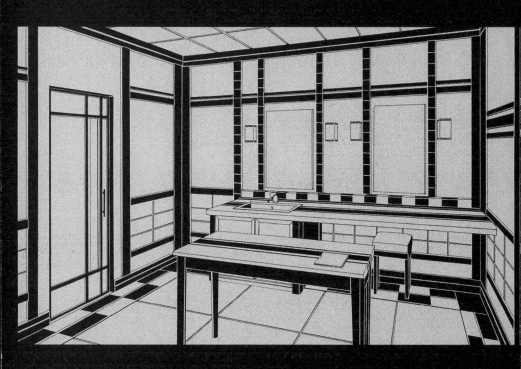

Thanks to all of you for picking up Volume 4 of *Kakegurui*.
I have an important announcement to make.
This volume is going on sale in Japan alongside the first volume of *Kakegurui Twin*,
which stars Mary Saotome. Kei Saiki-sensei is handling the art for that series, and
man—Mary's so cute! And so cool-looking too! She's wonderful, fascinating, and has
just a bit of that yuri feel to her as well!!
I hope you'll keep supporting both *Twin* and the original *Kakegurui*.

SPECIAL THANKS:

My editors · Kawamoto-sama · Imoutoko · Hg-sama ·
AO-sama · M-sama · U-sama

Toru Naomura (artist) December 2015

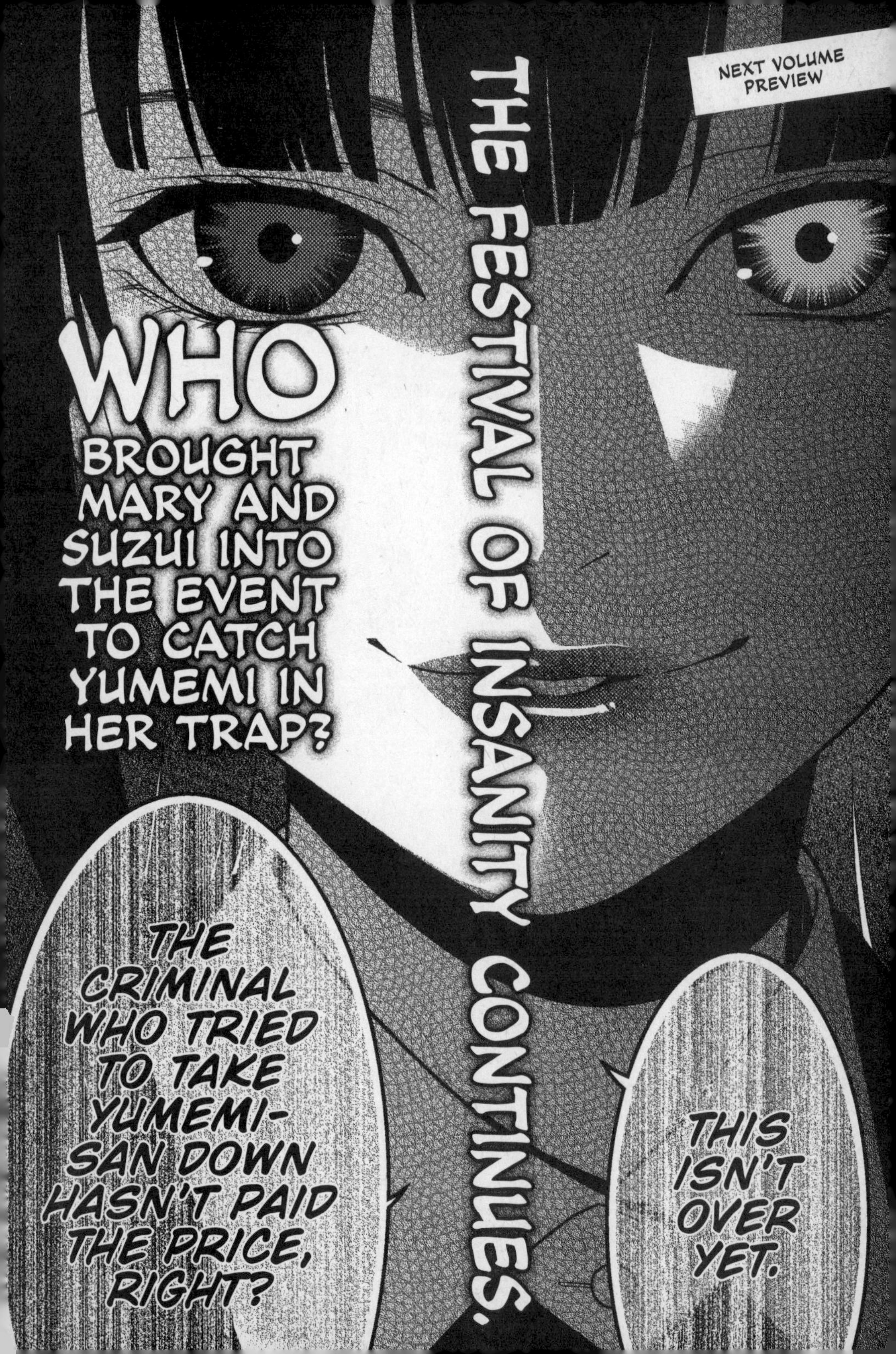
NEXT VOLUME PREVIEW
THE FESTIVAL OF INSANITY CONTINUES.
WHO BROUGHT MARY AND SUZUI INTO THE EVENT TO CATCH YUMEMI IN HER TRAP?
THIS ISN'T OVER YET.
THE CRIMINAL WHO TRIED TO TAKE YUMEMI-SAN DOWN HASN'T PAID THE PRICE, RIGHT?

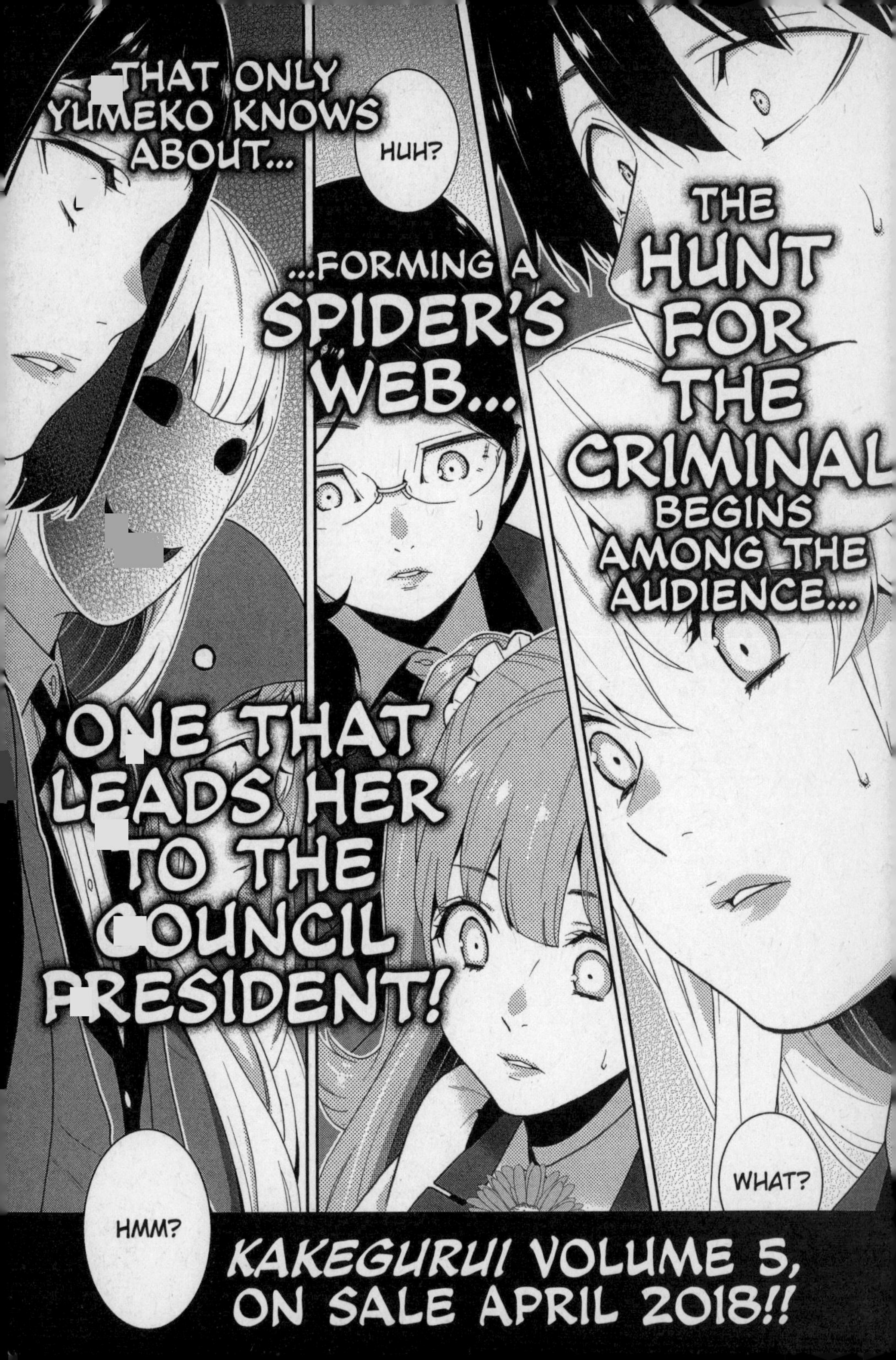
THE HUNT FOR THE CRIMINAL BEGINS AMONG THE AUDIENCE...
WHAT?
HUH?
...FORMING A SPIDER'S WEB...
THAT ONLY YUMEKO KNOWS ABOUT...
ONE THAT LEADS HER TO THE COUNCIL PRESIDENT!
HMM?
KAKEGURUI VOLUME 5, ON SALE APRIL 2018!!

MURDERER
IN THE STREETS, KILLER
IN THE SHEETS!

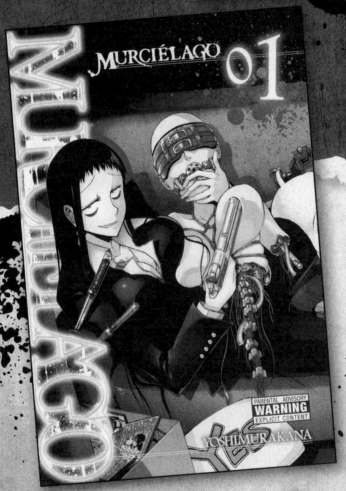

MURCIÉLAGO 01

YOSHIMURAKANA

PARENTAL ADVISORY
WARNING
EXPLICIT CONTENT

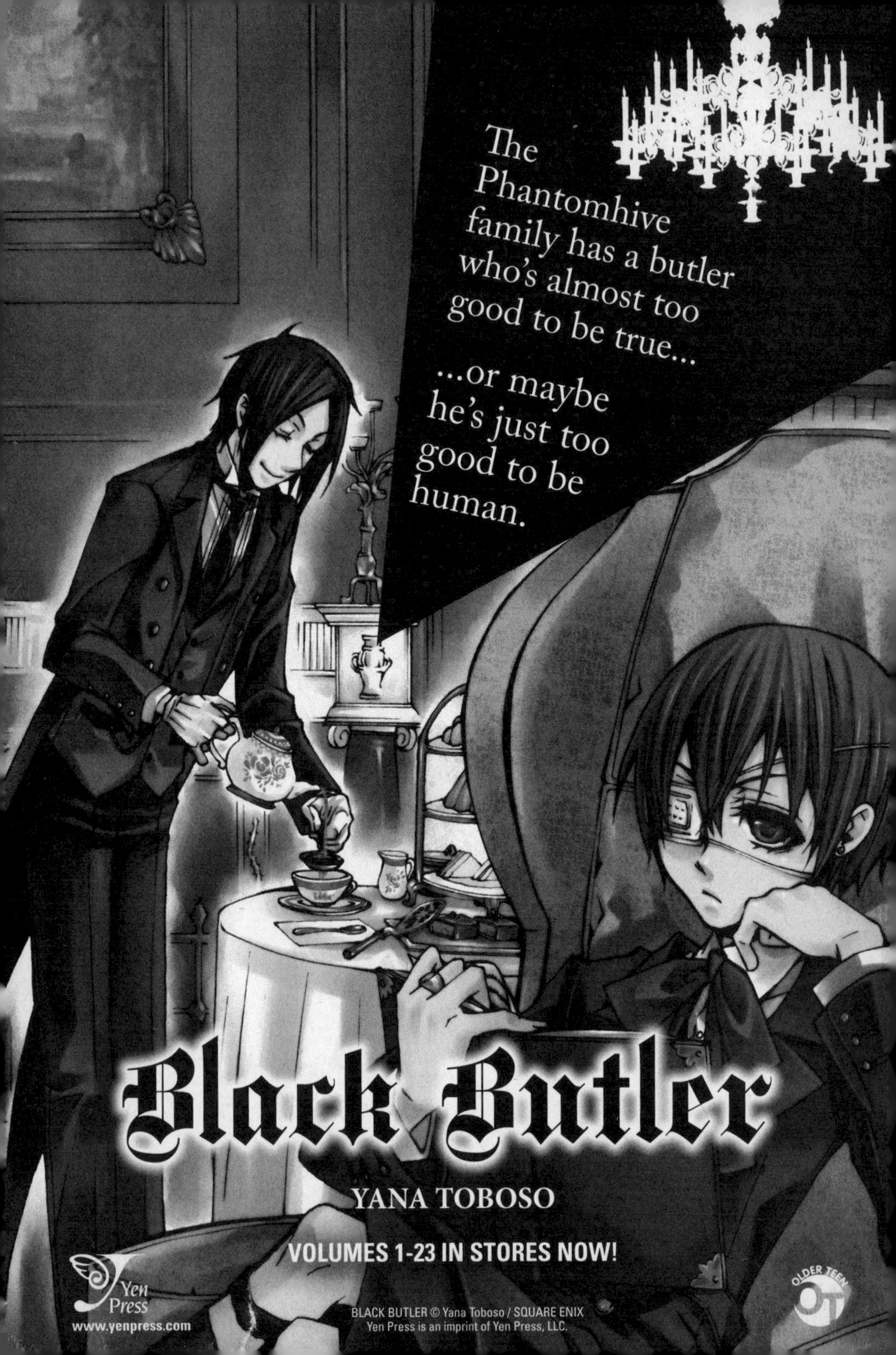
The Phantomhive family has a butler who's almost too good to be true...
...or maybe he's just too good to be human.
Black Butler
YANA TOBOSO
VOLUMES 1-23 IN STORES NOW!
Yen Press
www.yenpress.com
BLACK BUTLER © Yana Toboso / SQUARE ENIX
Yen Press is an imprint of Yen Press, LLC.
OLDER TEEN
OT

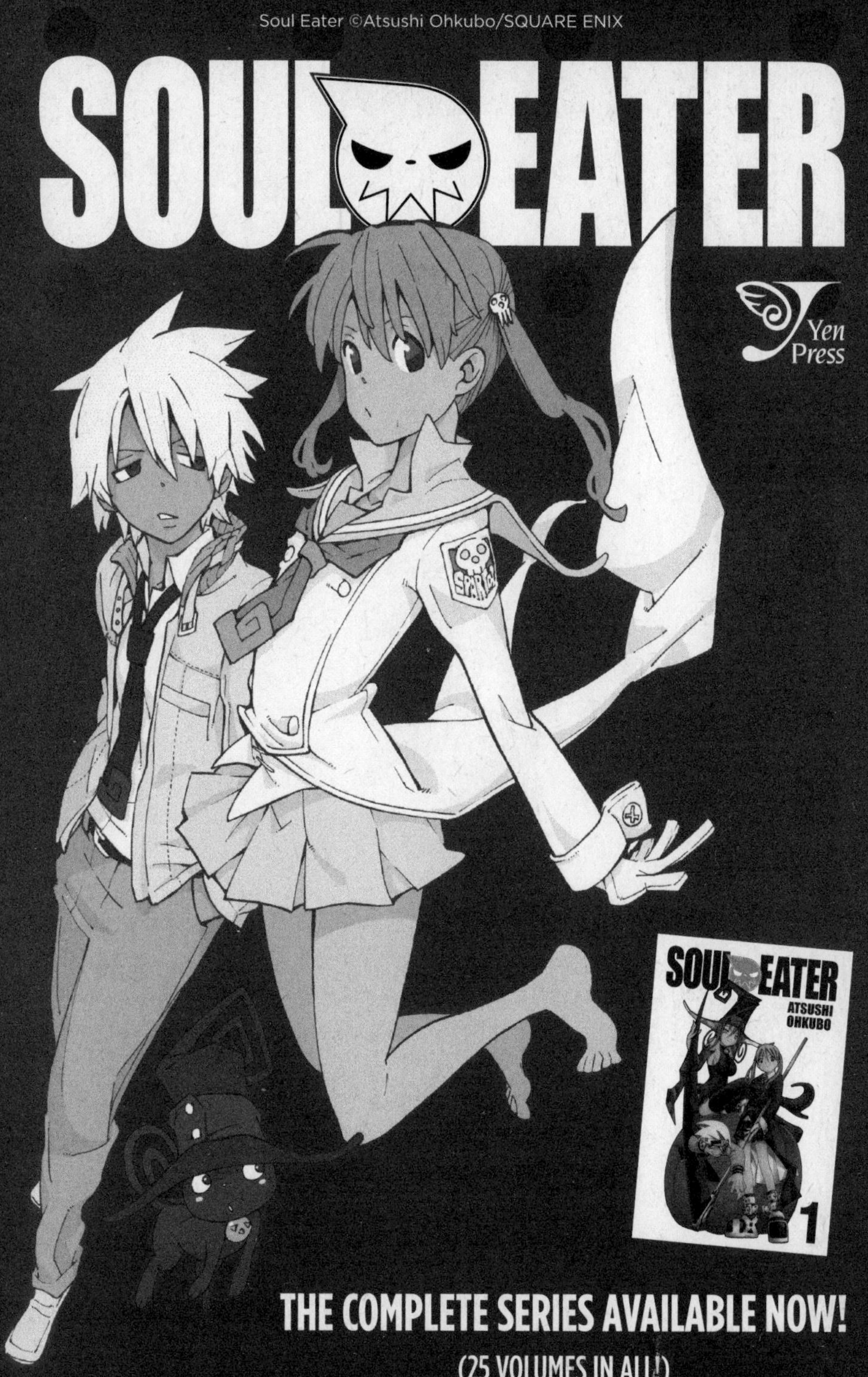
Soul Eater ©Atsushi Ohkubo/SQUARE ENIX
SOUL EATER
Yen Press
SOUL EATER
ATSUSHI OHKUBO
1
THE COMPLETE SERIES AVAILABLE NOW!
(25 VOLUMES IN ALL!)

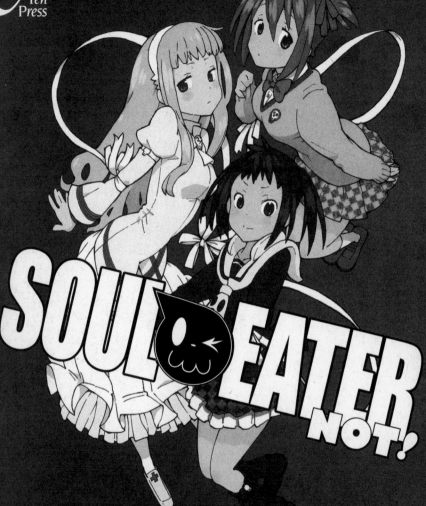

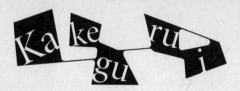

STORY: **Homura Kawamoto**
ART: **Toru Naomura**

Translation: Kevin Gifford
Lettering: Anthony Quintessenza

KAKEGURUI Vol. 4 ©2015 Homura Kawamoto, Toru Naomura/SQUARE ENIX CO., LTD. First published in Japan in 2015 by SQUARE ENIX CO., LTD. English translation rights arranged with SQUARE ENIX CO., LTD. and Yen Press, LLC through Tuttle-Mori Agency, Inc.

English translation ©2018 by SQUARE ENIX CO., LTD.

Yen Press
1290 Avenue of the Americas
New York, NY 10104

Visit us at yenpress.com
facebook.com/yenpress
twitter.com/yenpress
yenpress.tumblr.com
instagram.com/yenpress

First Yen Press Edition: January 2018
The chapters in this volume were originally published as ebooks by Yen Press.

Yen Press is an imprint of Yen Press, LLC.
The Yen Press name and logo are trademarks of Yen Press, LLC.

The publisher is not responsible for websites (or their content) that are not owned by the publisher.

Library of Congress Control Number: 2017939211

ISBNs: 978-0-316-48003-1 (paperback)
       978-0-316-48004-8 (ebook)

10 9 8 7 6 5 4 3 2 1

BVG

Printed in the United States of America